THE ENGLISH HOUSEKEEPER

LECTOR HOUSE PUBLIC DOMAIN WORKS

THE ENGLISH HOUSEKEEPER

ANNE COBBETT

ISBN: 978-93-89509-37-3

Published: 1851

LECTOR HOUSE LLP
E-MAIL: lectorpublishing@gmail.com

THE LARDER.

THE ENGLISH HOUSEKEEPER:

OR,

MANUAL OF DOMESTIC MANAGEMENT: CONTAINING ADVICE ON THE CONDUCT OF HOUSEHOLD AFFAIRS, AND PRACTICAL INSTRUCTIONS

CONCERNING

THE STORE-ROOM,	THE KITCHEN,
THE PANTRY,	THE CELLAR,
THE LARDER,	THE DAIRY.

THE WHOLE BEING INTENDED

FOR THE USE OF YOUNG LADIES WHO UNDERTAKE THE SUPERINTENDENCE OF THEIR OWN HOUSEKEEPING.

SIXTH EDITION.

(IMPROVED BY THE INTRODUCTION OF MANY NEW RECEIPTS.)

BY ANNE COBBETT.

1851.

CONTENTS

CONTENTS

CHAPTER VIII.

CHAPTER XXIX.

CHAPTER XXX.

CHAPTER XXXI.

CHAPTER XXXII.

CHAPTER XXXIII.

INTRODUCTION.

"She looketh well to the ways of her *Household*, and eateth not the bread of idleness. Her children arise up, and call her blessed: her husband also, and he praiseth her. Many daughters have done virtuously, but thou excellest them all."—Proverbs, Chap. xxxi., vs. 27, 28, & 29.

I have taken so much pains to make the following work deserving of the title it bears, that I could not, without affectation, pretend to undervalue my own performance, by anticipating doubts of its utility, or by expressing any fear lest my friends should be disappointed when they look into it. Every publication of this description is necessarily calculated to be of some essential service; for it must not only be practical in its descriptions and directions, but must relate to matters touching the daily and hourly wants of all mankind; and it will, of course, be approved according as it may happen to meet those wants.

As a mere Cookery-book, mine must submit to be placed in a lower rank than some others, because I do not profess to bring to light discoveries in the culinary art, neither do I design to favour epicurism. I have no pretension beyond that of advising young ladies who are their own housekeepers; and the receipts which will be found in my selection, are such as appeared to me suitable to any family of moderate style in living, and such as may be easily comprehended and put in practice. These have been carefully revised and amended in the present edition, and some others added.

While I am offering advice with respect to the manner of conducting domestic affairs, I cannot refrain from expressing my regret that so large a proportion of the young ladies of England are sadly deficient in that information, and in those practices of economy which are the most essentially necessary to their welfare as persons of influence and authority in a house. I am by no means singular in lamenting that the advantages of a knowledge of housekeeping seem to be so entirely lost sight of by those who have the responsibility of bringing up either their own or other people's daughters; and I find it frequently the subject of remark that the ladies of the present day have become incapable of being so skilful in the discharge of their domestic duties as the ladies of a former period were, in proportion as they have become more cultivated and more accomplished. But is it so? Are there now a greater proportion of women whose minds are really cultivated than there were formerly? Is there not rather a greater pretence of learning with less of it in reality? It is erroneous to suppose that persons of real learning look upon the minor duties of life with contempt, because of their learning; for, though learning does not, perhaps, give sense, it surely does not destroy it, and there is not only a want of sense, but a positive folly, in that affectation of refinement, and that assumption of superiority, which has led to the result now complained of. But the system of education which has prevailed of late years is certainly in fault; a system which assigns the same species of learning, indiscriminately, to young persons of every rank and degree, without distinction even as to ability. Such a method of bringing up has unavoidably been productive of very injurious effects; for, while it withdraws the daughters of farmers and tradespeople, and others, during a great part of their youth, from the practice of those homely arts which belong to their stations, it leaves them, in nine cases out of ten, without anything more than the mere fancy that they possess acquirements of a higher order.

The desire which many persons feel to give their children a better education than has been bestowed upon themselves is laudable, because it proceeds from sincere affection: but how often is the success equal to the motive which actuates? How often is the manner of attempting at all calculated for attaining the object so earnestly sought? An ambition to promote the welfare of children reconciles parents to part with them at that tender age when they ought to command more constant care than they generally need at a more advanced time of life; and this ambition is so strong that it will even cause little girls to be consigned to the blighting atmosphere of a crowded schoolroom, there to bewail the loss of the warm hearth, or the airy room of their own homes, and all the comforts which depend upon a mother's solicitude. With a view to their being educated, that is to say, fitted for the world, and for the discharge of their respective duties in it, girls are sent to school, and are there condemned to a dull course of lessons, before their minds have sufficient strength to imbibe any kind of learning that requires mental labour, and before their understandings are equal to any greater exertion than that of perceiving the difference between a roasted apple and a sugar-plum.

A knowledge of housekeeping is not difficult to attain. It needs no natural superiority of talent, and no painful application. It is rather a habit than a science, and, like the neatness so characteristic of English women, this knowledge rarely comes to perfection at all, unless it be partly formed in early life, and by means of our very earliest associations. Little girls are always prone to imitate the ways of older persons, particularly in housekeeping matters. They very soon begin to find amusement in learning to make preserves, pastry, and such things. Those children, therefore, who are brought up at home, and have the daily and hourly practice of domestic duties before their eyes, will naturally fall into habits of usefulness, and acquire, by degrees and imperceptibly, a knowledge of what belongs to home, which should constitute the elementary education of every woman who is not born to rank and to luxury. But the unhappy little creatures who drag through seven or more years of continuous monotony within the walls of a school, their minds taking little or no part in the tasks which their memories are racked upon, have but little chance of learning any thing which will benefit their after lives; for, those whose mothers knead the bread, churn the butter, and help to cook the dinner, have not the benefit of that sort of society that would teach them to apply their learning, that would call forth their acquirements, or that would be able to appreciate those acquirements when displayed. During the period which these children spend at school, their mother continues her old-fashioned occupations, and, as time passes on, she looks forward, perhaps, with cheering anticipations to the *help* which her daughters are to afford her. But alas! how often do these daughters return from school with false notions of the lives they are to lead, and with mistaken ideas of their own consequence, such as lead them to despise the humble occupations of their home, although their "education" may not have given them one single idea to justify any pretension of the kind. It is generally acknowledged, that girls educated at schools are seldom far advanced in learning. Where history and geography, and other sciences, are learnt by rote, "a page of Greece on Monday," a "page of Rome on Tuesday," a "page of Universal Biography on Wednesday," with occasional readings of the middle ages, of modern times, and application being made to maps, globes, charts, &c., to fill up the time which is not devoted to the fine arts (for it all goes on at once), the stock of real solid information which is gained by the end of the year, will be very scanty, or will probably have resolved itself into such a confused mass of imperfect information that all practical benefit may be despaired of. No wonder, if, after having undergone a course like this, a young girl is often found to have gained less from books than others have gained from vulgar report, and be puzzled to say whether it was Scipio or Washington who was the first President of the United States of America. They learn lessons, but they do not reason or think about what they are getting by heart; and many girls, whose education has cost a large sum of money, are unable to answer a question of name, place, or date, in their geography or history, without first running over a certain portion of one whole lesson, the sound of which has left a deeper impression on the ear, than its sense has left on the understanding. Just as, when wanting to ascertain the number of days in a particular month, we repeat the words, "Thirty days hath September," &c., thus recalling by means of the jingle of words, what of itself had slipped our memories.

Girls so educated are very much to be commiserated. They live, through that part of their lives in which the mind is most open to receive impressions, without any opportunity for exercising their powers of observation, till, at last, those powers fall into a state of inertness; and their education is finished without their having gained the least knowledge of what the world really is, or of the part which they are to be called upon to act in it. Having had no intimate association with persons really well informed, it is no matter of surprise, if they become conceited of their supposed attainments, or if they remain in ignorance of the fact, that a little music, a little drawing, and a very little French and Italian, are not sufficient to make an accomplished woman, and that merely going the round of primers will not, of itself, constitute what is looked for in a "good education." Nor is it, indeed, to be wondered at, if the home, which has been so cherished in recollection from one holiday time to another, fail to realise all the anticipations of pleasure and of happiness which the thought of it has excited. Its simple occupations are not of a kind to make them, as novelties, attractive to one who is *only* a fine lady; the want of capacity to fill domestic duties will, of course, render them rather disagreeable than otherwise; and it is but natural that young women who, during all the early part of their lives, have been unaccustomed to think of household cares, should entertain some degree of aversion to them, and feel dissatisfied when called upon to take a part in them. Many a father has repented that he did not rather lay up for his daughter, the money which has been expended to no better purpose than to cause her to repine at the condition in life in which he must leave her. And many a mother's pride, in the fancied superiority of her daughter, has been saddened by the recollection, not only that her daughter was incapable of helping her, but that the time must come when that incompetent daughter would be left to take care of herself.

My readers may imagine that I forget my proper theme: they may wish me to remember that this book professes only to aid those young ladies who are uninformed on this subject, *how to keep house*, and that I am diverging from that subject, and raising objections to a very common way of bringing up children. But when it is generally acknowledged that there is, in the ladies of the present day, a great want of skill as regards the affairs of their household, an ignorance, in fact, of some of their first duties, it cannot be impertinent for me to inquire, whether this want of skill, and this ignorance, be not properly ascribable to a defective, or even to a mischievous, course of education. I certainly do think that habits of usefulness, and the cultivation of talents, may be combined, but then the acquiring of the useful, and the cultivating of the finer accomplishments must proceed hand in hand. There are, doubtless, many who do not think it beneath them to be able to make a pudding, merely because they can execute a difficult piece of music, or sing with good taste; who do not regard these as things absolutely incongruous; and who do not consider, when they receive applause for excelling in fashionable powers to charm, that the offering carries with it an excuse for their being inefficient and helpless mistresses of families. There are, however, not a few, who do think that qualifications of a refined nature render it unbecoming in their possessors to give that personal superintendence to the affairs of the kitchen, of the store-room, and of all the other branches of household arrangement, which is so necessary, that, for the want of it, moderate fortunes often prove inadequate to the support of families in the middle rank. Young persons cannot be expected to entertain a proper estimation of the value of useful habits, as compared with the value of ornamental acquirements, unless they have grown up in the exercise of those habits. The idea that capability in the domestic, is incompatible with taste in the elegant accomplishments, is so deeply rooted in the minds of most persons who aspire to be fashionable, that I despair of the power to do much towards eradicating the fatal error. And yet, I would fain represent to parents, the wrong which is done to children by suffering this idea to plant itself in their minds; for it not only reduces young women to a standard of comparatively little consequence, by making them helpless in all the ordinary business of life, but it produces incidentally, a variety of injurious effects on the health, on the spirits, and even on the temper. It is proverbial, that the largest portion of happiness belongs not to the higher ranks of society; and the reason is, not that the rich and luxurious are, as a matter of course, unworthy and consequently unhappy; but that their minds are not diverted by necessary cares, that their amusements are easily obtained, and that the enjoyment of them is never interrupted by their having duties to perform. Pleasures fail to excite and interest the mind, unless they come in the way of relaxation. Therefore it is, that even in youth, something by way of employment is necessary to keep gaiety from subsiding into dulness; and in mature life nothing is more salutary than occupation. To have *something to do*, to be obliged to *be doing*, withdraws the mind from the contemplation of fancied sorrows, and prevents its being subdued by the recurrence of unavailing regrets. Women who have been accustomed, in their youth, to be industriously engaged and to contribute to the daily happiness of others, are sure to enjoy the greatest share of tranquillity and satisfaction in a review of days gone by, to show the most courage in adversity, the most patience in sickness, and to be the most cheerful and resigned under the infirmities of age; and those parents, therefore, who instil into the minds of their daughters the principle of *making themselves useful*, will confer upon them one of the greatest of blessings.

Let it not be supposed, however, that by *useful*, I mean that a woman should be a mere household drudge, that all her ideas should be confined within the limits of her domestic offices, or that her guests as well as her family, should be entertained by nothing better than details of the household. Ladies who have houses and servants to look after, should be capable of superintending the whole in a manner so systematic, as that they may have a due portion of their time, and of their thoughts, to give to other, and, if they deem them such, higher matters. I by no means recommend, as patterns, the fussy people, who are always busy and have never done, who let you know every thing that they have to do, and who, sometimes, do very little after all. Neither is it advisable to imitate, too closely, that class of housewives who are distinguished by the phrase—"very *particular:*" for even the virtue of neatness, when incessantly exercised, or manifested too much in matters of little moment, becomes an intruder upon comfort, and, consequently, offensive. What I recommend is, that quiet and orderly method of conducting the business of a house, which tends rather to conceal than to make an appearance of much to do, which puts all that part of the family, who are not immediately engaged in it, as little as possible out of the way, and which may enable strangers to remain under the roof without being constantly reminded of the trouble they occasion. Every woman who presides over a home, and who wishes to preserve its attraction, should bear in mind the many minute cares which all contribute to give to that home, not only the semblance, but the substance of enjoyment; and I earnestly impress upon my youthful readers the important fact, that, as far as mere fortune is concerned, those often prove to be the most poor in reality, who may have been thought to be the most rich. Competence and ease may be changed for narrowed circumstances, and a struggle may ensue, to stem a torrent of difficulties which follow in succession, and threaten to destroy the home which has been hitherto considered secure. Then she who has passed her life in total listlessness, possessing no acquirements but of a showy kind, and ignorant of what is wanted to preserve the foundation of a family's happiness; then such a woman will prove as unfitted to lighten sorrow, as she has been careless to avert it: for herself, she can but quail as difficulties assail her; for others, she can only seek for protection where, if she were capable, she might be of assistance; and, instead of aiding to alleviate distress, she will become the main cause of rendering the common burden intolerable.

How often do we see families stricken to the very dust, by the first, and perhaps only a slight blow, of misfortune; and this, merely for the want of a little of that practical knowledge, and that experience, which would have enabled them to husband their diminished means so that they might still supply sufficient to meet all real wants, and still procure every material comfort. From a want of this experience, some of the very best intentioned persons will so misapply the resources left to them, at one time laying out money where they ought to refrain altogether, and at another parting with more than the occasion requires, that, by degrees, those resources dwindle away to nothing before they seem to be aware of the natural consequences, and not only poverty, but destitution and misery are let into an abode where comparative ease and contentment might still have remained. The great art of economy in domestic life, is comprised in the two very homely phrases, *"to turn every thing to account,"* and *"to make the most of what you have."* But their meaning is often perverted, and the habit of *turning every thing to an account*, and of *making the most of every thing*, is ascribed to those who are actuated, not by a laudable desire to produce as much comfort as their circumstances will admit, but by an inclination to indulge in a strong propensity to stinginess. But of this class of persons I am far from being the advocate; between extravagance and parsimony the widest possible interval exists; and that economy, that management and application of means, which I deem perfectly consistent with the most rigid virtue and the most generous impulse, is of too admirable a character to partake either of the spendthrift's criminality or of the miser's meanness.

If my censures upon the present system of educating young ladies should appear to be presumptuous, I greatly fear that any disapproval of that which is now so universally adopted with regard to *the poor* will be still more unpopular; but it does appear to me that *there*, there exists a mistake also, which, perhaps, in its consequences, will prove still more fatal. It appears to me that something better might be done, more advantageous to both rich and poor, by educating the latter to be useful members of society; and I think that ladies who live in the country may have ample opportunities of training up good servants, by attending to the education of poor neighbours of their own sex. By *education*, I do not mean that kind of teaching which merely qualifies them for reading letters and words. Small literary accomplishments, accompanied by idle habits, are already but too common, though the fact is more generally known than acknowledged. Nor do I mean that sort of education which creates expectations of gaining a livelihood by any other means than those of honest industry; or which tends to raise the ideas of persons who are born to work above the duties which fortune has assigned to them. I mean such an education as shall better their condition, by making them better servants. In large establishments, where there are old and experienced persons in service, it is very much the custom to have younger ones as helpers, and thus the latter have the benefit of learning all the duties of the household; but these establishments are comparatively few in number. The fashion of the day is opposed to my opinion, and the same ladies who now condescend to teach poor children to read and write, because it is the fashion to do so, would, in many cases, think it beneath them to teach a little girl to make a pudding. It would, in a work of this nature, be a hopeless and presumptuous attempt, to argue against the all-powerful influence of fashion, against which the keenest shafts of invective and ridicule, and in short every weapon of satire, have been so often aimed in vain; but, all are not under the dominion of so senseless and so capricious a tyranny, and I have to regret my inability to set before my readers the benefits which mistresses of families would confer and receive, from bringing up young country girls to be good servants. There might always, in a country-house, be one or more young girls, according to the size of the establishment; to be placed under older servants, or be instructed by the mistress herself, in all household occupations, from the hardest work and most simple offices, to the more delicate arts of housekeeping, including needle-work. This practice would not only insure more good servants than there now are; but, young girls so trained would, by the force of hourly tuition and good example, imbibe a right sense of duty, and acquire good habits, before they could have had time to become vicious or unmanageable.

When ladies take the trouble to teach the poor to read and write, they mean well, no doubt, and think they are doing the best they can for their pupils. But teaching industry is more to the purpose; for when learning has been found insufficient to preserve the morals of princes, nobles, and gentry, how can it be supposed that it will preserve those of their dependents? The supposition is, in fact, injurious to the cause of true learning, since the system founded upon it has been attended by no moral improvement. Our well-being is best secured by an early habit of earning our bread by honest labour; and

> "Not to know at large of things remote
> From use, obscure, and subtle, but to know
> That which before us lies in daily life,
> Is the prime wisdom; what is more, is fume.
> Or emptiness, or fond impertinence,
> And renders us in things that most concern,
> Unpractis'd, unprepar'd, and still to seek."

A country girl, the daughter of a labourer, would, by making herself in some way practically useful to society, and gaining a respectable livelihood, be more profitably employed than in going through that long course of literary exercise which has, of late, been so generally bestowed on the children of poor people, but which, I fear, has not generally imparted to them much of what MILTON styles "the prime wisdom." It should also be considered, that the literary education of the poor, such as it is, cannot be much more than half completed at the age when the children cease to receive lessons from their charitable instructors. They are taught to read, to write a little, and perhaps something of the elements of arithmetic. The reading, however, is the principal attainment; and in this, they generally become well enough schooled before they are eleven, or, at most, twelve years of age. But alas! have they at that age, or at the age of thirteen or fourteen, been taught all that is necessary for girls so young to learn, with regard to the *choice of books*? With the use of *letters*, indeed, as the mere components of words, they have been made acquainted. But why have they been taught to read at all, unless there be some profit to be derived from their reading; and how can any profit be looked for from that reading, unless there be the same kind of pains taken to point out the proper objects of study as there have been to teach the little scholars to spell? Surely that advice which is required by all young persons in the pursuit of book-learning, is at least as necessary to those who can do no more than just read their own native language, as it is to those who are brought up in a superior way. The education of youth, among the higher and middle classes, does not terminate, or, at least, it never should, immediately on their leaving school. At that period, a fresh series of anxieties occur to the parent or the guardian, who is quite as sedulous as before, to finish that which has been, in fact, only begun at school. If this be not the case, how is it, that though the son may have been eight or ten years at the best schools, the father, after the schooling is ended, finds it necessary to consult the most discreet and experienced advisers, concerning the right guidance of his child in the course of his future studies? The attention paid to the studies of young ladies, after they come from school, is, to be sure, not precisely the same as that which parents think requisite for their sons. But, while the daughter has generally the advantage of being with her mother, or with some female relative much older than herself; and while the success in life of our sex does not so frequently depend upon literary acquirements, and the proper employment of them; yet under such circumstances, favourable as they are, we all know that there is still much wanting, both in the way of counsel and attractive example, from the parent or guardian, to render the learning which a young girl has acquired at school, of substantial service to her in after years. If the daughters of the rich require to be taught, not merely to read, but, also, *what* to read, why should not this be the case with the daughters of the poor? in whose fate, it is too often proved, that "a little learning is a dangerous thing," owing to the want of that discretion which is necessary to prevent the little learning becoming worthless, and even mischievous, to its possessor.

In the way of practical education, there are many things of importance to the poor, which ought to be taught them in early youth. At the age of fifteen or sixteen, a girl should already have learned many of the duties of a servant; for if her education up to that age have been neglected, she must necessarily, for the next three or four years of her life, be comparatively useless and little worthy of trust. The poor do not, as some may suppose, inhale with the air they breathe any of that knowledge which is necessary to make them useful in the houses of their parents or their employers. To learn cookery, in its various branches; making bread; milking, butter-making, and all the many things that belong to a dairy; household offices innumerable; besides the nice art of getting up fine linen, and plain work with the needle; not only requires considerable time, but, also, unless the learner be uncommonly quick and willing, great attention on the part of the person who undertakes to teach them. It is lamentable to see how deficient many female servants are in some things, the knowledge of which ought to be thought indispensable. Some are so ignorant of plain needle-work as to be incapable of making themselves a gown; and this, too, where they happen to be what the country-people call "scholars," from their ability to read a little, and to make an awkward use of the pen. A maid-servant who can assist her mistress in plain needle-work, is a really valuable person. Strange as it may seem, however, there are but few common servants who can do so, notwithstanding that superiority in learning by which the present generation of the labouring people are said to be distinguished from their predecessors.

With young servants, nothing has a better effect than *encouragement*. If they are, by nature, only good tempered, and blest with as much right principle as those who have not been spoiled generally possess, whatever you say or do in the way of encouraging them, can hardly fail to produce some good, though it may not always accomplish everything that you would desire. A cheerful tone in giving directions, a manner of address which conveys the idea of confidence in the willingness, as well as the ability, of the person directed, has great influence upon the minds of all young persons whose tempers and inclinations have not been warped by ill-usage, or soured by disappointment. Very young servants frequently take pride in their work, though of the most laborious kind, and many a young girl might be proud to improve in the more refined departments of housewifery, and would regard a little congratulation upon the lightness of her pastry, or the excellence of her cakes, as worth ten times all the thought and care which she had bestowed upon them. There is no mistress who does not acknowledge the importance of a servant who can assist in preserving, pickling, wine-making, and other things of this description, which demand both skill and labour, and which must, where there is no one but the mistress herself sufficiently acquainted with them to be trusted, take up much of her time and give her considerable trouble.

To teach poor children to become useful servants, may, perhaps, be thought a serious task; but it surely cannot be said that this sort of instruction is at all more difficult than that which is necessary to give them even a tolerable proficiency in the lowest branches of literature. The learning here recommended, seems naturally more inviting, as well as more needful, than that which is taught in the ordinary course of school education; and it possesses this advantage, that while its benefits are equally lasting, they are immediately perceptible. It is sometimes said that the poor are ungrateful, and that after all the pains and trouble which may have been taken in making them good servants, it often happens, that instead of testifying a proper sense of the obligation, they become restless, and desirous of leaving those who have had all the trouble of qualifying them for better places and higher wages. Servants cannot be prevented from bettering themselves, as they call it, but that constant changing of place which operates as one of the worst examples to young women who are at service, would become less frequent if their employments were occasionally varied by relaxation and amusement, and their services now and then rewarded by small presents. The influence of early habits is so universally felt and acknowledged, that it seems almost superfluous to ask why an early and industrious education of the poor, and the teaching of the youth of both sexes to look upon prosperity and right endeavour as inseparable, should not produce a taste, the reverse of that which leads to a discontented and unsettled existence.

It is equally the interest of the rich and of the poor, that the youthful inhabitants of the mansion and those of the cottage, should grow up with sentiments of mutual good will. If the poor are indebted to their opulent neighbours for the assistance which makes a hard lot tolerable, there exists a reciprocal obligation on the part of the rich, since they could not obtain the comforts and the luxuries which they enjoy, without the aid of those who are less fortunate than themselves. But there is another and superior motive, which ought to narrow the distance between the poor and the rich: the lady of the mansion, when she meets her washerwoman in the village church, must know that, in that place, she and the hard-working woman are equals. The lady of the mansion, when she beholds the ravages which but a few years of toil have wrought in the once blooming and healthful country girl, is astonished, perhaps, that her own looks and health have not undergone a similar change; but, she forgets that the pitiable creature before her has been exposed to the damp floors and steams of a wash-house, to the chill of a cold drying-ground, and the oppressive heat of an ironing stove, in order to earn her miserable portion of the necessaries of life. No wonder that her beauty has vanished; that her countenance betrays the marks of premature age, and that her air of cheerfulness is exchanged for that of a saddened resignation. But the lady of the mansion should not, in the confidence of her own happier fate, lose sight of the fact, that this poor and destitute creature is a *woman* as well as herself; that her poor inferior is liable to all those delicacies and weaknesses of constitution of which she herself is sensible; and that, in the eyes of their Maker, the peeress and the washerwoman hold equal rank.

The ingratitude of the poor is often made a pretext for neglecting to relieve their wants. But are not their superiors ungrateful? Is "the ingratitude of the world," of which philosophers of the earliest ages have said so much, confined to the lowly and unrefined? By no means. High birth and refinement in breeding do not, alone, ensure feelings of honour and of kindness to the heart, any more than they ensure common sense and sound judgment to the head; for these qualities seem to be in the very nature of some, while it passes the power of all art to implant them in others. It is for those who have known what adversity is to say whether they have not met with instances of devoted attachment, of generosity, and of every other good feeling, on the part of servants, at the very time when they have been depressed by the heart-sick sensation caused by the desertion of friends. Those have been unfortunate in their experience of human nature, who cannot bear testimony to the admirable conduct of servants in fulfilling that wearisome, and often most trying, but at the same time most imperative of all earthly duties, attendance upon a sick bed. Perhaps it has not occurred to most others, as it has to me, to witness such proofs of virtue in poor people. Among the truly charitable there are, no doubt, many in whom disgust has been excited by ingratitude; but has it been excited by the hard-working and the half-starving only? It is but a very limited acquaintance with this life, which can justify the unselfish and noble nature in denouncing the *poor*, for being ungrateful. Be this, however, as it may, one thing is certain, that no probability of disappointment, no apprehensions of an ungrateful return, ought to have any influence with the mind of a Christian, and that such obstacles were never yet a hinderance to any man or woman whose desire was to do good.

THE ENGLISH HOUSEKEEPER.

CHAPTER I.

General observations relating to Housekeeping, with remarks on the fitting up of a House, and conducting its affairs. On the choice and management of Servants.

It would be impossible to give rules for the management of a domestic establishment, because they would necessarily be subject to many and various exceptions, produced by various circumstances. But a few general observations, accompanied by remarks on the most important matters in domestic life, may not be unacceptable to young housekeepers.

In the young and thoughtless, a spirit of emulation, leading them to vie with those who are richer than themselves, is often the source of domestic unhappiness, by causing so much to be sacrificed to appearance, as to circumscribe the means of enjoying the substantial comforts of life. It sometimes manifests itself in houses, equipages, and retinues of servants; but amongst persons of moderate income, for whose use this work is principally intended, it is commonly displayed in costly furniture and expensive entertainments. Many young married women conceive the notion, that unless they have as fine a house, as expensive furniture, plate, china, and glass, as some others have, and give as fine entertainments as others give; in short, unless they make the appearance of living quite as well as their richer neighbours, they will not be held in equal estimation. It is not that they derive any real pleasure from the false appearance which they make; indeed, expensive furniture is but an annoyance to its possessor, if there be not a sufficient number of good servants to keep it in order. Where the whole family concur in this sort of pride, no mortification arises from difference of opinion, but the unanimity tends only to accelerate the ruin.

The young housekeeper should consider the serious consequences that are likely to result from setting out in a style of lavish expenditure, and she should remember that, while it is easy to extend, it is extremely difficult to reduce, her establishment. One expensive article requires another to correspond with it, and one expensive entertainment imposes the necessity of other equally expensive entertainments; for it requires no small share of moral courage to risk the loss of consequence which may result by its being surmised that we are not so well off, as we have been supposed to be. And when the time comes, as sooner or later it assuredly must, when the means are not adequate to the demands, what sacrifices are made, and what unseemly contrivances are resorted to, in order to keep up, to the last, a poor remnant of *"appearance!"* and, when this can no longer be effected, then comes the humiliation, with all the bitter feelings attendant upon *retrenchment*; of all which feelings, the bitterest is, the dread of being degraded in the world's estimation. To endure privations with resignation, to feel the want of habitual comforts, yet be grateful for the blessings which are left to us, is the duty of every Christian, and is the less arduous when the reverse of fortune which has befallen us, has not been produced by any fault of our own. But if, in addition to the distresses of adversity, the wife and the mother be doomed to writhe under the pang of self-reproach, great indeed must be her suffering, and one for which I can suggest no adequate relief. To the young and generous-minded, the hardest portion which accompanies reverses of fortune, is, the change which they sometimes produce in the behaviour of acquaintances. When we are become poorer than we were, and have lost the ability to entertain guests in the accustomed manner, it is painful to perceive some of those very people who have been the most hospitably entertained, and who, in our prosperity, have appeared the most attached to us, turn from us and our difficulties, while they banish from their minds the recollection of past kindness. To meet with indifference in those whose smiles have courted ours; to feel that we have thrown away sincere friendship upon mere heartlessness, is hard to be endured, even by the faultless, but how intolerable must it be, when aggravated by the consciousness that we have incurred it by our own misconduct. To the experienced, this is one of the severest vicissitudes of life; what, then, must it be to us, before we have acquired that equanimity of mind, which falls only to the lot of those who have passed through the ordeal of the world, and who have been amply compensated for the desertion of the many, by the sincerity, the warmth of heart, and the steadfastness of the few.

Houses and furniture properly belong to the extraordinary expenses of the household. When a young woman is called upon to exercise her judgment in the choice of a house, she must pause before she rejects one which, though she may consider it rather too small, might, nevertheless, be made to accommodate the family *well enough*, and might be fitted up at a less cost than a larger one. Such a house would require fewer servants, and would certainly present a better appearance, than one that is rather too large for the quantity, or for the style of its furniture, and is, perhaps, larger than is actually required for the number of its inhabitants. It is easier to remove from a small to a large house, when circumstances require it, than it is to remove from a large to a small one. It is so easy to increase our wants, and so difficult to reduce them, that young persons should begin the world with caution, and not multiply their wants, lest, in time, they lack the means of gratifying them.

In fitting up a house, the young housekeeper, who sets out with a determination to choose furniture suitable to her circumstances and station in life, will be content with that which is just *good enough*, rather than be induced to exceed her previous good intentions, and gratify her fancy at the expense of her comforts. She must never yield to the seductive reflection, that "*only* five pounds more cannot make much difference;" for, the same argument may be equally applied to the sofa, the tables, the carpet, the curtains, the grate, the fire-irons and fender; all of which are necessary to furnish a dining room; to say nothing of the lamps, the mirrors, and other articles of ornament, which fashion in some cases makes of absolute necessity. If "*only five pounds*" be given for some of these, and two, or even one pound, for others, more than is necessary, she will find that the "difference" is very great by the time that she has fitted up only one room.

The rage for vying with our superiors shows itself in the bad taste which encumbers houses with unsuitable furniture. Massive sideboards, and unwieldy chairs, occupy too much space in a small room, while draperies not only obscure the light, but have an inelegant appearance, unless the room be large and lofty, or in keeping with the size and weight of cornices, cords, tassels, and other ornaments, which give offence to the eye when too gorgeous or prominent. Of equal bad taste, is the habit of occasionally changing furniture, to suit the varying of fashions; which is so much the practice that even persons in trade, having families to provide for, change furniture, sufficiently good to serve its purpose for a lifetime, for other no handsomer, but a little more fashionable.

It is strange that persons pretending to gentility should not rather imitate the higher class of their superiors, who value their high-backed chairs the more because they are old, and would on no account exchange them for modern finery. When expensive furniture is introduced into the houses of persons of small fortune, the long upholsterer's bill rises like a phantom before the misplaced couches, ottomans, and ottoman sofas, crowded into small drawing rooms; and my feelings of regret become almost feelings of indignation on seeing plate, which belonged to fathers and mothers, or to grandfathers and grandmothers, and spoons which have touched those lips which spoke tenderness to our infancy, about to be bartered for the "Prince's," the "King's," or the "fiddle pattern," or for some other pattern that may happen to offer the newest temptation to vulgar taste.

Every young woman who has the good taste to wish that her house may be characterised by its simplicity, and be more remarkable for comfort than for show, will, if she wish to spare herself and her family much discomfort, avoid having show-rooms; such rooms, I mean, as are considered too fine to be habitually occupied by the family, and are, therefore, kept shut up; except when, on particular occasions, and perhaps only a few times in the year, a fire is lighted for the reception of company. Upon such occasions, children are seen to look about them as if they had never beheld the place before; the master of the house fidgets from one seat to another, as if he were anywhere but at home; and it is probable, that before the entertainment is over, the mistress of the house is heard to remark, that she is "never so comfortable as in the room she is accustomed to;" by which her friends discover that their visit has put her out of the way. True hospitality conceals from guests any trouble which their presence may unavoidably occasion; but in the luxurious taste of the times, there is little real hospitality left: friendly intercourse seems lost in ostentatious display, and in our vain attempts to equal, if not to outshine, each other. Most persons acknowledge this to be the case, and lament that it is so; yet few have the courage to pursue a different system.

There is no species of decoration which produces so much effect in ornamenting a house as flowers. The artificial productions of the painter and the upholsterer, the gilded ceilings, glittering mirrors, and couches of brocade, are more splendid and durable, and are worthy of admiration for their individual beauty and the ingenuity and industry which has produced them, but they have not the lively, gay, and varied attractions of flowers. Vases, whether gaudy or elegant, excite interest only as mere objects of curiosity, unless filled with flowers.

To point to any particular department of the household, as demanding the greatest share of attention, would tend rather to mislead than instruct; for a due proportion ought to be bestowed upon every department; where the mistress of the house is over particular on any one point, other matters, of equal importance, may be neglected.

Perfect and uniform neatness is indispensable, not only for comfort, but appearance. By uniform neatness, I mean, that nothing which presents itself, whether about the house, in the dress of mistress, children, or servants, should be left open to unfavourable remark. A young lady who relaxes in attention to her own dress, merely because she has more important cares after, than she had before her marriage, does wrong; but she whose studied attire forms a contrast to the little soiled fingers which are forbidden to approach it; she who strikes the beholder as having bestowed care on herself, while her children bear the appearance of neglect, does infinitely worse. To preserve the neatness of a house, there must be regular attention on the part of the mistress. I am a great enemy to the system of periodical scrubbings and general house-cleanings, which prevails to so great an extent, and especially in the country, where, when the appointed day comes round, carpets are taken up, and floors, even though they be delicately clean, are washed, whether the weather be suitable or otherwise, the health of the family being left to take its chance. The day of *general house-cleaning* is no other than a day of commotion and discomfort. One attendant evil is, the make-up dinner, which does not, perhaps, content all the family; and it is a singular piece of good fortune if friends do not select that very day for paying you a visit. It is certainly a more simple process to clean a house, than it is to keep a house clean; for mere labour is required for the one, while method is necessary for the other. But this method every young housekeeper should endeavour to acquire. Sweeping, dusting, and polishing, should proceed daily. Carpets should be swept every day with a hair broom; but only once a week with a carpet broom, because it wears them: and damp tea leaves should always be used, whether in sweeping carpets or boards, as they lay the dust, which would otherwise fly over the furniture, and again settle on the floor. Bed room carpets should be in different pieces, not nailed to the floor, for the convenience of shaking, which may then be done once in a week. Bed rooms should be swept every day, and a damp mop passed under the beds, chests of drawers, &c., &c., which will remove all the flue and dust, and prevent accumulation of dirt, so that the washing of boards will not be so often required during the winter. In summer, indeed, frequent washings refreshen the atmosphere, and are also beneficial in removing the collections of light dust which engender insects so difficult to get rid of.

Upon the subject of wet boards, I believe that my dislike to great scrubbings was acquired in that cleanest of cities, Philadelphia; where, though American servants do not and will not work so hard as English servants, yet, because it was the custom of the place, they were, notwithstanding severe cold, everlastingly scrubbing the stairs during the months of December and January. Some years afterwards, at Rome, one of the dirtiest of cities, and in the middle of summer, I recalled to mind, with a complacency I had never bestowed on them before, the scrubbing-brushes and the curd-white pails of Philadelphia, and marvelled, as every one must, that in wet and cold countries people wash their houses so much, and that, in hot and dry countries, they do not wash them at all.

With regard to the ordinary expenses of housekeeping, the most important branch of domestic duty which devolves upon the mistress is, to estimate and keep an exact account of the expenditure of her family. She may make this a simple affair by first ascertaining the sum of money to be allotted to it, and then making such arrangements as will confine the expenses rigidly *within* that sum. By keeping a strict account of every article for the first three months, and making a due allowance for casualties, she will be able to form an estimate for the year; and if she find she has exceeded in these three months the allotted sum, she must examine each article, and decide where she can best diminish the expense; and then, having this average to go by, she may calculate how much to allow each month for meat, bread, groceries, washing, and sundries. Having formed her plan, whatever excess circumstances may have required in one month, she must make up for in the next. I should not advise paying for everything at the moment, but rather once a week; for if a tradesman omit to keep an account of the money received for a particular article, he may, by mistake, make a charge for it, as something had upon trust. A weekly account has every advantage of ready money, and is a more convenient mode of payment. All tradesmen may be paid on a Monday morning, the bills receipted, endorsed, and put by in a portfolio or case (which should have the date of the year on the outside), and they can then be referred to as vouchers, or to refresh the memory as to the price of any particular article. It is a satisfaction, independently of the pecuniary benefit, for the head of a family to be able, at the end of the year, to account to herself for what she has done with her money.

Having, in the arrangement of her house, and in the choice of her servants, kept in view the two main objects, namely, the comfort of her family, and the care of her purse, the young housekeeper ought to commence her career, by strictly adhering to order and regularity in the performance of those duties which devolve peculiarly upon herself. If the mistress of a house be regular in the superintendence of her domestic affairs, if she proceed every day to each department at the appointed time, and never pass over any neglect, in such a manner as to give the servants an idea that it had escaped her observation; if, in short, she be regular herself, her servants must be so too, and she will find the business of housekeeping a matter of no difficulty, and of comparatively little labour.

The comfort and respectability of a house depend, in a great degree, upon the servants. Clean, neatly-dressed, and well-behaved servants, always impress a visitor with a favourable idea of the mistress of a house; while it is scarcely possible not to be somewhat prejudiced against her, if they be the reverse.

Servants who understand their work, and do it without being continually looked after, are invaluable; and, as regards wages, not to be compared with ignorant and incapable ones, who perform their services only as they are directed at every turn. A few pounds a year more to a good servant is not, therefore, a consideration; the addition in wages will occasion little additional cost; for, the bad servant consumes as much as the other, and she wastes or damages more.

The hours of meals should vary as little as possible; particularly the first meal of the day; for the work may be said to commence immediately after breakfast, and when that takes place one hour only, after the usual time, the whole business of the house is retarded. In even the most regular families, the time of dining may unavoidably be postponed. But this should happen as seldom as possible: for if the dinner ordered for five, be kept waiting till half-past six, one day, and, perhaps, later still another day, the cook may be prevented from performing some other part of her work, for which she had allotted the time; she will naturally be dissatisfied in having to consume that time in watching over the dinner; and if the dinner upon which she has, perhaps, exerted her utmost skill, be spoiled by waiting, she may be excused if she reproach herself for having taken so much trouble in its preparation. If the trial of her patience and temper be repeated, she will soon take little interest in pleasing her employers; she will take *her* turn to be irregular, and that, perhaps, on some occasion when it may produce inconvenience to the family. Under such circumstances, it would be unreasonable to find fault with the cook, who would only be following the bad example of those whose duty it is to preserve regularity. Their hours for going to bed, and getting up, should be as early as other arrangements will permit. But, those ought to be so regulated as to make it unnecessary that the servants should be kept up late, except on extraordinary occasions. Late dinners have, in a great measure, done away with hot suppers. Where these are not eaten, the labours of the twenty-four hours may be ended by ten o'clock at night; and that is the latest hour at which the servants of a family of the middle rank, and of regular habits, ought to remain up. Some one of the family should see that fires have been put out, and doors and windows secured.

The honesty of servants depends, principally, upon their bringing up. But it also depends much, with young servants especially, upon the temptations to be dishonest they may have had to contend with; and it is the duty of every master and mistress to put all such temptations out of their way, as much as possible. The practice of locking up does not, as a matter of course, imply *distrust*, but it denotes *care*; and surely carefulness is one of the first principles to impress upon the mind of a poor person. I would as scrupulously avoid anything which should lead a servant to imagine that a drawer or tea-chest was locked up from *her*, as I would avoid giving the same idea to an acquaintance; but it is a culpable practice to leave tea, sugar, wine, or other things, open at all times, or only now and then locked up. The *habit* is bad; and it is the result, not of generosity, but of negligence; it is also a habit which cannot fail to excite, in the minds of experienced and well-disposed servants, feelings rather of contempt, than of respect for their employers; while to the young, and more particularly to those of unsettled principles, it is nothing less than a temptation to crime. Little pilferings at the tea-chest, perhaps, have been the beginning of that which has ended in depriving a poor girl of her character, and, consequently, of all chance of gaining her bread by honest means. To suspect servants of being disposed to be dishonest merely because they are servants, is as silly as it is unfeeling. I should never hesitate to give my keys to a servant, when it happened to be inconvenient to me to leave company, any more than I should hesitate to entrust them to one of my own family; but such an act of confidence is far different in its effects, from that neglect which often proceeds from mere idleness, and, while it proclaims a disregard of the value of property, is the occasion of much waste, and, in the end, proves as ruinous to the employer as it is fatal in the way of example to servants.

That *"servants are plagues"* may be the fact; but when the hardships which belong to the life of a maid-servant are taken into consideration, the wonder is, that they are not less obedient to the will of their employers, and more callous to their displeasure, than we really find them. It is too much the habit to regard servants as inferior beings, hired and paid to perform certain services, but whose feelings are unworthy of the consideration of those upon whom they wait, for whom they cook, and whom they enable to sit at their ease, or to go about, and take their pleasure. True, they are paid for what they do; but how paid? Not in a degree adequate to their services. The double or the treble of what they are paid, would not compensate us for the discomfort of having to work for ourselves. Yet, "they are *paid* for it," is said in justification of unreasonable demands upon the time, strength, and patience of servants; when, in fact, the whole of the pay to a female servant consists of that food, without which she would be unable to work, and of a sum of money, barely sufficient to keep her clothed, which she is required to be, for the credit of the house she lives in. Ladies who shudder as they meet the cold air, in descending to their breakfast rooms, forget the sufferings of the female servant, who has, perhaps, gone to bed over-night exhausted by fatigue, but whose duty compels her to rise again, some hours before she is rested, to begin her work afresh, and to do over again all that had been done the day before. A lady who thinks her servant *sufficiently paid* for all she endures, has never known what it is to get up in the dark of a cold winter morning, and to spend half-an-hour on her knees, labouring to produce a polish on the bars of a grate, which bars were burnt black yesterday, and will be burnt black again to-day. Such a lady has never suffered from the drudgery of a kitchen, not from the scorching of a kitchen fire, either of which is sufficient to impair the constitution of any woman, independently of all that wearing of the spirits, which those exposed to such trials must experience.

It is true, also, that it is by their own choice that servants go to service; they are not compelled to do so by any other law than that of necessity; but starvation is their only alternative; and we should think it hard to be reduced to the alternative of either starving to death, in the bloom of our youth, and of quitting a world which was made for us, as well as for our more fortunate fellow beings, or of yielding up the whole of our lives, to promote the ease of those who deem us amply rewarded, in being fed and clothed, and suffered to repose from toil, at those times only when their wants happen not to require our attention.

The apprehension of lowering our dignity and encouraging disrespect, by giving way to familiarity with inferiors, is pleaded by some as an excuse for haughty and overbearing demeanour towards servants. But such as adopt that kind of demeanour are mistaken. There are few better judges of good breeding than servants. Their ideas upon this subject are not formed by rules, or by fashions; but they have generally, from observation, a remarkably correct knowledge both of what is due to themselves, and of what is most becoming to the dignity of their superiors. I have occasionally been astonished at the quickness with which a servant has made the discovery, that some upstart person, notwithstanding her lofty bearing, "was no lady." The behaviour which characterises such persons is more likely to give rise to contempt, in those who are beneath them, than any behaviour that is unaffectedly conciliating and kind. To be loved, and to be cheerfully served, is for those only who respect the feelings, and consult the comfort of their dependents; and, as a single trait is often sufficient to reveal the whole character, they will most assuredly be disappointed, who expect to meet with the qualities which conduce to the happiness of domestic life, in a woman who considers the feelings of a female servant as unworthy of the same consideration as that which she gives to the feelings of others of her own sex.

With regard to the general character and merits of servants, nothing is more common than the remark, that "servants are not so good as they used to be." This is surely an error. There cannot be a greater predisposition to misconduct in them now than formerly. It may be said, that there are more frequent instances of bad conduct; but this does not warrant the idea, that the servants of the present day have a degree of inborn viciousness from which those of times past were free. If all who rail at the negligences, the waste, the want of care, the dislike of work, and the liking for dress and for gadding, to which servants are as much addicted as their betters; if all such were themselves as free from fault as they would have their servants be, it would probably be found that the effect, what with precept and example combined, would be quite enough to banish this commonplace remark. The truth is, that the change which has taken place in the habits of the middle class, has produced a change, but a very natural change, in the habits of those of a more humble station. There exists now a greater degree of high living than formerly; and consequently, a want of frugality, a waste in all sorts of ways, formerly unknown. Persons of moderate income keep more company than persons of the same class used to keep; they imitate the late hours, and other fashionable habits which used to be reckoned among the privileges of their superiors in fortune, instead of wisely avoiding emulation in such things, and keeping to their own more simple, and less hazardous mode of life. What wonder, then, if we find the most humble copying those of the middling, when the middling are doing all they can to rival those of the highest rank.

Servants were formerly more the object of care with their employers than they have been of late. When ladies gave a considerable portion of their time to domestic duties, and prided themselves on their skill in household matters, they were not above maintaining a certain degree of friendly intercourse with their servants. This afforded opportunities for giving good counsel, and for superintending their conduct, and was a more efficient check upon them than "a good scolding now and then," which many think better than "being always on the watch."

In addressing myself to young persons, it may not be considered impertinent or foreign to the general purpose of this work, to offer a few remarks upon the subject of company. I do not mean in respect to the selection of friends and acquaintance, or the *kind* of visitors proper to be invited, but simply as to the mode of entertaining them, which must, necessarily, be a matter of importance in housekeeping, and, therefore, comes properly within the scope of domestic economy.

It should be a rule, not to invite such visitors as cannot be entertained without trespassing on the comforts and conveniences of the family. True hospitality may be enjoyed without much ceremony, and may be practised in the plainest manner; but when efforts to entertain *company* disturb the usual arrangements of a house, they are inconsistent with their object. Let nothing, therefore, be attempted which cannot be performed without difficulty; let nothing be provided which cannot be provided plentifully; let nothing which is necessary be wanting, and nothing produced which may seem to be out of place or uncalled for. Do nothing, in short, which you cannot really afford to do; and the result will be, that while you consult your own ease, you will, at the same time, ensure that freedom from restraint which contributes, more than all besides, to make visiting agreeable, and which never fails to create in your departing guest, those mixed feelings of regret at going, but of pleasure at the prospect of returning, which are amongst the most flattering acknowledgments that genuine hospitality can receive.

CHAPTER II.

The Store Room; the mode of fitting up, and the uses of it

Every housekeeper knows the value of a good Store-room; for it seems to be little less essential than a good kitchen. Few modern town residences, except those for large establishments, have a store-room sufficiently large to answer all its purposes.

In the country a good store-room is so indispensable that where there is none it ought to be built; it should be on the same floor with, and as near as possible to, the kitchen; and as this would be on the ground floor, it would be necessary to make a cellar underneath, or to raise the building a little distance from the ground, to prevent its being damp, above all things to be guarded against, in a place where stores are kept. It may, perhaps, be kept dry by flues from the kitchen fire; and this would be a saving of fuel and labour; but if not practicable, the room should have a fire-place.

If it be sufficiently large, and there be no other place for the purpose, there might be a closet, or press, for household linen. This should always be kept in a dry situation, and in some houses a small room is fitted up, with closets or presses round it, some of these having shelves or drawers for linen, and others with hooks, for a variety of things belonging to a family; but in this room there ought to be a fire-place, unless it be aired by one adjoining. In the store-room, there should be a closet or shelves for china and glass, not in every-day use. But as these ought to be free from dust, open shelves would not be so desirable as a closet; and if expense is not of importance, glass doors would be the most convenient. Preserves and pickles require air; they will ferment if shut up, or the place very warm; and, therefore, open shelves are best for them; and they should be at a convenient distance from the ground, so as not to be out of sight, for they ought to be examined frequently, and the coverings dusted. For bottles of green gooseberries, peas, or any kind of fruit preserved dry, without sugar, have shelves with holes in them, to turn the bottles with their necks downwards. This effectually excludes the air.

A dresser is a convenience in a store-room; or a table in the middle of the room may answer the purpose; but in either of these, or at the bottom of the linen press, there should be drawers for dusters, tea-cloths, &c., &c., unless they be kept in the Pantry.

There should be boxes for candles and soap, but as these smell, the store-boxes may be kept in a garret, or some dry place, and a smaller quantity in the store-room for immediate use. Late in the summer is the best time to provide the year's stock of candles and soap. Both are the better for being kept some time before they are used: and the latter should be cut in pieces the size required for the different household purposes, and left, before packed in the box, a few days exposed to the air; but not in a thorough draught, for that would cause the soap to crack. It is mismanagement to buy candles a few at a time, and soap just as it is wanted; and not good to buy cheap candles. The dearest articles are not always the best; but it is very certain that the best are the cheapest. Good candles afford more light than bad; and do not waste, particularly if they have been kept some time, even for a year.

There ought to be a place in the store-room appropriated to groceries, for they, too, should be laid in, not oftener than two or three times a year. The price of starch varies with the price of flour; and, therefore, as it keeps well, a stock should be laid in when flour is at a low price. Rice keeps very well, and is useful in a family, particularly in the country, where new milk and eggs are plenty. We once kept a quantity more than three years, by spreading a well-aired linen sheet in a box, and folding it over the rice, the sheet lifted out on the floor, once in two or three months, and the rice spread about upon the sheet for a day or two. This had the effect of keeping away the weevil. Jars and canisters, with closely fitting lids, for tea, sugar, coffee, cocoa, mustard, pepper, spices, and such things, will last many years. By giving, in the course of the year, one or two large orders, to any respectable shop, and always to the same one, you may pretty well depend upon being supplied with good articles; but not so, if you send here and there, and for small quantities at a time; besides the inconvenience of finding yourself, now and then, without the very thing which you want. To dispose of these things properly, they should be kept in a closet, some in earthen jars, others in tin or japan boxes; and the spices in little drawers very closely fitted. If drawers, which are preferable, they should be labelled.

As it may be convenient sometimes to perform little culinary matters in the store-room, there should be a rolling pin, pasteboard, and pestle and mortar kept there, in addition to those of the kitchen, and on this account a small marble slab would be very useful, for making pastry in hot weather. The fire-place might have an oven attached to it; for though it would be imprudent to heat the store-room, on account of preserves, &c., it may be occasionally used, when there is more cooking than usual. Besides which, in the season for making preserves, a hot plate in the store-room would be found useful. Weights and scales of various sizes are absolutely necessary, that the housekeeper may be able to ascertain the weight of the largest joint of meat, as well as of the smallest quantity of spice. Care should be taken to keep these in good order.—A hanging shelf is also a good thing in a store-room. Here the flour-bin may find a place, if there be no other more suitable.

A store-room of this description is not adapted for keeping fruit; it would be too warm, besides that the fruit might prove injurious to other stores, from the smell which it occasions. There are various methods of keeping apples through the winter; but scarcely any other will be found to succeed so well as that of making layers of fruit, and layers of perfectly fresh and dry straw, in hampers, boxes, or the corner of a dry room. The apples should be examined every now and then, the specked ones taken away for use, the others wiped, and covered up again. In hard frosts, windows that have no shutters could be covered with rugs, old carpet, or mats, and something of the same kind spread over the apples. When we were in America, we were surprised to find that our neighbours took so little care to preserve their apples, during the three months of unremitting hard frost, which occur in their winter season. They merely laid their apples on the floor of a spare room, sometimes of the barn, or of an outhouse, each sort by itself, and then covered them with a linen sheet. The people told us that their apples never became frozen, and attributed this to the dryness of the atmosphere. Apples and pears may also be preserved in the following way. Gather them on a dry day: wipe, and roll them, singly, in very soft paper, then pack them in jars, each containing about a gallon. Put a cover on the jar, and cement it closely, so as to keep out the air; and place the jar in a dry cellar. When a jar is opened, the fruit will eat the better for being taken out of the paper, and exposed to the air of a warm room for two or three days. Large baking pears may be suspended by their stalks on lines, placed across near the ceiling of a room. There are many ways of preserving grapes; but the best way is, to gather them with about five or six inches of the branch to each bunch, to seal the end with common sealing wax, and hang them to lines in a dry room. Examine them frequently, and cut out the mouldy berries. Nuts of all kinds may be preserved in jars, the covers cemented, the jars in a dry cellar.

In this short sketch of what a store-room ought to be, even in the plainest houses in the country, many things requisite to the fitting up of a complete one are omitted. But one thing more necessary to be observed than any other, must not be omitted; which is, that it must be always in order, and everything kept in its proper place, or the main object in having it will be defeated. A store-room out of order can be compared to nothing but a drawer in a state of confusion. A lady once dressing in haste, to keep an appointment for which she was already too late, needed the assistance of all about her, to aid in her search for different articles necessary to complete her toilet. I sought a pair of gloves, and discovered many single ones of various sorts and colours, but no two to form a perfect match. And with this ill success must have ended my labours, if the drawer had not been regularly *put to rights*: and by the time that scarfs were folded, ribands rolled, collars smoothed, and scissors disentangled from sewing silk, half a dozen gloves were paired.

The saving of time occasioned by observing order, and the waste of time occasioned by want of order, are incalculable. A general putting to rights, every now and then, does not answer the purpose, because, in that case, it is sure to happen that some things will find new places; and persons coming in a hurry be unable to find them. The mistress of a house, when she sends her servant or a child to a store-room, should be able to say precisely where what she wants may be found. Negligence, and its companion disorder, are the two demons of housekeeping. Once admit them, and, like the moth, they gradually but completely destroy.

CHAPTER III.

The Pantry; the uses of it, with Receipts for Cleaning Plate and Fur-
niture.

WHAT is commonly called the *Butler's Pantry*, does not of necessity imply the presence of a butler; nor does it require to be spacious, when the china and glass not in daily use are kept in the store-room. Where women servants only are kept, the care of the pantry belongs either to the parlourmaid or the housemaid, and the same servant usually performs the office of laying the cloth, and waiting at table: which is always done better by women than by men servants, except it be the higher order of men servants, those who are in the daily practice of it, and whose occupation is in the house. The same hands which, in the morning, rubbed down the horses, swept the stable, cleaned the harness, and blackened the shoes, seem unfit to be employed in placing dishes on the dining-table, folding up napkins, and handling tea-things. It is almost impossible that occupations so widely differing should be equally well suited to one and the same person. The employing of men servants in work which properly belongs to women is highly objectionable; and nothing renders travelling in the South of France and Italy so disagreeable as being waited on by men, acting as housemaids and chambermaids. If, indeed, men were employed to scrub the floor, wash the stone halls, and clean the dirty doorsteps in London, the lives of many female servants might be saved. But the more delicate occupations, such as wiping glasses, trimming candles, and waiting in the parlour, seem more suitable for women.

Some women servants, it is true, never learn to wait at table well; but, then, others are very expert at it. Short people are generally the most nimble, but it is desirable that the servant who waits at table be tall, for the convenience of setting on and taking off dishes; and it requires long arms to carry heavy mahogany trays. Practice is as necessary to good waiting as it is in any of the higher domestic occupations. The mistress, therefore, should require the same particularity in preparing the table, arranging the sideboard, and waiting at dinner, when her family dines alone, as she requires when there are visitors; because, in the latter case, an increase in number gives sufficient additional trouble to a servant, without her being thrown into confusion by having to do what she may have forgotten, from being out of practice.

There is one item of expenditure in housekeeping which should not be too narrowly restricted, and that is the washing of table-cloths and napkins. The fineness is not so much a matter of consideration with me: neither should I desire a clean table-cloth every day, merely for the sake of the change; but, if at all soiled, I would rather not see it on the table again. It is a very neat practice to spread a napkin on the centre of the table, large or small according to the size of the latter, and to remove it with the meat. In Italy this napkin is clean every day, and I have seen it folded in a three-cornered shape, and then crimped at the edges with the thumb and finger, which, when the napkin was spread out, gave it a pretty appearance. It is also a neat practice to place the dessert on the table cloth, and a convenient one too, where there are few servants, because the cloth saves the table; and rubbing spots out of dining tables, day after day, seems waste of labour. But the cloth must be preserved from gravy spots, or it will disgrace the dessert. A baize between two cloths is sometimes used, and this, being rolled up with the upper cloth and removed with the dinner, leaves the under cloth for the dessert. A table cloth *once folded* may be laid over the one which is spread, and then removed with the dinner. A table cloth press is a convenience.

The fitting up of the pantry must, in a great measure, be regulated by the style of the establishment, but, in any case, there should be a dresser, furnished with drawers, one for table cloths, napkins and mats (unless all these be kept in sideboard drawers); another for tea cloths, glass cloths, dusters, &c. &c., and another drawer lined with baize, for the plate which is in use. Plate-leathers, flannels and brushes, kept in a bag; and the cloths and brushes used in cleaning furniture, in another bag, to preserve them from dust. A small sink, with the water laid on, indispensable. There should also be a horse, or lines, for drying tea and glass cloths upon.

China and glass, whether plain or of the finest kind, require to be kept equally clean; and the servant whose business this is ought to have soft cloths for the purpose. China should be washed in warm water, with a piece of flannel, and wiped with a clean and soft cloth, or it will look dull. Glass washed in cold water, drained nearly dry, and then wiped; if the cloth be not clean and dry, the glasses will not look clear. For cut glass a brush, because a cloth will not reach into the crevices to polish it; and dull looking salts, or other cut glass, spoil the appearance of a table. Wash lamps and lustres with soap and cold water. When looking glasses are become tarnished and dull, thump them over with a linen bag containing powdered blue, and wipe it off with a soft cloth.

Paper trays are the best, considering the small difference in the price, compared with the great difference in the appearance: it would be better to save in many other things, than to hear tea-things, glasses, or snuffers, jingle on japan. Paper trays are very durable, if taken care of. They will seldom require washing; but when they do, the water should only be lukewarm, for if hot water be poured on them the paper will blister. Wipe clean with a wet cloth, and when dry, dust a little flour over, and wipe that off with a soft cloth. To prevent their being scratched, keep tea-boards and trays in green baize cases, under the dresser of the pantry, or, if convenient, hung against the wall, to be out of the way, when not in use.

Plate, plain, handsome, old or new, looks badly, if not perfectly clean and polished. Washing is of great consequence; and if in cold soft water, wiped dry with a linen cloth, and then polished with leather, it will not want any other cleaning oftener than once a week. Unskilful servants may do great injury by using improper things to polish plate, or by rubbing it too hard, for that may bend it. Plate should be kept covered up, when not in use, to preserve it from tarnish. Tea pots, coffee pots, sugar bowls, cream jugs, candlesticks, and all large things, each in a separate bag of cloth, baize, or leather; a lined basket for that which is in daily use, preserves it from scratches. Where there is neither butler, nor housekeeper, to take charge of it, the mistress of the house usually has the plate basket taken at night into her own room, or that of some one of the family, where it may, occasionally, be looked over and compared with the inventory, kept in the basket. If a spoon or any article be missing, it should be immediately inquired after; the effect of this will be that the servant who has the care of these things will take more care of them for the future. It has happened to us to have spoons found, at different times, in the pig-sty, which had been thrown out in the wash. If they had not been discovered there, the servant, who was only careless, might have been suspected of dishonesty.

To clean Plate.

Having ready two leathers, and a soft plate brush for crevices, and the plate being washed clean, which it always should be first, rub it with a mixture of prepared chalk, bought at the chemist's, and spirits of wine; let it dry, rub it off with flannel, and polish with leather. I find this the best way of all.

Much of the labour necessary to keep tables in good order might be saved, if mats were used, when jugs of hot water are placed on the table; and, also, if the servant were brought to apply a duster, the instant any accident had occurred to cause a stain. For this purpose a clean and white duster should always be in readiness. Rosewood and all polished, japanned, or other ornamental furniture, is best *dusted* with a silk handkerchief, and wiped with a soft leather. China and all ornaments dusted with clean leathers.

So little furniture is now used which is not *French polished*, that I shall only give the plainest receipt I know of, for cleaning mahogany. Take out ink spots with salts of lemon; wet the spot with water, put on enough to cover it, let it be a quarter of an hour, and if not disappeared, put a little more. Wash the table clean with stale beer, let it dry, then brush it well with a clean furniture brush. To polish it, use the following FURNITURE PASTE:—½ lb. beeswax, turpentine to moisten it, *or* spirits of wine, melt it, stirring well, and put by in a jar for use. Rub some on with a soft cloth, rub it off directly, and polish with another soft cloth.

Nothing betrays slovenliness and want of attention more than ill-used and badly cleaned knives and forks. Plate, glass and china, however common, may be made to answer every purpose; but knives and forks ought to be good in quality, or they soon wear out, and nothing looks so bad on a table as bad knives and forks, and when good they are so expensive that it is unpardonable not to take care of them. Carving knives are of great consequence; there should be a judicious assortment of them, to suit various joints, or different carvers, and particular attention paid to their cleaning and sharpening. When it can be done, knives and forks should be cleaned immediately after they have been used; but when not, they ought, if possible, to be dipped in warm (not hot) water, wiped dry, and laid by till the time of cleaning comes. After bath brick has been used, dip the handles into lukewarm water, or wipe them with a soaped flannel, and then with a dry soft cloth. Inexperienced men servants seldom *wipe* knives and forks sufficiently; but it is next to impossible for a woman to clean them well, and it is a masculine occupation. To preserve those not in daily use from rust, rub with mutton fat, roll each one in brown paper, and keep in a dry place. A good knife-board indispensable; covered with leather saves the steel, but the knives not so sharp as if cleaned on a board, and bath brick. Both knives and forks are the better for being occasionally plunged into fresh fine earth, for a few minutes. It sweetens them.

Knife-trays do not always have so much care as they ought to have. Out of sight when in the dining-room, they are often neglected in the pantry; but they ought to be as clean as the waiters on which glasses are handed. The tray made of basket work and lined with tin, is best; there should be a clean cloth spread in it, before it is brought into the parlour, and also one in the second tray to receive the knives and forks, as they are taken from the table.

CHAPTER IV.

The Larder; with Directions for Keeping and Salting Meat. Seasons
for Meat, Poultry, Game, Fish and Vegetables

THE LARDER

A GOOD larder is essential to every house. It should have a free circulation of air through it, and not be exposed to the sun. If it can be so contrived, the larder ought to be near the kitchen, for the convenience of the cook. For a family of moderate style of living it need not be very roomy. There should be large and strong hooks for meat and poultry; a hanging shelf so placed as for the cook to reach it with ease; and a safe, either attached to the wall, or upon a stand, for dishes of cold meat, pastry, or anything which would be exposed to dust and flies on the shelf. Wire covers should be provided for this purpose, and in hot weather, when it may be necessary to place dishes of meat on a brick floor, these covers will be found to answer every purpose of a safe. There should be a pan, with a cover, for bread, another for butter, and one for cheese. A shelf for common earthenware bowls, dishes, &c., &c., &c. Cold meat, and all things left from the dinner, should be put away in common brown or yellow ware; there ought to be an ample supply of these. Tubs and pans for salted meat sometimes stand in the dairy, but it is not the proper place for them, for meat ought not to be kept in a dairy.

Meat should be examined every day in cold, and oftener in warm weather, as it sometimes taints very soon. Scrape off the outside, if the least appearance of mould, on mutton, beef, or venison; and flour the scraped parts. By well peppering meat you may keep away flies, which cause so much destruction in a short time. But a very coarse cheese-cloth, wrapped round the joint, is more effectual, if the meat is to be dressed soon. Remove the kidneys, and all the suet, from loins which are wanted to hang long, in warm or close weather, and carefully wipe and flour that part of the meat. Before you put meat which is rather stale to the fire, wipe it with a cloth dipped in vinegar. A joint of beef, mutton, or venison, may be saved by being wrapped in a cloth and buried, over night, in a hole dug in fresh mould. Neither veal, pork, or lamb should be kept long.

Poultry and game keep for some length of time, if the weather be dry and cold, but if moist or warm, will be more liable to taint, than venison or any kind of meat, except veal. A piece of charcoal put inside of any kind of poultry will greatly assist to preserve it. Poultry should be picked, drawn and cropped. Do not wash, but wipe it clean, and sprinkle the parts most likely to taint with powdered loaf sugar, salt, and pepper. As I should reject the use of all chemical processes, for the preservation of meat, I do not recommend them to others.

Frost has a great effect upon meat, poultry, and game. Some cooks will not be persuaded of the necessity for its being completely *thawed before it is put near the fire*; yet it neither roasts, boils, nor eats well, unless this be done. If slightly frozen, the meat may be recovered, by being five or six hours in the kitchen; *not* near the fire. Another method is, to plunge a joint into a tub of *cold* water, let it remain two or three hours, or even longer, and the ice will appear on the outside. Meat should be cooked immediately after it has been thawed, for it will keep no longer.

If the tastes of all persons were simple and unvitiated, there would be little occasion for the cook's ingenuity to preserve meat after it has begun to putrefy. An objection to meat in that state, does not arise merely from distaste, but from a conviction of its being most unwholesome. There may have been a difference of opinion among the scientific upon this subject: but, it seems now to be generally considered by those who best understand such matters, that when meat has become poisonous to the air, it is no longer good and nutritious food. The fashion of eating meat *à la cannibale*, or half raw, being happily on the decline, we may now venture to express our dislike to eat things which are half decomposed, without incurring the charge of vulgarity.

SALTING AND CURING MEAT.

The Counties of England differ materially in their modes of curing bacon and pork; but the palm of excellency in bacon has so long been decreed to Hampshire, that I shall give no other receipts for it, but such as are practised in that, and the adjoining counties. The best method of keeping, feeding, and killing pigs, is detailed in COBBETT's *Cottage Economy*; and there, also, will be found directions for salting and smoking the flitches, in the way commonly practised in the farm-houses in Hampshire. The *smoking* of bacon is an important affair, and experience is requisite to give any thing like perfection in the art. The process should not be too slow nor too much hurried. The skin should be made of a dark brown colour, but not black; for by smoking the bacon till it becomes black, it will also be made hard, and cease to have any flavour but that of rust.—Before they are dressed, both bacon and hams require to be soaked in water; the former an hour or two, the latter, all night, or longer, if very dry. But, according to some, the best way to soak a ham is to bury it in the earth, for one, two, or three nights and days, according to its state of dryness.

Meat will not take salt well either in frosty or in warm weather. Every thing depends upon the first rubbing; and the salt, or pickle, should not only be well rubbed in, but this is best done by a hard hand. The following general direction for salting meat may be relied on:—"6 lbs. of salt, 1 lb. of coarse sugar, and 4 oz. of saltpetre, boiled in 4 gallons of water, skimmed and allowed to cool, forms a very strong pickle, which will preserve any meat completely immersed in it. To effect this, which is essential, either a heavy board or flat stone must be laid upon the meat. The same pickle may be used repeatedly, provided it be boiled up occasionally with additional salt to restore its strength, diminished by the combination of part of the salt with the meat, and by the dilution of the pickle by the juices of the meat extracted. By boiling, the *albumen*, which would cause the pickle to spoil, is coagulated and rises in the form of scum, which must be carefully removed."

It is a good practice to wash meat before it is salted. This is not generally done; but pieces of pork, and, more particularly, beef and tongues, should first lie in cold spring water, and then be well washed to cleanse them from all impurities, in order to ensure their being free from taint; after which, drain the meat, and it will take the salt much quicker for the washing.—Examine it well; and be careful to take all the kernels out of beef.

Some persons like salted meat to be red. For this purpose, saltpetre is necessary. Otherwise, the less use is made of it the better, as it tends to harden the meat. Sweet herbs, spices, and even garlic, may be rubbed into hams and tongues, with the pickle, according to taste. Bay salt gives a nice flavour. Sugar is generally used in curing hams, tongues and beef; for the two latter some recommend lump sugar, others treacle, to make the meat eat short.

In cold weather salt should be warmed before the fire. Indeed, some use it quite hot. This causes it to penetrate more readily into the meat than it does when rendered hard and dry by frost.

Salting troughs or tubs should be clean, and in an airy place. After meat of any kind has been once well rubbed, keep it covered close, not only with the lid of the vessel, but, in addition, with the thick folds of some woollen article, in order to exclude the air. This is recommended by good housekeepers; yet in Hampshire the trough is sometimes left uncovered, the flitches purposely exposed to the air.

To cure Bacon.

As soon as the hog is cut up, sprinkle salt thickly over the flitches, and let them lie on a brick floor all night. Then wipe the salt off, and lay them in a salting trough. For a large flitch of bacon, allow 2 gallons of salt, 1 lb. of bay salt, 4 cakes of salt prunella, a ¼ lb. of saltpetre, and 1 lb. of common moist sugar; divide this mixture into two parts; rub one half into it the first day, and rub it in *well*. The following day rub the other half in, and continue to rub and turn the flitch every day for three weeks. Then hang the flitches to drain, roll them in bran, and hang them to smoke, in a wood-fire chimney. The more quickly, in reason, they are smoked, the better the bacon will taste.

To cure a Ham.

Let a leg of pork hang for three days; then beat it with a rolling pin, and rub into it 1 oz. of saltpetre finely powdered, and mixed with a small quantity of common salt; let it lie all night. Make the following pickle: a quart of stale strong beer, ½ lb. of bay salt, ½ lb. of common salt, and the same of brown sugar; boil this twenty minutes, then wipe the ham dry from the salt, and with a wooden ladle, pour the pickle, by degrees, and as hot as possible, over the ham; and as it cools, rub it well into every part. Rub and turn it every day, for a week; then hang it, a fortnight, in a wood-smoke chimney. When you take it down, sprinkle black pepper over the bone, and into the holes, to keep it safe from hoppers, and hang it up in a thick paper bag.

Another.

For one of 16 lb. weight. Rub the rind side of the ham with ¼ lb. of brown sugar, then rub it with 1 lb. of salt, and put it in the salting-pan, then rub a little of the sugar, and 1 oz. of saltpetre, and 1 oz. salt prunel, pounded, on the lean side, and press it down; in three days turn it and rub it well with the salt in the pan, then turn it in the pickle for three weeks; take it out, scrape it well, dry it with a clean cloth, rub it slightly with a little salt, and hang it up to dry.

Another.

Beat the ham well on the fleshy side with a rolling pin, then rub into it, on every part, 1 oz. of saltpetre, and let it lie one night. Then take a ½ pint of common salt, and a ¼ pint of bay salt, and 1 lb. of coarse sugar or treacle; mix these ingredients, and make them very hot in a stew-pan, and rub in well for an hour. Then take ½ a pint more of common salt and lay all over the ham, and let it lie on till it melts to brine; keep the ham in the pickle three weeks or a month, till you see it shrink. This is sufficient for a large ham.

Another, said to be equal to the Westphalian.

Rub a large fat ham well, with 2 oz. of pounded saltpetre, 1 oz. of bay salt, and a ¼ lb. of lump sugar: let it lie two days. Prepare a pickle as follows: boil in 2 quarts of stale ale, 1 lb. of bay salt, 2 lb. of common salt, ¾ lb. of lump sugar, 2 oz. of salt prunella, 1 oz. of pounded black pepper, and ½ an oz. of cloves; boil this well, and pour it boiling hot over the ham. Rub and turn it every day for three weeks or a month; then smoke it for about a fortnight.

To cure a Mutton Ham.

A hind quarter must be cut into the shape of a ham: rub into it the following mixture: ¼ lb. saltpetre, ¼ lb. bay salt, 1 lb. common salt, and ¼ lb. loaf sugar; rub well, every other day, for a fortnight, then take it out, press it under a weight for one day, then hang it to smoke ten or fifteen days. It will require long soaking, if kept any length of time, before it is dressed. Boil very gently, three hours. It is eaten cut in slices, and these broiled for breakfast or lunch.—*Or*; the ham smoked longer, not boiled, but slices very thinly shaved to eat by way of relish at breakfast.

To pickle Pork.

For a hog of 10 score.—When it is quite cold, and cut up in pieces, have well mixed 2 gallons of common salt, and 1½ lb. of saltpetre; with this, rub well each piece of pork, and as you rub, pack it in a salting tub, and sprinkle salt between each layer. Put a heavy weight on the top of the cover, to prevent the meat's swimming. If kept close and tight in this way, it will keep for a year or two.

Leg of Pork.

Proceed as above, salt in proportion, but leave out the saltpetre if you choose. The hand and *spring* also, in the same way—and a week sufficient for either. Rub and turn them every day.

Pig's Head in the same way, but it will require two weeks.

To pickle a Tongue.

Rub the tongue over with common salt; and cut a slit in the root, so that the salt may penetrate. Drain the tongue next day, and rub it over with 2 oz. of bay salt, 2 oz. of saltpetre, and 2 oz. of lump or coarse sugar, all mixed together. This pickle should be poured over the tongue, with a spoon, every day, as there will not be sufficient liquor to cover it. It will be ready to dress in three weeks or a month.

To salt Beef.

Be sure to take out the *kernels*, and also be sure to fill up the holes with salt, as well as those which the butcher's skewers have made. In frosty weather, take care that the meat be not frozen; also, to warm the salt before the fire, or in a frying pan.

For a piece of 20 lb. weight.—Sprinkle the meat with salt, and let it lie twenty-four hours; then hang it up to drain. Take 1 oz. of saltpetre, a ½ oz. of salt prunella, a ¼ lb. of very coarse sugar, 6 oz. of common salt, all finely powdered, and rub it well into the beef. Rub and turn it every day. It will be ready to dress in ten days, but may be kept longer.

To salt a Round of Beef.

For one of 30 lb. weight.—Rub common salt well into it all over and in every part, cover it well with salt: rub it well next day, pouring the brine over the meat. Repeat this every day for a fortnight, when it will be ready. Let it drain for 15 minutes, when you are going to cook it. You may, if you wish it to look red, add 4 oz. salt prunel, and 1 lb. saltpetre to the pickle.

An Edge Bone.

To one of 10 or 12 lb. weight allow ¾ lb. of salt, and 1 oz. of moist sugar. Rub these well into the meat. Repeat the rubbing every day, turning the meat also, and it will be ready to dress in four or five days.

Tongue Beef.

After the tongues are taken out of the pickle, wash and wipe dry a piece of flank or brisket of beef; sprinkle with salt, and let it lie a night; then hang it to drain, rub in a little fresh salt, and put the beef into the pickle; rub and turn it every day for three or four days, and it will be ready to dress, and if the pickle have been previously well prepared, will be found to have a very fine flavour.

To smoke Beef.

Cut a round into pieces of 5 lb. weight each, and salt them very well; when sufficiently salted, hang the pieces in a wood-smoke chimney to dry, and let them hang three or four weeks. This may be grated, for breakfast or luncheon. *Another.*—Cut a leg of beef like a ham, and to one of 14 lb. make a pickle of 1 lb. salt, 1 lb. brown sugar, 1 oz. saltpetre, and 1 oz. bay salt. Rub and turn the ham every day for a month, then roll it in bran and smoke it. Hang it in a dry place. Broil it in slices.

To make pickle for Brawn.

To rather more than a sufficient quantity of water to cover it, put 7 or 8 handsful of bran, a few bay leaves, also salt enough to give a strong relish; boil this an hour and a half, then strain it. When cold, pour the pickle from the sediment into a pan, and put the meat into it.

Any of these pickles may be used again. First boil it up and take off all the scum.

THE SEASONS FOR MEAT, POULTRY, GAME, AND VEGETABLES.

It is always the best plan to deal with a respectable butcher, and to keep to the same one. He will find his interest in providing his regular customers with good meat, and the *best* is always the *cheapest*, even though it may cost a little more money.

Beef is best and cheapest from Michaelmas to Midsummer.

Veal is best and cheapest from March to July.

Mutton is best from Christmas to Midsummer.

Grass Lamb is best from Easter to June.

House Lamb comes in in February.

Poultry is in the greatest perfection, when it is in the greatest plenty, which it is about September.

Chickens come in the beginning of April, but they may be had all the year round.

Fowls are dearest in April, May, and June, but they may be had all the year round, and are cheapest in September, October, and November.

Capons are finest at Christmas.

Poulards, with *eggs*, come in in March.

Green Geese come in in March, and continue till September.

Geese are in full season in September, and continue till February.

Turkey Poults come in in April, and continue till June.

Turkeys are in season from September till March, and are cheapest in October and November.

Ducks are in season from June till February.

Wild Ducks, Widgeons, Teal, Plovers, Pintails, Larks, Snipes, Woodcocks, from the end of October till the end of March.

Tame Pigeons are in season all the year, *Wild Pigeons* from March till September.

Pea-Fowl (young ones) from January till June.

Partridges from 1st September till January.

Pheasants from 1st October till January.

Grouse from the 12th of August till Christmas, also *Black Cocks* and *Grey Hens*.

Guinea Fowls from the end of January till May; their eggs are much more delicate than common ones.

Hares from September to March.

Leverets from March to September.

Rabbits all the year round.

Fish.

The seasons of Fish frequently vary; therefore the surest way to have it good is to confide in the honesty of respectable fishmongers; unless, indeed, you are well acquainted with the several sorts, and have frequent practice in the choosing of it. No fish when out of season can be wholesome food.

Turbot is in season from September to May. Fish of this kind do not all spawn at the same time; therefore, there are good as well as bad all the year round. The finest are brought from the Dutch coast. The belly of a Turbot should be cream coloured, and upon pressing your finger on this part, it should spring up. A Turbot eats the better for being kept two or three days. Where there is any apprehension of its not keeping, a little salt may be sprinkled on it, and the fish hung in a cool dry place.

Salmon.—This favourite fish is the most unwholesome of all. It ought never to be eaten unless perfectly fresh, and in season. Salmon is in season from Christmas till September. The Severn Salmon, indeed, is in season in November, but it is then obtained only in small quantities. This, and the Thames Salmon, are considered the best. That which comes from Scotland, packed in ice, is not so good. *Salmon Peel* are very nice flavoured, but much less rich than large Salmon; come in June.

Cod is in perfection at Christmas; but it comes in, generally, in October; in the months of February and March it is poor, but in April and May it becomes finer. The Dogger Bank Cod are considered the best. Good Cod fish are known by the yellow spots on a pure white skin. In cold weather they will keep a day or two.

Skate, Haddocks, Soles, Plaice, and *Flounders* are in season in January, as well as *Smelts* and *Prawns*. In February, *Lobsters* and *Herrings* become more plentiful; *Haddocks* not in such good flavour as they were. In March *Salmon* becomes plentiful, but is still dear. And in this month the *John Dory* comes in.

In April *Smelts* and *Whiting* are plentiful; and *Mackerel* and *Mullet* come in; also river *Trout*.

In May *Oysters* go out of season, and *Cod* becomes not so good; excepting these, all the fish that was in season at Christmas, is in perfection in this month.

In June *Salmon, Turbot, Brill, Skate, Halibut, Lobsters, Crabs, Prawns, Soles, Eels* and *Whiting* are plentiful and cheap. Middling sized Lobsters are best, and must weigh heavy to be good. The best Crabs measure about eight inches across the shoulders. The silver eel is the best, and, next to that, the copper-brown backed eel. A humane method of putting this fish to death is to run a sharp-pointed skewer or fine knitting needle into the spinal marrow, through the back part of the skin, and life will instantly cease.

In July fish of all sorts plentiful, except Oysters, and about at the cheapest. Cod not in much estimation.

In the months of August and September, particularly the former, fish is considered more decidedly unwholesome than at any other time of the year, and more especially in London. *Oysters* come in, and *Turbot* and *Salmon* go out of season. In choosing Oysters, natives are best; they should be eaten as soon after they are opened as possible. There are various ways of *keeping* and *feeding* oysters, for which see Index.

In October *Cod* comes in good season, also *Haddocks, Brill, Tench,* and every sort of shell fish.

In November most sorts of fish are to be got, but all are dear. *Oysters* are excellent in this month.

Fresh Herrings from November to January.

River Eels all the year.

Red Mullet come in May.

Flounders and *Plaice* in June.

Sprats beginning of November.

Gurnet is best in the spring.

Sturgeon in June.

Yarmouth Mackerel from May till August.

Vegetables.

Artichokes are in season from July to October.

Jerusalem Artichokes from September till June.

Asparagus, forced, may be obtained in January; the natural growth, it comes in about the middle of April, and continues through May, June, and July.

French Beans, forced, may be obtained in February, of the natural growth, the beginning of July; and they continue in succession through August.

Red Beet is in season all the year.

Scotch Cale in November.

Brocoli in October.

Cabbage of most sorts in May, June, July, and August.

Cardoons from November till March.

Carrots come in in May.

Cauliflowers, the beginning of June.

Celery, the beginning of September.

Corn Salad, in May.

Cucumbers may be forced as early as March; of their natural growth they come in July, and are plentiful in August and September.

Endive comes in in June, and continues through the winter.

Leeks come in in September, and continue till the Spring.

Lettuce, both the Coss and the Cabbage, come in about April, and continue to the end of August.

Onions, for keeping, in August.

Parsley, all the year.

Parsnips come in in October; but they are not good until the frost has touched them.

Peas, the earliest forced, come in about the beginning of May; of their natural growth, about the beginning of June, and continue till the end of August.

Potatoes, forced, in the beginning of March; and the earliest of natural growth in May.

Radishes, about the beginning of March.

Small Salad, in May and June; but may be had all the year.

Salsify and *Scorzonera*, in July and August.

Sea Kale may be found as early as December or January, but of the natural growth it comes in in April and May.

Eschalots, for keeping, in August and three following months.

Spring Spinach, in March, April, and three following months.

Winter Spinach from October through the winter.

Turnips, of the garden, in May; but the field Turnips, which are best, in October.

CHAPTER V.

The Kitchen, with observations upon the fitting it up

THE benefit of a good kitchen is well known to every housekeeper, but it is not every mistress that is aware of the importance of having a good cook. I have seen kitchens which, though fitted up with every convenience, and certainly at considerable expense, yet failed to send forth good dinners, merely because the lady of the house was not happy in her choice of a cook. I do not in the least admire gourmands, or gourmandism; and yet I would be more particular in selecting the servant who is to perform the business of preparing the food of the family, than I should deem it necessary to be in selecting any of the other servants. In large establishments there is a greater quantity of cookery to be performed, and, consequently, a greater quantity of waste is likely to be caused by unskilful cooks, than there can be in small families; but even in the latter considerable waste may be the consequence of saving a few pounds a year in the wages of a cook. An experienced cook knows the value of the articles submitted to her care; and she knows how to turn many things to account which a person unacquainted with cooking would throw away. A good cook knows how to convert the remains of one dinner into various dishes to form the greater part of another dinner; and she will, also, be more capable than the other of forwarding her mistress's charitable intentions; for her capability in cooking will enable her to take advantage of everything which can be spared from the consumption of the family, to be converted into nourishing food for the poor, for those of her own class who have not the comfort of a home such as she herself enjoys. The cook who knows how to preserve the pot-liquor of fresh meat to make soup, will, whenever she boils mutton, fowls, or rabbits, &c., &c., carefully scum it, and, by adding peas, other vegetables, or crusts of bread, and proper seasonings, make some tolerable soup for poor people, out of materials which would otherwise be thrown away.

To be a good cook she must take pleasure in her occupation; for the requisite painstaking cannot be expected from a person who dislikes the fire, or who entertains a disgust for the various processes necessary to convert meat into savoury dishes. But a cook who takes pride in sending a dinner well dressed to table, may be *depended upon*, and that is of great importance to the mistress of a house: for though Englishmen may not be such connoisseurs in eating as Frenchmen, I question whether French husbands are more dissatisfied with a badly-cooked dinner than English husbands are. Dr. KITCHENER observes, "God sends us victuals, but *who* sends us cooks?" And the observation is not confined to the Doctor, for the walls of many a dining-room have echoed it, to the great discomfiture of the lady presiding at the head of the table. Ladies might, if they would, be obliged to confess that many ill humours had been occasioned by either under or over roasted meat, cold plates, or blunt knives; and perhaps these *are* grounds for complaint. Of the same importance as the cooking is neatness in serving the dinner, for there is a vast difference in its appearance if neatly and properly arranged in hot dishes, the vegetables and sauces suitable to the meat, and *hot*—there is a vast difference between a dinner so served, and one a part of which is either too much or too little cooked, the meat parting from the bone in one case, or looking as if barely warmed through in the other case; the gravy chilled and turning to grease, some of the vegetables watery, and others crisped, while the edges of the dishes are slopped, and the block-tin covers look dull. A leg of mutton or piece of beef, either boiled or roasted—so commonly the dinner of a plain-living family—requires as much skill and nicety as the most complicated made dishes; and a plain dinner well cooked and served is as tempting to the appetite as it is creditable to the mistress of the house, who invariably suffers in the estimation of her guests for the want of ability in her servants. The elegance of the drawing-room they have just left is forgotten by those who are suffocating from the over-peppered soup; and the coldness of the plate on which is handed a piece of turbot bearing a reddish hue, may hold a place in the memory of a visitor, to the total obliteration of the winning graces, and agreeable conversation, of the lady at the head of the table.

It is impossible to give particular directions for fitting up a kitchen, because so much must depend upon the number of servants, and upon what is required in the way of cookery. It was the fashion formerly to adorn it with a quantity of copper saucepans, stewpans, &c., &c., very expensive, and troublesome to keep clean. Many of these articles, which were regularly scoured once a week, were not, perhaps, used once in the year. A young lady ought, if she has a good cook, to be guided by her, in some measure, in the purchase of kitchen utensils; for the accommodation of the cook, if she be a reasonable person, ought to be consulted. But, where there is no kitchen-maid to clean them, the fewer coppers and tins the better. It is the best plan to buy, at first, only just enough for use, and to replace these with new ones as they wear out; but all stewpans, saucepans, frying-pans, &c., &c., should be kept in good order—that is to say, clean and in good repair.

Some of the best cooks say that iron and block tin answer every purpose. There is an useful, but somewhat expensive, article, called the *Bain-marie*, for heating made dishes and soups, and keeping them hot for any length of time, without over-cooking them. A *Bain-marie* will be found very useful to persons who are in the habit of having made dishes. A *braising* kettle and a *stock-pot* also; and two or three cast-iron *Digesters*, of from one to two gallons, for soups and gravies. Saucepans should be washed and scoured as soon as possible after they have been used: wood ashes, or very fine sand, may be used. They should be rinsed in clean water, wiped dry (or they will rust), and then be turned down on a clean shelf. The upper rim may be kept bright, but it seems labour lost to scour that part where the fire reaches; besides which, the more they are scoured the more quickly they wear out. Copper utensils must be well tinned, or they become poisonous. Never allow anything to be put by in a copper vessel; but the fatal consequences of neglect in this particular are too well known for it to be necessary here to say much in the way of caution.

The fire-place is a matter of great importance. I have not witnessed the operations of many of the steam cooking apparatuses, which the last thirty years have produced, but the few I have seen do not give me satisfaction. It is certainly desirable that every *possible* saving should be made in the consumption of coals; but it is *not possible* to have cooking in perfection, without a proper degree of heat; and, as far as my observation has gone, meat cannot be well roasted unless before a good fire. I should save in many things rather than in coals; and am often puzzled to account for the false economy which leads persons to be sparing of their fuel, whilst they are lavish in other things infinitely less essential. A cook has many trials of her temper, but none so difficult to bear as the annoyance of a bad fire; for she cannot cook her dinner well, however much she may fret herself in the endeavour; and the waste caused by spoiling meat, fish, poultry, game, &c., is scarcely made up for by saving a few shillings in coals. "Economy in fuel" is so popular, that every species of invention is resorted to, in order to go without fire; and the price of coals is talked of in a fine drawing room, where the shivering guest turns, and often in vain, to seek comfort from the fire, which, alas! the brightly polished grate does not contain. The beauty of the cold marble structure which rises above it, and is reflected in the opposite mirror, is a poor compensation for the want of warmth. I advise young housekeepers to bear in mind, that of the many things which may be saved in a house, without lessening its comforts, firing is *not* one.

It is best to lay in coals in the month of August or September, to last until the spring. They should be of the best kind; paid for in ready money, to prevent an additional charge for credit. The first year of housekeeping will give a pretty correct average to go by: and then the consumption should be watched, but not too rigidly.

To return to the fire-place.—Perhaps there is no apparatus more convenient for a family of moderate style of living than the common kitchen range, that which has a boiler for hot water on one side, and an oven on the other side. It is a great convenience to have a constant supply of hot water, and an advantage to possess the means of baking a pie, pudding, or cake; and this may always be done, when there is a large fire for boiling or roasting. There is a great difference in the construction of these little ovens. We have had several, and only three which answered; and these were all, I believe, by different makers.—A *Hot plate* is also an excellent thing, as it requires but little fire to keep it sufficiently hot for any thing requiring gradual cooking; and is convenient for making preserves, which should never be exposed to the fierceness of a fire. The charcoal stoves are useful, and so easily constructed that a kitchen should not be without one. There is a very nice thing, called a *Dutch Stove*, but I do not know whether it is much in use in England. On a rather solid frame-work, with four legs, about a foot from the ground, is raised a round brick-work, open at the top sufficiently deep to receive charcoal, and in the front, a little place to take out the ashes; on the top is a trivet, upon which the stew-pan, or preserving-pan, or whatever it may be, is placed. This is easily moved about, and in the summer could be placed anywhere in the cool, and would, therefore, be very convenient for making preserves.—Where there is much cooking, a *Steamer* is convenient; it may be attached to the boiler of the range. I have seen lamb and mutton which had been steamed, and which in appearance was more delicate than when boiled, and equally well flavoured. But there is an *uncertainty* in cooking meat by steam, and, besides, there is no liquor for soup. Puddings cook well by steam.—The *Jack* is an article of great consequence, and also a troublesome one, being frequently out of repair. A *Bottle-jack* answers very well for a small family; and where there is a good *meat screen* (which is indispensable), a stout nail and a skein of worsted will, provided the cook be not called away from the kitchen, be found to answer the purpose of a spit.

There are now so many excellent weighing-machines, of simple construction, that there ought to be one in every kitchen, to weigh joints of meat as they come from the butcher, and this will enable the cook to weigh flour, butter, sugar, spices, &c., &c.

The cook should be allowed a sufficiency of kitchen cloths and brushes, suitable to her work. Plates and dishes will not look clear and bright unless rinsed in clean water, after they are washed, then drained, and wiped dry with a cloth which is not greasy. A handful of bran in the water will produce a fine polish on crockery ware.

As they do not cost much, there need be no hesitation to allow plenty of jelly-bags, straining cloths, tapes, &c. &c. These should be very clean, and scalded in hot water before they are used.

There should be a table in the middle of the kitchen, or so situated as not to be exposed to a current of air, to arrange the dishes upon, that blunders may not be committed in placing them upon the dining-table. Much of the pleasure which the lady at the head of her table may feel at seeing her guests around her, is destroyed by the awkward mistakes of servants in waiting; who, when they discover that they have done wrong, frequently become too frightened and confused to repair the error they have committed.

The cook in a small family should have charge of the beer; and where there are no men servants, it should be rather good than weak, for the better in quality, the more care will be taken of it. When more is drawn than is wanted, a burnt crust will keep it fresh from one meal to another, but for a longer time it should be put into a bottle, and corked close; it would be well for the cook to keep a few different sized bottles, so that the beer may not stand to become flat before she bottle it.

A clock, in or near the kitchen, will tend to promote punctuality. But the lady herself should see to its being regulated, or this piece of furniture may do more harm than good. There is nothing fitter to be under lock and key than the clock, for, however true to time, when not interfered with, it is often made to bear false testimony. That good understanding which sometimes subsists between the clock and the cook, and which is brought about by the instrumentality of a broom-handle, or some such magic, should be noted by every prudent housekeeper as one of the things to be guarded against.

The kitchen chimney should be frequently swept; besides which, the cook should, once or twice a week, sweep it as far as she can reach; for where there are large fires in old houses, accidents sometimes occur; and the falling of ever so little soot will sometimes spoil a dinner.

Every lady ought to make a receipt-book for herself. Neither my receipts nor those of any cookery book can be supposed to give equal satisfaction to every palate. After performing any piece of cookery according to the directions given in a book, a person of common intelligence would be able to discover whatever was displeasing to the taste, and easily alter the receipt, and so enter it in her own book that the cook could not err in following it. This plan would be found to save much trouble.

As soon after breakfast as she conveniently can, the mistress of a house should repair to the kitchen; which ought to be swept, the fire-place cleaned, tea-kettles, coffee-pots, and anything else used in preparing the breakfast, put in their appropriate places, and the cook ready to receive her orders for the day. Without being parsimonious, the mistress should see, with her own eyes, every morning, whatever cold meat, remains of pastry, bread, butter, &c., &c., there may be in the larder, that she may be able to judge of the additional provision required. Having done that, she should proceed to the store-room, to give the cook, the housemaid, and others, such stores as they may require for the day. This will occupy but very little time, if done regularly every morning; and having done this, she should proceed to make her purchases at once, lest visitors, or any accidental circumstance, cause her to be late in her marketing, and so derange the regularity of the dinner hour, the servants' work, &c., &c. Many ladies, in consequence of their own ill health, or that of their children, are compelled to employ their servants to market for them; but when they can avoid doing so it is better. I do not say this from a suspicion that either tradespeople or servants are always likely to take advantage of an opportunity to impose upon their customers or their employers, but because this important part of household management ought to be conducted by some one of the family, who must necessarily be more interested in it than servants can be. Besides, more judgment is required in marketing than all servants possess. A servant, for instance, is sent to a fishmonger's for a certain quantity of fish, and she obeys the order given her and brings home the fish, but at a higher price, perhaps, than her mistress expected. Now if the lady had gone herself, and found that the weather, or any other circumstance, had raised the price of fish for that day, she would probably have made a less expensive one suit her purpose, or turned to the Butcher or Poulterer to supply her table. Also it is a hindrance to a servant to be sent here and there during the early part of the day, not to mention the benefit which the lady of the house would derive by being compelled to be out of doors, and in exercise, for even a short time, every day.

Although I like French cookery, I am not sufficiently acquainted with the interior of French kitchens to know whether we should improve in the fitting up of ours by imitating our neighbours. When I was abroad, and had opportunities of informing myself upon this subject, I had not the present work in contemplation. And though it is the object of travellers in general to inquire into almost every thing while passing through a foreign country, it happened once to me to meet with so much discouragement, when prying into the culinary department of a large Hotel in the south of France, that I hesitated to enter a foreign kitchen again. I was then on the way to Italy, and from what was afterwards told me respecting the kitchens of the latter country, I have reason to think that my resolution was not unwise, since, had it been overcome by fresh curiosity, I might have been induced to starve from too intimate knowledge of the mode in which the dishes of our table were prepared. We had, at the hotel I am speaking of, fared sumptuously for three days. There were, among other things, the finest poultry and the most delicate pastry imaginable. But some chicken broth was wanted for an invalid of our party, and the landlord suggested that if Mademoiselle would herself give directions to the cook, the broth might, perhaps, be the better made; and he went, accordingly, to announce my intended visit to the important person who commanded in the kitchen. Upon receiving intimation that all was ready, I descended, and was introduced to the said cook, who met me at the door of a large, lofty, vaulted apartment, the walls of which were black, not from any effect of antiquity, but from those of modern smoke, and decorated with a variety of copper utensils, all nearly as black on their outsides as the walls on which they hung. Of what hue their insides might be I did not ascertain; and, at the moment, my attention was suddenly diverted by the cook, who, begging me to be seated, placed a chair by the side of a large, wild-looking fire-place. I had not expected to see a tall, thin and bony, or a short and fat woman, like the cook of an English kitchen; I imagined a man, somewhat advanced in age, and retaining some traces of the *ancien regime*, with large features and a small body, with grizzly and half-powdered hair, and, perhaps, a pigtail; at all events, with slippers down at heel, hands unclean, and a large snuffbox. It was, therefore, not without surprise that I found the very contrary of this in the personage who, dressed in a white apron, white sleeves, and white night cap of unexceptionable cleanness, and bowing with a grace that would have done credit to the most accomplished *petit maître* of the last century, proceeded to relate how he had been instructed in the art of making chicken broth by an English *Miledi*, who in passing into Italy for the benefit of her health, had staid some weeks at the Hotel de l'Europe. His detail of the process of broth-making was minute, and no doubt scientific, but unhappily for the narrator, it was interrupted by his producing a delicate white fowl, which he without ceremony laid on the kitchen table, which stood in the middle of the room, and rivalled the very walls themselves in blackness. I was assured, by the first glance at this table, by reason of the fragments of fish, fowl, and pastry, strewed over it, that the same piece of furniture served every purpose of *chopping-block* and *paste-board*. When, therefore, under these circumstances, I saw the preparation for the broth just going to commence, the exclamation of "Dirty pigs!" was making its way to my lips, and I, in order to avoid outraging the ears of French politeness, in the spot of all France most famous for the romantic, made the best of my way out of the kitchen, and endeavoured, when the next dinner-time arrived, to forget that I had ever seen it. Whenever afterwards the figure of this black table appeared to my fancy, like a spectre rising to warn me against tasteful and delicate looking *entremets*, I strove to forget the reality; but I never recovered the feeling of perfect security in what I was about to eat until the sea again rolled between me and the kitchen of the Hotel de l'Europe, and I again actually saw the clear bright fire, the whitened hearth, the yellow-ochred walls, the polished tins, the clean-scrubbed tables and chairs, and the white dresser cloths, of the kitchen, such as I had always been used to see at my own home.

CHAPTER VI.

*Directions for Jointing, Trussing and Carving, with plates of Animals
and various Joints*

Below will be found the figures of the five larger animals, followed by a reference to each, by which the reader, who is not already experienced, may observe the names of all the principal joints, as well as the part of the animal from which the joint is cut. No book that I am acquainted with, except that of Mrs. Rundell, has taken any notice of this subject, though it is a matter of considerable importance, and one as to which many a young housekeeper often wishes for information.

Venison.

1. Shoulder.   4. Breast.
2. Neck.   5. Scrag.
3. Haunch.

Beef.

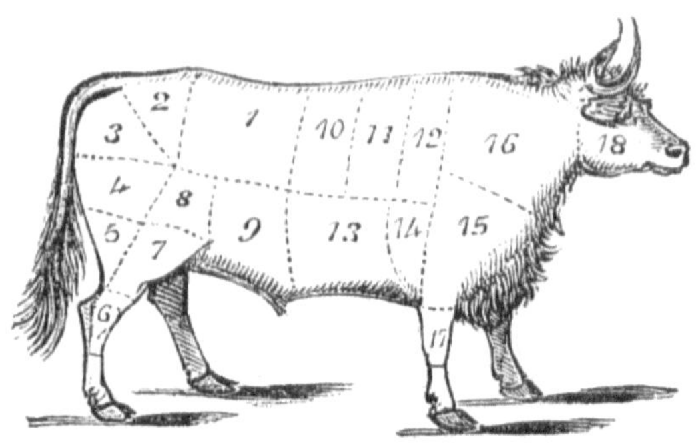

1. Sirloin.
2. Rump.
3. Edge Bone.
4. Buttock.
5. Mouse Buttock.
6. Leg.
7. Thick Flank.
8. Veiny Piece.
9. Thin Flank.

10. Fore Rib: 7 Ribs.
11. Middle Rib: 4 Ribs.
12. Chuck Rib: 2 Ribs.
13. Brisket.
14. Shoulder, or Leg of Mutton Piece.
15. Clod.
16. Neck, or Sticking Piece.
17. Shin.
18. Cheek.

Mutton.

1. Leg.
2. Shoulder.
3. Loin, Best End.
4. Loin, Chump End.

5. Neck, Best End.
6. Breast.
7. Neck, Scrag End.

Note. A Chine is two Loins; and a Saddle is two Loins, and two Necks of the Best End.

Veal.

1. Loin, Best End.
2. Fillet.
3. Loin, Chump End.
4. Hind Knuckle.
5. Neck, Best End.

6. Breast, Best End.
7. Blade Bone, or Oyster-part.
8. Fore Knuckle.
9. Breast, Brisket End.
10. Neck, Scrag End.

Pork.

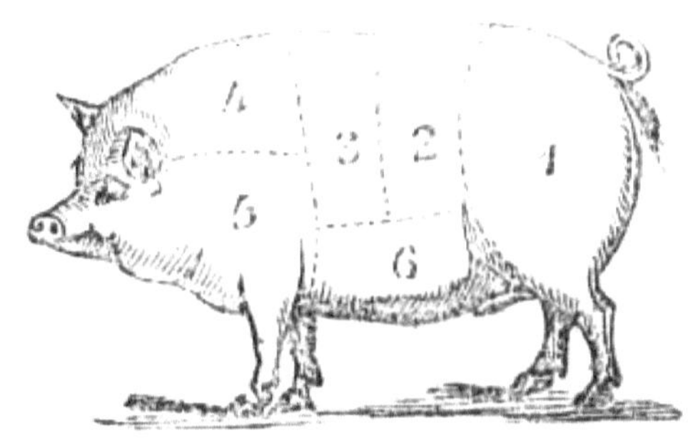

1. Leg.
2. Hind Loin.
3. Fore Loin.
4. Spare Rib.
5. Hand.
6. Belly or Spring.

Cod's Head.—Fig. 1.

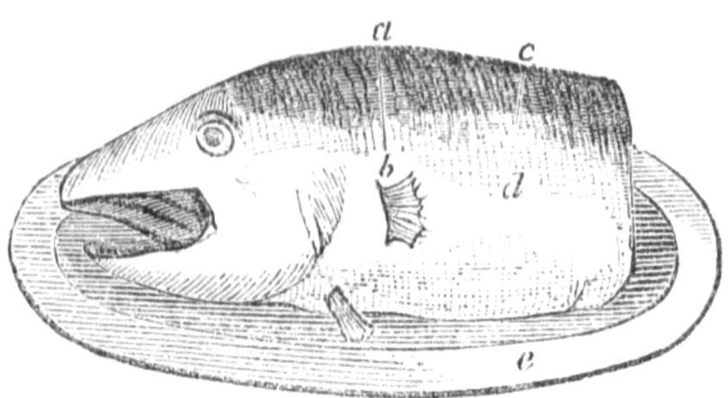

Cod's Head (*Fig. 1*) is a dish in carving which you have nothing to study beyond that preference for particular parts of the fish which some persons entertain. The solid parts are helped by cutting through with the fish trowel from *a* to *b* and from *c* to *d*, and so on, from the jaw-bone to the further end of the shoulder. The *sound* lies on the inside, and to obtain this, you must raise up the thin part of the fish, near the letter *e*.—This dish never looks so well as when served dry, and the fish on a napkin neatly folded, and garnished with sprigs of parsley.

Haunch of Venison.—Fig. 2.

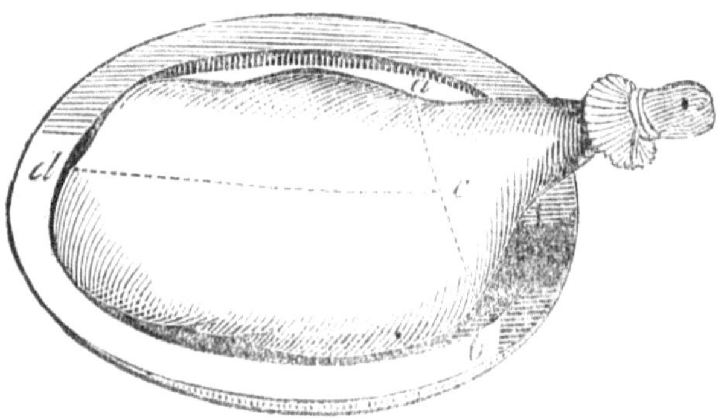

Haunch of Venison is cut (as in *Fig. 2.*) first in the line *a* to *b*. This first cut is the means of getting much of the gravy of the joint. Then turning the dish longwise towards him, the carver should put the knife in at *c*, and cut, as deep as the bone will allow, to *d*, and take out slices on either side of the line in this direction. The fat of venison becomes cold so very rapidly, that it is advisable, when convenient, to have some means of giving it renewed warmth after the joint comes to table. For this purpose, some use water plates, which have the effect of rendering the meat infinitely nicer than it would be in a half chilled state.

Haunch of Mutton is carved in the same way as *Venison*.

Saddle of Mutton.—Fig. 3.

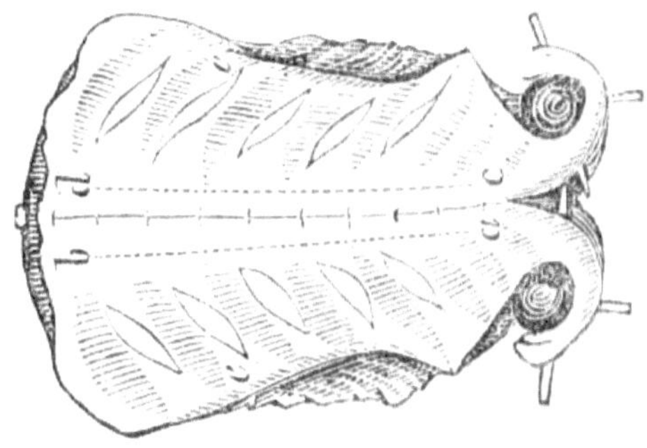

Saddle of Mutton. This is prepared for roasting as in *Fig.* 3, the *tail* being split in two, each half twisted back, and skewered, with one of the kidneys enclosed. You carve this by cutting, in straight lines, on each side of the backbone, as from *a* to *b*, from *c* to *d*. If the saddle be a fine one, there will be fat on every part of it; but there is always more on the sides (*ee*) than in the centre.

Edge Bone of Beef.—Fig. 4.

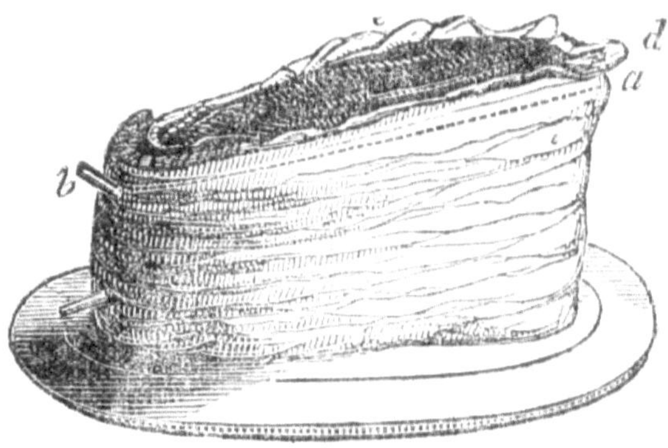

Edge Bone of Beef, like the Round of Beef, is easily carved. But care should be taken, with both of these, to carve neatly; for if the meat be cut in thick slices or in pieces of awkward shape, the effect will be both to cause waste and to render the dish, while it lasts, uninviting. Cut slices, as thin as you please, from *a* to *b* (*Fig.* 4). The best part of the fat will be found on one side of the meat, from about *c* to *d*. The most delicate is at *c*.

Fore Quarter of Lamb.—Fig. 5.

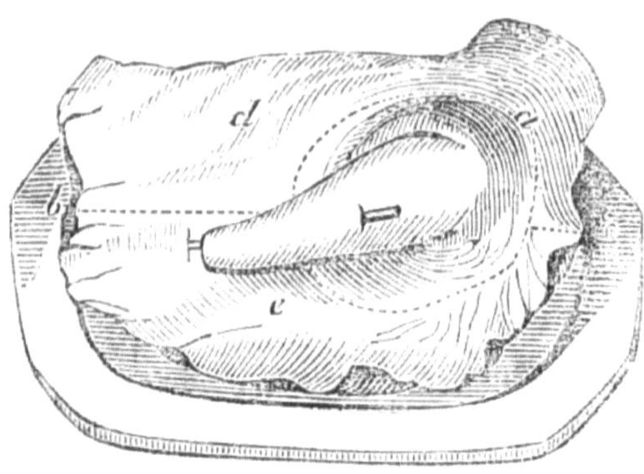

Fore Quarter of Lamb is first to be cut so as to divide the *shoulder* from the rest of the quarter, which is called the *target*. For this purpose, put the fork firmly into the shoulder joint, and then cut underneath the blade-bone beginning at *a* (*Fig. 5*), and continue all round in the direction of a circular line, and pretty close to the under part of the blade-bone. Some people like to cut the shoulder large, while others take off no more meat with it than is barely necessary to remove the blade-bone. It is most convenient to place the shoulder on a separate dish. This is carved in the same way as the shoulder of mutton. (See *Fig. 7*.) When the shoulder is removed, a lemon may be squeezed over that part of the remainder of the joint where the knife had passed: this gives a flavour to the meat which is generally approved.—Then, proceed to cut completely through from *b* to *c*, following the line across the bones as cracked by the butcher; and this will divide the ribs (*d*) from the brisket (*e*). Tastes vary in giving preference to the ribs or to the brisket.

Leg of Mutton.—Fig. 6.

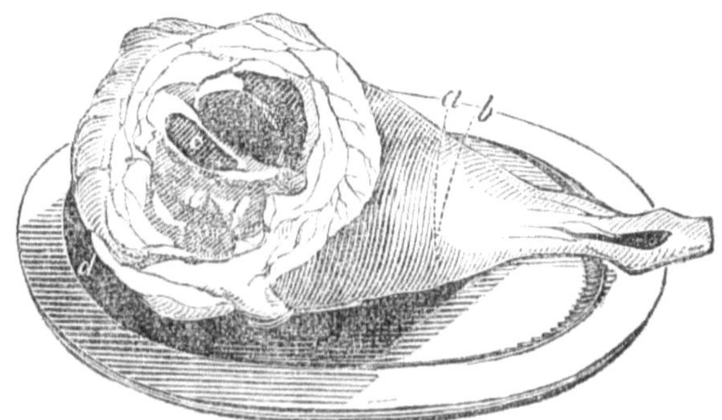

Leg of Mutton, either boiled or roasted, is carved as in *Fig. 6*. You begin, by taking slices from the most meaty part, which is done by making cuts straight across the joint, and quite down to the bone (*a*, *b*), and thus continuing on towards the thick end, till you come to *c*, the *cramp-bone* (or, as some call it, the *edge-bone*).

Some mutton is superfluously fat on every part of the leg. The most delicate fat, however, is always that which is attached to the outside, about the thick end. After cutting as above directed, turn the joint over, and cut longwise the leg, as with a haunch of venison (see *Fig. 1*). Some people like the *knuckle*, that part which lies to the right of *b*, though this is always the driest and the leanest. A few nice slices may be taken at *d*, by cutting across that end: these are not juicy, but the grain of the meat is fine; and here there is also some nice fat.

Shoulder of Mutton.—Fig. 7.

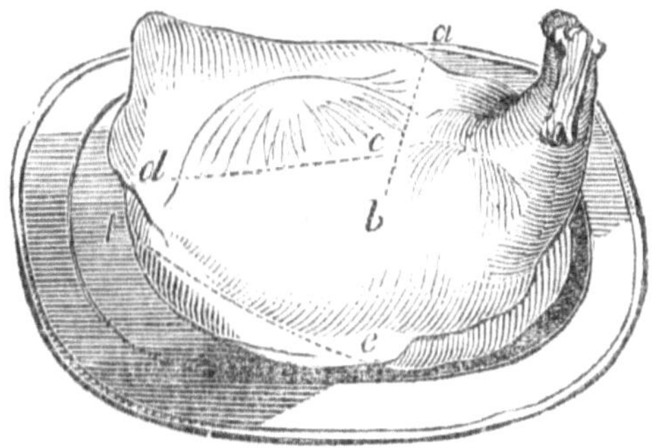

Shoulder of Mutton.—Cut first from *a* to *b* (*Fig. 7*) as deep as the bone will permit, and take out slices on each side of this line. Then cut in a line with and on both sides of the ridges of the blade-bone, which will be found running in the direction *c* to *d*. The meat of this part is some of the most delicate, but there is not much of it. You may get some nice slices between *e* and *f*, though these will sometimes be very fat. Turn the joint over, and take slices from the flat surface of the under part: these are the coarsest, yet some think the best.—In small families it is sometimes the practice to cut the under side while hot; this leaves the joint better looking for the next day.

Ham.—Fig. 8.

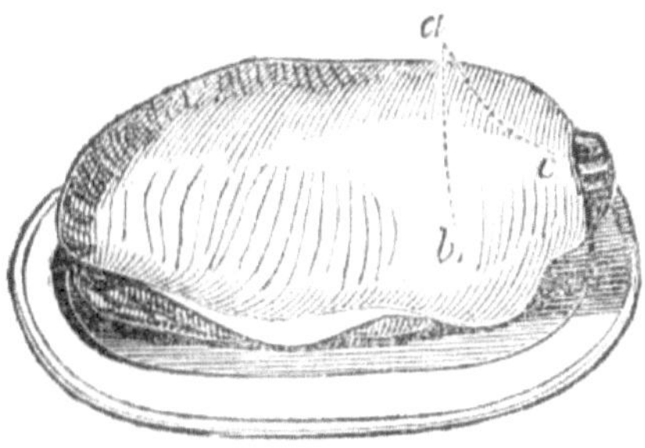

Ham is generally cut by making a deep incision across the top of it, as from *a* to *b*, and down to the bone. Those who like the *knuckle* end, which is the most lean and dry, may cut towards *c*; but the prime part of the ham is that between *a* and the thick end. Some prefer carving hams with a more slanting cut, beginning in a direction as from *a* to *c*, and so continuing throughout to the thick end. The slanting mode is, however, apt to be very wasteful, unless the carver be careful not to take away too much fat in proportion to the lean.

Sucking Pig should always be cut up by the cook; at least, the principal parts should be divided before the dish is served. First, take off the *head* immediately behind the ears: then cut the body in two, by carrying the knife quite through from the neck to the tail. The *legs* and the *shoulders* must next be removed from the sides, and each of them cut in two at their respective joints. The *sides* may either be sent to table whole, or cut up: if the latter, separate the whole length of each side into three or four pieces. The *head* should be split in two, and the lower jaws divided from the upper part of it; let the *ears* be cut off. In serving, a neat cook will take care to arrange the different parts thus separated so that they may appear, upon the dish, as little uneven and confused as possible. The sides, whether whole or in several pieces, should be laid parallel with each other; the legs and shoulders on the outer side of these, and opposite to the parts to which they have respectively belonged; and the portions of the head, and the ears, may be placed, some at one end, and some at the other end, or, as taste may suggest, at the sides of the dish.

Hare, or Rabbit, for Roasting.—Fig. 9.

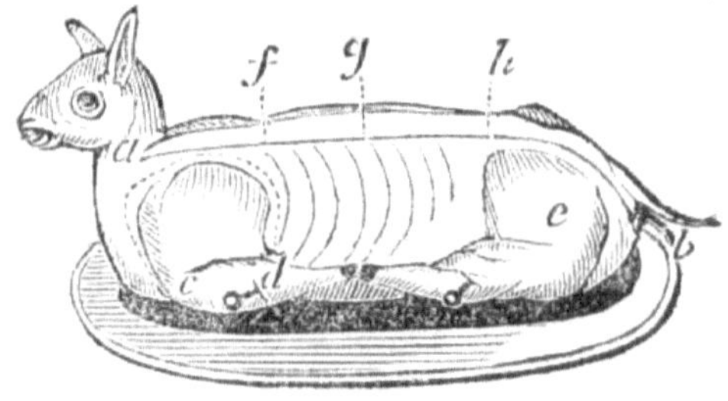

Hare, or Rabbit, for Roasting, is prepared for the spit as in *Fig. 9.*—To carve: begin by cutting through near to the back-bone, from *a* to *b*; then make a corresponding cut on the other side of the back-bone; leaving the *back* and the *head* in one distinct piece. Cut off the *legs* at the hip joint (*e*), and take off the *wing* nearly as you would the wing of a bird, carrying the knife round the circular line (*c*). The *ribs* are of little importance, as they are bare of meat. Divide the *back* into three or four portions, as pointed out by the letters *f g h*. The *head* is then to be cut off, and the lower jaws divided from the upper. By splitting the upper part of the head in the middle you have the *brains*, which are prized by epicures. The comparative goodness of different parts of a hare, will depend much on the age, and also upon the cooking. The back and the legs are always the best. The wing of a young hare is nice; but this is not so good in an old one, and particularly if it be not thoroughly well done. The carving of a *rabbit* is pretty much the same as that of a hare: there is much less difficulty, however, with the former; and it would always save a good deal of trouble, as well as delay, if hares which are not quite young were sent to table already cut up.

Rabbit, for Boiling.—Fig. 10.

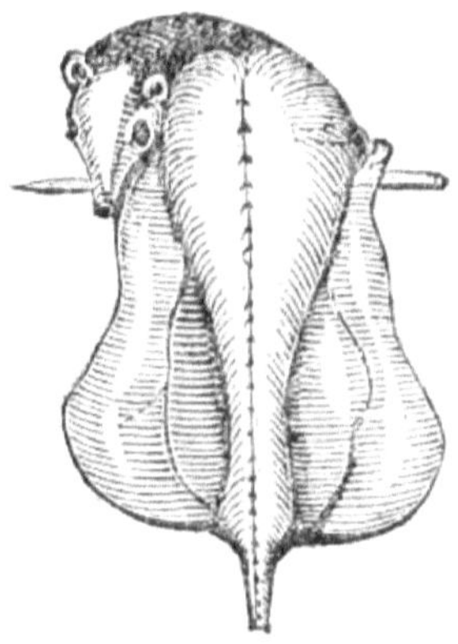

Rabbit, for Boiling, should be trussed, according to the newest fashion, as in *Fig. 10*. Cut off the *ears* close to the head, and cut off the *feet* at the foot-joint. Cut off the *tail*. Then make an incision on each side of the backbone, at the *rump-end*, about an inch and a half long. This will enable you to stretch the legs further towards the head. Bring the *wings* as close to the body as you can, and bring the legs close to the outside of the wings. The *head* should be bent round to one side, in order that, by running one skewer through the legs, wings and mouth, you may thus secure all and have the rabbit completely and compactly trussed.

Turkey, for Roasting.—Fig. 11.

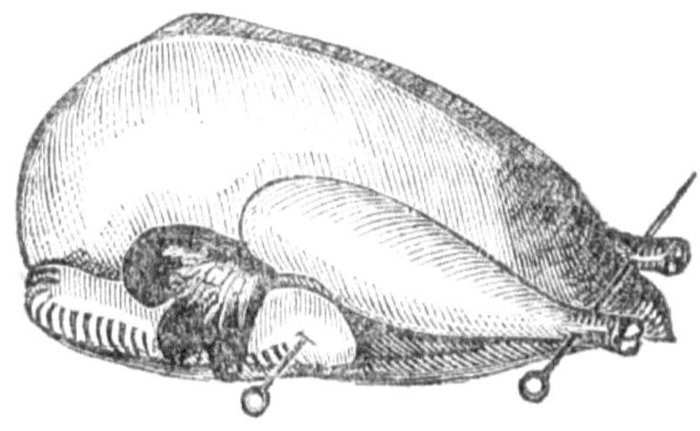

Turkey for Roasting, is sometimes trussed with the *feet* on; and it is sometimes brought to table with the *head* as well as the feet. But such trussing is exceedingly ugly, and altogether unworthy of a good cook. The manner here described (see *Fig. 11*) is the most approved. If the breast-bone be sharp, it should be beaten down, to make the bird appear as plump as possible.—See *Carving*, in observations on *Fig. 15*.

Goose.—Fig. 12.

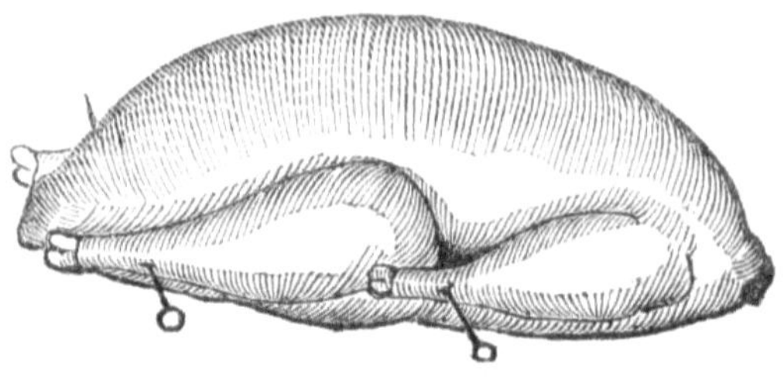

Goose.—For Carving, see observations on *Fig. 15.*

Fowls, for Roasting.—Fig. 13 & 14.

Fig. 13.   Fig. 14.

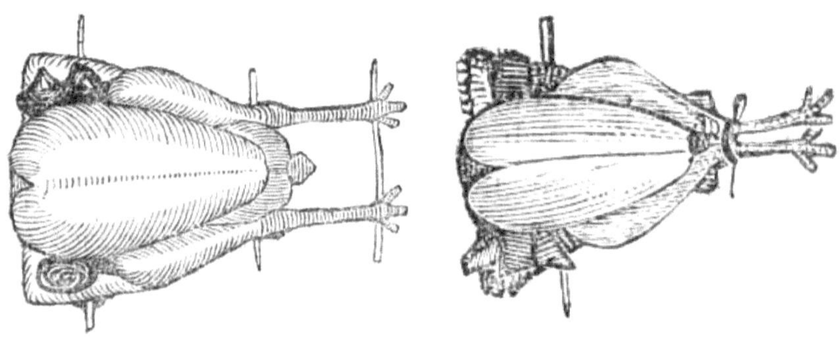

Fowls, for Roasting.—The most modern way of trussing these is as in *Figs. 13* and *14.* If it be but a chicken, or a small fowl, a single skewer through the wings, and the legs simply tied, as in *Fig. 14,* will be sufficient. But a large fowl is best kept in shape by the other method (*Fig. 13*).—See *Carving,* in observations on *Fig. 15.*

Turkey or Fowl for Boiling.—Fig. 15.

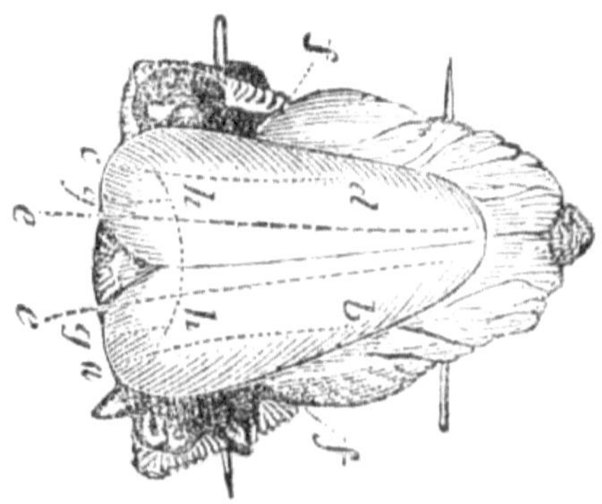

Turkey or Fowl, for Boiling.—For boiling, turkeys and fowls should, according to the newest fashion, both be trussed in the same way. There is nothing peculiar in this way, excepting as to the legs, which are to be trussed *within the apron*. To do this, the cook must first cut off the feet, and then, putting her fingers into the inside of the fowl, separate the skin of the leg from the flesh, all the way to the extreme joint. The leg, being drawn back, will thus remain, as it were, in a bag, within the apron; and, if this be properly done, there need be no other break in the skin than what has been occasioned at the joint by cutting the feet. If it be a turkey, or a large fowl, the form may be better preserved, by putting a skewer through the legs as well as through the wings (*see Fig. 15*). But with small fowls there needs no skewer for the legs. All skewers used in trussing should be taken out before the dish comes to table. To carve fowls, turkeys, &c., see *Fig. 15*. Begin by taking off the *wings*, cutting from *a* to *b*, *c* to *d*. Next the *legs*, putting your knife in at *ff*. Then, if it be a large bird, you will help slices from the breast (*e e*). But with the smaller birds, as chickens, partridges, &c., a considerable portion of the breast should come off with the wing, and then there is not enough left to spare any thing more from the breast-bone. *The merry-thought*, situated at the point of the breast-bone, is taken off by cutting straight across at *h h*. In helping, recollect that the *liver-wing* is commonly thought more of than the other. The *breast-bone* is divided from the back by simply cutting through the ribs on each side of the fowl. The *neck-bones* are at *g g*; but for these see *Fig. 16*, and the directions for carving the *back*.

Back of a Fowl. — Fig. 16.

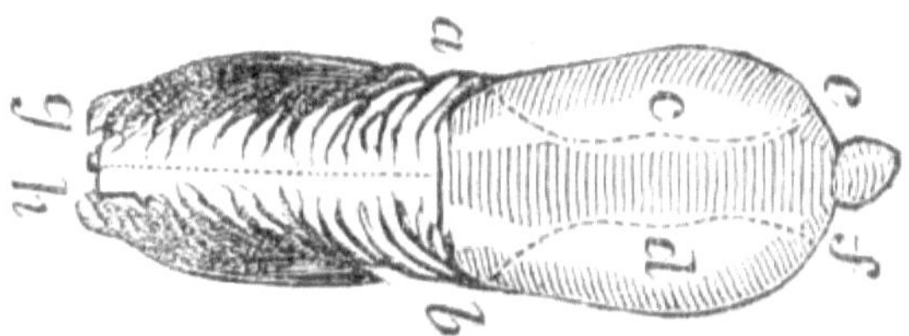

Rest your knife firmly on the centre of the back, at the same time turning either end up with your fork, and this part will easily break in two at *a b*. The *side-bones* are at *c d*; and to remove these, some people put the point of the knife in at midway the line, just opposite to *c d*; others at the rump end of the bones *e f*. The *neck-bones* (at *g h*) are the most difficult part of the task. These must be taken off before the breast is divided from the back; they adhere very closely, and require the knife to be held firmly on the body of the fowl, while the fork is employed to twist them off.

Duck.—Fig. 17.

Breast.   *Back.*

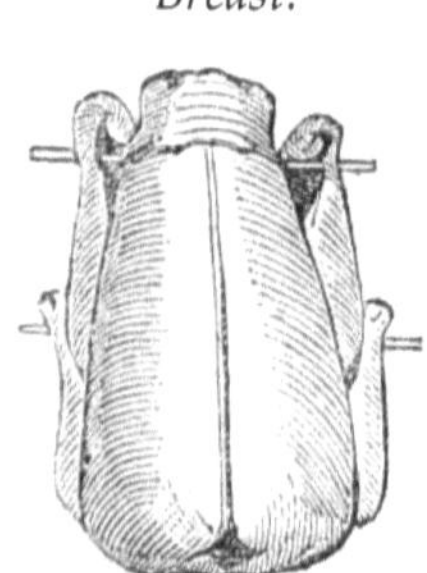   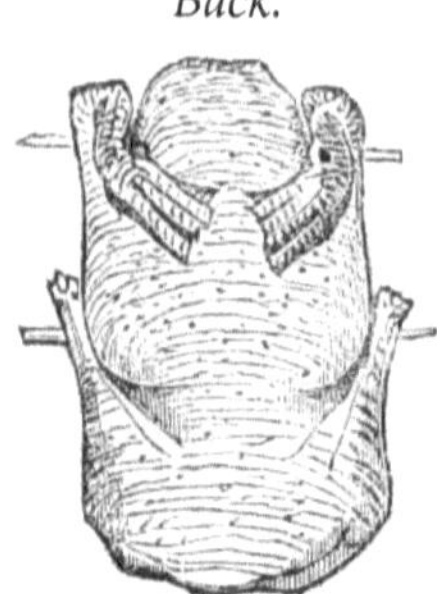

Duck.—This should be trussed as in *Fig. 17*. The *leg* is twisted at the joint, and the *feet* (with the *claws* only cut off) are turned over, and so brought to lie flat on the rump.—For *Carving*, see observations on *Fig. 15*.

Pheasant.—Fig. 18.

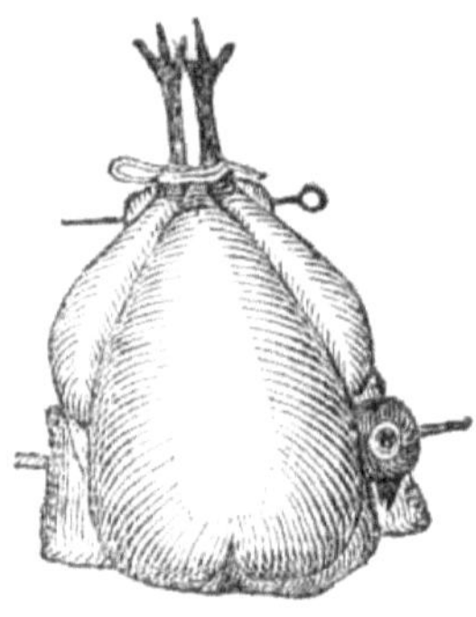

Partridge.—Fig. 19.

Pheasant and Partridge.—These two are trussed nearly in one way, as in *Figs. 18* and *19*, excepting, that the *legs* of the partridge are raised, and tied together over the apron, crossing each other. For *Carving*, see observations on *Fig. 15*.

CHAPTER VII.

General Instructions for Boiling, followed by Directions for Boiling various Joints

THERE is no branch of cookery which requires more nicety than plain boiling, though, from its simplicity, some cooks think it does not. They think that to put a piece of meat into water, and to make that boil for a given length of time, is all that is needful; but it is not so. To boil a leg of mutton, or a fowl, properly, requires as much care as to compound a made dish. Meat which is poor and tough cannot be made tender and fine flavoured by boiling; but that which was, to all appearance, very fine meat before it was put into the pot, has often been taken out really good for nothing. And many a Butcher and Poulterer have been blamed, when the fault was not theirs.

Meat should be put into cold water, enough to keep it *well* covered. The longer in reason it is coming to a boil, the better, as a gradual heating produces tenderness, and causes a separation from the meat of the grosser particles, which rise in the shape of scum to the surface, and which should be carefully taken off. The finest leg of mutton must be disgusting, if garnished with flakes of black scum. Care should be taken to watch the first moment of the scum's appearing in order to remove it, and then, by throwing in a little salt, the remainder will be caused to rise; and if the fast boiling of the water render the scumming difficult, pour in a very little cold water. The practice of boiling meat, such as poultry, veal, and lamb, in floured cloths, to keep it white, must have been the invention of lazy cooks, if not of tasteless and extravagant housewives; for the meat is rendered less juicy, and the liquor in which it has been boiled, so good for broth or gravy, must be lost.

When the pot has been well scummed, and no more scum to be seen, set in such a situation on, or by, the fire, that it may continue to boil *gently* and *regularly*, for the time required; and see that it do not stop boiling altogether at one time, and then be hurried to a wallop at another time, for this dries up the juices, hardens the meat, and tears it. A kettle of boiling water should be at hand, in order to replenish the pot, as the quantity diminishes, taking heed not to exceed the original quantity, namely, enough to *cover* the meat, for the less water, the better the broth will be.

Salted meat, if very salt, and all smoked meat, should be washed, and in some cases, *soaked* before it is boiled. If too little salted, it must not be either washed or scraped, and may be put on to boil in water a little heated, because a slow process would help to freshen it.

No positive rule can be given for the time required to boil meat, any more than to roast, for much depends on its freshness, and a piece of *solid* meat requires a longer time to boil than a joint of equal weight but of less thickness. Salted and smoked meat require longer boiling than fresh meat, veal longer than beef, mutton, or lamb; and pork, though ever so little salted, still longer than veal. A leg of mutton which has hung long will boil in less time than one which is quite or nearly fresh; but then the former ought not to be boiled at all, but roasted, for the fire takes away mustiness, and all the impurities with which the boiling water would only tend still more to impregnate the meat. A quarter of an hour, and a quart of water, to every pound of meat, is the rule of boiling, but practice must teach this, as well as many other important parts of culinary science. By a little care and attention, a cook will soon gain sufficient experience to preserve her from the risk of sending a joint to table too little, or too much done.

When meat is sufficiently boiled, take it up directly; and if it have to wait, stand it over the pot it was cooked in, to keep it hot; remaining in the water will sodden it.

The next thing for consideration, after that of cooking the meat properly, is the turning to account the liquor in which it is boiled. This, be the meat what it may, is good as a foundation for *Soups* or *Gravies* unless it be the liquor of ham or bacon, and that can only be used in small quantities, to flavour. The liquor of pork makes good pease soup. When such liquor is not wanted for the family, it may always, at a trifling expense, be converted into wholesome and nourishing food for the poor. (*See cookery for the poor.*)

Round of Beef.

If too large a joint to dress whole, for a small family, or where cold meat is not liked, it may be cut into two or even three pieces, taking care to give to each piece a due portion of fat; skewer it up tightly, of a good shape, then bind it with strong coarse tape, or strips of linen. The vessel roomy, the beef placed on a fish drainer (as should all large joints), and care taken to keep it covered with water. Three hours for a piece of 12 lbs. About three hours and a half to 16 lbs., and so on, in proportion. Put in carrots and turnips two hours after the meat. See that there be no scum left on, before you send it to table. Garnish with sliced carrots, and serve mashed turnips or greens, in a separate dish. Also dumplings, if approved.

The whole round, if 30 lbs. weight, will require to boil five hours. But remember, that the *boiling* should be only steady *simmering*. Place the vessel over the fire, that the water may come to a boil; then draw it to the side, and never let it cease to simmer. Have a kettle of boiling water by the side, to fill up with.

Edge Bone of Beef.

One of 20 lbs. weight will require to boil three hours and a half. One of 10 lbs. weight will be done in two hours. The soft fat is best hot, the hard fat cold.

Brisket of Beef.

This being a long, awkward joint, may be cut in two; it requires longer boiling than the edge bone; five hours not too much for a large piece. (See *Beef to Press*.)

For *Bouilli* and other ways of cooking beef, see the *Index*.

Leg of Mutton.

This joint should be kept from two days to a week. Cut out the pipe, and carefully wipe the meat to clear it of all mustiness. Chop but a very small piece off the shank. Boil carrots and turnips with it if you *like*, but the former will not improve the colour; and do not put them in before the pot has been carefully scummed. A leg of 9 lbs. will take three hours *slow* boiling. Garnish with slices of carrot, or a rim of mashed turnip. Serve caper sauce in a boat. *Walnut* also is good, in place of capers. If chickens or a fowl be wanted for the same dinner, they may boil in the same vessel with the mutton, but not with vegetables. The *broth* will be better for this addition. If broth be wanted the same day, put into the water, as soon as it has been scummed, some barley or rice, and after it has boiled one hour and a half, lift out the mutton and place it by the fire, covered to keep warm; take the lid off the pot, and let it boil quickly till the liquor be reduced to the quantity you desire; put in turnips and carrots, in small pieces, a head of celery, and a little parsley; return the mutton, and boil it slowly half an hour. — A leg of mutton, if too large to cook at once, may be divided into two; roast the fillet and boil the shank. *Or*: you may take cutlets off the large end two days running, and then dress the shank. — Tongue is good with boiled mutton.

Neck of Mutton.

Should be very much trimmed of its fat, and, if from 3 to 5 lbs. weight, boil *slowly* two hours; it will likewise make very good broth, as the leg. Garnish and serve in the same way. — Some do not cut off any of the fat, until after it is cooked, then pare it off, and put it by: this, shred finely, makes light pudding crust.

Leg of Lamb.

A delicate dish, if nicely boiled, served with parsley and butter, and garnished with sprigs of cauliflower, brocoli, or spinach. A dish of the latter should be served with it. (*See in the Index*.) If small, the loin may be cut into steaks, fried, and placed round the leg, lightly garnished with crisped parsley; or they may be placed round mashed potatoes, in another dish. A leg of 5 lbs. should *simmer* gently two hours, counting from the time it is first put on, in cold water.

Calf's Head.

Wash it well in several waters, and soak it in warm water for a quarter of an hour, but first take the brains out, and having well washed, let them soak in cold water with a little salt for an hour. *Half* the head (without the skin), will require *gentle* boiling two hours; with the skin, another hour. Put it on in cold water. Boil 8 or 10 sage leaves, and the same quantity in bulk of parsley, half an hour, then drain, chop very fine, and spread them on a plate. Scald and peel the skin off the brains, put them into a saucepan with plenty of cold water: when it boils, carefully scum it, and let it boil gently fifteen minutes; chop the brains, but not very fine, and put them into a small saucepan with the parsley and sage, also 2 table-spoonsful of thin melted butter, a little salt, and, if you like, cayenne and lemon juice. Take the tongue out of the head, trim off the roots, skin and place it in the middle of a dish, the brains round it. Pour parsley and butter over the head, garnish with broiled rashers of bacon. Serve ham, bacon, or pork, and greens. Save a quart of the liquor to make sauce for the hash (*which see*). A very good sauce for this, eaten in France, is as follows: 2 table-spoonsful of chopped eschalots, 1 of parsley, 1 of tarragon and chervil, 1 of salt, a little pepper, 6 table-spoonsful of salad oil, 1 of vinegar: mix well together and serve cold.

Veal.

In some parts of England a boiled fillet is considered a delicacy. It should not be large. Stuff it the same as for roasting (*which see*), or with the forcemeat directed for boiled turkey. Serve white sauce, and garnish with slices of lemon and barberries. — The neck is good boiled, and eaten with parsley and butter.

Pork.

This must be exceedingly well done. Wash and scrape a leg, and let it lie in cold water a quarter of an hour to whiten; put it on to boil in cold water; do not let it boil fast, because the knuckle will be broken to pieces, before the thick part of the meat is done. Be careful to take off all the scum, and let a leg of 7 lbs. weight simmer three hours. If to eat cold, do not cut it in the middle, because that will allow too much gravy to be lost, but cut from the knuckle, and it will eat more tender. Peas pudding with leg of pork, also parsnips, carrots, turnips or greens, and mashed potatoes.

Petit-Toes.

Put a thin slice of bacon at the bottom of a stew-pan, with a little broth or thin melted butter, a blade of mace, a few peppercorns, and a sprig of thyme; in this boil the feet, the heart, liver and lights, till tender; the three latter will be done first; take them out and mince them fine: put this mince and the feet into another saucepan with some good gravy thickened with butter rolled in flour, season with pepper, salt, and a small quantity of walnut and mushroom catsup; let it simmer five minutes. While this is cooking prepare some sippets of toasted bread, lay them round a dish, pour the mince and sauce into the middle, and having split the feet, lay them lightly on the top. — A little cream may be added. (*See to fry.*)

Poultry.

Be careful in picking, that the skin be not broken. Some cooks wash poultry, but if wiping will be sufficient, it is best not washed. Chickens and fowls will keep two or three days, except in very hot weather. A fowl put on in cold water, should simmer by the side of the fire, from twenty-five minutes to half an hour. Some cooks boil a little fresh suet sliced, and also slices of lemon peel, with fowl. Some boil them in milk and water. The water must be well scummed.

Boiled Fowls with white sauce, or mushroom, oyster, celery, liver, or lemon sauce, or parsley and butter. A pretty remove of fish or soup, is, a small tongue in the centre, a boiled chicken on each side, and small heads of brocoli, with a few asparagus and French beans to fill the spaces. Serve any of the above sauces.— Always ham, bacon or tongue, and some sort of green vegetable, with fowl and turkey; chine with the latter. Garnish with slices of lemon.

Ducks.

Choose fine fat ones. Some persons salt them slightly, for two days, others boil them without. Smother them with onions, or serve onion sauce.

Turkey.

Let it hang four days, and take care not to blacken it in singeing. It is usual to fill the crop of a turkey with forcemeat (*see forcemeats*), or with a stuffing of bread-crumbs, suet shred fine, a little parsley, thyme, and lemon peel, chopped fine, nutmeg, pepper, and salt, the whole mixed together by an egg. In America it is the practice to stuff turkeys with oysters chopped and mixed with bread-crumbs. About 4 would be sufficient. A large turkey, with the crop filled, requires two hours *slow* boiling; not filled, half an hour less; and a small hen turkey an hour. Serve with oyster or celery sauce, and either chine, bacon or tongue. The forcemeat may be enriched by grated tongue or ham, chopped veal, an anchovy and a little bit of eschalot. (*See to hash, also grill.*)

Rabbits.

A full-sized one will boil in half an hour; an old one above an hour. Some use *milk* and water. Serve with onion sauce poured over; or a sauce made of melted butter, and the livers, previously boiled, and minced small, with a little parsley. Lay slices of lemon round the dish. Ham or Bacon.

Bacon

Should be well washed and scraped, and old bacon soaked in cold water. After coming slowly to a boil, let a piece of 4 lbs. simmer by the fire two hours, if young and fresh cured, less time. Some cooks put fat bacon into hot water, and lean into cold. Take off the rind and set it before the fire to dry up the oozing fat. Strew bread-raspings over.

Ham.

The main thing to be attended to is the previous soaking, and the requisite time must be left to the discretion of the cook, for, whereas one night would be sufficient for a small and tender ham, if very old and dry, less than four days and four nights will scarcely be enough. The water should be changed every day, and the night before it is boiled, scrape well, pour warm water over it, and trim off all the rusty, ill-looking, bits, then lay it in the water again. Scum the pot, and let the ham *simmer from three to five* hours, according to its weight. When done, take the skin off gently, and after covering the ham with bread-raspings, set it before the fire, to crisp it. Twist writing paper round the shank, and garnish with greens, or little heaps of bread-raspings. The liquor, if well scummed at first, may be strained or put by, and if you boil fowls or veal on the following day, you may put the two liquors together, boil them rapidly down; add pepper, mace, eschalot, and a faggot of herbs, and you will have a highly relishing gravy. Some persons contend that the practice of boiling a ham until half cooked, and then finishing by *baking* it, improves the flavour. (*See to bake meat.*)

Tongue.

If you buy it salted, learn how long it has been in pickle, for according to that it must soak. If old and hard, twenty-four hours will not be too much. Have plenty of water, and let it be a full hour in coming to a boil; then *simmer gently* for three hours; longer if very large. The root is an excellent ingredient for peas soup.

Tripe.

Cut in cutlets, or not, as you choose, and simmer it in milk and water till quite tender. Peel and boil a dozen button onions, put the tripe in a deep dish with some of the sauce, and the onions on the top; or you may boil it in plain water. Mustard sauce is good.—As all persons would not choose onions, you may serve onion sauce as directed for rabbits (*which see*). Serve rashers of bacon, if approved.

Cow-Heel.

When well boiled, cut into nice pieces, egg, bread crumb, and fry them of a light brown, and serve with fried onions or any piquant sauce. Is very good only boiled, and served with parsley and butter.

CHAPTER VIII.

General Instructions for Roasting, followed by Directions for Roast-
ing particular Joints

For roasting, meat should be kept longer than for boiling, or it will not, though ever so good, eat well. The proper length of time depends upon the state of the weather, and the age of the animal when killed, for young meat bears keeping less time than old meat. Two days of hot weather will do as much to render meat fit for the spit, as a week of cold weather.

Next after the state of the meat, the thing of most consequence is preparing the fire, which ought to be made up (of the size required by the length and breadth of the joint) half an hour before the meat is put down. It should not at first be exposed to a fierce fire. Let there be a backing of wetted cinders or small coals: this tends to throw the heat in front; lay large coals on the top, smaller ones between the bars, give the fire time to draw, and it will be clear. Before you put down the meat, stir the fire, clear it at the bottom, and see that it be free from smoke in front.

Some cooks make a practice of washing meat, with salt and water, then wiping it dry, before it is roasted. Where there is mustiness, or slimy appearance, it should be wiped off with a wet cloth, otherwise much washing is neither necessary nor beneficial. See that it be properly jointed; if there be too much fat, cut it off (it is better for puddings, in the shape of suet, than dripping); cover the meat with kitchen paper, *tied* on with twine, and not fastened by *pins*; see also, that the spit be bright and clean, and take care to run it through the meat, in the right place, at once, for the more the meat is perforated, the greater chance will be given for the escape of the gravy. Great nicety is required in spitting, that the joint may be accurately balanced. In the absence of spits and smoke-jacks, a bottle-jack, or a stout nail with a strong string or skein of worsted, will dangle a joint, and if the fire be made proportionably high to the length of the joint, there is no better mode of roasting. A strong skewer must be run in, at each end of the joint, in order to turn it.

The larger the joint the greater distance it should, at first, be from the fire, that the outside may not be shrivelled up before the middle is warmed. A quarter of an hour to a pound of meat, is the rule for roasting, and it admits of the same exceptions as in the case of boiling, with this addition, that fat meat takes longer than lean meat, as do pork and veal longer than any other kind. Fillets and legs, on account of their solidness, longer than loins and breasts. Much depends upon the situation of the fire-place, and whether the joint be exposed to draughts of cold air, or whether it be preserved from them, and the fire assisted, by a meat screen. Where there is none, a contrivance must be resorted to, by way of substitute, such as small wooden horses, or chairs, with cloths hung over them; these will keep off the cold, but a meat screen, lined with tin, keeps in the heat, and acts as a reflector. — Twice, or if the roast be large, oftener, remove the pan, pour off the dripping (it ought to be strained), draw the spit to a distance, and stir the fire, bring forward the hot coals, and put fresh at the back. Be careful that cinders do not reach the dripping-pan, for the smoke which they cause to rise from the fat, gives a disagreeable flavour to the meat, besides the injury to the dripping. (*See Dripping.*)—When the meat is nearly done, the steams will draw towards the fire; take the paper off, and move the joint nearer to the fire, particularly the ends, if they want more cooking; sprinkle salt lightly over the roast; then pour off all the remaining dripping, dredge flour *very lightly* over the joint, and baste with a very little fresh butter, which will not injure the gravy in the pan, but give a delicate froth to the meat. To the gravy now flowing from the meat, the best addition is a teacupful of boiling water. (*See Gravies.*)

With a clear strong fire (and meat cannot be well roasted without a strong fire), time allowed for gradual cooking, a cook may ensure for her roasts that fine pale brown colour, to produce which is esteemed one of the greatest proofs of a cook's skill.

Sirloin of Beef.

After reading the foregoing observations, the cook must gain, by observation and practice, that experience which will enable her to send this very best of joints to table, done enough, yet not overdone. A piece of 15 lbs. weight will require nearly four hours to cook it well: cover it with two half sheets of foolscap paper, and put it near to the fire for a few minutes; then rub it well over with butter, and draw it back to a distance (provided always that there is a very *good, steady* fire); and in this case do not baste at all, but put some boiling water into the dripping-pan when you first put the meat down, and this, by the time the meat is done, will be good gravy, after you have poured the fat off. The older fashion is to baste with dripping as soon as you put it down, and continue the basting every quarter of an hour; but I think the other method gives the meat the most delicate taste and appearance. However, a cook should try both ways, and afterwards follow the one which best suits the taste of her employers.

The old fashion of Yorkshire pudding with roast beef is too good a one to be abandoned, though its substitute of potatoe pudding is not to be rejected. Garnish with finely scraped horseradish. — Where cold roast beef is not liked, or if too underdone to eat cold, slices may be gently simmered over the fire in gravy or broth, or a very little water, and a little pepper and salt, eschalot vinegar, or some sort of catsup. The sirloin always came to table whole in the house in which I was brought up; therefore, I am able to give instructions for cooking it. No spit will carry round a whole sirloin; it must be *dangled,* and one which weighs (after great part of the suet has been taken out) 40 lbs. will roast in five hours, for it is no thicker than a piece of 10 lbs. weight. The fire must be large and high, the heat, of course, very great. Many a cook's complexion, to say nothing of her temper, has suffered in the cause of our "noble sirloins." If the inside, or tender-loin, be taken out leaving all the fat to roast with the joint, this part may be cooked to resemble hare. For this purpose, spread some hare stuffing over the beef, roll that up tightly with tape, and tie it on the spit. Send this to table with the sauces for roast hare. When the whole joint is roasted, the inside will be sufficiently underdone to make hashes. If only a part of the sirloin be cooked, the inside is best eaten hot, as it is not so good cold as the upper side.—Roast beef bones should be taken care of, for soup and gravy, and used before they become musty.

Rump of Beef.

Roast in the same manner. *Half* of this joint makes a nice family dish. Parboiled potatoes, browned in the dripping-pan are good.

Ribs of Beef.

Roasted the same as the sirloin. But it requires to be basted. Is a better joint to eat cold than sirloin. 15 or 20 lbs. weight, three hours or more, according to the size. Paper the fat and the thin part. Another way is to take out the bones, lay the meat flat, and beat it with a rolling pin; soak it in two thirds of vinegar and one of water, or, better still, white wine in place of vinegar, a night; next day cover it with a rich forcemeat, of veal, suet, grated ham, lemon peel, and mixed spices. Roll it tightly up, fasten with small skewers and tape, and roast it, basting constantly with butter, and serve with venison sauce.—*Or:* you may take out the bones, roll the meat up like a fillet of veal, lard it, then roast and serve with tomata sauce.

Leg, Loin, Haunch, Saddle, and Shoulder of Mutton.

Cut out the pipe that runs along the back bone, wipe off all mustiness. Rather a *quick* fire is required for mutton, particularly if it have been kept. Roast in the same manner as beef. Paper it, and baste every twenty minutes till the last half hour, when lightly sprinkle with salt, baste with *butter*, and dredge flour lightly over, and as soon as the froth rises, take it up. Onion, sweet sauce, or currant jelly, are eaten with mutton. Some think it an improvement to the *haunch* and *saddle* to take the skin off; to do this you must beat it well with a rolling pin, slip the skin with a sharp knife from the meat, and with a cloth pull it off nearly to the shank. Some put a thin paste over, as directed for venison, others paper only, and the latter is sufficient, if the cook baste enough, and do not let it burn.—A good sauce for roast mutton is made by putting 2 glasses of port wine, 1 of Reading sauce, and a tea-spoonful of garlic vinegar into a small saucepan, and pouring the contents hot over the joint just before serving it.

Haunch of Mutton.

To dress as Venison.—Keep it as long as you can, then rub with the following, and let it lie in it, thirty-six hours. Mix 2 oz. of coarse sugar, 1 oz. of salt, and ½ oz. of saltpetre. A taste somewhat peculiar to our house, and of American growth, is stewed cranberries, as sauce with roast mutton, and I recommend the trial to all who can procure good cranberries. Tomata sauce is also good with roast mutton.

Bullock's Heart.

Soak it well in lukewarm water to disgorge, dry and stuff the interior with a veal stuffing, and roast it two hours. *Calves'* and *Sheep's* heart the same.

Tongue.

Stick a fresh tongue all over with cloves, roast it, baste with butter, and serve with port wine sauce, and currant jelly.

Sucking Pig.

The age at which it ought to be killed is a matter of dispute; some say at twelve days old, others at three weeks; but all agree that the sooner it is cooked after, the better. After the inside is taken out, wash the pig well with cold water. Cut off the feet at the first joint, leaving the skin long enough to turn neatly over. Prepare a stuffing as follows: ½ oz. of mild sage, 2 onions, parboiled and chopped fine, a tea-cup full of grated bread crumbs, 2 oz. of good butter, and some pepper, cayenne and salt; put this into the pig, and carefully sew the slit up. Some cooks baste, at first, with salt and water, and then keep brushing the pig with a brush of feathers, dipped in salad oil. Others tie a piece of butter in muslin, and diligently rub the crackling with it; either is good. It should be dredged with flour, soon after it is put down, and the rubbing with butter or oil never cease, or the skin will not be crisp. The fire should be brisk, and a pig iron used, or the pig will be unequally cooked, for the middle will be burnt up, before the two ends are done. A good-sized one will take two hours. A pig should never go whole to table. Take the spit from the fire, and place it across a dish, then with a sharp knife cut the head off, cut down the back, and slip the spit out. Lay it back to back in your dish, and the ears, one at each end, which ought to be quite crisp. For sauce, clear beef, or veal gravy, with a squeeze of lemon, and, if approved, the brains and liver, or a little of the stuffing out of the pig, mixed in it, also a very little finely chopped sage. Apple sauce and currant sauce are not yet out of fashion for roast pig. Chili or eschalot vinegar is an improvement to pig-sauce. The easiest way is to *bake it*. (See *Baking.*)

Venison, Haunch or Shoulder.

This will hang three weeks with care, but must be watched. Wet it as little as possible; a damp cloth, only, should be used to cleanse it. Butter a sheet of kitchen paper, and tie it over the fat side of the joint, then lay over that a paste of about ½ an inch thick of flour and water; tie another sheet of paper over that, fasten all on firmly, and rub butter over the outside paper, that the fire may not catch it. Baste well, and keep up a strong clear fire. A haunch of from 20 to 25 lbs. weight, in a paste, will take from four to five hours, and not be overdone. Half an hour before it is ready take off the coverings, and put it nearer the fire to brown and froth. Baste with fresh butter, and lightly dredge it with flour. For sauce, currant jelly in heated port wine, in one boat, and clear drawn, unspiced gravy, in another. (*See Gravies.*) Raspberry vinegar may be used in making sauce for venison. Some epicures like eschalots or small onions, served with venison, hare, or any meat, eaten with sweet sauce. — The shoulder, breast, and neck, are all roasted, but the two latter are best in pies; and if lean, may be used in soup.—Serve French beans, and currant jelly.

Fawn.

This should, like a sucking-pig, be dressed soon after it is killed. When quite young, it is trussed and stuffed like hare. But it is best, when large enough, cut in quarters, and dressed like lamb. The hind quarter is the best. It may be half roasted, and then hashed like hare or venison.—*Or*: in pies the same as venison. It may also be baked. Venison sauce.

Veal

Must have a strong and brisk fire. It must not only be *well done through*, but be of a nice brown. For the fillet a stuffing of forcemeat made thus: two parts of stale bread-crumbs, one part suet, marrow or fresh butter, a little parsley boiled for a minute and chopped fine, 2 tea-spoonsful of grated lemon peel, a little nutmeg, a very little cayenne and some salt, the whole to be worked to a proper consistence, with yolks of 2 or 3 eggs. Many things may be used in flavouring stuffing, such as grated ham, beef, sausages, pickled oysters, anchovy, sweet herbs, eschalots, mushrooms, truffles, morels, currie powder and cayenne. The fillet should be covered with paper, and securely fastened in a nice shape. Baste well, and half an hour before you take it up, remove the paper, and bring the meat nearer the fire, to brown it. Garnish with slices of lemon. When in the dish, pour some thin melted butter over it, to mix with its own gravy. A fillet of 15 lbs. weight will require 4 hours' roasting. Serve sausages, ham, or bacon, and greens.

Shoulder of Veal.

Stuff it, using more suet or butter than for the fillet. Serve and garnish the same. From three hours to three and a half.

Loin of Veal

Must be well jointed. The kidney fat papered, or it will be lost. Toast half the round of a loaf, and place it in the dish under the kidney part, and serve and garnish the same as the fillet. About three hours.

Breast of Veal.

Keep it covered with the caul till nearly done, for that will preserve the meat from being scorched, and will also enrich it.—From one hour and a half to two hours. Some put in a very delicate stuffing.

Neck, best end.

Two hours to roast.

Lamb.

Lamb must be young, to be good, and requires no keeping to make it tender. It is roasted in *quarters*, or *saddles, legs*, and *shoulders;* must be well done, but does not require a strong fire. Put oiled paper over a fore quarter. One of 10 lbs. weight will require two hours.—When the shoulder is removed, the carver ought to sprinkle some salt, squeeze ½ a lemon, and pour a little melted butter (it *may* have finely chopped parsley in it), over the target, and then replace the shoulder for a few minutes.—Mint sauce; and garnish with crisp parsley, sprigs of parsley, sprigs of cauliflower, or alternate slices of lemon and sprigs of water cress.—Serve salad, spinach, French beans, cauliflower or green peas. (*See Sauces.*)

Pork

Requires a very strong fire, and must be well done.

Leg of Pork.

Make a slit in the shank, and put in a stuffing of mild sage, and parboiled onions, chopped fine, also pepper, salt, grated stale bread-crumbs, a piece of butter, a tea-spoonful of made mustard, and an egg to cement the whole, then sew it up. Rub the skin often all over with salad oil or fresh butter, while the roast is going on. The skin must be scored about twenty minutes after the pork is put down. A leg of 8 lbs. about three hours. Serve onion sauce, mustard, or apple sauce. (*See Sauces.*)

Spare Rib.

When put to the fire, dust some flour over, and baste gently with some butter. Have some sage leaves dried and rubbed through a hair sieve, and about a quarter of an hour before the meat is done, sprinkle this over it, just after the last basting with butter. Apple sauce; mashed potatoes.

Loin and Griskin.

Score the loin, and, if you like, stuff it as the leg, or mix powdered sage and finely-chopped onion with the basting. A loin of 5 lbs. two hours; if very fat, half an hour longer. A griskin of 7 or 8 lbs. one hour and a half. Either of these may be baked. Score the rind, rub over it well with butter or oil, and stand it in a common earthen dish, with potatoes peeled and cut in quarters; and, if you like, add some apples also, and two or three onions previously parboiled and cut up. Dress the pork round with these when you serve it. *Apples roasted*, and sent to table in their skins, are very good with pork.

Turkey.

It is not a good practice to wash poultry, only to wipe it out quite clean; but if it be *necessary* to wash it, then dredge flour over before you put it down to the fire.

A turkey ought to hang as long as the weather will allow. Take care, in drawing, not to break the gall bag, for no washing would cure the mischief. It is still the custom, in some counties, to send a roast turkey to table with its head on. Press down the breast-bone. Fill the craw with a stuffing as follows: a large cup of bread-crumbs, 2 oz. minced beef suet, a little parsley (always parboiled, as well as onions, for stuffings), a little grated lemon peel, two or three sprigs of thyme, some nutmeg, pepper and salt; mix the whole well, and cement it with an egg. Add, if you choose, parboiled oysters (a few), or a little grated ham. Do not stuff too full, and keep back some of the stuffing to make little balls, to fry and garnish with, unless you have sausages. Paper the breast. Score the gizzard, dip it in melted butter, and then in bread-crumbs, fix it under the pinion, cover it with buttered paper, and be sure that it has its share of basting, as well as the liver, which must be placed under the other pinion. The fire must be the same as for beef. Keep the turkey at a distance from the fire, at first, that the breast and legs may be done. A very large one will require three hours, and is never so good as a moderate sized one, such as will roast in little more than one hour and a half. Dredge with flour, and baste with fresh butter, or wash it with salt butter. Half an hour before it is done, take off the paper, to let the turkey brown, and when the steam draws towards the fire, lightly dredge it with flour; then put a good sized piece of butter in the basting ladle, hold it over the turkey, and let it drop over it as it melts. This will give a finer froth than basting from the dripping-pan. Clear gravy in the dish, and more in a tureen, with egg, bread, or oyster sauce, in another. Chine and greens.

Capons and common Fowls.

Roasted the same as turkeys, and stuffed, if the size will admit. A large, full-grown fowl will take about one hour and a quarter; a chicken from thirty to forty minutes. The sauces for fowls are, gravy, parsley, and butter, either with or without the liver (roasted) chopped up in it, or mushroom, bread or egg sauce. Three or four slices of fat bacon, not too thick, may be attached by skewers to the breast of a fowl, and is an improvement to a large one.

Goose.

Well wash and dry it in a cloth; then stuff it with four onions, parboiled, a fourth of their bulk in sage, and half, or, if you like it, the whole of the liver; parboil these together slightly, and mix them with the crumb of a penny loaf and an egg. *Or*, prepare a stuffing of six good onions, two or three apples, and some sage; chop these together quite fine, season with pepper and salt, and warm it in a saucepan sufficient to half cook it. Put the stuffing in the goose, tie that tightly at both ends, when on the spit: keep it papered the first hour, and baste with a little dripping. Froth it the same as turkey. The fire must be kept brisk. A large goose will require two hours. Take it up before the breast falls. Its own gravy is not good. Serve a good gravy flavoured with port wine, or cider, and walnut catsup, also a ta-ble-spoonful of made mustard.—It is a good plan for the cook to cut up the goose, remove the joints separately on another *hot* dish, then pour the gravy boiling hot over. This may not be fashionable, but it preserves the goose from eating *greasy*, saves the lady of the house trouble, and insures its being hot when helped. Serve apple sauce.—Some persons like goose stuffed with potatoes, previously boiled, then mashed without butter, and well peppered and salted.

Green Geese

Will roast in half an hour; are not stuffed. Put a good sized piece of butter inside, pepper and salt. Froth and brown nicely. Gooseberry sauce.

Ducks

Will keep three days, but are better dressed the day they are killed. Ducks may be stuffed or not (the same as geese), according to taste. But if two are roasted, one may be stuffed, and the other merely seasoned inside, with pepper, salt, an eschalot, and cayenne, if liked. Serve green peas with ducks. From three quarters to an hour will roast them. Baste well, and give a good froth. (*See Sauces and Force-meats.*) Some persons squeeze a lemon over the breasts when dished.

Wild Ducks

Take from twenty-five minutes to half an hour. Have a clear brisk fire. They are, generally, preferred underdone, but brown outside. Cut slices in the breast, and squeeze in lemon juice with cayenne; *or* put an oz. of butter into a stew-pan with a little cayenne, the rind of an orange cut thin and previously blanched in boiling water, and the juice of a lemon; warm this over the fire, and when melted, but not oiled, pour it over the duck and serve. (*See Sauces.*)

Pheasants, Partridges, Guinea and Pea-fowl,

Require a brisk fire. All are trussed in the same way, and the heads left on. Make a slit in the back of the neck to take out the craw; do not turn the head under the wing, but truss it like a fowl, and fasten the neck to its side with a skewer. Thirty minutes will roast a young pheasant, and forty or fifty minutes a full grown one. Good sized partridges take nearly as long. Baste with butter, and froth them. Clear, well-flavoured gravy, in which there should be a tea-spoonful of the essence of ham. Also bread sauce.

French cooks lard all these. (*See to Lard.*) They also have a method of dressing them thus: lay slices of lemon over the breast, and upon these, slices of fat bacon, cover with paper, and roast them. Another way is to fill the bird with a delicate stuffing of veal, grated ham, lemon grated, and spice; then roast it.

Woodcocks, Snipes, and Ortolans,

Should be kept as long as they are good. Do not draw woodcocks, for the trail is considered a delicacy, nor cut off their heads. They should be tied to a bird spit, or dangled singly. The fire must be clear. Twenty or thirty minutes is enough for woodcocks, and less for the rest, in proportion to their size. Lay some slices of toasted bread, the crust cut off, in the dripping-pan, to dish them on. Serve melted butter. Garnish with slices of lemon.—In France they stuff woodcocks with truffles, and other things, then roast, or stew them.

Grouse, Black Game, Plovers, Rails, Quails, Widgeons and Teal,

Are roasted the same as partridges, the head of grouse twisted under the wing. Do not let them be over-done. A rich gravy, and bread sauce. Garnish with fried bread-crumbs.

Pigeons.

Clean them as soon as killed, and the sooner they are dressed the better. Wash them very well, stuff each with a piece of butter the size of an egg, a few bread-crumbs, a little parsley, and the liver chopped, if you like: season well with pepper and salt. Roast twenty-five or thirty minutes. Pour into the dish a little thin melted butter, with or without the parsley, to mix with their own gravy. Serve bread or rice sauce, or parsley and butter. They may be served on a thin toast. Wood-pigeons should hang till tender, then roasted and served in rich gravy. They require less roasting than tame pigeons.

Larks, Wheat-ears, and other Small Birds.

Some of these are nice eating, particularly the *Wheat-ear*, which, from its superior flavour, has been called the English ortolan. A roast of small birds is so much the fashion in France, that you seldom travel many days together without finding it one of the principal dishes of the supper table. In the autumn, and, indeed, through the winter, you will constantly see a partridge, or a woodcock, served up in the midst of a numerous company of blackbirds, thrushes, larks, and a variety of such small birds; a truly "dainty dish to set before a king." This custom is re-markable because there is a comparative scarcity of small birds in France, whilst we in England are overstocked with them. The *sparrow-pudding* is *known* in many country places, but is not often seen. Indeed, in this land of beef and mutton, it would be hard if these little creatures could not be left to sing and build their nests in peace. With the French there is such an avidity for all sorts of small birds, that a string of them is one of the most ordinary articles in the larder. Nothing that flies in France above the order of humming-birds in its size, is too insignificant to come within the scope of the sportsman's ambition, and the purveyor's nets and springes. I am not sure whether our exquisite neighbours ever proceed so far as to devour sweet Philomel herself; but they certainly do what would be deemed still more shocking in England, making no exception in favour of that little bird, to injure which is here a sort of crime; they kill the robins and cook them by dozens at a time. The Forest of Ardennes abounds in them, and in the season the traveller may fare sumptuously upon these pretty little creatures, without being aware of what he is eating. Lovers of delicacies might find it worth their while to travel in the countries where the vine and the fig-tree abound. There the small birds feed and fatten on the grapes, even in the winter, for, long after the conclusion of the vintage, refuse grapes may always be found hanging. This food, so superior to our blackberries, hips and haws, may well cause the flavour of the birds to be in the highest perfection: for the fruit is so nutritious that the labouring people almost entirely live upon it through one whole season of the year. In Sicily the grapes will keep for months after they are quite ripe, hanging on the vines in the open air. There is a little bird, about the size of the nightingale, called the *fig-pecker*, from its feeding upon the figs. This is one of the most prized delicacies of the south of France and Italy.—All the above-named birds require to be well cleaned. Then put them on a bird-spit or skewer, and tie that on another spit, or dangle it before the fire. Baste constantly with good butter, and strew sifted bread-crumbs over as they roast. French cooks generally put a thin small slice of bacon over the breast of each bird, bringing it over each wing. Fifteen minutes will roast them. Serve larks on bread-crumbs, and garnish with slices of lemon.—*Or*: dip the birds into a batter, then roll them in bread-crumbs.

Hare

Should, unless a leveret, hang several days, to become tender. Cooks differ as to the proper method of keeping it. Some keep it unpaunched, while others see that it is paunched instantly, wiped clean and dry inside, and then let it hang as many as eight days. If really an *old* hare, it should be made into soup at once, for it will never be tender enough to roast. The heart and liver should be taken out as soon as possible, washed, scraped, parboiled, and kept for the stuffing. Most cooks maintain the practice of soaking hares for two hours in water, but more are rendered dry and tasteless by this method than would be so naturally. A slit should be cut in the neck, to let the blood out, and the hare be washed in several different waters. Prepare a rich and relishing stuffing, as follows: the grated crumb of a penny loaf, a ¼ lb. beef suet, or 3 oz. of marrow, a small quantity of parsley and eschalot, a tea-spoonful of grated lemon-peel, the same of nutmeg, salt, pepper, and the liver chopped, mix all together with the yolk of an egg; and an anchovy, if approved; put it inside the hare, and sew it up. For basting, most cooks use milk and water till within twenty minutes, or thereabouts, of the hare being done, and then baste with butter. But a cook of ours, first basted it with milk and water, for about ten minutes, to draw away the blood, then with ale, and for the last half hour with fresh dripping, until about five minutes before the hare was taken up, when she basted with butter to give a froth, having previously lightly floured it. Where cream and eggs abound, you may, after the hare has been basted with butter, empty the dripping pan, and baste with warm cream, and the yolk of an egg mixed in it. A good-sized hare will take one hour and a quarter to roast. Serve good gravy in a tureen, and currant jelly, or some piquant sauce. (*See Sauces.*) Kid is dressed the same way.

Rabbit

Is roasted in the same manner as hare; in addition to the stuffing, put three or four slices, cut very thin, of bacon. Liver sauce.

CHAPTER IX.

Directions for Baking

SOME joints of meat bake to advantage. It is convenient, occasionally, to send the dinner out to be cooked, and the meat which suffers least from such cookery ought to be selected; veal is good baked, so is pork, a sucking pig, a goose, and a duck; but not mutton. Some pieces of beef bake well, with peeled potatoes under to catch the gravy, and brown. Some sorts of fish also bake well. (*See Fish in the Index.*)

Breast, Loin, Fillet, or Shoulder of Veal.

The two last stuffed with forcemeat; put the joint on a stand in a deep baking dish, and stick bits of butter over the top. The heat of the oven strong, but not fierce. Baste often; when nearly done, sprinkle salt over, and ten minutes before it is taken out, dredge with flour.

Pig.

Put it in a shallow baking dish, wrap the ears and tail in buttered paper; send a good sized piece of butter tied in muslin, for the baker to rub over it frequently.

Goose and Duck.

Prepare as for roasting: put them on a stand, and turn them when half done. — *Wild Goose* the same, with a piece of suet inside.

Ham.

Boil it till half done, then cover it with a paste of flour and water, and set it in an oven, hot enough for bread, till you think it done.

Ox Cheek.

Cover with a strong seasoning of pepper, salt, and minced onion. Bake three or four hours, according to its size, then set it by till next day, take off the fat, and warm it as you want it. A *Shin of beef* in the same way.

Hare and Rabbit.

Prepare as for roasting, and baste it constantly with butter. The stuffing should be rich.

A Fawn.

Put a caul over and set it in the oven; about a quarter of an hour before it is done, take off the caul and baste well with butter. It will bake in the same time that a pig requires.

Meat pies require the oven to be as hot as for joints of meat, yet they should not be scorched. They also require time to soak through, or the meat will not be done.

Fish pies require half an hour less baking than the same sized meat pies.

Great nicety is required in baking fruit pies and light pastry. All these ought to be baked at home; when the precise heat of the oven, required, may be attained, which it rarely can be at the bakehouse. Pastry suffers, too, in being exposed to the air on its way to the oven; and it ought not to wait long before it is baked.

Pork.

Any joint will bake well. It must be scored. Rub it over with oil, or stick bits of butter all over it. Put it on a stand, and put peeled potatoes under it; also, you may put onions and apples. Sprinkle dry sage over, before you serve it. Stuff the pork, or not, as you choose.

CHAPTER X.

Directions for Broiling

THIS is seldom excelled in, though it appears simple, and is of general utility; for few like to dine on cold meat, and none dislike a broil. There is no economy in broiling, but such meat, poultry, or game, as cannot be hashed with advantage, had best be broiled.

The great art in broiling is to have a suitable fire. It must be strong, bright, and clear, and entirely free from smoke; if half burnt down, so much the better. Have two gridirons, one for meat and poultry, the other for fish. Those which hang before the fire are useful. A gridiron should be rubbed clean immediately after being used, not set aside with a particle of grease or soot attached to it. Just before you lay meat on, after you have made it hot, rub the gridiron with a piece of fresh suet, if for meat; if for fish, rub with chalk. A pair of steak-tongs is indispensable. Above all things, it is necessary that the broil be served immediately, closely covered on its way from the fire to the table, and that the plates and the dish be hot.

Beef Steaks.

These are eaten in perfection in England only, and, it is said, best in the Chop-houses in London, where daily practice makes the cooking perfect, and because in London the best beef may always be procured. No skill in broiling will render tough meat tender. Steaks are best from the middle of the rump (unless it be the under part of the sirloin), after the meat has been killed five days (if the weather permit), or even longer. They should be of about ¾ of an inch in thickness; beat them a very little. Sprinkle a little salt over the fire, lay the steaks on the hot gridiron, turn them frequently, and when the fat blazes and smokes much, quickly remove the gridiron for an instant, till it be over, and the steak will be sufficiently done, in from ten to fifteen minutes. Have a hot dish by the side of the fire; and, to gratify the taste of some persons, rub it with a piece of eschalot; at all events let the dish be *hot*, and as you turn the steaks, if there be any gravy at the top, drop it into the dish. Before you dish them, put a piece of fresh butter, and a spoonful of catsup in the dish; then sprinkle the dish with a little salt, lay the steaks in the dish, and turn them once or twice, to express the gravy. Garnish with horse-radish, or pickles. Oyster, and many other sauces may be served; some beef steak eaters say that its own gravy, pepper and salt, are all that a good beef steak requires, unless it be a little sliced raw onion or tarragon; others like fried onions.

Beef Steaks, with Potatoes.

Beat them flat; season on both sides with pepper, salt, and such mixed spices as you choose; dip the steaks in melted butter, lay them on the gridiron, and broil them, as directed in the last receipt. Have a little finely-rubbed parsley, or chopped eschalot, a piece of butter, and some pepper and salt, in a hot dish; when the steaks are done, lay them in it, turn them once or twice, and arrange slices of potatoes fried, round them. *Or*: spread mashed potatoes quite hot in the dish, and lay the steaks on.

Blade bone of Veal.

Broil it till quite done. Serve it with stewed mushrooms, or a garnish of pickled mushrooms and slices of lemon.

Mutton and Lamb Chops, also Rabbit and Fowl cut up, Sweetbread and Kidneys.

These may all be broiled in the same way as plain beef steak. Take care that the fat which drops from mutton and lamb, does not smoke the chops; where there is danger, take off the gridiron, and hold it aslant over the fire. Kidneys must, to prevent their curling, be stretched on a skewer. They may be dressed in a more savoury way, thus: dip them in egg, then in a mixture of bread-crumbs, and savoury herbs, before you put them on the gridiron. For mutton, a piece of butter in a hot dish, with a little catsup, is good sauce; but no catsup for lamb; cucumber sauce is better.—(*See Blade bone of Pork.*)

Pork Chops

Require a very strong fire, and more cooking than mutton, for they must be well done, about a quarter of an hour; cut them once to ascertain the state they are in. Mix in a *little* gravy, rather thin than rich, a spoonful of made mustard; pour this quite hot, over the chops, in the dish, to mix with their own gravy; then strew over them a little dry sage, rubbed small, and some chopped eschalot. Pork chops may be dressed in a Dutch oven.

Blade bone of Pork.

Cut it with a small quantity of meat to it: lay it on the gridiron, and when nearly done, pepper and salt it well, then rub a piece of butter over, and serve it directly. Mutton in the same way.

Chickens and Pigeons.

After a chicken is picked, singed and washed, or wiped clean, truss, and lay it open, by splitting down the back; season the inside with pepper and salt, and lay that side on the gridiron, at a greater distance from the fire than you put a steak, for it will take longer to cook; at least half an hour is necessary for a good sized chicken. From time to time remove the chicken from the fire, and rub it over with a piece of butter, tied in muslin. Run a knife into the breast to ascertain if it be done. The gizzard should be scored, well seasoned, broiled and divided, to garnish the chicken, with the liver, and slices of lemon. Serve mushroom sauce or parsley and butter. You may egg the chicken and strew grated bread over it, and broil till it is of a fine brown; take care that the fleshy side is not burnt. Pigeons are broiled in the same way, or may be done whole; in which case truss and put inside each a large piece of butter, pepper and salt, tie close at both ends, lay them on the gridiron, and turn them frequently. You may brush them with egg, and roll them in bread-crumbs and chopped parsley, with which mixture dredge them whilst broiling. Parsley and butter in the dish, with mushroom catsup, if you like. Stewed mushrooms are served with these, or pickled mushrooms as garnish. Chickens should be skinned before they are broiled for a sick person.

Partridges.

Prepare as above, and place them in a frying-pan in which you have melted a little very delicate dripping, or butter; let them stay ten minutes; turn them once, finish on the gridiron; this makes them more firm than they would otherwise be. Poor man's sauce (*see Sauces*) is good with all broiled birds.

(*See in Index for Devils, also in Made Dishes, for Cutlets.*)

Note.—Sauce Robert is good with all broils.

CHAPTER XI.

Not so difficult to *fry* as it is to *broil* well, and it is quite as good, for some things, but the fat must be good. Lard, butter, dripping, topfat (i.e. the cake of fat which is taken off soup or broth, when it has stood a night), oil, and suet, are all good for frying. If butter, suet and dripping be clarified, the pan will not be so apt to burn, and the fat will be more delicate. Housekeepers lose much of their credit by neglecting this, and similar niceties. The pan should be thick at the bottom: an oval shape is best, particularly for fish. The fire not fierce, as fat soon scorches, and the meat may be burnt, before it is half cooked; neither must it be too slack, for then the meat will be soddened; and if fish, of a bad colour, and not crisp. Ascertain the heat by throwing a bit of bread in; if the pan be too hot the bread will be burnt up. The fat in which veal, lamb or sweetbreads have been fried, will do for fish; let it stand to settle, then pour the top carefully from the sediment, and put it by. Fritters, pastry or sweet things, must be fried in good butter, lard or oil.

Care is required to fry fish well, and is attainable only by practice. To ascertain the heat of the pan, dip the tail of the fish into the boiling fat, and if it crisps quickly, the pan is ready.

Fries, as well as broils, served hot, as soon as off the fire, or they will be spoiled.

To Clarify Butter.

Cut in pieces, and put it into a jar: set that in a kettle of boiling water, to melt; skim carefully, take the jar out of the water, let the butter cool a little, then pour it gently off, keeping back the milky sediment.

Suet.

Chop beef, mutton, or veal suet, take off all skin and fibrous parts, melt it *slowly*, as in the last receipt, or in a Dutch oven, before the fire. Strain, and pour it off: beef or mutton dripping may be done the same way, and is good for peas soup, and for plain pastry. For soup, it may be seasoned, after it is melted and strained. A piece of charcoal will remove a rancid taste, put into the melting fat, and stirred round a few minutes. Use butter or lard in frying white meat.

Beef Steaks and Mutton Chops

Must be fried in butter. Steaks the size directed for broiling will be done in from ten to fifteen minutes. When nearly done, cover with a dish and let the pan remain five minutes by the fire, after you take it off. Then lay the steaks in a hot dish, and add to the gravy in the pan a piece of butter rolled in flour, a glass of port wine, or some catsup, a very little water, pepper, salt, a little minced eschalot or onion; let this boil, then pour it over the steaks. Garnish with horse-radish, and serve mashed potatoes and pickles. (*See Made Dishes, for Cutlets.*)

Veal Cutlets

May be cut from the fillet or the loin, ½ an inch thick: brush them over with egg, cover with bread-crumbs, and fry of a nice light brown, in a good deal of butter or lard. You may, if you choose, add to the bread-crumbs, a mixture of parsley, lemon thyme, lemon peel, and a little nutmeg and cayenne. When done place the cutlets in a hot dish, while you make some gravy in the pan; pour all the fat out, and pour in ¼ pint of boiling water, the same of melted butter, and let it boil till thickish, then add Harvey sauce, white wine, and any other sauce you like: strain this over the cutlets. Garnish with rashers of bacon, curled parsley, and slices of bacon. Cutlets, *without gravy*, may be served round mashed potatoes.

Lamb and Pork Chops.

Pork chops may be cut from neck or loin. Fry the same as veal, either plain or egged. Garnish with slices of lemon, or crisped parsley. Pork chops, egged, are improved, to some persons' tastes, by a little finely chopped onion and sage. You may make a sauce thus: put the chops on a dish, keep hot while you pour part of the fat from the pan, stir in a tea-spoonful of flour, moisten ½ pint of water, or broth, a table-spoonful of vinegar, a little salt and pepper, and 6 small gherkins or slices (or *for lamb, pickled mushrooms*), put the chops back into the pan to re-warm in the sauce, and serve it altogether. You may add mustard to the sauce; also, chopped onions, for pork. If there be no herbs used before, you may sprinkle dried parsley over lamb chops in the dish; also, lemon peel.

Sausages.

Some suppose that these do not require fat to fry them. It should be butter or dripping, not lard (a little for beef or pork, more for veal), and sausages ought to cook slowly, that they may be done, without being scorched, and not burst. Prick them with a darning needle to prevent this, but gradual heating is the best preventative. Drain, *very* lightly flour, and set them before the fire to froth. For dinner or supper, serve mashed potatoes with sausages.

Rabbits

Must be young, either tame or wild. Carve in joints, brush these with egg, and dip them in bread-crumbs, in which there may be, if you like it, some dried parsley, grated ham or lemon peel; fry nicely and serve with rashers; make some gravy in the pan as directed for veal cutlets.

Eggs with Ham or Bacon.

Soak the slices, of ham or bacon, in lukewarm water, and dry them in the folds of a cloth; and they will be less hard than fried bacon usually is. The pan used to fry eggs should be delicately clean. A good method is, to melt a little fat in the pan, pour that off, and then, whilst the pan is quite hot, rub it hard with a cloth. Let the bacon be nearly done, and if the fat be burnt, pour that off, and put in some fresh; then slip the eggs gently in. When they are done lay the slices of bacon in a dish, trim the eggs, and lay them on the bacon. The eggs may be fried in one pan, and the bacon in another; some prefer the latter broiled. For breakfast, slices of ham or bacon should not be broiled or fried, but toasted before the fire.

Sweetbreads.

Parboil them while fresh, and then fry them in long slices, or whole, in plain butter; or else egged, covered with bread-crumbs, and seasoned with lemon peel, pepper, and a sprig of basil. Garnish with crisped parsley, and lemon sliced: serve on a toast, with either parsley and butter, or plain butter, and a very little walnut, mushroom or any other catsup. Garnish with small slices of crisped bacon. (*See Made Dishes.*)

Ox, Calves', and Lamb's Liver, and Pig's Harslet,

Must be quite sound. Cut the liver in long thin slices, soak in water, then dry them in a cloth, flour, and season with pepper, salt, a little onion, or eschalot and sage, chopped fine. Fry the slices in butter or lard, of a light brown, and when nearly done, put into the pan some slices of bacon. When you take the liver and bacon out of the pan, pour in a tea-cupful of boiling water, dredge some flour in, let it boil up, and pour this gravy over the liver. You may fry a handful of parsley in the gravy. You may improve this gravy, by adding to it pepper, salt, a wine-glass of vinegar, lump of sugar, and a tea-spoonful of made mustard. Garnish with crisped parsley; serve mashed potatoes, or better still, stewed cucumbers. Of the pig's harslet, the lights, sweetbread, and heart may be parboiled, cut up, and fried with the liver. *Or:*—After the fashion of *Herefordshire*, cut in slices, 2 inches thick, the liver, griskins, heart, kidney, lights, crow, and some fat of bacon; rub these slices well with a seasoning, composed of onions, apples, a *little* sage, and plenty of pepper and salt; then put them on a small spit in alternate slices of lean and fat, cover all over with a pig's caul, and roast it three hours, or more, if the harslet be large. When done, remove the caul and pour a kettle of boiling water over. Make some gravy of the water that has been poured over, and flavour it with port wine, cyder, and walnut catsup. Serve apple sauce. *Harslet* is very good stewed in just enough water to make gravy, and seasoned well. A little cayenne.

Tripe.

Boiled tender, cut in long narrow slips, these dipped in a batter of egg and flour, and, if you like, a little minced onion and salt. Fry from seven to ten minutes, of a light brown. Serve, if approved of, onion sauce.—(*Cow-Heel the same.*)

To Fry Parsley.

After it has been washed and picked, shake the parsley backwards and forwards in a cloth till dry; then put it into a pan of hot fat, and fry it quickly of a light brown; take it out with a slice the moment it is crisp—it will be spoiled if done too much. Lay it on a sieve before the fire. Herbs, lemon peel, and onions, must always be chopped fine before they are mixed with bread-crumbs to fry. *Or*: Spread it on paper in a Dutch oven before the fire, and turn it often till it is crisp.

To Fry Bread Sippets.

Cut a slice of bread about a ¼ inch thick, divide it into pieces of any shape you like. Make some fat quite hot, in the frying-pan, put in the sippets, and fry of a light brown; take them up with a slice, and drain them before the fire ten minutes. Take care the pan be not hot enough to burn.

To Fry Bread Crumbs.

The bread two days old: rub it into very smooth crumbs, put them into a stew-pan with some butter; set it near a moderate fire, and stir them constantly with a wooden spoon, till of a fine light brown; spread them on a sieve to drain, and stir occasionally. Serve with roasted sweetbreads, small birds, and game, if approved. (*See Made Dishes.*)

CHAPTER XII.

General Instructions for the making of Soups and Broths, and Directions relating to particular sorts

The prejudice against French soup, arising from a belief that it must be *maigre*, is as ridiculous as was the assuming that all Frenchmen are the small, thin, miserable looking creatures which they used to be represented in caricatures. Soup is nourishing, and also economical, as it converts into palatable food, the coarser parts of meat, all trimmings, and much that could not be cooked with effect in any other way.

The French excel, merely because they take such pains in making soup, and not from the quality or quantity of their ingredients. A little meat with slow and regular boiling, will produce richer soup, than double the quantity, if the soup kettle be suffered to boil fast one quarter of an hour, and to stop boiling altogether the next quarter of an hour.—The fault most common in English soup is, the want of the juice of meat, caused by too quick and irregular boiling, to remedy which want, recourse is had to pepper, herbs, and wine. It is very easy to vary the *sort* of soup, by making a good clear *stock*, or what the French call *bouillon*, and the next or following days, flavour it, or add vegetable ingredients to your taste. Soup made solely of brown meat or game, without vegetables, will keep better than that made of veal, fowl, any vegetable substance, or fish. As the French are great economists in their kitchens, and are most scientific cooks, it may not be amiss to recommend their practice.

Read the directions for boiling meat, for they must be observed in the first process of soup making. Always use the softest water; and, as a general rule, give a quart to a pound of meat for soup, rather less for gravy. Place the soup-kettle over a moderate fire, that the meat may be gradually heated through, which will cause it to swell and become tender; also the water will penetrate into it, and extract all the gross particles, which will then go off in scum. If it be suffered to boil up quickly, it will be just as if scorched before the fire, and will never yield any gravy.—After the soup has been near to a boil for half an hour, let it boil *gently*, to throw up the scum; remove that carefully, and when you think no more will appear, put in the vegetables and a little salt: these will cause more scum to rise; watch and take it off, then cover the pot close, and place it so, by the fire, that it may boil or *simmer* gently, and not vary its rate of boiling. From four to six hours may be enough, but an hour more would not be too much, for the bare meat and vegetables; all flavouring ingredients should be allowed the shortest possible time, because their flavour evaporates in boiling. Great extravagance is often committed for the want of attention to this, for a larger quantity of costly ingredients is used, than need be if they were put in just at the proper time. It may be necessary to put in *some* of these things earlier than others; but this must rest with the discretion of the cook. Remember that where catsup is used, care must be observed not to give so much salt as where there is none.

If the soup waste much in boiling, add boiling water. Keep the lid close, and remove it as seldom as possible, because so much of the flavour escapes by that means. If the soup be over-watered, leave the lid half way off, that some of it may evaporate in steam.

French cooks, I believe, invariably brown the meat and vegetables first, thus: put a good piece of butter in a stew or frying-pan, then the meat and vegetables and a little water (no seasoning), set it over a sharp fire, turn it frequently that none of it may burn, or the flavour will be spoiled; when it is all browned, put your quantity of water to it. The soup may, perhaps, have a finer flavour, but it will not be so clear, for after the meat has been fried the scum will not be extracted from it in boiling.

Thickening may be made of bread-raspings. But that most commonly used, is flour rubbed in butter or fat skimmings. Flour or meal is coloured, spread on a plate, in a Dutch oven before the fire. Turn it with a spoon till it is of the colour you wish. Keep covered close, for use. Potato flour, a table-spoonful, mixed smooth in a cup of water, is a nice thickening. Barley and oatmeal, also Indian corn meal, in the same quantity. Thickening should be put in after that scumming has taken place which the vegetables have made necessary. But the French mode of thickening soup is best of all. (*See Roux.*)

Some persons boil vegetables by themselves to a mash, and pulp them through a sieve into the soup. This helps to thicken it. The fatter the meat, the more of green vegetables, such as leeks and greens, may be used. Meat should not be very fat, nor yet all lean, for soup.

No seasoning whatever, except salt, should be given to plain stock, if not to be eaten the day it is made. Thickened soup requires a greater quantity of flavouring ingredients than clear soup, as the thickening material absorbs a portion of the flavouring.—Take care not to over-season, for this is a common fault. Of wine, the quantity should not exceed a wine-glassful to a quart. The sort must depend upon taste, but claret is best for brown soup; Madeira for Mock Turtle; Brandy is used in soup, and so is lump sugar. Vegetable soup requires a little cayenne.

Soup or stock to be eaten on the following day, should stand by the side of the fire a quarter of an hour to settle, before it is strained; the fat skimmed carefully off, and put by. Strain the stock into an unglazed vessel. In hot weather, let it stand in a cool place; if you wish to keep it three or four days, boil it up every day. When you rewarm it, take off the cake of fat at the top, and hold back the sediment. Be careful in warming soup, that it do not get smoked. Also remember that it should but just come to a boil, and be taken off the fire, for every bubble tends to flatten its flavour. When macaroni, or other paste, or any kind of green vegetable, is added at the time of re-warming the soup, of course time must be given for such addition to be cooked; it is best partly cooked by itself first.

Ham is used for making stock; but except for ragouts, or sauces very highly flavoured, I should reject it.

When cream is added, it must be boiled first, or it will curdle. Pour it in by degrees, stirring all the while.

The French use earthenware soup-kettles, and some prefer them to the cast-iron digester, or stock-pot. Tammis cloths (bought at the oil shops) are better for straining than sieves.

Never use stale meat for broth or soup. Vegetables as fresh as possible. The older and drier the onion, the stronger its flavour.

Plain Stock.

Having read the foregoing directions, get a leg or shin of beef, break it in two or three places, wash it, and cut some nice pieces to eat. Cover with water, and boil it slowly. If you wish it to be very good, add an old fowl, rabbit, any trimmings of meat, or gizzards of poultry, or bones, but mind that whatever it be, it is quite fresh; take care that you take off the first scum as it rises, then put in salt, and a large carrot, a head of celery, two turnips, and two onions. Simmer this so gently as not to waste the liquor, from four to five hours, then strain as directed.—Rabbits are excellent in making stock. More onions may be used than I have given directions for in this receipt; indeed, where their flavour is not objected to, it is scarcely possible to use too many, for nothing enriches soup and gravy so much. The meat of shin of beef is excellent for your family dinner; before what is cut into smallish pieces are cooked too much, take them out and keep hot to serve with a little of the soup poured over, as sauce. Serve pickles.

Soup and Bouilli.

About 5 lbs. of fresh, juicy rump, or flank of beef, four quarts of water, let it come slowly to a boil, put in a heaped table-spoonful of salt, taking off all the scum carefully; put in three carrots, four turnips, two leeks, one head of celery, three onions (one burnt), three cloves in each, a small bunch of herbs; this should boil very gently five hours. All the vegetables cut or sliced. Some persons like a small cabbage cut up in this. Serve the bouilli garnished with the vegetables; put slices of bread in your tureen and pour the soup over, without straining. Tomata sauce is good with bouilli.

Good Plain Stock.

7 lbs. of knuckle of veal cut in pieces, five inches in diameter, also ¾ lb. of lean ham, cut in dice, put ¼ lb. of butter into a stew-pan, turn it round, then put in the meat, two onions, four cloves in each, a turnip, carrot, leek and a head of celery. Cover the pan and keep skimming its contents over a sharp fire, until there be a thick white glaze that will adhere to the spoon; then put in four quarts of soft water, and when coming to a boil, set it on one side of the fire, that it may *simmer* for three hours. Skim off the fat, and strain it.

Very good Clear Gravy Soup.

First heat, then rub with a coarse cloth, a good-sized stew-pan or stock-pot, then rub the bottom and sides with a marrow, or a large piece of butter. Lay in about 6 or 7 lbs. of shin of beef chopped across, a knuckle or scrag of veal, four shanks or the knuckle part of a leg of mutton, and any trimmings of meat, game or poultry you have, a slice of carrot, a head of celery, two onions, two leeks, and turnip sliced, and two table-spoonsful of salt. Let this catch, not burn, over a rather brisk fire, and add five quarts of soft water. When it has been carefully scummed once, give it a pint of cold water, to throw up more scum. Simmer slowly full four hours. Place it by the side of the hearth to settle, skim off the fat, and strain it. Of this soup, which ought to be very clear, are made many sorts, on following days, thus:—

Vermicelli.—Boil the quantity you wish to use, in a little water, till nearly cooked enough, then put it into the clear soup, when you put that on the fire to re-warm. *Brown thickening, which see, in the Index.*

Maccaroni Soup.—The same as the last, but do not make it too thick. Boil the maccaroni till rather more than three parts cooked, and put it into the soup to finish while that is heating. Cream is an improvement. Serve grated parmesan. *White thickening.*

Carrot or Turnip Soup.—Cut red carrots in thin strips, boil them till tender, and put them into clear soup, when it is rewarmed. *Or:* Boil six or eight carrots quite tender, then pulp them through a sieve into the soup. Scoop turnips into little balls, or cut them in any shapes you like, boil them till tender, and put into the soup. *Brown thickening.*

Celery and Asparagus Soup.—Cut these in pieces rather more than ½ an inch in length, and boil them gently, till tender, then put them into clear gravy soup. Cream may be used if the thickening be white.

Julienne Soup.—Cut leeks and celery in squares, turnips and carrots in strips, boil them till tender, and put into clear brown soup. *Or:* Cut carrots and turnips in strips, put a large tea-cupful of these into a stewpan with ½ lb. of butter, and shake it over the fire till they are tender and look transparent, then pour in the stock; add young peas, two onions, two leeks, a small lettuce, some sorrel and chervil, all these cut small; simmer gently till the vegetables are cooked, then put in three lumps of sugar.

Clear Herb Soup.

Cut up what herbs you like the flavour of; also leeks, celery, carrots, turnips, cabbage, lettuce, and young onions, in preference to old ones, a handful of young peas, put the whole into boiling water, and give them just a scald. Drain them on a sieve, put them into some clear stock, and simmer slowly till the roots are tender. Season with salt, and a very little cayenne, if you choose.

A Clear Soup.

Cut 6 lbs. of gravy beef small, put it into a large stewpan, with two onions, a small carrot and turnip, a head of celery, a bunch of sweet herbs, and a pint of water. Stew slowly an hour, add nine pints of boiling water. Simmer it slowly six hours, strain, and let it stand till next day. Take off the fat, pour it from the sediment, and boil up with whatever flavouring ingredient you choose. This may be made *Julienne* by putting in the mixture of vegetables as directed above. Also *Ox-tail* by adding one to it.

Brown Soup.

Make this as clear gravy soup, and strain it. Then fry to a nice brown 2 lbs. rump steaks, cut in small pieces, drain them from the fat, and put them in the soup. Let them simmer an hour, add salt, pepper, and cayenne to taste, also a wine-glassful of any catsup you like, and when done, let it stand by the fire, to allow the fat to rise; take that off, and serve the soup with the steaks.

Plain White Soup.

Soak a large knuckle of veal, put it into the soup-kettle with 2 fowls skinned, or a rabbit, ¼ lb. of lean undressed bacon or ham, a bunch of lemon thyme, 2 onions, 1 carrot, 1 turnip, a head of celery, a few white peppercorns, and 2 blades of mace, cover with water, and boil for two hours and a half, and strain. This should form a jelly. To re-warm it, take off the top fat, clear the soup from the sediment, and put it in a stewpan. Add vermicelli or maccaroni, previously boiled, till nearly done.

Another White Soup.

Fry 2½ lbs. veal, and ¼ lb. ham or bacon, with a faggot of herbs, 2 onions, a parsnip cut small, and a head of celery. When the gravy is drawn, pour upon it 2 quarts of water, and 2 quarts of skim milk. Boil it slowly an hour and a half. Add 2 table-spoonfuls of oatmeal, rubbed smooth in a tea-cupful of broth. Boil half an hour, then strain it into the tureen. *Cow heel* and *calf's feet* are good in making white soup; also rabbits, in place of fowls. When veal is dear, use lean beef.

Another with herbs.

Boil a quart of beef and a quart of veal stock together, with a table-spoonful of chopped tarragon, and one of chervil; when tender, have ready a coffee-cupful of cream and three eggs beaten together, stir them gently in, and keep stirring till cooked, but do not let it boil.

Lorraine Soup.

Blanch ½ lb. of sweet and 1 oz. bitter almonds, pound them in a mortar, with a very little water, to a paste. Take all the white part of a cold roast fowl, skin and mince it very fine, with the yolks of 3 hard-boiled eggs, and some fine bread-crumbs; put this into a pint of *plain white soup*, with a large piece of lemon peel, and a little mace and nutmeg; let it come to a boil, add a quart more of the same stock boiling hot, and after it has simmered a few minutes, strain the soup, and add, by degrees, a quart of cream which has been boiled.

Onion Soup.

The number of onions must depend upon taste; if 10 or 12, chop and stew them, in a saucepan, with a good piece of butter; stew them gradually, and when done, add some good stock: salt, pepper, and cayenne, if the stock be not already seasoned. This may be strained, and a pint of boiling cream added, to make it more delicate.—*Another*: cut small silver onions in rings, fry them of a light colour, drain and cook them for twenty minutes in *clear gravy soup*. Serve toasted sippets.

Onion Soup Maigre.

Fry in clarified butter 12 large onions, 2 heads of celery, a large carrot and a turnip, all chopped. When soft, pulp them through a sieve, into 2 quarts of boiled water, thickened with 4 or 5 oz. of butter, worked up with potato flour, and seasoned with mace and white peppercorns, 2 lumps of sugar, or you may thicken with the beat yolks of 4 eggs. Bread sippets in the tureen.

Green Peas Soup.

An old-fashioned, but good receipt. Boil quite soft, 3 pints of green peas, and work them through a hair sieve. Put into the water in which the peas were boiled, 3 large slices of ham, a small knuckle of veal, a few beet leaves shred small, a turnip, 2 carrots, and a little more water. Boil an hour and a half. Then strain the liquor into a bowl, and mix it with the pulp. Put in a little juice of spinach, which is obtained by squeezing the spinach, after it has been boiled, through a cloth. This will give a good colour. Then give it a gentle boil, to take off the taste of the spinach, slice in the whitest part of a head of celery, and a lump of sugar the size of a walnut. Cut a slice of bread into little square pieces, a slice of bacon in the same manner, and fry together in fresh butter, of a light brown. Cut a large lettuce in slices, fry that, after the other, then put them all together into the tureen. Have ready boiled, a pint of young peas, put them also into the tureen, and pour the soup over.—Onions may be added if approved.—Serve toasted bread, and also dry powdered mint.

Green Pea or Asparagus Soup.

Put 5 pints of peas, with ½ lb. of butter and ¼ lb. lean ham, in dice, into a stew-pan with two onions cut up and a little parsley, moisten it with water, and keep stirring or shaking over a sharp fire; when quite tender put in a thickening of flour rubbed smooth with water or broth, and having stirred that well in, add 3 quarts of any stock you have; whatever salt and pepper you think is required, also cayenne if you like, and 3 lumps of sugar: boil ten minutes and strain it. This may be served at once; or, after you have strained it, you may boil it up again with ½ pint of boiling milk, skim it, and serve on crisp sippets. *Asparagus* the same way: keep back part of the heads, and boil them separately, not very tender, cut them in pointed pieces, and put into the strained soup.

Artichoke Soup.

Wash and peel 2 doz. Jerusalem artichokes, and cut them in thin slices. Put 2 large onions, 1 turnip, a head of celery, 2 bay leaves, a sprig of thyme, and 1 lb. of lean ham into a stew-pan, with ½ lb. butter, stir all the time, and let it fry over a slow fire 20 minutes; it will form a white glaze, then take it off, and put it all with the artichokes into a stew-pan with a pint of thin broth or soft water, and simmer it, till all the vegetables are quite tender, then put in 3 table-spoonsful of flour rubbed smooth with broth, mix well together; add 3 quarts of good stock and a pint of boiled milk, a tea-spoonful of salt, the same of sugar, let it just boil up, then strain it, and boil it up again with mushroom catsup, and a glass of white wine; and pour it over fried bread in the tureen.

A good Maigre Soup.

Melt slowly, in a stew-pan, ¾ lb. butter, put in a head of celery, 1 carrot, and 1 turnip sliced, shake them well and let them brown; add three quarts of boiling water, 1½ pint of young peas, and some black pepper; when these are done, let it settle, strain the soup into another stew-pan, leaving all sediment; put it on again with 3 large onions in slices, another head of celery, and 3 turnips and carrots in pretty shapes. Boil slowly till done, then serve the soup.

Yellow Peas Soup

Should soak the night before, and if old, again in the morning, in lukewarm water. Allow 1½ lb. to 4 quarts of soft water, with 3 lbs. of lean sinewy beef, or fresh trimmings of meat, poultry, or roast beef bones, a small piece of pickled pork, the shank of a bacon or mutton ham, or the root of a tongue a little salted, and soaked and washed; also 2 carrots, 2 turnips, and 6 rather small onions. Scum well, as soon as it boils, and stir the peas up from the bottom; add another quart of boiling water, or the liquor of any boiled meat. (Pot liquor should always be saved for peas soup.) Let it simmer till the peas will pulp. Then strain through a coarse sieve. Take the onions out from the pulp, and put the latter back into the soup, with a fresh head of celery, or a large tea-spoonful of celery seed, tied in muslin, and some salt and pepper. Simmer it, if thin, three-quarters of an hour, to thicken it; then put it into the tureen, let it stand covered a few minutes, and remove the fat which will have gathered on the top. Shake dried mint or parsley over the soup, and serve with dice of toasted bread. — This soup may be made in a very economical way, by the means of pot liquor, roast beef bones, fragments of meat, and fresh clarified dripping. The liquor in which a leg of pork has been boiled, should be saved for peas soup. — Very little pieces of boiled pork may be served in peas soup, also cucumbers cut and fried, or bacon cut and fried. A pickled herring is used to give flavour, when there is no pot liquor. Peas soup is very good quite maigre; the water must be soft, and the peas boiled long and slowly, before they are pulped.

Carrot Soup plain.

Scrape and wash six large carrots, and peel off the outsides quite thick; put these into a soup-kettle, with a large head of celery, an onion cut thin, two quarts of soft water, or pot liquor, and, if you have them, roast beef bones. After this has been boiled and scummed, set it by the fire, keep it close covered and simmer it gently two hours. Strain through a sieve, and pulp the vegetables, with a wooden spoon, into a clean saucepan, and as much broth as will make it as thick as peas soup; season with salt and pepper. Make it hot, and send it to table. Add what spices you like. Serve toasted bread, either fried or plain.—*Celery* and *Turnip* soup the same way. When celery cannot be procured, the seed pounded fine, about ½ a drachm, put in a quarter of an hour, will give the flavour of two heads of celery.

Mock Turtle Soup.

Make it the day before it is wanted. Get a good sized calf's head, the skin on, scald and split it, take out the brains, and the bones of the nose, and lay it in lukewarm water to soak. Change the water often, to draw out the blood and slime. When the head is quite clean, put it into a stew-pan with rather more soft cold water than to cover it. Let it come to a boil rather quickly, and scum well. Then boil gently, rather more than half an hour. Take out the head, place it in a dish, and when cold, cut it into small neat pieces: skin the tongue, and cut it up. Keep the meat covered, and set it by till the next day. Put all the bones and refuse parts of the head into the soup-kettle, in the liquor in which it was boiled, with a knuckle of veal broken, and about 3 lbs. shin of beef, but the latter must be soaked first. Let this boil, then take off all the scum, and simmer it gently from four hours and a half to six hours, strain it into a pan, and set it by. When you want to make the soup, take off the cake of fat, and pour the stock into a large stew-pan, holding back the sediment; set it on the fire, let it come quickly to a boil, then throw in a little salt to facilitate the rising of whatever scum there may still be, and take this off. Put in from 10 to 12 sliced onions, browned in the frying-pan; also a few sprigs of fried sage, a few leaves of sweet basil, and the peel of a large lemon, not fried; a little cayenne, black pepper to your taste, a very little allspice, three blades of mace, some cloves, one eschalot, and the thickening; which latter may be of flour worked up in butter, or of brown *roux* (which *see in the Index*). Let it simmer nearly two hours, or till it taste strong, and be of a good colour; pass it gently through a hair-sieve into another stew-pan, and put into that the cut up pieces of head, and what wine you choose, Madeira, sherry, or claret, about a wine-glassful of either of the two former, to a quart of soup. When the meat is tender, the soup is done, and from half to three-quarters of an hour ought to cook it.

Have ready 12 each of forcemeat and egg balls to serve in the tureen. *Forcemeat balls* are made of veal or fowl, suet and parsley, all minced very fine, mixed with bread-crumbs, salt, pepper, cayenne, lemon-peel, nutmeg, and allspice, and wetted with yoke of egg, to make up into balls. Fry of a light brown, and lay them in a small sieve to drain before you put them in the tureen. *Egg balls* are eggs boiled hard, the yoke taken from the white and pounded well in a mortar, a little salt added, and as much raw yolk of egg and flour as will bind these into balls, not bigger than a marble. Put them into the soup soon enough to cook them. Before you serve the soup, squeeze the juice of a lemon into the tureen.

Some persons put ox palates, in slices, in mock turtle; pickled cucumbers cut very thin may also be an improvement. The above is not an expensive receipt, though, perhaps, quite rich enough. *Cheaper Mock Turtle* may be made of cow-heels or calf's feet, stewed gently, strained, and the liquor added to plain stock of beef, an onion, and what herbs and other seasonings you like. Cut up the feet, and put them into the soup, just before you serve it. Add lemon juice and wine, if you like.

Hare Soup.

The hare must be quite fresh. Cut it up (washed, but not soaked), put it in a stewpan, with six middling-sized onions (two burnt), two bay leaves, a blade of mace, three cloves, a bunch of parsley, a little sweet basil, thyme, and celery, also a little broth, plain stock, or, if you have neither, soft water, to cover the meat. If you desire it to be very good, add 1 lb. of gravy beef, notched and browned first; when it has come to a boil, and been scummed, put in three quarts of water, and simmer, if the hare be young, three hours; if old, longer. Strain it, set the best pieces cut rather small apart, to serve in the tureen, and cut all the meat off the other parts, to pound with soaked crumb of bread, to give thickness to the soup. When this is put into the strained soup, season it to your taste, and add catsup and port wine; also fried forcemeat balls, if you like.

Another, and a better.

If you happen to have two hares, one old and tough, the other young, cut up the first and put it on in three quarts of water, with three onions, two anchovies, six cloves, a blade of mace, a teaspoonful of salt, half a one of cayenne, and simmer it four hours. Meantime, roast the other hare, properly stuffed, till half done, then cut it up, and put it all, with the stuffing, into the soup, and let it simmer gently nearly an hour. You will have kept back some of the best pieces to serve in the soup the next day, unless you prefer it clear without any meat, in which case put it all in. Next day, when you re-warm it, add a tumbler of port wine. Not having the old hare, two rabbits may be found very good.

Rabbit Soup.

Cut up the rabbits, and if two, put the pieces into water sufficient to cover them; let it boil slowly, and take off all the scum; when no more rises, add two quarts of good stock (or soft water), prepared of shin of beef and veal, or of knuckle of veal alone, or of trimmings of veal and two or three shanks of mutton: this stock must be already flavoured with onions or eschalots, white peppercorns, and mace; simmer gently till the meat is quite tender, and then put it by till next day. Take off all fat before you re-warm it; take out the liver, rub it through a sieve, moisten with a little flour and butter, and add to the soup, also a teacupful of Port, the same of white wine, a table-spoonful of walnut catsup, and lemon pickle.

Game and Venison Soup,

May be made of any and of every kind of game. Skin the birds; if large ones, carve them; if small ones, only split down the back; fry them, with slices of ham or bacon, and a *little* sliced onion and carrot. Drain the pieces, lay them in a stewpan with some good *stock*, a head of celery, a little chopped parsley, and what seasonings you like. Stew gently for an hour. If venison be at hand, fry some small steaks, and stew with the birds. Serve the meat in the soup, taking out the ham.

Another, and plainer.

In the season, and in houses where game abounds, make soup as follows: cut the meat off the breasts of any cold birds, and pound it in a mortar. Boil the legs, and all the bones, in whatever broth you have, for an hour. Boil four large turnips to a mash, and pulp them to the pounded meat, mix these well, then strain in the broth, by degrees, and let it stand close by the fire, in the stew-pan, but do not let it boil. Season to your taste. Just before you serve it, beat the yolks of 6 eggs in a pint of cream, and pass through a sieve; then put the soup on the fire, and as it is coming to a boil, stir in the cream, and keep stirring a few minutes, but do not let it quite boil, or it will curdle.

Stewed Knuckle of Veal and Soup,

May be made of the breast, shoulder-blade, or scrag, but best of the knuckle. Cut it in three pieces: wash, break, and place it on skewers, in the stew-pan, with 1 lb. of streaked bacon, a head of celery, 4 onions, 2 carrots, 1 turnip, a bunch of parsley and lemon thyme, and a few black and Jamaica peppercorns. Cover the meat with water, and let it simmer till quite tender. Strain the soup, put it on the fire again, and season and thicken it to your taste. Either serve the meat in the tureen with the soup, or put it in a dish with the bacon, and the vegetables round it. You may pour parsley and butter over the meat, or serve it in a boat. A little rice flour is good to thicken with. Some have whole rice boiled, as for eating, and put to the soup when it is returned to the fire. Others use vermicelli. Eggs and cream beaten together and strained, would enrich this soup; when you put them in, stir all the time, and take off the soup before it quite boils.

Mulligatawny Soup.

Put a few slices of bacon into a stew-pan with a knuckle of veal, and no vegetables; simmer an hour and three quarters; cut about 2½ lbs. of breast of veal into rather small pieces, add the bones, and gristly parts of the breast, to the knuckle which is stewing; fry the pieces of meat, and 6 sliced onions, in a stew-pan, with a piece of good clarified dripping or butter. Strain the stock if done, and put the fry to it, set it on the fire, and scum carefully; simmer it an hour. Have ready mixed in a batter, 2 dessert-spoonsful of curry powder, the same of lightly browned flour, and salt and cayenne as you choose; add them to the soup. Simmer the meat till quite tender. You may have 2 chickens parboiled, and use them in place of the breast of veal. The above receipt is a plain one.

Another and richer.

Make a strong stock of a knuckle of veal, roast beef bones, a ham bone, a faggot of sweet herbs, 2 carrots, 4 turnips, 8 onions, 1 clove of garlic, 3 heads of celery, previously fried in butter, 6 cloves, some black pepper, salt, cayenne, mace, and mushroom powder; stew it all in 5 quarts of water, eight hours, then strain through a fine sieve. When cold take off all the fat, and if the stock be not rich enough, add to 3 quarts, a pint of good gravy; rub 3 table-spoonsful of curry powder, 1 of ground rice, and 1 of turmeric with some butter and flour, then moisten with a little stock, and add it by degrees to the rest, and simmer it two hours. Add 2 or 3 wine-glassfuls of sherry or Madeira, 1 of oyster, 1 of walnut pickle, 1 of eschalot or chili vinegar, 2 table-spoonsful of soy, 2 of Harvey or Reading sauce, and 1 of essence of anchovy; simmer it a few minutes. Have ready 2 chickens, or a rabbit, parboiled, then browned in fresh butter, or pieces of ox-tail previously cooked, add whichever of these it may be to the soup, simmer it again till the meat be cooked, then squeeze in the juice of a lemon and serve. Serve rice, cayenne, chili vinegar, and pickles.—*Cold Arrack*, or *Rum Punch*, after mulligatawny.

Ox-Tail Soup.

Three tails will make a good sized tureen-ful of soup; it is very strengthening, is considered an elegant, and is by no means an expensive soup. Have the tails divided at the points, rub with suet, and soak them in lukewarm water. Lay them in a stew-pan with 6 onions, a turnip, 2 carrots, some peppercorns, and 3 quarts of soft water. Let it simmer two hours and a half; take out the tails, cut them in small pieces, thicken it brown, then strain it into a fresh stew-pan, put in the pieces of meat, boil up and skim it; put more pepper, if wanted, and either catsup, or Port wine.

Grouse Soup.

Roast 3 birds, cut off all the meat, reserve some nice pieces to serve in the tureen; put the bones and all the rest into 2 quarts of good stock, and boil them half an hour; then pound the meat in a mortar; put a large onion, ½ a carrot and turnip, cut up, into a stew-pan with ½ lb. butter, 2 sprigs each of parsley, thyme, 2 bay leaves, 6 peppercorns, and ½ a blade of mace, and stir them a few minutes over the fire; then add a pint of stock, and stew it all till tender, put in the pounded meat, and 4 oz. of flour rubbed smooth, and the soup, mix it all well together, simmer it 20 minutes, stirring all the while; if required, add salt, and a table-spoonful of sugar; strain it into another stew-pan, boil it up, skim it well, and pour into the tureen over the reserved slices of meat, and some fried pieces of bread, cut in any shape you please. The *stock* for the above is good made of 4 or 5 lbs. of beef and 1 or 2 rabbits, according to the quantity, and the richness you require. I should put a large wine-glassful of Port into a moderate sized tureen-ful.

Partridge and Pheasant Soup.

The same as the above.

Poacher's Soup.

This excellent soup may be made of any kind of game. About 4 lbs. of any of the coarse parts of venison, beef, or the same weight in shanks, or lean mutton, for the stock; boil in it celery, onions, carrots, turnips, what herbs you like, and ¼ oz. of mixed black and Jamaica peppers. Simmer three hours, then strain it. Skin and cut up a black cock, a woodcock, a pheasant, half a hare, a rabbit, a brace of partridges, or grouse, or slices of venison; any one, or parts of several of these, according to what you may require and what game you may have. Season the meat with such mixed spices as you like, then flour and fry it in the frying-pan, or put them, at once, into the strained stock, for the frying process is not actually necessary. Put in with the pieces of meat, about 10 small onions, 2 heads of celery cut up, and 6 peeled potatoes; when the stock comes to a boil, add a small white cabbage, or a lettuce quartered, black pepper, salt, and allspice if you like. Simmer till the meat be tender. If the meat be composed of small birds, the vegetables must be put into the soup and cooked before the meat, for *that* must not be *overdone*. This may be enriched by wine, catsup, anchovies, and forcemeat balls.

Scotch Barley Broth.

About 4 lbs. of mutton to 4 quarts of water, and ¼ lb. of Scotch barley (more or less according to taste), a large spoonful of salt, also a large cup of soaked split peas, if in season. Scum carefully, and let the broth boil slowly an hour. Then add 2 carrots, 2 turnips, cut small, 3 onions, or 3 leeks sliced, and a head of celery, or a bunch of parsley, and some green or split peas. When these are done, season to your taste. This may be made of beef, with greens instead of turnips. The meat, if mutton, is served in a dish, with parsley and butter; and the vegetables in the soup. Remove the fat from the top before you serve.

Hotchpotch, a German dish.

Cut 6 lbs. of either beef or mutton, or both, into nice shaped pieces, and put to them as much water as you require soup. Boil and scum well, then put in carrots and turnips sliced, parsley chopped, leeks and German greens cut up, suiting the quantity to the meat. Serve all together.

A Pepper Pot.

Three quarts of water, 2 lbs. of mutton or veal, and a small piece of lean bacon; a fowl if you have it; as many carrots, turnips, and onions as you like, and a tea-cupful of rice. Scum well, season highly, and let it stand a little before you serve it, to take off the fat.

Scotch Cock-a-leekie.

Make a stock of 5 lbs. of shin of beef, strain, and put to it a large fowl trussed for boiling, and when it boils, put in six leeks (blanched), in pieces an inch long. In half an hour put in six more leeks and the seasoning; if these leeks do not make the soup thick enough, put more. When the fowl is done, serve it in the soup.

Mutton Broth.

Put 2 lbs. of scrag of mutton into a saucepan, with just enough water to cover, and when that is near boiling, pour it off, and carefully take all the scum off the meat; then put it back into the saucepan with four pints of boiling water, a table-spoonful of grits, a little salt, and an onion; set it over a slow fire, scum well, and then put in two turnips, and simmer it slowly two hours. (*See Cooking for the Sick.*)

Veal Broth.

The knuckle is best, but the scrag is good. A gallon of water to the knuckle, add an onion, a blade of mace and salt. Carefully scum, and boil it gently till the meat be thoroughly done, and the liquor greatly reduced. Add vermicelli or rice.

Chicken Broth

Should simmer very gently, and its strength will be in proportion to the quantity of water. A good-sized chicken will make a quart of very good broth. As this is seldom made except for invalids, neither onion, carrot, nor turnip ought to be used. A bunch of parsley may be boiled in the broth, then taken out and chopped fine. Skim the fat off the broth, and serve the parsley in it.

Milk Soup.

Boil two quarts with a little salt, cinnamon, and sugar. Lay thin slices of toasted bread in a tureen, pour a little hot milk over them, and cover close that they may soak. Beat the yolks of five eggs, add them by degrees to the milk; stir it over the fire till it thickens, take it off instantly or it will curdle; pour it into the tureen upon the bread. You may stir into the boiling milk a ¼ lb. of sweet almonds, and a few bitter ones, all blanched. In France *buttermilk* is cooked in this way, and poured on thin slices of boiled apples, spread in a tureen.

Ox-Head Soup.

Put half an ox cheek into a tub of cold water, and let it soak two hours. Take it out, break the bones not already broken, and wash it well in lukewarm water. Then put it in a pot, cover with cold water, and let it boil; scum carefully, put in salt, one head of celery, one turnip, two carrots, two large onions (one burnt), a bay leaf, two dozen berries of black pepper, the same of allspice, a good handful of parsley, some marjoram, savory, and lemon thyme; cover the soup kettle close, and set it over a slow fire. As the liquor is coming to a boil, scum will rise, take that off, and let the soup stew gently by the fire three hours. Then take out the head, pour the soup through a fine sieve into a stone-ware pan, and set both by till the next day. Cut the meat into small pieces, skim all fat from the top of the liquor, and put about two quarts of it, all the meat, and a head of celery cut up and fried with an onion, into a clean saucepan, and simmer it half an hour. Cayenne may be added, a glass of white wine, or a table-spoonful of brandy.

Giblet Soup.

Scald two sets of fresh giblets, and pick them very clean. Cut off the noses, split the heads, and divide the gizzards and necks into small pieces; crack the bones of the legs, put all into a stewpan, and cover them with cold water. When it boils scum well, and put in three sprigs each of lemon thyme, winter savory, or marjoram, and a little bunch of parsley; also twenty berries of allspice, and the same of black pepper, in a muslin bag; let this *stew very gently*, till the gizzards are tender, which will be in about an hour and a half. Lift out the giblets with a skimmer, or spoon with holes, into a tureen, and keep it, covered, by the fire. Melt 1½ oz. of fresh butter in a clean saucepan, stir in enough flour to make a paste, and pour in, by degrees, a ladleful of the giblet liquor, and the rest by degrees, and boil it ten minutes, stirring all the time. Skim and strain the soup through a fine sieve into a bason. Rince the stewpan, return the soup into it, and add a glass of Port wine, a tablespoonful of mushroom catsup, and a little salt. Give it one boil up, put the giblets in to get hot, and serve it.—You may make this much better by using plain stock in place of water, and a ham bone. You may add a pint of Madeira also; squeeze a small Seville orange into the tureen, and add three lumps of sugar and a little cayenne.

Soup Maigre.

Cut the white part of eight-loaved lettuces small as dice, wash and drain them, also a handful of purslain, the same of parsley. Cut six large cucumbers into pieces the size of a crown piece, peel and mince four large onions, and have three pints of young peas. Put ¾ lb. of fresh butter into a stewpan, brown it of a high colour, and put in all the vegetables, with thirty whole peppers, and stew it ten minutes, stirring all the time, to prevent burning. Add a gallon of boiling water, and one or two French rolls, cut in three pieces, and toasted of a light brown. Cover the stew-pan, and let the soup stew gradually two hours. Put in ½ drachm of beaten mace, two cloves bruised, nutmeg and salt to your taste; boil it up, and just before you serve, squeeze the juice of one lemon into it: do not strain it.—Soup may be made of any, and of every sort of vegetable, in the same manner, but they must be thoroughly cooked. Cream is an improvement, and French rolls, if not stewed in the soup, may be cut in slices, toasted, and put into the tureen before the soup.

Stock for Fish Soup.

This may be made of either meat or fish, the latter for maigre days. If meat, make it the same as for meat soup. If fish be used, it may be cod's head, haddocks, whitings, eels, skate, and all white fish. Boil the fish for stock in two quarts of water, with two onions, some salt, a piece of lemon peel, and a bunch of sweet herbs. Scum carefully, and strain it. If the soup is to be brown, you may brown the fish for stock in the frying-pan before you boil it. Fish stock will not keep.

Lobster Soup.

For this there should be a good stock, of beef, ham, onions, and fresh fish trimmings; strain it and pulp back the onions. Pound the spawn and all the body of the lobster, and stir it smoothly into the soup. Cut all the meat of the claws in small pieces, and put it in the soup also. Add cayenne, white pepper, and a glass of sherry. Or—Having a stock of fish prepared, cut up the meat of the lobster in pieces, and mix the coral with it. Bruise the spawn with a little flour in a mortar, wet it with a little of the strained stock, and mix it by degrees into the rest. Take half of the cut up meat and coral, add oysters, an anchovy, a blade of mace, nutmeg, lemon peel grated, and a little cayenne; pound all together, with the yolks of two eggs, and a very little flour, and make forcemeat balls for the soup; fry or brown them in a Dutch oven, or use them without being browned or fried. Put the balls and the remainder of the cut up meat into the soup, let it simmer half an hour, then serve it, first squeezing half a lemon or Seville orange in the tureen. Madeira may be added.

Oyster Soup.

Veal makes the most delicate stock; it should be strong and clear: put to it a quart of the hard part of fresh juicy oysters, which have been pounded in a mortar with the yolks of six hard-boiled eggs. Simmer for half an hour, then strain it into a fresh stewpan, and put in another quart or more of oysters, trimmed, and washed from their shells, also some mace and cayenne, and let it simmer ten minutes. Beat the yolks of three eggs, take out a little soup in a cup, let it cool, mix it by degrees with the eggs, and stir into the soup, having first drawn that aside from the fire; stir all the time until you send it to table, or it will curdle. Give this soup any additional flavour you like. The oysters put in whole, may be first run on fine wire skewers, and fried.

Another Maigre.

Into four pints of water put five onions fried in butter, some mace, salt, pepper, and what herbs you like, in a small quantity. When this has boiled, and been carefully scummed, put in 1 lb. of fresh butter, a few mushrooms, and a 100 oysters; thicken with vermicelli, and let the soup boil gently a quarter of an hour.

Cray Fish Soup.

If to be maigre, the stock must be made of fish alone; it must be quite fresh, and 3 lbs. will make two quarts; put in an onion or two, and some black and Jamaica peppers. Boil the fish to a mash, and keep straining the liquor till clear. About four dozen cray fish will be enough, pick and stew them in the soup, after it has been strained, till done; add a little cayenne, and the spawn of a lobster pounded, and stirred in to thicken as well as flavour the soup. *Prawns, cockles,* and *muscles,* in the same way. It may be made of meat stock, and flavoured to be richer.

Eel Soup.

To 3 lbs. of eels, cut in pieces, allow three quarts of water; after this has boiled and been scummed, add two rather large crusts of toasted bread, eight blades of mace, three onions, a few whole peppercorns, and a faggot of herbs. Let this boil gently till half wasted, and then serve it with dice of toasted bread. You may add ¼ pint of cream, with a dessert-spoonful of flour, rubbed smooth in it. (*For fish forcemeats see in the Index.*)

CHAPTER XIII.

Instructions for Boiling, Frying, Baking, Pickling and Potting Fish

To Boil.

THE fish-kettle ought to be roomy: the water should, according to some, be cold, and spring water, and be slow in coming to a boil. I incline to this: according to others, it ought to be hot at the time of putting in the fish, upon the supposition that the shorter time it is in water the better. Experience must, however, be the best instructor; and much depends on the size, and sort of the fish. A handful of salt in the water, helps to draw the slime from the fish, and gives it firmness. Vinegar is used for the latter purpose, particularly for cod and turbot.—When the water boils, take off the scum, and place the fish-kettle by the side of the fire, to simmer gently; the usual allowance of time is twelve minutes to the pound, but there is no certain rule. Run a sharp knife into the thick part, and if it divide easily from the bone, it is done. When you think the fish done, lift up the strainer, and place it across the kettle to drain, and if it have to wait, put a heated cover on it, and over that, several folds of flannel; this is the best substitute for a *Bain Marie*. It must not stay an instant in water, after it is done. Serve on a fish drainer, which, as well as the dish, ought to be quite hot, for half cold fish is very bad. Crisp parsley, slices of lemon and barberries, also picked red cabbage, are used to garnish.

Some cooks say that *salt fish* should scarcely *boil* at all, but remain till tender, in hot water, just coming to a boil; put it on in cold water, and let it be a long time heating through.

Stock for gravy, for stewing, or sauce, is made of meat or fish, according to whether it be to be maigre or not. Any white fish, and the trimmings of all quite fresh fish, may be used. These may be browned first, in the frying-pan, then put into 1 or 2 quarts of water, according to the quantity you require, with a bunch of sweet herbs, onion, eschalot, mace, and lemon peel; boil it and scum well; then strain it, and put in the fish to stew. Fish stock is best made on the morning it is wanted. *Court Bouillon*, for boiling or stewing fish, is as follows: to a gallon of water, a handful of salt, 2 onions, 2 carrots, and eschalots, a bunch of parsley, thyme, and basil, 2 bay leaves, 12 peppercorns, and 6 cloves, also a large piece of butter. Stew, then strain it. This may be enriched as required. It keeps well, and is a good basis for stock.

To Fry.

This is rather difficult, and requires exceeding care and attention. Some people consider that lard is essential, but clarified dripping is as good. Oil is used in countries where the olive tree grows. Wash, and lay the fish in the folds of a clean cloth, for it must be quite dry. Flour it lightly, if to be covered with bread-crumbs, for if not quite dry, the bread will not adhere to it. The crumbs of stale bread; or to be very delicate in appearance, use biscuit powder. Having floured the fish, brush over with yolk and white of egg, then strew over the crumbs or powder, so as to cover every part of the fish. The frying-pan of an oval shape. The fire hot, but not fierce. If not hot enough, the fish will be soddened, if too hot, it will catch and burn. There should be fat enough to cover the fish; let it boil, (for frying is, in fact, *boiling in fat,*) skim it with an egg slice, as it becomes hot, then dip the tail of the fish in to ascertain the heat; if it become crisp at once the pan is ready, then lay in the fish. When done, lay it before the fire to dry, either on whity brown paper or a soft cloth; turn it two or three times, and if the frying fat has not been sufficiently hot, this will, in some measure, remedy the defect.—Fat in which veal or lamb has been fried may be used for fish, when it has settled long enough to be poured from the sediment.

Turbot to Boil.

First wash well, and soak it in salt and water; when quite clean, score the skin of the back, or the belly will crack when the fish begins to swell. Do not take off the fins, as they are a delicacy. Place it on a fish-strainer, in a roomy turbot-kettle, the back downwards. You may rub it over with lemon juice, to keep it white. Cover the fish with cold water, and throw in salt. Allow 1 lb. salt to a gallon and a half of water. It should be quite half an hour in coming to a boil, scum well, then draw the kettle to the side, and if a fish of 10 lbs. weight (larger are not so good), let it simmer 30 minutes, but if it do not simmer *gently* the fish will be spoiled and the skin cracked. When done, garnish with slices of lemon, scraped horse-radish, parsley, barberries, whole capers, or the pea of a lobster, forced through a sieve. A very few smelts or sprats fried, laid round the turbot. Lobster sauce is most esteemed, but shrimp or anchovy sauce answer very well. (*See to dress Cold Turbot.*)

Brill.

The same as turbot, except that you put it into boiling water, the flesh being softer. *Or:* parboiled, covered with egg and crumbs, and browned before the fire, or in the frying-pan. If 6 lbs. simmer it ½ an hour, but when it begins to crack it is done.

John Dory.

The same as brill.

Sole to Boil.

Wash clean, cover it with cold water, put in a handful of salt, and let it come gently to a boil, take off the scum, and set the fish-kettle aside; let it simmer very gently five minutes, and it is done, unless very large, then eight or ten minutes. Oyster sauce.

Cod to Boil.

Wash clean, and rub the inside with salt; cover it with water, in the kettle. A small fish will be done in fifteen minutes after the water boils; a large one will take half an hour; but the tail being much thinner than the thick part, it will be done too much if boiled all at once; therefore, the best way is to cut the tail in slices, to fry, and garnish the head and shoulders, or serve separately. Lay the roe on one side, the liver on the other side of the fish. Serve oyster, shrimp sauce, or plain melted butter; also scalloped oysters.—Garnish with lemon, and horse-radish. If the fish be in *slices*, the water should be made to boil as soon as possible after they are in it, and 10 minutes will cook them: pour shrimp or anchovy sauce over the slices. If you wish it to be rich, having some clear broth, put in a boned anchovy, some pickled oysters, chopped fine, pepper, salt, a glass of Port wine, and a thickening of butter and flour; boil this up, skim it, and pour over the slices of cod.

Cod to Boil Crimp.

Put it into boiling hot salt and water, draw it to the side, and let it simmer 15 or 20 minutes, according to its size. Slices less. Oyster sauce.

Salt Cod and Ling.

Soak it, according to the time it has been salted. If hard and dry, two nights, changing the water two or three times. The best *Dogger Bank* split fish require less. Let there be plenty of water, and the fish a long time in becoming heated through. Then simmer *very gently*, or it will be tough. Garnish with hard-boiled eggs, in quarters. Serve egg sauce, parsnips, or beet-root.

Cod to Fry.

Cut in thick slices; flour or egg, and cover with bread-crumbs or biscuit powder. Fry in hot dripping or lard.

Cod's Head and Shoulders.

Wash clean, then quickly dash boiling water over it, which will cause the slime to ooze out; this should be carefully removed with a knife, but take care not to break the skin; wipe the head clean, and lay it on a strainer, in a turbot-kettle of boiling water; put in salt and a tea-cupful of vinegar. Take care that it is quite covered. Simmer from thirty to forty minutes. Drain, and put it into a rather deep dish; glaze it with beaten yolk of egg, strew bread-crumbs, pepper, salt, and lemon-peel over, stick in bits of butter, and brown it before the fire; baste with butter, constantly strewing more bread-crumbs and chopped parsley over.—A rich sauce for this is made as follows; have a quart of beef or veal stock; or, if to be maigre, a rich well-seasoned fish stock; thicken with flour rubbed in butter, and strain it; add 50 oysters, picked and bearded, or the hard meat of a boiled lobster cut up, and the soft part pounded, 2 glasses of sherry, and the juice of a lemon. Boil it altogether, five minutes, skim and pour part into the dish where the fish is: the rest serve in a sauce tureen. It may be garnished with fried smelts, flounders, or oysters. The French stuff it with meat or fish forcemeat, with some balls of the same fried, as a garnish. — *Cold cod* may be dressed as cold turbot. The head may be baked; bits of butter stuck all over it.

Cod Sounds.

Scald, clean, and rub them with salt; take off the outer coat, and parboil, then flour and broil them. Pour over a thickened gravy, which has a tea-spoonful of made mustard, cayenne, and what other seasoning you like. — *Or*, fried, and served with the same kind of sauce. — *Or*, dressed in *ragout*, parboiled, cut in pieces, and stewed in good gravy, or in white sauce. Serve mustard and lemon.

Cabeached Cod.

Boil vinegar enough to cover the pieces of fish, a little mace, a few pepper-corns, a few cloves, and a little salt; when this is cold put a tea-cupful of olive oil. Cut the tail part of a cod fish in slices, rub pepper and salt on each, fry them in oil, then lay them on a plate to cool; when cold, put them into a pan or jar, and pour the pickle over. If you like, lay thin slices of onion between the fish. *Salmon* is good in this way. Serve salad with this.

Cod to Stew.

Lay three slices of cod in a stewpan, with ½ pint of weak white wine, *not* sweet, 6 oz. butter, two dozen oysters and their liquor, three blades of mace, salt, pepper, and a few crumbs of bread; stew this gently, and thicken with flour before you serve it.

Salmon to Boil,

Should be well cleaned and scaled (the less washing the better), and cut open as little as possible. Let there be water enough to well cover the fish, and salt in the proportion of 1 lb. to a gallon and a half. When it begins to boil, scum well, and put the fish in; for most cooks, I believe, are of opinion that salmon eats *firmer* when put on in hot or boiling water. A fish of 10 lbs. will take a full hour, or a little more, but it must only simmer all the time. Let the drainer be hot, put a folded napkin on it, and serve the fish directly. Garnish with curled parsley, horseradish, or slices of lemon. Serve shrimp, anchovy, or lobster sauce, also plain melted butter. Cucumber, and also salad, are eaten with salmon.

To boil Crimp.

Cut off the head, with about two inches of the neck, and clean the fish, opening it as little as possible, and do not cut it up the breast; also cut off the tail. Then cut the fish in circular slices, wash them, and lay them in salt and water. Put the head and tail on the strainer of the kettle, and pour in boiling water, with a little salt, and a very little vinegar; boil it five minutes, then put in the slices, and boil fifteen minutes, scumming all the time. Put the head and tail in the middle of the dish, the slices round. Sauces the same as the last. — Mustard is good with salmon.

Salmon to Grill.

Split the salmon, and endeavour not to mangle it in taking out the bone. Cut it into fillets four inches in breadth. Dry, but do not beat or press them, in the folds of a linen cloth, or dust them with flour to dry them. Have a clear fire, as for steaks, rub the gridiron with chalk, lay on the slices, and turn them occasionally. Serve very hot, with anchovy or shrimp sauce. French cooks steep the slices in oil, cover them with seasonings and fine herbs, and broil them, basting the while with oil. Caper sauce with this. Salmon may be thus prepared, then *fried*.—Some put the slices in paper to broil.

Salmon, Trout, Haddock, or Gurnet to bake.

Mix a seasoning of salt, pepper, and allspice, and rub a little in the fish. If a small salmon, turn the tail round to the mouth, and run a skewer through the fish to keep it in form. Place it on a stand, in a deep dish, cover with bits of butter, and strew the remainder of the seasoning over. Put it in the oven (an American or Dutch oven, before the fire, is very good for this), and baste occasionally with the liquor which runs from it. Garnish and serve the same sauce as boiled salmon. *Slices* of salmon may be baked this way.—Or: make it richer as follows: boil in a quart of vinegar, a piece of butter, 2 onions, the same of eschalot and carrots, a bunch of parsley, a sprig of thyme, a bay leaf, some basil, cloves, and allspice. Having cleaned and scaled the fish, fill it with fish forcemeat, sew it up, turn the tail into the mouth and skewer it. Place it on a stand in a baking dish, and pour the liquor over. Baste it from time to time. When the fish is done, pour off the liquor, and boil it up with an anchovy, cayenne, lemon juice, and a little thickening of butter rolled in flour. Place the fish in a rather deep dish, and strain the liquor round it. A *salmon peel* is best suited to this, being less rich than large salmon. (*See Haddock to stew.*)

Salmon to Pickle.

Cut the fish in pieces, not very small, and boil them in a little water and salt, scumming carefully all the time. When done, lift the fish out into a pan, and boil the liquor up with vinegar and spices to your taste, with black pepper, mace and ginger. Pour it cold over the fish.—Or: into the best vinegar, put 1 pint of white wine (supposing there to be 2 quarts of liquor or water to 1 of vinegar), add mace, ginger, horse-radish, cloves, allspice, a bay leaf, a sprig of lemon thyme, salt, and pepper. Pour it cold over the fish. Put away carefully, in a vegetable dish, any salmon left at table, strew over it ½ a salt-spoonful of cayenne; boil 12 allspice in a pint of white wine vinegar, and pour it scalding hot over the salmon. Keep it in a cool place.

Salmon to Dry.

Cut the fish down, take out the roe, and rub the whole with common salt; let it hang twenty-four hours to drain. Pound 3 oz. saltpetre, 2 oz. bay salt, and 2 oz. coarse sugar; rub these into the salmon, and lay it on a large dish for two days; then rub with common salt, and in twenty-four hours it will be fit to dry. Drain it, wipe it dry, stretch it open and fasten it with pieces of stick, in order that it may dry equally; hang it in a chimney corner where wood or peat is burnt, and it will be smoked in five days. Broil slices for breakfast. If too much smoked, or too dry, soak the slices in lukewarm water, before you broil them. To make this more relishing, dip the slices in oil, then in a seasoning of herbs and spices, and broil them.

Salmon to Collar.

Clean, scale, and bone the fish, then season it highly with mace, cloves, pepper and salt, roll it up into a handsome collar, and bandage it; then bake it with vinegar and butter, or simmer in vinegar and water. Serve melted butter, and anchovy sauce.

Salmon to Pot.

Do not wash, but clean with a cloth, and scale the fish, rub with salt, and let it lie three hours; then drain, and cut it into pieces. Sprinkle over them a seasoning of mace, black and Jamaica pepper, pounded, and lay them in a dish; cover them with melted butter, and set the dish in the oven. When done, drain the fat from the fish, and lay the pieces into little pots; when cold, cover with clarified butter.

Sturgeon

Is generally roasted or baked, if the former, tie a piece of 3 or 4 lbs. on a lark spit, and fasten that to a large one, baste with butter, and serve with a rich meat or maigre gravy highly flavoured. Serve besides, or instead of gravy, oyster, lobster, or anchovy sauce. *Slices* of sturgeon may be egged, rolled in bread-crumbs, seasonings, and herbs, then broiled in buttered papers. Also it is *stewed* in good beef gravy.

Skate.

This should be broad, thick, and of a bluish cream colour. It must be quite fresh, if to be crimp, and put on in hot water. It will keep, in cold weather, two or three days, but will eat tender. Shrimp, lobster, or caper sauce, parsley and butter, or onion sauce.—*Or*: put into a stew-pan ½ pint of water, ½ pint of vinegar, all the trimmings of the skate, two onions, a clove of garlic, some parsley, and a little basil. Boil till the trimmings are cooked to a mash, then strain and put the skate into the liquor; it should just come to a boil, and stand by the side of the fire ten minutes. Garnish with the liver. Serve caper sauce.

Skate to Fry.

Parboil it first, then cut in thin slices, and dip them in egg and bread-crumbs. Then either fried or broiled. Both ways skate is good *cold,* with mustard, pepper, oil and vinegar.

Thornback and Maids.

Dress the same as Skate.

Trout to Boil.

Put a good-sized fish into boiling water, in which there is a handful of salt, and simmer gently 20 minutes. Melted butter plain, or with chopped gherkins.

Haddock to Boil.

The night before, fill the eyes with salt, and hang the fish up. *Or*, for a few hours before cooking, sprinkle them with salt. Serve egg sauce. It may be stuffed, as in the next receipt.

Haddocks to Stew, Bake, or Roast.

If you have six small ones, take the heads, tails and trimmings of all, and one whole fish, boil these in a quart of water or broth, with an onion, sweet herbs, and cayenne; boil well, and thicken with brown flour; add spices, and mushroom catsup, or essence of anchovy; strain this, boil again, and skim well; then lay in the rest of your haddocks, cut in pieces. If there require more sauce, add as much as is necessary, of any broth or gravy you have; some oysters, or oyster-pickle. When done, take the fish out with a slice, lay it in a dish, and pour the sauce, which ought to be thick, round. This fish may be stuffed with meat, or rich forcemeat, and dressed whole in the above gravy.—*Another*: the fish being well cleaned, dry it, and put in the stuffing directed for fillet of veal; tie the tail to the mouth, put the haddock in a pie-dish, rub it over with flour, half fill the dish with veal stock, and bake it in a slow oven 40 minutes. A glass of white wine, or half a one of brandy, oyster-pickle, or lemon juice, either of these may be used, according to taste. *Gurnet* the same. *To Roast*: Stuff a good-sized one with veal stuffing, and dangle it before the fire; baste with butter, and when nearly done, take the gravy out of the pan, skim off the fat, then boil up the gravy with pepper, salt, and a wine-glassful of Port wine.

Haddocks to Bake, quite plain.

Boil and mash some potatoes. Season the fish, and put a piece of butter inside, lay it in the middle of the dish, and put a thick border of the potatoes round. Brush over the whole with egg, stick bits of butter over the fish, and bake for half an hour; when in the oven a short time, pour a little melted butter and catsup in the dish.

Haddock or Mackerel to Broil.

Split the fish, bone the haddock, salt it, and hang it for two days in the chimney corner.

Haddocks, Soles, Flounders, Plaice, Perch, Tench, Trout, Whitings, and Herrings to Fry.

Haddocks, soles, and generally whitings, are skinned. Plaice wiped, not washed, and must lie three or four hours after being rubbed with salt. When the fish is cleaned and wiped dry, dust with flour, and lay it gently into the boiling fat; having first egged and dipped it into bread-crumbs. The fat may be either lard, butter, dripping, or oil. Turn it carefully, lift it out when done, and lay it on a sheet of paper in a sieve, whilst you fry the rest; or put it before the fire, if it require drying. Garnish with curled parsley, and slices of lemon. Serve very hot. Shrimp or anchovy sauce, and plain butter. *Whitings* and *haddocks* should have the tail skewered into the mouth.

Mackerel and Herrings to Boil.

The fresher these are eaten the better. They require a great deal of cleaning. Choose soft roes to boil. A small mackerel will be done in a quarter of an hour. When the eye starts it is done, and should not stand in the water. Serve fennel boiled and chopped, in melted butter, and garnish with lumps of chopped fennel. Both these may be broiled, whole or split, and sprinkled during the cooking with chopped herbs and seasonings.

Mackerel and Herrings to Bake.

Choose fine ones, in season, cut off the heads and take out the roes. Pound together some mace, nutmeg, Jamaica pepper, cloves, and salt; put a little of this into each fish, then put a layer of them into a pan, and a layer of the mixture upon them, then another layer of fish, and so on. Fill the vessel with vinegar, and tie over close with brown paper. Bake them 6 or 8 hours. To be eaten cold.

Mackerel and Herrings to Pickle.

The same as salmon.—*Or*: as follows: get them as fresh as possible. Take off the heads, split the fish open, and lay them in salt and water an hour; prepare the following pickle: for 1½ dozen mackerel, take 1 lb. common and 1 lb. bay salt, 1 oz. saltpetre, 1 oz. lump sugar broken, and mix well together. Take the fish out of the water, drain and wipe them. Sprinkle a little salt over them, put a layer into a jar or cask (the skin side downwards), then a layer of the mixture, till the vessel is full. Press it down, and cover close. Ready in three months.

Red Herrings and Sardinias to Broil.

Open and trim them, skin them or not, as you like. If hard, soak in lukewarm water. Broil them, either over or before the fire, and rub butter over as they broil.

Carp, Perch, and Tench to Stew.

If very large, divide the fish. Rub the inside with salt and mixed spices, stick in a few cloves, and a blade or two of mace, in pieces, lay them in a stew-pan, and cover with good fish, or meat stock. Put in 2 onions, an anchovy chopped, cayenne, 3 glasses of claret, or 2 of Port. When done, take the fish up, and keep it hot, while you thicken the gravy with butter and browned flour; add mushroom catsup, oyster-pickle, chili vinegar, or the juice of a lemon; simmer the sauce, skim and pour it over the fish. The roe may be kept back and fried, to garnish the fish, with sippets of bread fried. Use horse-radish and slices of lemon also, to garnish. Where meat gravy is not used, more wine is required.—*Cod's skull, Soles, Eels, Flounders, Trout, Whitings and fillets of Turbot, Cod and Halibut,* may be dressed the same way. *Or*: having parboiled the fish, brown it in the frying-pan, and stew it in good gravy seasoned with sweet marjoram, lemon thyme, basil, onions, pepper, salt, and spices: when nearly done, thicken the sauce, and flavour it, with a small portion each, of Worcester, Harvey's and Reading sauces, soy, anchovy sauce, oyster-pickle, catsup, and an equal portion of Port and white wine. The carp's blood should not be omitted.

Carp and Pike (or Jack) to Boil or Bake.

If to be maigre, make a forcemeat of the yolks of 3 eggs, some oysters bearded, 3 anchovies, an onion and some parsley, all chopped; mace, black pepper, allspice, and salt, pounded; mix this with biscuit flour, or crumbs of bread, and the fish being well cleaned and scaled, fill it with the stuffing, and sew it up. If to bake, lay it in a deep dish, stick butter over, and baste plentifully, as it bakes, in a moderate oven. Serve anchovy sauce. *Or*: you may take the fish out, and keep it hot, whilst you make a rich sauce thus: thicken the gravy in the dish, and boil it up with parsley and sweet herbs; then strain it, add made mustard, a glass of Port wine, and one of chili or any other flavouring vinegar, also pounded mace, salt, and cayenne. Pour this over the fish.

Eels to Stew.

Skin and cut them in pieces. They may be egged and rolled in bread-crumbs, or merely floured. If to be maigre, stew them in fish stock; if otherwise, in good clear beef gravy, in which seasoning herbs, and roots have been boiled. Stew the fish gently, until done, then take them out, keep them hot, and thicken the gravy with browned flour, or what you like; add a glass of white wine, and one of mushroom catsup, also a spoonful of made mustard; boil it up, strain and pour it over the fish. Garnish with scraped horse-radish, and barberries. *Whiting*, also *slices of Turbot*, in the same way.

Lampreys to Stew.

After cleaning the fish carefully, remove the cartilage which runs down the back, and season well with cloves, mace, nutmeg, allspice, a tea-spoonful of mushroom powder, a little black pepper and cayenne; put it into a stew-pan with good gravy to cover it, and sherry or Madeira; keep the pan covered till the fish is tender, then take it out, and keep it hot while you boil up the liquor with essence of anchovy, lemon pickle, Gloucester sauce, and thickening; add the juice of a lemon, a spoonful of made mustard, 1 of soy, and 1 of chili vinegar. Fry the spawn to put round the fish.

Eels to Fry.

They should always be *gently parboiled*, before they are either fried or broiled, then allowed to be cold, before they are cut up; but if very small, turn the tail round to the mouth, and fry it whole. Rub with a mixture of spices, brush with egg, and cover them with bread-crumbs. Fry of a light brown, and lay them on a sieve to drain.—Small eels are sometimes boiled, and served with dried sage and parsley strewed over.

Eels to Collar.

Choose a large eel. Slit open the belly and take out the bone. Rub it well with a mixture of pepper, salt, parsley, sage, thyme, and lemon peel. Roll up, quite tight, and bind it with tape; then boil it gently, in salt, a little vinegar, and water to cover it, till tender. It will keep in the pickle it was boiled in.

Eels to Spitchcock.

They are not skinned, but well cleaned, and rubbed with salt. Take out the bone, wash and dry them in a cloth. Either cut in pieces, or roll them round and cook them whole. First (parboiled) dip the fish into a thick batter of eggs, chopped parsley, sage, eschalot, lemon peel, pepper and salt; then roll them in bread-crumbs or biscuit powder, dip again in batter, and again in the crumbs. Broil over a clear fire. Garnish with curled parsley or slices of lemon, and serve anchovy sauce, or butter flavoured with cucumber vinegar.

Trout to Stew.

The fish being cleaned, put it into a stew-pan, with half champagne and half rhenish, or half moselle and half sherry, in all a tumbler full; season with pepper, salt, an onion with 3 cloves in it, and a very little parsley and thyme, also a crust of bread. When the fish is done, lift it out whilst you thicken the sauce; bruise the bread, but if that be not enough, add a little flour rubbed smooth, and a bit of butter, boil it up and pour over the trout in the dish. Garnish with sliced lemon and fried bread.

Sprats, Smelts, and Gudgeon to Bake, Boil, or Fry.

Rub the gridiron with chalk or mutton suet, and set it over a clear fire. Run a long thin skewer through the heads of the sprats, and lay them on the gridiron. They should be eaten quite hot.—To *bake*, lay them in a deep dish, strew bits of butter, pepper, salt and spices over, cover with vinegar, and set them in the oven.—To *fry*, dip them in batter, then in a mixture of seasoning, chopped herbs, and biscuit powder, and fry them.

Allice or Shad.

These are broiled and eaten with caper sauce.

Red Mullet.

The inside is not taken out. Wash the outside of the fish, fold it in oiled paper, lay in a rather shallow dish, and bake it gently. Make a sauce of the liquor, a piece of butter rolled in flour, a little anchovy essence, and a glass of sherry. Boil it up, and serve in a tureen. Send the fish to table in the paper.

Water Souchy.

Eels, whitings, soles, flounders, and mackerel are generally used. Stew it in clear fish stock, until done, eight minutes will be enough; add cayenne, catsup, an anchovy, and any other flavouring ingredient; let it boil up, skim, and serve hot altogether in a tureen.

Pipers to dress.

Stuff the fish with a forcemeat of suet, bread-crumbs, 2 eggs, chopped parsley, pepper, salt and cayenne. Skewer the tail in the mouth, flour and egg the fish, and bake in a hot oven. Drain it, and serve with Dutch sauce.

Cray Fish to Boil.

Boil in the shell; five minutes is enough. Some cooks put a bunch of herbs in the water. Serve on a napkin.

Lobsters and Crabs to Boil.

Have plenty of water, make it quite salt, brush the lobster or crab, and put it in. From forty to fifty minutes for the middling size, more if very large, less if very small. They will throw up a great deal of scum, which must be taken off. Wipe the lobster with a damp cloth, rub a piece of butter over, then wipe it with a dry cloth. Take off the large claws, and crack them; split down the tail, and place the whole neatly in a dish. A very nice sauce, as follows: boil hard 2 eggs, pound the yolk in a mortar, with a little vinegar, and the spawn of the lobster, make it quite smooth, add a large spoonful of salad oil, 3 spoonsful of good vinegar, a tea-spoonful of made mustard, and a little cayenne and salt.

Lobster or Crab, to eat hot.

Cut the meat in pieces, or mince it fine; season with spices, nutmeg, cayenne and salt, and warm it in a little good gravy, thickened: or if maigre, fish stock, or just enough water to moisten the meat, and a good-sized piece of butter rolled in flour, a little cream, and some catsup. Serve on toasted sippets; or have the shell of a lobster or crab cleaned, and serve the meat in it. — *Another way* is, not to warm the mince *over* the fire, but to put it into the shell, and set that before the fire in a Dutch oven, strew some fine bread-crumbs or biscuit powder over all, and stick some bits of butter over that; brown with a salamander, and serve quite hot. *Prawns* the same way. — Lobster is sometimes fricasseed, in rich veal gravy; or with cream, and yolk of egg. Garnish with pickled cucumber, or other pickle. — Lobster may be cooked as follows: chop the meat of a large one, and mix with it a very little lemon peel, pepper, salt, nutmeg, butter, cream, and crumbs of stale bread; roll this well, and divide it into small quantities; put each one into light puff paste, the size of sausages, rub them over with yolk of egg, then with bread-crumbs; fry of a yellow brown, and serve with crisped parsley. — *Or:* wash and clean some spinach and put it into a saucepan, with the meat of a lobster, or a pint of picked shrimps cut small, an onion, a clove of garlic minced, salt and cayenne; when nearly done, add 2 onions sliced and fried; cover close a few minutes; garnish with slices of lemon.

Lobsters and Crabs to Pot.

Parboil the fish, cut it into small pieces, put a layer into a potting can, or deep tin dish, sprinkle salt, pepper, cayenne and pounded mace over, then a layer of the spawn and coral, then a layer of the meat, and so on, till all is in, press it down, pour melted butter over, and put it half an hour in a slow oven. Let it then get cold, take off the butter, take out the meat and pack it into small pots; clarify the butter, and pour over. The butter left may turn to account in sauces, as it will be highly flavoured. If for sandwiches, the meat must be pounded in a mortar before it is baked, that it may spread more easily.

Prawns, Shrimps, and Cray Fish to Pot.

Boil them in salt and water, pick them carefully, then pound in a mortar, with, to 1 lb. fish, a salt-spoonful of mace, the same of allspice, half the quantity of salt and cayenne, the ¼ of a nutmeg grated, and butter to make it a thick paste. Put into pots, pour clarified butter over, and tie it down close.

Prawns and Shrimps to Butter.

Take them out of their shells, and warm them in gravy, with a bit of butter rolled in flour, nutmeg, salt, and pepper. Simmer it a little, stir all the time, and serve with toasted sippets.

Prawns or Cray Fish in Jelly.

Make a good calf's-feet or cow-heel jelly, and boil in it some trimmings of cod, turbot, and skate, a little horse-radish, lemon peel, an onion, a piece of pounded mace, grated nutmeg and grated tongue, hung beef, or ham. Boil it well, strain, and let it get cold. Take off the fat, pour the jelly from the sediment, and boil it up with 2 glasses of white wine, and the whites of 4 eggs whisked to a froth. Do not stir this as it boils. When done, let it stand a quarter of an hour to settle; then pass it through a jelly bag: pour some of it into a mould, or deep dish, to become firm; then stick in the fish, neatly picked, in any form you like, and fill up the dish with jelly. When quite cold, turn it out.

Fish Cake.

Pick the fish from the bones, add 1 lb. of mashed potatoes to 2 lbs. fish, a little white pepper, mace, cayenne, and lemon peel; flavour either with essence of anchovy, of lobster, of shrimp, or of oyster, according to taste and the sort of fish; add Harvey's or Camp or Gloucester sauce, also lemon pickle and eschalot vinegar, to your taste: mix the whole with a little melted butter and an egg, dip in breadcrumbs, and fry of a light brown. Use no salt with the above sauces.—*Another*: Having some cold boiled fish, add to it the third of its weight in bread-crumbs, a little butter beaten with a spoon, a small onion, parboiled and minced fine, pepper, salt, and the whites of 2 eggs to bind; mixed well together, make it in the form of a thick cake, and fry on both sides of a light brown: stew it in good gravy, made from either meat or fish stock, and flavoured with onion, pepper, and salt. Thicken the sauce, and add mushroom catsup.

Fish to Pull.

When cold, pick the fish clean from the bones, and to 1 lb. add two ta-ble-spoonsful of anchovy, two of lemon pickle, one of Harvey's, one of Camp sauce, one of chili vinegar, a little cayenne, white pepper, and mace; when nearly hot, add a piece of butter rolled in flour to thicken it, then make it quite hot, put it in a dish, grate bread-crumbs over, and baste with melted butter, to moisten them, then brown with a salamander, or in a Dutch oven, or on a tin before the fire, with a Scotch bonnet behind it.—*Or*: Pick from the bones, in flakes, any cold or boiled fish, salmon, cod, turbot, sole, skate or pike; and to 1 lb. fish, add ½ pint of cream, or ¼ lb. of butter, a table-spoonful of mustard, the same of essence of anchovy, mushroom catsup, any flavouring sauce you like, salt and pepper; heat it in a saucepan, put it into a hot dish, strew crumbs of bread over, moisten the top with thin melted butter, and brown in a Dutch oven.

A Salmagundi.

Wash and cut open, then take out the meat from the bones of two large her-rings, mince the fish with cold chicken, two hard-boiled eggs, one onion, a boned anchovy, and a little grated ham, season with cayenne, vinegar, and oil, salt, if nec-essary; and serve the mince, garnished with heaps of chopped boiled egg, parsley and pickles, also spun butter.

Oysters to Stew.

Choose plump natives, beard and stew two dozen in their own liquor, till just coming to a boil; take them out and lay them in a dish, whilst you strain the liquor into a saucepan; add a little piece of butter rubbed in flour, a blade of mace, a few peppercorns, lemon peel, three table-spoonsful of cream, and a little cayenne. Lay the oysters in, cover the saucepan, and let them simmer five minutes, very gently. Have toasted sippets in a deep dish, take out the oysters when done with a silver spoon, lay them in and pour the gravy over.—The French strew grated parmesan over the oysters, before the sauce. *Oysters to Grill.*—Toss them in a stew-pan in a little of their own liquor, a piece of butter, and a little chopped parsley, but do not let them boil. Clean their own shells, lay an oyster in each, and some little bits of butter. Put the shells on the gridiron, in two minutes they will be done. *Oysters to Brown.*—Open carefully, lift them out of their liquor, and dip each one in yolk of egg, beaten up with flour, pepper and salt, then brown them in a frying-pan, with a piece of butter; take them out, pour the liquor into the pan, thicken with a piece of butter rolled in flour, add a little catsup, minced lemon peel, and parsley, let it boil up, put in the oysters, and stir them in it a few minutes. Serve on toasted sippets. *Oysters to Fry.*—Make a batter of three or four eggs, a table-spoonful of flour, a tea-spoonful of salt, and the ¼ of one of cayenne, also a very little mace. Cover the oysters well with this, and fry in boiling lard of a light brown; then grate toasted or brown bread over them, and put before the fire for three minutes in a Dutch oven. *Oysters or Cockles to Scallop.*—Stew the oysters in their own gravy. Have ready some bread-crumbs, put a layer into the scallop shells, or dish, moist-en with the oyster liquor, and put some little bits of butter, then a layer of oysters, then of crumbs, till the shell is full; a light sprinkling of salt, pepper, and cayenne;

let bread-crumbs be at the top, and lay on some little bits of butter. Brown before the fire in a Dutch oven. *Cold fish* may be re-cooked in this way for supper or luncheon. *Oysters in Dean Swift's way.*—Wash the shells clean, and put the oysters, unopened, into an earthen pot, with their hollow sides downwards; set the pot, covered, in a kettle of water, and make that boil. Do not let the water get into the shells; three or four minutes will cook the oysters.

Oysters to Keep.

Wash them clean, lay them, bottom downwards, into a tub, and cover them with strong salt and water, in the proportion of a large handful of salt to a pail of water. Some persons sprinkle them with flour or oatmeal; this fattens them, but does not always improve the flavour.

See in the Index for *Curry of Fish*.

CHAPTER XIV.

General Instructions for Made Dishes, and Directions relative to particular Dishes

WHAT is generally understood in England to represent a "made dish" is something too rich, or too highly seasoned, to be available for a family dinner; but this is an error. Made dishes are not of necessity rich or costly, but judgment is required in compounding them, and, by a little practice, a cook will acquire this judgment, and then will be able to convert the remains of joints, and much that would not appear to advantage if plainly cooked, into nice palatable dishes. It is the proper application of seasonings and flavouring ingredients, and not the superabundance of them, which constitutes the excellence of "made dishes." — (*See in the Index for Sauces.*)

It has been directed, in making soup, that it must not boil fast. Made dishes should never boil at all; *very* gentle simmering, and the lid of the stewpan must not be removed, after the necessary scumming is over. Time should be allowed for gradual cooking, and that over, the stewpan ought to stand by the fire a few minutes, that the fat risen to the top be taken off, before the dish is served. Indeed, ragouts are better made the day before, because then the fat is more completely taken off. Shake the stewpan if there be danger of burning, but if the lid be removed, the savoury steams escape, and also much of the succulent qualities of the meat.

Great delicacy is required in re-warming made dishes; they should be merely heated through; and the safest mode is to place the stewpan in a vessel of boiling water.

All made dishes require gravy, more or less good, and, in most houses, this, by a little previous forethought, may always be ready; for if the liquor in which meat has been boiled be saved, that seasoned, flavoured, and thickened, the cook will always be provided with gravy for a ragout or fricassee. (*See the Chapter on Soup, and also that on Gravy.*)

The following is a good store gravy. — Boil a ham, or part of one, in water to cover it, with four onions, a clove of garlic, six eschalots, a bay leaf, a bunch of sweet herbs, six cloves, and a few peppercorns. Keep the pot covered, and let it simmer three hours. The liquor is strained, and kept till poultry or meat of any kind is boiled; put the two together, and boil down fast till reduced to three pints; when cold, it will be a jelly, and suits any sort of ragout or hash.

Every cook ought to learn the art of *larding,* and also of *braising,* as they are both used in made dishes.

To Lard.

Have larding pins of various sizes. Cut strips of bacon, with a sharp knife, put one into the pin, pierce the skin and a very little of the flesh, and draw it through; the rows may be either near together or far apart. The bacon is sometimes rolled in seasonings to suit the meat.

To Blanch, either Meat or Vegetables.

This gives plumpness as well as whiteness. Put whatever it be into a saucepan with cold water to cover, and let it come to a boil; take it out, plunge it into cold water, and let it remain till cold.

To Braise.

This is, in fact, to stew in highly seasoned fat. Poultry must be trussed as for boiling. Either lard, or stuff it, with good forcemeat, and provide a thick-bottomed stew-pan, large enough to hold it. Line this with slices of bacon, or fat beef, sliced onion, carrot, and turnip. Strew in a few chopped herbs, salt, mace, black and Jamaica pepper, 2 bay leaves, and a clove of garlic. (The seasoning to suit the meat.) Lay the meat in, and cover it, first with the same quantity of herbs and spices as above, then with thin slices of bacon, and, over all, white paper; wrap a cloth about the lid of the stew-pan, and press it down, setting a weight on the top. Place the stew-pan over a slow fire, and put embers on the lid. The cooking process should be very slow. Braised joints are generally glazed.

To Glaze.

When the meat is sufficiently cooked, take it out of the stew-pan and keep it covered. Strain the gravy into a clean stew-pan, put it on the fire, and let it boil quickly, uncovered, a few minutes; brush the meat over with this, let it cool, and then brush again. What is not used may be kept in a jar tied down, in a cool place.—*Fowls, Hams,* and *Tongues,* cooked by plain boiling, are often glazed, to be eaten cold.—*Another way* is, to prepare a glaze beforehand, for *Hams, Tongues,* or *Fricandeaux,* thus: break the bone of a knuckle of veal, cut the meat in pieces, the same with shin of beef, add any poultry or game trimmings, and a few slices of bacon; put them in a stew-pan over a quick fire, and let them *catch,* then put in a little broth of cow-heels, or calf's-head, or feet. Let this stew to a strong jelly; then strain, and put it by in jars. It may be flavoured to suit the dish, at the time it is heated to be used. Glaze should be heated in a vessel of boiling water, and when quite hot, brushed over the meat. When *cream* is used, it should be first heated (not boil), poured in by degrees, and stirred, to prevent curdling. In making a stew, remember to let it stand by the fire nearly ten minutes, not simmering, that you may remove the fat, before you put in the thickening. The *flour* for this should be of the finest kind, well dried. For *Ragouts,* you may brown it, before the fire, or in the oven, and keep it ready prepared. It is convenient to keep spices ready pounded; the quantity so prepared, as to be proportioned to the usual consumption. *Kitchen pepper* is: 1 oz. ginger, ½ oz. each, of nutmeg, black and Jamaica pepper, and cinnamon; pound or grind, and keep them in small phials, corked, and labelled. For *white sauces*, white pepper, nutmeg, mace, and grated lemon peel, in equal proportion, may also be kept prepared; cayenne, added or not, as taste requires; cayenne is used in preparations of brains, kidneys, or liver. Made dishes are sometimes served on a *Purée* of mushrooms or vegetables. This is: boiled to a mash, just thicker than a sauce, and much used in French cookery. To *Marinade* is to *steep* meat or fish, in a mixture of wine, vinegar, herbs and spices.

Onions, small silver ones, are blanched, peeled and boiled in good broth to serve as garnish to *bouilli* and many other made dishes; or not blanched, but stewed with butter, if to be brown. When very strong you may parboil them with a turnip, for a stew, or forcemeat.

Some persons use *brandy* in made dishes. *Wine* in the proportion of a wine-glassful to a pint of gravy; the quantity of brandy small in proportion.

Truffles and *Morells* are a valuable addition to gravy and soup. Wash 1 oz. of each, boil them five minutes in water, then put them and the liquor into the stew.

Rump of Beef to Stew, Ragout, or Braise.

Cut out the bone, break it, and put it on in cold water, with any trimmings you can cut off the rump; season with onion, sweet herbs, a carrot, and a turnip. Scum, and let it simmer an hour; then strain it into the stew-pan in which you stew the beef. Season the rump highly with kitchen pepper (*which see*), and cayenne; skewer and bind it with tape. Lay skewers at the bottom of the stew-pan, place the meat upon them, and pour the gravy over. When it has simmered, rather more than an hour, turn it, put in a carrot, turnip, and 3 onions, all sliced, an eschalot, and a glass of flavouring vinegar. Keep the lid quite close, and let it simmer 2 hours. Before you take it up, put in a little catsup, made mustard, and some brown *roux*, or butter rolled in flour, to thicken the gravy.—*Or*: having taken out the bone, lard the beef with fat bacon, and stew it for as many hours, as the beef weighs pounds, in good gravy, or plain water, with vegetables and seasoning, as in the other receipt, to which you may add a head of celery. This dish should be nicely garnished; for which purpose have carrots boiled, and cut into any shapes you like, also button onions, Brussels sprouts, sprigs of cauliflower, &c., &c.; a border of mashed potatoes round the meat, and carrot or green vegetables disposed upon it, is also nice. Stewed tomatas also, or tomata sauce.

Brisket of Beef to Stew.

Wash, then rub the beef with salt and vinegar, put it into a stew-pan to just hold it, with water or broth; when it boils scum well, and let it stew an hour; add carrots, turnips, and onions, cut up. Stew it 6 hours, take out the bones, skim the gravy, add butter rolled in flour, a little catsup and mixed spices. Put the meat into a dish; add made mustard, and more catsup, to the gravy, pour some into the dish, and the rest in a tureen. This may be enriched by walnut and mushroom catsup, truffles, morells, and Port wine; also, carrots and turnips cut in shapes, boiled separately, and, when the meat is dished, spread over and round it. Serve pickles.

Beef, or Veal à la Mode.

The rump, the thick part of the flank, the mouse buttock, and the clod, are dressed as follows; take from 8 to 10 lbs. beef, rub well with mixed spices and salt, and dredge it with flour. Put some skewers at the bottom of a stew-pan, and on them thin slices of bacon, 2 table-spoonsful of vinegar, and a pint of good gravy or broth; then put in the beef, and more bacon. Cover close, and let it stew slowly 3 hours; then turn the meat, and put in cloves, black and Jamaica peppers, 2 bay leaves, and a few mushrooms, or catsup, also a few button onions, browned in the frying-pan, and a head of celery. Let it stew till the meat is tender, then take out the bay leaves, put in a tea-cupful of Port wine, and serve the meat with the gravy in the dish. The gravy will have thickened to a glaze. Some cooks lard the beef with thick slices of fat bacon, first dipped in vinegar, then in a mixture ready prepared, of black pepper, allspice, a clove and parsley, chives, thyme, savoury and knotted marjoram, all chopped very fine. Serve *salad* or *cucumber*. When veal is dressed this way (the breast is best), flavour with oyster catsup, lemon peel, lemon pickle, mace, bay leaf, and white wine. Garnish with pickled mushrooms, barberries, and lemon. This may be cooked in the oven, in a baking dish with a close fitting lid.

Beef to Collar.

The thin flank is best; the meat young, tender, not very fat. Rub it with salt and a very little saltpetre, lay it across a deep dish one night, to drain; rub in a mixture of brown sugar, salt, pounded pepper and allspice; let it lie a week in the pickle; rub and turn it every day. Then take out the bones, cut off the coarse and gristly parts, and the inner skin, dry it, and spread over the inside some chopped herbs of whatever flavour you choose, and mixed spices; roll it up as tight as you can, and bind with tape; allow it four or five hours' slow, but constant boiling. When done press it under a heavy weight, and put by to eat cold. It is sometimes served hot.

Bœuf Royale.

Bone the brisket, then scoop holes or cut slits in the meat, about an inch asunder, fill one with small rolls of fat bacon, a second with chopped parsley and sweet herbs, seasoned with pepper and salt, the third with oyster cut small and powdered with a very little mace and nutmeg. When all the apertures are stuffed, tie up the meat in a roll, put it into a baking pan, pour over it a pint of sherry, quite hot, and six cloves, flour the meat, cover close and set it in the oven for three hours; pour off the gravy, and put it by to cool that you may skim off the fat; if it is not already in a jelly, which it should be, boil it a little longer. Serve the beef cold, and the jelly round it.

Beef to Fricandeau.

Lard a piece of lean beef with strips of bacon, seasoned with salt, pepper, cloves, mace, and allspice; put it into a stew-pan, with a pint of broth, a faggot of herbs, parsley, half a clove of garlic (if you like), one eschalot, four cloves, pepper and salt. Let it stew till tender, take it out and keep hot by the fire; strain the gravy, and boil it quickly, till reduced to a glaze; and glaze the larded side of the beef.

Serve on stewed sorrel or cucumbers.

Ox Cheek to Stew.

Having washed the cheek, tie it up round, and stew it in good gravy, or water, with two bay leaves, a little garlic (if approved), two onions, mushrooms, two turnips, two carrots, half a small cabbage, a bunch of sweet herbs, six whole peppers, a little allspice, and a blade of mace. Scum well, and when nearly done, take out the cheek, cut off the tapes, put it into a fresh stew-pan; strain the liquor, skim off the fat, add lemon juice, or vinegar, salt, cayenne, and catsup; whisk in some white of egg to clear it, pour it through a strainer, to the cheek; and stew it till quite tender.

Ox Palates.

Parboil them till the upper skin will easily come off, and either divide, or cut them in slices. Stew them slowly, in gravy thickened with browned flour, with a little minced eschalot or onion, or a spoonful of onion pickle, some catsup, and cayenne. If to be dressed high, add wine, mushrooms, truffles, and morells to the sauce, and forcemeat balls in the dish. Stewed cucumbers with this. — *Beef skirts* the same way. — *Or*: boil the palates in milk, and serve them in white sauce, flavoured with mushroom powder and mace.

To Pickle Ox Palates.

Clean and simmer them in water, scum well, then put as much mace, cloves, pepper, salt, and sweet herbs, as will make them highly seasoned, and let them boil gently 4 hours, or till quite tender; then take the skin off, cut them into small pieces, and set them by, to cool. Cover them with a pickle of half white wine, half vinegar, and spices as above: when this is cold, strain it, and pour over the palates; add 2 bay leaves, if you like. Cover very close.

Bouilli.

See this in direction for soup. But if to be dressed without soup, boil a piece of the flank or brisket in water to cover it, with a sufficiency of cut carrot and turnip to garnish, also a head of celery and 12 or 16 button onions, browned; add a small table-spoonful of black and Jamaica peppers tied in muslin; simmer it gently; and it requires a long time to cook it enough. When it has boiled till tender, take out enough of the liquor to make sauce; thicken it with brown *roux*, or flour rubbed in butter, add catsup, cayenne, and made mustard. Garnish with the vegetables. Caper, walnut, or tomata sauce. Pickled gherkins on the table.

Tongue to Stew.

Cut off the root, and boil a salted tongue tender enough to peel. Stew it in good gravy, with herbs, celery, soy, mushroom catsup, and cayenne. To be very rich this is served with truffles, morells, and mushrooms. Lard it if you like. — *Or*: put the tongue into a pan that will just hold it, strew over a mixture of pepper, cloves, mace, and allspice, and thin slices of butter, put a coarse paste over, and bake it slowly, till you think a straw will pass through it. To eat cold.

Ox Tails to Stew.

Divide them at the joints. Scald or parboil, then brown them in a stew-pan, with a little piece of butter, to keep from burning. Stew them slowly till tender, in broth or water, enough to make sufficient gravy, seasoned with salt, pepper, cayenne, chopped parsley, and a spoonful of made mustard. Thicken the gravy with brown flour. If you approve, put into the stew three onions (one brown), two carrots, and a bay leaf; or you may boil some cut carrots and turnips, stew them in melted butter, and serve round the pieces of meat in the gravy.

Irish Stew.

This excellent dish is made of mutton or beef. Chops cut from a loin or neck of mutton, trimmed of most of the fat, and well seasoned with salt, pepper, and spices. Parboil and skin as many potatoes as you think enough, the proportion is 4 lbs. weight to 2 lbs. of meat. Peel 8 or 10 onions (for 4 lbs. meat), lay some sliced suet at the bottom of the stew-pan, or a tea-cupful of melted butter, put in a layer of potatoes sliced, a layer of chops, slice a layer of onions over, then potatoes and mutton, and so on, the top layer potato; pour in half a pint of broth or water. A shank or small piece of ham is an improvement. This should stew very slowly; when the meat is tender the potatoes *may* be boiled to a mash, therefore have some boiled whole, by themselves. Beef steaks, and any of the coarser parts, make a better stew than mutton.

Rump Steaks to Stew.

The steaks should be of one thickness, about ¾ of an inch. Put about 1 oz. of butter into a stew-pan, and 2 onions sliced, lay in the steaks, and let them brown nicely on one side, then turn them to brown on the other side. Boil a large tea-cup-ful of button onions three quarters of an hour, strain, and pour the liquor over the steaks; if not enough to cover them, put a little more water or broth, add salt, and 10 peppercorns. Stew them very gently half an hour, then strain off as much of the liquor as you want for sauce; put it into a saucepan, thicken with brown flour, or *roux*, add catsup, a little cayenne, also a glass of red wine. Lay the steaks in a dish, and pour the sauce over. The boiled onions may be laid over the steaks. Mush-rooms stewed with steaks are an improvement; 2 or 3 tomatas, also, will help to enrich the stew, and about 4 pickled walnuts may be put in. Harvey's and Reading sauces may be used to flavour, also chili or eschalot vinegar. *With Cucumbers, or Potatoes.*—Having your steak either broiled or fried, pour over it the following:—3 large cucumbers and 3 onions, pared, sliced, browned in the frying-pan, and then stewed till tender in ½ pint of gravy or water.—*Or:* cut the under side of the sirloin into steaks, broil them three parts, rub a piece of butter over each, and finish in the Dutch oven: serve them on potatoes, parboiled, cut in slices and browned.—*Italian Steak:* have a large tender one, season it with salt, pepper, and onion, or eschalot: put it, without any water, into an iron stew-pan, with a close-fitting lid, and set it by the side of a strong fire, but do not let it burn: in 2 hours, or a little more, it will be tender: serve, in its own gravy.

Rolled Beef Steaks.

Prepare a forcemeat of the breast of a fowl, ½ lb. veal, ¼ lb. ham, fat and lean, the kidney of a loin of veal, and a sweetbread, all cut very small, also a few truffles and morells stewed, an eschalot, a little parsley, thyme and grated lemon peel, the yolks of 2 eggs, ½ a nutmeg and ¼ pint of cream, stir this mixture over the fire ten minutes, then spread it on very tender steaks, roll them up and skewer them; fry them of a fine brown, then take them from the fat, and stew them a quarter of an hour with a pint of beef gravy, a spoonful of catsup, a wine-glassful of Port wine, and, if you can, a few mushrooms. Cut the steaks in two, serve them the cut side uppermost, and the gravy round. Garnish with lemon or pickled mushrooms.— The forcemeat may be less rich, according to what you have.

A *fillet of beef*, namely, the under cut of the rump, makes very nice steaks; cut in pieces ¼ inch in thickness, put them on the gridiron over a sharp fire, season them whilst broiling with pepper and salt, and turn them often, to keep the gravy in. Make a sauce of the yolks of 4 eggs, ½ lb. butter, in slices, salt, pepper, the juice of ½ a lemon, and a little chopped parsley; keep stirring it over the fire in every direction, till rather thick, then take it off and keep stirring until the butter is melted; if too thick, add milk or cream, and pour round the steak.

Beef Olives.

Cut slices, of ½ an inch thick, about 5 long, and 3 inches broad. Beat, dip them in egg, then in a seasoning of chopped herbs, bread-crumbs, salt, mixed spices, and a little finely shred suet. Roll up and fasten them with thread. These may be roasted in a Dutch oven, or stewed in clear gravy, after being browned in the frying pan. Thicken the gravy, and add catsup and walnut pickle; dish the olives, skim, and pour the gravy hot over them. They may be made of slices of cold roast beef, forcemeat spread over them, and when neatly tied up, stewed in gravy, or boiling water, with brown flour rubbed in butter, to thicken it.—*Or*: spread on the slices of beef this mixture; mashed potatoes worked to a paste, with cream, the yolks of 2 eggs, and 1 spoonful of flour, seasoned with salt and pepper; when this is spread on the slices, strew over each a very little finely chopped onion, parsley, and mushrooms; roll the olives up, fry in butter, or bake in a Dutch oven.

Beef Marrow Bones.

Fill up the opening with a piece of paste, tie a floured cloth over that, and place them upright in the pot. Two hours' boiling. Serve on a napkin, with slices of dry toast.

Beef Heart.

Soak it and cut off the lobes. Put in a good stuffing, and roast, or bake it, two hours. Serve gravy and currant jelly.—When cold, hash it like hare.

Hunter's Beef.

Take the bone out of a round, and rub in the following mixture, all in fine powder: ¼ lb. saltpetre, ¼ lb. lump sugar, 1 oz. cloves, 2 nutmegs, and 3 handfuls of salt; this for 25 lbs.; rub and turn it every day, till you think it salted enough to boil; take it out of the brine, wipe it with a sponge, and bind up firmly with tape. If you choose, a stuffing may be put into the place where the bone came out. Put the meat into an earthenware pan just to hold it, with a pint of broth or thin melted butter; put some pieces of butter or suet on the top of the beef, lay folds of brown paper over the pan, or a coarse crust is still better, and bake it at least five hours. This is generally eaten cold, but it may be eaten hot. The gravy left in the pan is preserved to flavour soups and sauces. It may be made of the *Ribs*: rub into a piece of 12 lbs., boned, 4 oz. bay salt, 3 oz. saltpetre, ½ lb. coarse brown sugar, 2 lbs. salt, and a teacupful of juniper berries bruised: rub and turn every day for three weeks, then bake it, covered with a coarse paste.

Hamburgh Beef.

Rub a rump or round of beef well with brown sugar, and let it lie five days; turn it each day. Sponge, and rub into it a mixture of 4 oz. common salt, 4 oz. bay salt, and 2 oz. saltpetre, well beaten, and spices to your taste. Rub and turn it every other day, for a fortnight: then roll up, tie it, put it in a cloth, then under a heavy weight; that done, hang for a week in a wood-smoke chimney. Cut pieces to boil as it is wanted, and when boiled enough, press the meat again under a weight, to eat cold.

Hung Beef.

Rub the best end of the ribs well with lump sugar, or treacle, and saltpetre; on the third day rub with common salt and saltpetre; rub and turn it every day for a week; let it lie a fortnight, turning it every other day, pouring the brine over. Take it out, wipe, and dust bran over, then hang it to dry (not smoke) six or eight weeks.

Bœuf à la Flamande.

Lard a piece of ribs of beef of 8 lbs. weight, and braise it over a slow fire, a slice of bacon under and over it; then add a pint of fresh mushrooms, 2 lbs. truffles, 2 doz. forcemeat balls, made with plenty of eggs, and ½ pint Madeira. Carrots and turnips, cut small, boiled separately in broth till quite tender, also silver onions as directed for made dishes; all or any of these may be laid over the beef.

Beef to Press.

Bone the brisket, flank, or ribs, and rub it with a mixture of salt, sugar, and spices; let it be a week, then boil till tender, and press it under a heavy weight till cold.

Beef to Hash, or Mince.

Cut thin slices of the underdone part, leaving aside the gristly parts and burnt outside to make gravy, with the bones; put these on in a quart of water, pepper, salt, two onions, a little allspice, cayenne, sweet herbs, and parsley: when the water has wasted one half, thicken with flour, mixing it in by degrees, a little at a time; when this has boiled up, skim off the fat, set it by the side of the fire to settle, strain it into another saucepan, and put it again on the fire; add mushroom catsup, pickle, or whatever ingredient you choose; when hot, put in the slices of meat, and all the gravy left of the joint; let the meat slowly warm through, but not *boil*, or it will become hard; a very few minutes will be sufficient. Toasted sippets round the dish. You may add any flavouring sauce you choose; eschalot vinegar is good, but use no onion. A table-spoonful of curry paste makes it a good curry.

Beef Cecils.

Mince cold meat very finely, and mix it with bread-crumbs, chopped onion, parsley, pepper, and salt. Put it into a stew-pan with a very little melted butter, and walnut pickle, stir it over the fire a few minutes, pour it in a dish, and when cool, put enough flour to make it into balls, the shape and size of large eggs; brush with egg, roll them in bread-crumbs, and brown before the fire. Pour good gravy over them. The minced beef may be warmed in scallop shells, between layers of mashed potatoes, or only a layer spread thinly over the top, and little bits of butter stuck on, and then browned before the fire: this may be moistened with any gravy you have, or walnut pickle.—*Or*: you may serve the mince on toasted bread, or under poached eggs. Chopped *onions*, previously parboiled, make this more relishing to some persons' tastes.

Beef Collops.

Cut thin slices of very tender beef, divide them in pieces three inches long, beat them with the blade of a knife, and flour them; fry them in butter three minutes, then stew them in a pint of water or gravy; if water add salt and pepper, half a pickled walnut, 3 small gherkins, or a table-spoonful of capers, a lump of butter and flour to thicken it. Take care it do not boil, but stew gently. The pickles all cut small.—*Or*: do not stew, but fry them in butter with 1 onion in slices, till cooked, about ten minutes; then put them in a hot dish, keep that covered, while you boil up in the pan a table-spoonful of boiling water, a tea-spoonful of lemon pickle, of oyster pickle, walnut catsup, soy and made mustard; pour all hot over the collops.

Beef en Miroton.

Cut thin slices of cold boiled (not salted), or roast beef, or tongue. Put 6 onions chopped into a saucepan with ¼ lb. of butter, turn it round frequently, and in a few minutes add a little flour mixed in a tea-cup of broth, and a wine-glass of white wine; let it be on the fire until the onions are cooked; then put in the meat with salt, pepper, and a spoonful of vinegar. After one boil, stir in a spoonful of made mustard, and serve it; the edge of each slice lying a little over the other round the dish.

Bubble and Squeak.

Cold boiled beef is best, but roast meat is very good. Cut it in thin slices, pepper well and fry them in butter, then keep them hot, while you fry some boiled cabbage, chopped; when done, put this high in the middle of the dish, and lay the slices of meat round: if you like, an equal portion of cold potatoes, chopped and fried with the cabbage. Serve thick melted butter, with pickled cucumbers, or onion or capers, and a little made mustard. *Veal* may be cooked this way, with spinach instead of cabbage.—*Or*: what is more delicate, cut bits of cold veal without any skin, about an inch long, and warm them in the frying pan with the white part of a boiled cauliflower in little bits, ½ pint of cream, and a light sprinkling of salt and cayenne.

Beef to Pot.

Lean meat is best. Salt, and let it lie two days. Drain, season with pepper, and spices; bake it in a slow oven. When done, drain it from the gravy, and set it before the fire, to draw the moisture from it. Tear in pieces, and beat it up well in a mortar, with mixed spices, and enough oiled butter to make it the proper consistence. Flavour with mushroom powder, anchovy or minced eschalot. Put it into potting-cans, and pour clarified butter over, which may afterwards be used for various purposes. *Potted Beef* is generally made of meat which has been used to make clear gravy, *or* the remains of a joint.

Mock Hare.

Put the inside of a sirloin of beef into an earthen pan, cover it with Port wine, and let it lie 24 hours: then spread over it a forcemeat of veal, suet, and anchovies, chopped, also grated bread, mace, pepper, and mushroom powder, lemon peel, lemon thyme, eschalot, and the yolks of two eggs: roll up the beef tight, and roast it, by dangling before the fire: baste with the wine in which it was soaked, till half done, then with cream, or milk and butter, and froth it, till well coated, like hare. Serve a rich gravy, flavoured with walnut or mushroom catsup, and a table-spoonful of eschalot vinegar. Sweet sauce.—*Or*: a cold uncut inside of a roasted sirloin may be re-warmed whole, in gravy flavoured with eschalot vinegar, walnut or mushroom catsup, and Port wine.

Fillet of Veal to Stew.

Stuff it with a good forcemeat, roll tightly, and skewer it. Lay skewers at the bottom of a stew-pan, place the meat on them, put in a quart of broth, or soft water, lay some bits of butter on the top of the fillet, cover the stew-pan close, after taking off all the scum, and let it simmer slowly till the meat is tender; take it out, strain the sauce, thicken it, and put it on the fire to re-warm; season with white pepper, mace, nutmeg, a glass of white wine, and the juice of a lemon, pour it hot over the meat; lay slices of lemon, forcemeat balls, pickled mushrooms, or fresh ones stewed, over the meat, and round the dish. Serve white sauce.—This dish is made more savoury if you put mushrooms, and ham or tongue, in the forcemeat. Also, you make it richer by putting the best part of a boiled tongue, whole, where you take the bone out, fill up the cavities round the fillet with forcemeat; tie it up in a good shape, and either stew or bake it, in gravy, as above; or roast it, basting well. This may be served with a wall of mashed potatoes round, and that ornamented with pieces of tongue and bacon, cut in dice, alternately, with sprigs of green vegetable; or pieces of stewed cucumber; or Jerusalem artichokes cooked in white sauce; or garnish with lumps of young green peas.

Neck of Veal to Braise.

Lard the best end with bacon rolled in a mixture of parsley, salt, pepper, and nutmeg: put it into a stew-pan with the scrag end, a slice of lean ham, 1 onion, 2 carrots, and 2 heads of celery, nearly cover with water, and stew it till tender, about two hours. Strain off the liquor, and put the larded veal (the upper side downwards) into another stew-pan, in which you have browned a piece of butter, then set it over the fire, till the meat is sufficiently coloured; keep it hot in a dish whilst you boil up quickly a little of the strained liquor; skim it, put in a glass of Madeira, some orange or lemon juice, and pour it hot over the veal. Garnish with slices of lemon. — This joint may be covered with a veal caul and roasted; ten minutes before it is done, uncover it to brown. Serve it on sorrel sauce, celery, or asparagus tops: or with mushrooms fricasseed, or in sauce.

Breast of Veal to Stew, Ragout, or Collar.

An elegant dish for the second course. Put on the scrag and any bones of veal you have, to make gravy; put a well seasoned forcemeat into the thin part, sew it in; egg the top of the breast, brown it before the fire, and let it stew in the strained gravy an hour; when done, take it out and keep it hot over boiling water, while you thicken the sauce, and put to it 50 oysters cut up, a few mushrooms chopped, lemon juice, white pepper and mace; or catsup and anchovy sauce may be used to flavour it; also cream, white wine, truffles, and morells, at discretion. Pour the sauce hot over the meat, and garnish with slices of lemon and forcemeat balls, also pickled mushrooms. — A *Scrag* of veal is very good, stewed in thin broth or water, till very tender; make a sauce of celery, boiled in two waters to make it white, then put into very thick melted butter, stir in a coffee-cupful of cream, shake it two minutes over the fire, and pour it over the veal. *Or* tomata or onion sauce. *To Ragout* — Make a little gravy of the scrag and bones of the breast, cut the meat into neat pieces, rather long than broad, and brown them in fresh butter. Drain off the fat, and stew them in the gravy, with a bunch of sweet herbs, a piece of lemon peel, a few cloves, a blade of mace, two onions, white pepper, salt, and a little allspice. Simmer slowly, keeping it covered close. When done, take out the meat, skim off the fat, strain and thicken the gravy, add the juice of a lemon and a glass of white wine, and pour it hot over the veal, holding back the sediment. *Breast* and *neck of veal* may be stewed in water, or weak broth, without forcemeat. *Veal* is sometimes stewed with green peas, chopped lettuce, and young onions. — *Lamb* may be dressed this way, and served with cucumber sauce. — *Rabbit* the same, with white onion sauce. *To Collar* — Bone it, take off the skin, and beat the meat with a rolling pin; season it with pepper, salt, pounded mace, and a mixture of herbs, chopped very fine, then lay on thick slices of ham or 2 calves' tongues, boiled and skinned; bind it up in a cloth, and fasten it well with tape. Simmer it in enough water to cover it, over a slow fire, till quite tender, which will be about three hours and a half; then put it under a weight till cold. You may put in, in different parts, pigs' and calves' feet boiled and taken from the bones; also yolk of hard-boiled egg, grated ham, chopped parsley, and slices of beet root. *Collared Veal to be eaten Hot*—Spread a forcemeat over the breast (boned), then roll, bind it up tight, and stew it in water or weak broth. Serve it in good veal gravy, or on fricasseed mushrooms, and artichoke bottoms. This is sometimes roasted.

Veal Olives or Veal Rolls.

Cut long thin slices and beat them, lay on each one a very thin slice of bacon, and then a layer of highly seasoned forcemeat, in which there is a little eschalot. Roll them tight the size of two fingers 3 inches long; fasten them with a skewer, rub egg over, and either fry them of a light brown, or stew them, slowly, in gravy. Add a wine-glassful of white wine, and a little lemon juice.—If you do not choose the bacon, put only forcemeat strongly flavoured with ham; or grate ham thickly over the slices. Garnish with fried balls and pickled mushrooms.

Scotch Collops.

Cut small slices of the fillet, flour and brown them in fresh butter in the frying-pan, and simmer them very gently in a little weak broth or boiling water; when nearly done, add the juice of a lemon, a spoonful of catsup, a little mace, pepper and salt; take out the collops, keep them hot in the dish; thicken the sauce with browned flour, and pour it hot over the collops; garnish with curled slices of bacon.

Veal en Fricandeau.

The fat fleshy side of the knuckle, a little thin slice from the fillet, or the lean part of the neck boned. Take off the skin, beat the meat flat, and stuff with forcemeat; lard it, or not, as you like. Lay some slices of bacon at the bottom of a stew-pan, the veal on them, and slices of bacon on the top; put in 1½ pint of broth, or water, the bones of the meat, or 2 shanks of mutton; a bunch of herbs, 1 turnip, 1 carrot, 3 onions sliced, a blade of mace, 2 bay leaves, some white pepper, and lastly, more slices of bacon. Let this stew slowly, after being scummed, two hours, keeping the stew-pan closely covered, except when you baste the upper side of the fricandeau. The meat ought to be cooked to eat with a spoon. Take it out, when done, and keep it hot while you take all the bones out of the gravy, skim off the fat, and let it boil quickly till it thickens, and becomes a glaze; pour it over the meat. Mushrooms, morells and truffles may be added. Sorrel or tomata sauce.—*Another*: put the veal into a stew-pan, the larded side uppermost, add 2 tumblers of water, 2 carrots and onions in slices, 2 cloves, pepper and salt to taste, and a bunch of parsley: boil slowly three hours and a half; then brown the veal with a salamander; served with stewed mushrooms.

Knuckle of Veal to Ragout, or with Rice.

Break the bone and put it into a stew-pan with water to make a quart of broth, with the skin, gristles, and trimmings of the meat, a bunch of parsley, a head of celery, one onion, one turnip, one carrot, and a small bunch of lemon thyme; this being ready, cut the meat off the knuckle, the cross way of the grain, in slices smaller than cutlets, season with salt and kitchen pepper, dredge with flour, and brown them in another stew-pan. Then strain the broth, pour it over them, and stew it *very* slowly half an hour; thicken the gravy with white *roux*, and add the juice of half a lemon. *With Rice*—Cut off steaks for cutlets, or a pie, so as to leave no more meat on the bone than will be eaten hot. Break and wash the shank bone; put it into a stew-pan, with two quarts of water, salt, an onion, a blade of mace, and a bunch of parsley. When it boils, scum well, put in ¼ lb. of well-washed rice, and stew it at least two hours. Put the meat in a deep dish, and lay the drained rice round. Serve bacon and greens.

Granadin of Veal.

Line a dish, or shape, with veal caul, letting it hang over the sides of the dish; put in, first a layer of thin slices of bacon, then a layer of forcemeat, made of herbs, suet, and crumbs of bread, then a layer of thin slices of veal, well seasoned, and so on till the dish is filled; turn the caul over the whole, tie a paper over the dish, and bake it. Mushrooms may be added. When done, turn it out of the dish, and serve with a clear brown gravy.

Veal à la Daube.

Cut off the chump, and take out the edge-bone of a loin of veal; raise the skin and put in a forcemeat; bind the loin up with tape, cover with slices of bacon, and put it into a stew-pan, with all the bones and trimmings, one or two shanks of mutton, and just cover with water, or broth; a bunch of sweet herbs, two anchovies, some white pepper, and a blade of mace. Put a cloth over the stew-pan, and fit the lid tight, with a weight on the top. Simmer it slowly two hours, but shake the pan occasionally. The gravy will have become a strong glaze; take out the veal, the bacon, and herbs; glaze the veal, and serve it with tomata or mushroom sauce, or stewed mushrooms.

Veal to Haricot.

Shorten the bones of the best end of the neck; you may cut it in chops, or dress it whole. Stew it in good brown gravy, and when nearly done, add a pint of green peas, a large cucumber pared and sliced, a blanched lettuce quartered, pepper, salt, a very little cayenne, and boiling water, or broth, to cover the stew. Simmer it till the vegetables are done, put the meat in a hash dish, and pour the stew over. Forcemeat balls to garnish, if you choose.

Veal Cutlets à la Maintenon.

See Mutton Steaks à la Maintenon; or cook them without paper as follows: first flatten, and then season them with mixed spices, dipped in egg first, then in breadcrumbs mixed with powdered sweet herbs, grated nutmeg, and lemon peel. Broil them over a quick, clear fire, and serve directly they are done, with good gravy well flavoured with different sauces; or catsup in melted butter, or mushroom sauce. Garnish with lemon and curled parsley. They may be dressed in the Dutch oven, moistened, from time to time, with melted butter. The fat should be first pared off pretty closely. Serve pickles.

Calf's Heart.

Stuff it with a rich forcemeat, put the caul, or a well buttered paper over, and roast it an hour. Pour a sauce of melted butter and catsup over it.—*Or*: stuff, and brown it in a stew-pan, with a little butter, or a slice of bacon under it; put in enough broth or water to make a very little gravy, and let it simmer gently till done; take out the bacon, simmer and thicken the gravy, and pour it over the heart. Sweet sauce, or currant jelly.—*Sheep's* hearts are very nice, in the same way; a wine-glassful of catsup, or of Port wine, in the gravy.

Calf's Pluck.

Parboil half the liver and lights, and mince them. Stuff the heart with force-meat, cover with the caul, or a buttered paper, or, instead of either, lay some slices of bacon on, and bake it. Simmer the mince of the liver in gravy or broth, add salt, pepper, chopped parsley, the juice of a lemon and catsup: fry the rest of the liver in slices, with parsley. When done, put the mince in a dish, the heart in the middle, the slices round. Garnish with fried parsley, or toasted sippets.—*Or*: cut the liver into oblong slices an inch thick, turn these round, and fasten with thread, or form them into any shape you like. Chop onions very fine, also mushrooms and pars-ley, fry these in butter, pepper and salt; then dredge flour over the pieces of liver, and put them into the frying-pan; when done enough, lay them in a dish, pepper slightly and keep them hot, whilst you pour enough broth or boiling water into the frying-pan to moisten the herbs; stew this a few minutes, and pour it over the liver. A nice supper or breakfast dish.—*Lamb's pluck* the same way.—*Calf's liver* is very good stewed. This is made rich, according to the herbs, spices, and sauces used. Chili vinegar is good.

Veal Sweetbreads.

Parboil a very little, then divide and stew them in veal broth, or milk and water. When done, season the sauce with salt and white pepper, and thicken with flour; add a little hot cream, and pour it over the sweetbreads.—*Or*: when par-boiled, egg the sweetbreads, dip them in a seasoned mixture of bread-crumbs, and chopped herbs; roast them gently in a Dutch oven, and pour over a sauce of melt-ed butter and catsup.—*Or*: do not parboil, but brown them, in a stew-pan, with a piece of butter, then pour over just enough good gravy to cover them; let them simmer gently, till done, add salt, pepper, allspice and mushroom catsup; take out the sweetbreads, thicken the sauce with browned flour, and strain it over them. Mushroom sauce and melted butter are served with sweetbreads.—*Or*: par-roast before the fire, cut them in thin slices, then baste with thin melted butter, strew bread-crumbs over, and finish by broiling before the fire.—Truffles and morells may be added to enrich the gravy.

Calf's Tails.

Clean and parboil the tails, brown them in butter, then drain and stew them in good broth, with a bunch of parsley, a few onions, and a bay leaf. Green peas, sliced cucumber, or lettuce, may be added and served altogether, when done, and the fat skimmed off.

Calf's Head.

Wash and soak it in warm water, take out the brains, and the black part of the eyes. Boil it in a large fish-kettle, with plenty of water and some salt. Scum well, and let it simmer gently nearly two hours. Lift it out, carefully sponge it to take off any scum that may have adhered, take out the tongue, and slightly score the head, in diamonds; brush it with egg, and sprinkle it with a mixture of bread-crumbs, herbs, pepper, salt and spices; strew some little bits of butter over, and put it in the Dutch oven to brown. Wash and parboil the brains; skin, and chop them with parsley and sage (parboiled); add pepper and salt, with melted butter, to a little more than moisten it, add the juice of a lemon, and a small quantity of cayenne; turn this a few minutes over the fire: skin the tongue, place it in the middle of a small dish, the brains round it; garnish with very small sprigs of curled parsley, and slices of lemon; serve the head in another dish, garnish the same. Serve melted butter and parsley. If you have boiled the whole head, half may be dressed as above, and the other half as follows:—cut the meat into neat pieces along with the tongue, and re-warm it in a little good broth, well seasoned with spices and lemon peel; when it is done, put in the juice of a lemon, pour it into your dish, lay the half head on it, garnish with brain cakes and lemon.—*Calf's Head to Stew*—Prepare it as in the last receipt to boil; take out the bones, put in a delicate forcemeat, tie it up carefully, and stew it in veal broth or water; season well with mace, mushroom powder and a very little cayenne. Stew very slowly, and when done, serve it with fried forcemeat balls, and a fricassee of mushrooms. It may be enriched to almost any degree, by flavouring sauces, truffles and morells, also oysters. *A Collared Calf's Head* in the same way: when boned season as in the last receipt; put parsley in a thick layer, then thick slices of ham or the tongue, roll it up, tie as firmly as you can in a cloth and boil it, and put it under a weight till cold.

Brain Cakes.

Take off all the fibres and skins which hang about the brains and scald them; beat them in a bason, with the yolks of two eggs (or more, according to the quantity of brains), one spoonful of flour, the same of bread-crumbs, a little lemon peel grated, and two tea-spoonsful of chopped parsley; add pepper, salt, nutmeg, and what spices you like; beat well together, with enough melted butter to make a batter; then drop it, in small cakes, into boiling lard, and fry of a light brown. Calf's or lamb's brains, in this way, for garnishing, or a small side dish. *Brains à la Maître d'Hotel*: Skin the brains and soak them in several waters, then boil them in salt and water, with a little piece of butter, and a table-spoonful of vinegar. Fry in butter, some thin slices of bread, in the shape of scollop shells. Lay these in a dish, the brains divided in two on them, and pour over a Maître d'Hotel sauce.

Calf's Head to Fricassee, and to Hash.

First parboil, then cut the meat into small pieces, and stew it, in a very little of the liquor in which it was boiled, or in rich white gravy, seasoned with white pepper, salt, onion and sweet herbs. Simmer gently, and, when nearly done, thicken with butter, rolled in flour, and just before you dish it, add a tea-cupful of hot cream, or the yolks of two eggs beaten; let it simmer, but not boil. Garnish with brain cakes, or curled slices of bacon.—*To Hash*: Calf's head cold, makes an excellent hash, and may be enriched to any degree, by adding to the following plain hash, some highly flavouring ingredients, such as sweetbreads, truffles, artichoke bottoms, button mushrooms, forcemeat and egg balls.—Cut the head and the tongue into slices. Take rather more than a quart of the liquor in which it was boiled, two shanks of mutton, or bones or trimmings of veal, and of the head; a bunch of sweet herbs, parsley, one large onion, a piece of lemon peel and some white pepper; boil this slowly, so that it may not waste too much, till it is well flavoured gravy, then thicken it with butter rubbed in flour, and strain it into a clean saucepan, add pounded mace, a large spoonful of oyster catsup or lemon pickle, sherry, and any sauce you like; put in the slices of meat, and warm them by gently simmering. Garnish with forcemeat balls, curled slices of bacon, or fried bread, in sippets, or brain cakes.

Mock Turtle.

Soak a large head, with the skin on, in hot water, then parboil it, in sufficient water to cover it, with a bunch of sweet herbs, 2 onions and a carrot; and after it has boiled to throw up the scum, simmer it gently half an hour. Then take the head out and let it get nearly cold before you cut it up. Take out the black parts of the eyes, and cut the other part into thin round slices, the gristly parts of the head into strips, and the peeled tongue into dice or square bits. Put the bones and trimmings of the head back into the stew-pan, and keep it simmering by the fire. Fry some minced eschalot or onion, in plenty of butter dredged with browned flour; then put it into a clean stew-pan, with all the cut meat, toss it over the fire a few minutes, then strain into it, a sufficient quantity of the stock to make the dish a stew-soup; season with pounded mace, pepper, salt, and a pint of Madeira; simmer it very slowly, till the meat is done, add a large spoonful of catsup or soy, a little chopped basil, tarragon and parsley. It must be skimmed before it is served; add the juice of a lemon, and pour it into a tureen. Forcemeat balls may be used as garnish: this is made richer by a cow heel, and also, by sweetbreads parboiled, or oysters and anchovies being added.

Veal to Mince.

Cold veal is generally used to mince, but undressed meat is the most savoury. Mince it finely, only the white part, and heat it in a little broth, or water (a piece of butter rolled in flour, if the latter), salt, white pepper, pounded mace, and plenty of finely chopped or grated lemon peel; when warm, put to it a small coffee-cupful of hot cream, and serve with sippets round the dish. This preparation does for *patties* or *cecils* or *scallops*, the same as directed for *beef*.—You may mix with the mince some stewed mushrooms. *Veal* may be *hashed* the same as beef; adding to the gravy, mace, nutmeg, and lemon peel.

Veal to Pot.

Season a thick slice of an undressed fillet, with mace, peppercorns and 3 cloves, bake or stew nearly four hours, pound it quite small in a mortar, with salt, and butter sufficient, just melted. Put it in pots, and cover with clarified butter. A portion of ham is an improvement.

Veal Cake.

Boil 8 eggs hard, cut two in half, the others in rings, put some of the latter and the halves round the bottom of a deep dish or shallow mould, and between each, a light sprig of parsley to make a layer; then a layer of very thin small pieces of cold veal, ham or tongue, and sprigs of parsley between, and more egg, moisten as you go on with a very good savoury jelly, flavoured with cayenne.—*Or*: make a very pretty dish; having boiled two calf's feet or a cow heel for jelly, or other purpose, put some nice little bits of the meat at the bottom of a deep round pudding mould, and little bits of ham or tongue and sprigs of parsley between, season to taste, then another layer, till full, moisten as you go on with some of the liquor. Set in a rather cool oven just to stiffen, then in a cool place, and turn it out of the shape. Bunches of barberries to garnish it.

Mutton to Haricot.

Cut the neck or loin, into chops, and trim off all the fat and bones. Have 3 pints of good broth, in which a turnip, carrot, bunch of parsley and 3 onions have been boiled. Season the chops well with kitchen pepper, and flour them; then brown them in the frying-pan, with a piece of butter, put them in a stew-pan, and pour the strained broth over. Let them stew very slowly half an hour, then put in 2 large carrots, cut in slices, and notched on the edges, 10 or 12 pieces of turnip, cut in fanciful shapes, 6 button onions, previously half roasted in the frying-pan, or parboiled, also a head of celery, cut up. When the chops are tender, skim the gravy, thicken it with browned flour; add pepper and salt, and a table-spoonful of walnut catsup, the same of camp sauce, of universal sauce, of chili or eschalot vinegar, and a wine-glassful of either Port or white wine. Lay the chops in a hash dish, the vegetables on them, and pour the gravy hot over. *Cucumbers* sliced, *endive* parboiled and cut up, or *haricots* parboiled, are good in this. *Veal cutlets*, *beef steaks*, and *lamb chops*, in the same way. Young lettuces and celery are more suitable to veal than turnip and carrot. Garnish with pickled mushrooms.

Leg of Mutton with Carrots.

Lard the leg and put it in a stew-pan just large enough to hold it, with a piece of butter. Set it over the fire five or ten minutes, and turn it to every side; take it out, and mix in the saucepan, with the butter, a spoonful of flour, and two tea-cupsful of broth or boiling water; let this simmer, turning the saucepan often; put in the mutton, and fill up with broth or boiling water; add salt and pepper, and a small bunch of herbs. Boil it slowly two hours, then put in a large plate of carrots cut in small pieces, and browned in another saucepan. Boil the mutton another hour after the carrots are added, and then serve it. Any lean joint of mutton may be cooked in this way.

Loin of Mutton to Roll or to Stew.

Keep it till quite tender, take out the bones, and put them on in water to cover them, with an onion and herbs, to make a good gravy. Season the meat highly with black and Jamaica pepper, mace, nutmeg and cloves, and let it lie all night. Flatten the meat with a rolling-pin, and cover it with a forcemeat, as directed for roast hare; roll it up and bind with tape; bake it in a slow oven, or half roast it before the fire, and baste from time to time with the made gravy. Let it get cold, skim off the fat which will have settled on it, dredge it with flour, then finish the cooking by stewing it in the gravy with which you basted, which must be carefully preserved, after the roasting or baking be over. When cooked enough, put to the gravy an anchovy pounded, a wine-glass of catsup, one of Port wine, and a table-spoonful of lemon pickle. Mushrooms are an improvement.—*The Loin* may be boned, larded, stuffed with forcemeat, then rolled, and stewed in white stock, with plenty of delicate vegetables, and served with spinach round it, and a sharp sauce.

Shoulder of Mutton.

The same as the loin; or stuffed with oysters solely (bearded); the meat rolled up, bound with tape, and stewed in broth, with a few peppercorns, a head of celery, and one or two onions. When done, take off the tape, and pour oyster sauce over.—*Or*: half roast a well-kept shoulder of mutton, let it get nearly cold, then score it on both sides, put it in a Dutch oven, before the fire, with a clean dish under to catch the gravy, and let it continue to roast. Bone and chop four anchovies, melt them in the basting ladle, add pepper and salt, then mix it into ½ pint of hot gravy, ¼ pint of Port wine, a spoonful of mushroom, the same of walnut catsup, and ½ a spoonful of lemon pickle; baste the meat with this as it roasts; when done, lay it on a clean hot dish, skim the dropped gravy, heat it, if necessary, and pour over the mutton.—*Or*: bone the shoulder, and steep it in wine, vinegar, herbs, and spices; have ready a stuffing, in which there are either oysters or mushrooms, put it in, cover the shoulder with a veal caul, and braise it. Serve with venison gravy, and sauce. Some like the flavour of garlic in this.

Breast of Mutton to Grill.

Cut off all fat which will not be eaten with the lean, score that in diamonds, and season with pepper and salt. Brush it with egg, and strew a mixture of bread-crumbs and chopped parsley over. Either roast or broil it in a Dutch oven, baste well with butter, strewing more crumbs and parsley over. Serve with chopped walnut or capers in butter.

Neck of Mutton to Stew.

Cut off some of the fat, and the meat into chops, put it into a stew-pan with water or broth to cover it, pepper, salt, an onion, and what herbs you like, cover close, and let it stew very gently; when half the water is wasted, put it by the side to let the fat rise, take that off, put in ½ pint claret, 12 oysters, and let it stew till quite tender; take out the herbs, thicken the gravy, and add the juice of ½ a lemon, and what catsup you like.

To Dress Kidneys.

Skin and split mutton kidneys, rub with salt and pepper, and pin them out with small wire skewers, to keep them open. Dip in melted butter, then lay them on the gridiron, the inside downwards first, that when you turn them the gravy may be saved. Put the kidneys in a very hot dish, and pour melted butter into each one.—*Or*: cut a fresh kidney into slices or mouthfuls; soak in warm water and well dry them, dust them with flour, and then brown with butter in the frying-pan: put them in a stew-pan with the white of 3 young onions chopped, salt, pepper, parsley, a table-spoonful of eschalot vinegar, and then let them simmer till the kidney is quite done. Mushroom or walnut catsup may be used. Serve mustard with this.—*Or*: mince the kidney and season well with salt, pepper, and cayenne; fry this, and moisten it with gravy or boiling water, or use what catsup or flavouring vinegar you like. Serve on a hot dish for breakfast.—*Or*: put the mince into a stew-pan with a bunch of sweet herbs and an onion tied up in muslin, as soon as it is just browned cover with boiling water and let it simmer 3 hours, then take out the herbs, and sprinkle over the mince a table-spoonful of sweet herbs in powder.

Mutton or Lamb Chops and Collops.

Cutlets for a supper or breakfast dish may be cut from a rather underdone leg: put a good sized piece of butter in the frying-pan, when hot lay the slices of meat in, and turn them often till done, then take them out and keep them hot, while you make a little gravy in the pan, of parsley, other herbs if you like, and a very little broth or boiling water; any flavouring sauce you have, and cayenne. The gravy should be thick of herbs; dish the cutlets in the centre, and the herbs round.—*Or*: pare and slice some cucumbers, sprinkle them with salt and pepper, pour a little vinegar over, and let them lie an hour; then stew them with the collops in broth, enough to make sufficient gravy; season with catsup and what flavouring ingredient you prefer, skim the gravy when the meat is done, and serve in a hash dish.—*Or*: chop the leaves of 6 sprigs of parsley with 2 eschalots, very fine, season with salt and cayenne, and mix all well together with a table-spoonful of salad oil, cover the cutlets on both sides with this, then shake grated bread-crumbs over, and fry them in fresh butter.

Cutlets à la Maintenon.

Lightly season and lay them in a pan with 3 table-spoonsful of oil; fry over a moderate fire till 3 parts cooked, then take them out, and fry 2 table-spoonsful of chopped onions of a light brown, pour off the oil and put in a pint of good brown sauce, 3 table-spoonsful of tomata sauce, a tea-cupful of chopped parsley, a little sugar, nutmeg, pepper and salt, reduce it till rather thick, then put in the cutlets for about 5 minutes: take them out, let them be cold in the sauce, and fold each one (the gravy about it), in white paper (oiled), and broil them 10 minutes over a moderate fire. Serve in the papers.

Sauces for cutlets may be made of oysters, mushrooms, tomatas, anchovies, &c., &c., by stewing them in gravy, suitably seasoned; always add some lump sugar. Serve with Jerusalem artichokes, cooked in white sauce, round them: *or*, a bunch of asparagus in the centre, the cutlets round, and more grass cut in points to garnish: *or*, French beans or peas the same way: *or* (a very pretty dish), divide in 8 or 10 pieces 2 nicely boiled small cauliflowers, and put them into a saucepan with a tea-cupful of white sauce, a tea-spoonful of lump sugar, and a little salt; when it boils, pour in the yolk of an egg mixed with 4 table-spoonsful of cream, and serve it as above.

Mutton to Hash.

When a leg of mutton comes from the table, cut slices to hash the next day, and leave them in the gravy; if the joint be underdone, all the better. Make a gravy of the gristles, trimmings and any bones of mutton, pepper, salt, parsley, and 1 or 2 cut onions; skim off the fat, strain it, and put in the meat (having well floured each slice), with salt to your taste, and cayenne: simmer very gently about five minutes, to warm the meat through, and serve with toasted sippets round the dish. This may have walnut catsup or any other you choose: or 2 pickled walnuts, cut up, and a little of the liquor; or, and this is a great improvement, when the gravy is ready, put in 4 tomatas, and simmer for a quarter of an hour before you put in the meat. Stewed mushrooms are a nice accompaniment. Mutton may be minced and warmed in a pulp of cucumbers or endive, which has been stewed in weak broth.—*Or*: put a good sized piece of butter into a stewpan with ½ pint of mushrooms, ½ an eschalot minced, and boil them gently; then mix in, by degrees, a table-spoonful flour, ½ pint broth, and stew till all the flavour be extracted; let it cool a little, and put in some minced underdone mutton, to heat through, without boiling.

Hunter's Pie.

Line a mould with mashed potatoes, fill it with slices of cold beef or mutton, or mutton or lamb chops, well seasoned, cover with mashed potatoes, and bake it. Some add a very little minced onion.

Leg of Lamb with Vegetables.

Cut the loin of a small hind quarter into chops, and fry them. Boil the leg, delicately white, place it in the middle of the dish, a border of spinach round, and the fried chops upon that.—*Or*: instead of spinach, put a sprig of boiled cauliflower between each chop. Pour hot melted butter over the leg.—*Or*: season the chops, brush them with egg, and roll them in a mixture of bread-crumbs, chopped parsley, grated lemon peel, nutmeg, and salt; fry them in butter, and pour over a good gravy, with oysters or mushrooms. Serve hot; garnish with forcemeat balls.

Breast of Lamb.

Stew it in good broth twenty minutes, let it cool, then score it in diamonds. Season well with pepper, salt, and mixed spices; dredge flour over, stick on some little bits of butter, finish in the Dutch oven, and serve on spinach, stewed cucumbers, or green peas.

Lamb Cutlets and Steaks.

Flatten, season, and stew them in veal broth, and a little milk; season with white pepper and mace. When nearly done, thicken the sauce with mushroom powder, a bit of butter rolled in flour, and add a tea-cupful of hot cream.—*Lamb Chops with Potatoes*—Cut handsome chops from the neck, and trim the bone. Season, egg, and dip them in bread-crumbs and parsley, and fry of a pale yellow. Mash some potatoes thin, with butter or cream, place this high in the centre of a dish, score it, and arrange the chops round, leaning each one on the side of the adjoining one. Garnish with lemon slices, and pickled mushrooms.

Shoulder of Lamb Stuffed.

Take out the bone, and fill the vacancy with forcemeat. This may be roasted; or, if to be rich, stewed in good gravy, or braised. Glaze it, if you like, and serve with sorrel, or tomata sauce.—*Or*: parboiled, allowed to cool, scored in diamonds, seasoned with pepper, salt, and kitchen pepper, and finished on the gridiron, or in a Dutch oven. *Sauce Robert*, mushroom, or sorrel sauce, or a clear gravy. *Or*: bone a small shoulder, lard the under side, with strips of bacon, rolled in a mixture of cloves, mace, cinnamon, nutmeg, pepper, and salt, in small proportions. Roll the meat up, tie, and stew it in veal broth: or braise, and then glaze it. Serve it on cucumbers stewed in cream, or on stewed mushrooms.

Lamb's Head

May be dressed the same as *Calf's Head*.—*Or*: parboil, then score, season and egg it, cover with a mixture of bread-crumbs and parsley, and brown it before the fire. Mince part of the liver, the tongue, and heart, and stew till tender, in a little broth or water, with pepper and salt. Fry the rest of the liver with parsley. Put the mince in a dish, the head on it, and the fried liver round.

Lamb Fricassee.

Cut the best part of the brisket into square pieces of 4 inches each; wash, dry, and flour them. Simmer for ten minutes 4 oz. butter, 1 of fat bacon, and some parsley, then put in the meat, an onion cut small, pepper, salt, and the juice of half a lemon: simmer this two hours, then add the yolks of two eggs, shake the pan over the fire five minutes, and serve it.

Lamb's Sweetbreads.

Blanch, then stew them in clear gravy twenty minutes; put in white pepper, salt, and mace; thicken with butter rolled in flour, and add the yolks of two eggs well beaten, and stirred into a coffee-cup of cream, a little nutmeg and finely chopped parsley; pour the cream and eggs in by degrees, then heat it over the fire, but stir all the time. *Veal sweetbreads* in the same way. The best mode of re-warming *Lamb* is to *broil*, either over or before the fire.

Venison to Hash.

Cut in thin slices, and warm it in its own gravy; season with pepper, salt, mace, grated lemon peel, one wine-glassful of port and white wine mixed, and a table-spoonful each, of mushroom and walnut catsup and soy. Serve toasted sippets round it. If lean, mix with it some thin small slices of the firm fat of mutton. Cold venison may be minced and dressed as directed for beef.

Shoulder of Venison to Stew.

If too lean to roast, then bone and flatten it, lay over some thin slices of fat, well-flavoured mutton; season well with white pepper, salt, and mixed spices, roll it up tight, bind with tape, and stew it slowly in beef or mutton gravy, in a stew-pan which will just hold it; the lid close. When nearly done, put in a very little cayenne, allspice, and ½ pint of claret or Port. Stew three hours. Take off the tape, place the meat in a dish, and strain the gravy over. Venison sauce.

Venison Collops and Steaks.

A good way to dress what is too lean to roast well. Having cut thin long slices from the haunch, neck, or loin; make a good gravy of the bones and trimmings, strain it into a small stew-pan, put in a little piece of butter rolled in flour to thicken it, then a very little lemon, a wine-glassful of port or claret, pepper, salt, cayenne, and nutmeg; whilst this simmers gently, fry the collops, and pour the sauce hot over. You may add tarragon or eschalot vinegar, also soy and mushroom catsup. Garnish with fried crumbs. Season the steaks, and dip them in melted butter, then in bread-crumbs, and broil them in buttered papers, over a quick fire. Serve very hot, with good gravy in a tureen.

Pig to Collar.

It should be three or four weeks older than for roasting. Bone it, and season well with mixed spices; then spread over a layer of thin forcemeat of herbs, hard-boiled eggs, chopped fine, and a *little* suet, then a layer of thin slices of veal, a layer of seasoning, and so on; roll it up, tie in a cloth, and stew it three hours, in just enough water to cover the pig. It will then require to be tied tighter at each end, and put under a weight till cold.

Pork to Roll.

Bone the neck, spread over the inside a forcemeat of sage, crumbs, salt, pepper, and a very little allspice. Tie it up, and roast very slowly.

Pork Chops with Onions.

Season the chops on both sides with pepper and salt, brush them over with olive oil, and roll them in bread-crumbs; put them on the gridiron, taking care that the fire be clear, and do not turn the chops more than once. Put 12 large onions in slices, into a saucepan with a large piece of butter, turn the saucepan frequently that the onions may imbibe the butter equally; add half a tea-cupful of boiling water, some pepper and salt, and let the onions simmer three quarters of an hour; strain and mix with them a little made mustard. Place the onions in a dish and the chops on them.

Pig's Head Roasted.

Divide the head of a young porker in half, take out the brains and clean the inside; stuff it with bread-crumbs, sweet herbs, lemon peel, a very little suet, and an egg, to bind it, tie the head up carefully, and roast it. Serve with brain and currant sauce.

Pig's Feet and Ears soused.

Clean carefully, soak them some hours, then boil them tender, and when cold pour over the following pickle: some of the liquor they were boiled in, ¼ part of vinegar and some salt. Cut the feet in two, slice the ears, dip them in batter and fry them. Serve melted butter, vinegar and mustard.

To Fricassee.

Boil, and when cold cut in pieces, and simmer them in a very little veal broth, with onion, mace and lemon peel; just before you serve it, add a little cream, and a bit of butter rolled in flour.

Corned Pork with Peas.

Put a large piece of butter into a stew-pan with half a table-spoonful of flour, and when it is melted add a tea-cupful of boiling water, chopped herbs and pepper. Wash in three waters a small piece of corned pork, put it in the stew-pan, and when it has cooked half an hour add three pints of green peas, and let it cook one hour. Take out the herbs and pork, pass the rest through a sieve; serve the peas round the pork.

Hare to Jug.

A tender young hare is better jugged than an old one, but one that is too old to roast, may be good jugged. Cut it in rather small pieces, season with salt and pepper, and you may lard them if you like, if not put into the jar two slices of good bacon, then put in the pieces of hare with the following mixture; half a tea-spoonful of cayenne, a blade of mace and a very small bunch of sweet herbs, four silver onions, one stuck with six cloves, two wine-glassfuls of Port wine, half a pint of water, or thin broth, and a table-spoonful of currant jelly. Set the jug in a saucepan of boiling water, or put it in the oven for two or three hours, according to its age. Lay the meat on a dish before the fire, strain the liquor, boil it up, and pour hot over the hare; you may add lemon juice, walnut or mushroom catsup, and another glass of Port wine.—*Or*: you may put 2 lbs. of coarse beef in, to make the gravy better. This, and especially if the hare be an old one, will require an hour longer.

Hare to Stew.

Cut off the legs and shoulders, cut down the back and divide each side into three. Season these with pepper, salt, and mixed spices, and steep them 4 or 5 hours in eschalot vinegar, and 2 or 3 bay leaves. Make about 1½ pint of good gravy, of beef or mutton stock, the neck, head, liver, heart and trimmings of the hare, 3 onions, a carrot, a bunch of sweet herbs, 12 black peppers, the same of allspice, and a slice of bacon, in small pieces. Strain this into a clean stew-pan, and put the hare and the vinegar into it; let it stew slowly, until done. If required, add salt, more spices, and cayenne; also good sauces, and Port wine if you choose. Thicken with browned flour. An *old hare* may be larded and stewed in a braise.

Hare to Hash.

Into a pint of gravy put 2 silver onions, 4 cloves, and a very little salt and cayenne, simmer gently till the flavour of the spice and vegetables is extracted, then take them out, add 2 table-spoonsful of red currant jelly, the same of Port wine, and when quite hot, put in the slices of hare, and any stuffing there may be. Serve it hot with sippets and currant jelly.

Rabbits with fine herbs.

Joint 2 white young rabbits, and fry the pieces in butter with some rasped bacon, a handful of chopped mushrooms, parsley, eschalot, pepper, salt, and allspice; when of a nice brown put it into a stew-pan, with a tea-cupful of good gravy and a tea-spoonful of flour. Stew slowly till done, skim and strain the sauce, and serve it hot about the meat; the livers minced and cooked with it. When you serve it, add the juice of ½ a lemon and a very little cayenne.

Rabbits to Fricassee.

Cut them in joints and parboil them; take off the skin, and stew them in gravy of knuckle of veal, lean ham, sweet herbs, mace, nutmeg, white pepper, lemon peel and mushroom powder; when the meat is tender, thicken the gravy with the yolks of 3 or 4 eggs in a pint of cream; stir in gradually 2 table-spoonsful of oyster, 1 of lemon pickle, and 1 of essence of anchovy. Serve very hot. Stewed mushrooms are good with this. Garnish with slices of lemon and pickled barberries.

Rabbit, Hare, and Game to Pot.

Rabbit must be seasoned with pepper, salt, cayenne, mace, and allspice, all in fine powder.—*Hare* with salt, pepper, and mace.—*Partridges*, with mace, allspice, white pepper, and salt in fine powder.—Read directions to pot beef, and proceed in the same way.

Turkey to Braise.

Truss it as for boiling: put 3 onions, a carrot, turnip, and a head of celery, all sliced, at the bottom of a stew-pan, with a bunch of parsley, a sprig of thyme, 2 bay leaves, 3 cloves, and a blade of mace, also ½ lb. of lean ham, and 2 lbs. of veal cut small, put in 2 quarts of water, and then the turkey (the breast downwards), cover close, and let it simmer over a slow fire about two hours, according to its size; then take it up, and keep it hot, strain the stock into a stew-pan, boil it over the fire, and skim off all the fat; have 2 oz. butter melted in another stew-pan, stir in enough flour to make it thickish, and keep stirring till it is cooked enough, but keep it white, then take it from the fire, and keep stirring till half cold, pour in the stock, add a little sugar, and boil it all up, stirring all the time: place the turkey on the dish, with either some cauliflower heads or Brussels sprouts round it, and pour the sauce over.

Fowls, with Mushroom Sauce.

Braise them the same as directed for turkey, and when the stock is strained into the stew-pan, put in some mushrooms, and stew it till they are cooked, add lump sugar, and, at the last, stir in the yolk of 1 egg, beat up with a table-spoonful of cream, take it off the fire, and pour over the fowl in the dish. — *Or*: do not braise, but stew the fowl, in good stock, and when done, thicken the gravy, and put in enough button mushrooms; serve mushroom sauce with this, or a white fricassee of mushrooms round it. — *Fowl with Oysters*: the same as either of the above, using oysters in the place of mushrooms.

Fowl to Force.

Bone, then stuff a large fowl with a forcemeat made of ¼ lb. of veal, fowl, or turkey; 2 oz. grated ham, 2 oz. yolk of hard-boiled egg, lemon peel, mixed spices, and cayenne to taste; beat the whole in a mortar, to a paste, adding 2 raw eggs to bind it. Sew up the fowl, form it into its own natural shape, draw in the legs, and truss the wings. Stew it slowly in clear white broth; when nearly done, thicken the sauce with butter, rolled in flour; just before you serve it, add a little hot cream, by degrees, to the sauce, stirring all the time. Squeeze the juice of a lemon into a dish, lay the fowl in the centre, and pour the sauce over it. — *Or*: the stuffing may be of pork sausage, and the fowl roasted; serve good gravy in the dish, and bread sauce in a tureen.

Chickens, Pigeons, or Rabbits, to Braise.

Bone and stuff them as directed in the last receipt, and lay slices of bacon on them. Brown a few sliced onions in a stew-pan, and add all the bones and trim-mings, with, if you can, two shanks or a scrag of mutton, or a shank of veal, a bunch of sweet herbs, mace, and a pint of broth or soft water; simmer gently one hour. Then put in the chicken, cover the lid of the stew-pan with a cloth in thick folds, and let it stew very gently till done. If you wish to glaze the chicken, pigeon, or rabbit, take it out, and keep it hot while you strain the gravy, and boil it quickly to a jelly; glaze the chicken, and serve with a brown fricassee of mushrooms.

Chickens to Fricassee.

Cut them up, and season the joints with mixed spices and white pepper. Put into a pint of clear gravy or stock, two onions, three blades of mace, a large piece of lemon peel, and a bunch of sweet herbs. When ready put in the chickens, and stew them gently half an hour, covered close. When done, take them out, keep hot over boiling water, strain the sauce, thicken it with butter rolled in flour, and add salt and nutmeg. Just before you serve it, pour in, by degrees, ¼ pint of cream, heated, and the yolks of two eggs, beaten; keep stirring least it curdle, and do not let it boil: pour it over the chickens. A glass of white wine may be added. Garnish with lemon. You may put into the stew-pan, a quarter of an hour after the chickens, some quite young green peas and lettuce. — The French *Fricassée Naturel* is as follows: cut up the chickens, blanch them in hot water a few minutes, then dip them into cold water, and put them into a stew-pan with 4 oz. butter, parsley, green onions, and a tea-cupful of trimmed button mushrooms, to warm through, and slightly brown; add salt and white pepper, and dredge flour over them; then put in a little of the liquor they were blanched in, and let it simmer half an hour, or till the chickens are done: take them out, and keep hot, strain the sauce, give it a quick boil, add the yolks of two eggs, and pour it over the chickens.

Fowl à la Chingara.

Cut a fat fowl down the back and breast, then across, to be in four equal parts. Melt a very little piece of butter in a stew-pan, put in four slices from the thickest part of a boiled ham, then the fowl, and stew it gently, till done; take out, keep it hot, pour the fat off the glaze at the bottom of the stew-pan, and pour in a little good gravy, salt, pepper, and cayenne. Simmer gently a few minutes, during which, fry, in the fat you have poured off, four toasts, dust over them a little pepper and salt, place them in a dish, a quarter of the fowl on each; either with the ham or not. Skim the sauce, and serve in a tureen.

Cold Fowl or Turkey to Pull.

Take off the skin, and pull the meat off the breast and wings, in long flakes; brown these in the frying-pan with a piece of butter, drain them from the fat, put them into a saucepan with a little gravy previously seasoned with salt, pepper, nutmeg and mace. Simmer gently, to warm the meat; during which, score and season the legs, if turkey, and broil them, with the sidebones and back. Thicken the sauce with the yolks of two eggs, and add a tea-cupful of hot cream. Serve the hash in the middle, the broil round. Garnish with toasted sippets. Mushroom sauce good with this. *Boudins* are made thus: mince the meat which is left on fowl or turkey; put a tea-spoonful of chopped onion and a piece of butter into a stew-pan and turn it over the fire, for a minute or two, then put in a table-spoonful of flour and mix it well, a pint of stock and the mince, season with pepper, salt, and sugar; simmer it till heated through, and then stir quickly in, the yolks of three eggs well beaten, stir it over the fire, but do not let it boil, and pour it out on a dish to get cold; divide it into equal parts, and roll them round or to your fancy, egg and bread-crumb them two or three times, and fry of a light brown. These may be flavoured with ham, tongue or mushroom cut up in the mince.

Goose or Hare to Braise.

Stuff it for roasting, lay thin slices of bacon over it; line a stew-pan with bacon, put the goose and giblets in the centre, 5 or 6 onions, 2 carrots and turnips, a clove of garlic, all sliced, salt, black and Jamaica peppers, 2 bay leaves, and a slight sprinkling of finely chopped herbs. Moisten with boiling water. Lay a sheet of paper over, cover close, lay a folded cloth over the lid, put a weight on the top to keep it tight, and stew gently. (*See instructions for braising.*) Apple, pear, or currant jelly sauce.

Turkey or Hare en Daube.

Lard the breast and legs of the turkey with strips of bacon, with salt, pepper, spices, and herbs; and lay slices of bacon over the breast. Line a stew-pan with bacon, and put in the turkey, with a hock of ham or a calf's foot (both if you can), also the head and feet of the turkey, 4 onions, 2 carrots, young onions, a few sprigs of thyme, a bunch of parsley, and 6 cloves; moisten this, with a tea-cupful of melted butter, and cover it with white paper. Simmer it five hours; take it off the fire, and let it stand by the side twenty minutes, or half an hour. Take out the turkey, strain the gravy, and boil it down quickly; beat up an egg, stir it into the gravy, put it on the fire, and let it come nearly to a boil, then stand by the side of the fire half an hour, and it will be a jelly; strain it again if not clear, and pour it over the turkey.

Pigeons to Stew.

Put a piece of butter, rolled in flour, a little chopped parsley, and the liver, into each pigeon, truss, then place them on slices of bacon, in a stew-pan; cover with more slices of bacon, and stew them three quarters of an hour. Serve good brown gravy. Stewed mushrooms, if liked. Garnish with sprigs of boiled cauliflower, or small heads of brocoli. *Or*: add bread-crumbs to the stuffing, truss them for roasting, and brown them in the frying-pan; then put them into the stew-pan, with good stock of beef, flavoured with herbs, mace, anchovies, mushroom powder, onions, and pepper; stew till tender, then add oyster, mushroom and walnut catsup, Port and white wine, soy, Gloucester and camp sauces. Garnish with egg balls and pickled mushrooms.—*Or*: first stuff them with bread-crumbs, spices, parsley, and a little fresh butter; half roast them in a Dutch oven, and finish in the stew-pan, in good gravy; to which wine, lemon peel, and mushrooms may be added. Pour it over the pigeons. Asparagus may be laid round and between them.—*Pigeons in Jelly*—Pick, wash, and singe two plump pigeons; leave the heads and feet on, clean them well, clip the nails close to the claws, and truss them, propping the heads up with skewers; season inside with pepper and salt, and a bit of butter in each. Put a quart of the liquor of boiled knuckle of veal, or calf's head or feet, into a baking-dish, with a slice of lean ham, a blade of mace, a faggot of sweet herbs, white pepper, lemon peel, and the pigeons. Bake them in a moderate oven; when done, take them out of the jelly, and set by to get cold, but cover them to preserve their colour. Skim the fat off the jelly when cold, then boil it up with the whites of 2 eggs beaten, to clear it, and strain through a bag. Place the pigeons in a dish, the clear jelly round, and over them, in rough heaps. Instead of baking, you may roast the pigeons, and when cold, put a sprig of anything you like into their bills, place them on some of the jelly, and heap more of it round.—*Pigeons in Forcemeat*— Spread a savoury forcemeat in a dish, then in layers, very thin slices of fat bacon, young pigeons cut up, sliced sweetbreads blanched, 2 palates boiled tender and cut up, mushrooms, asparagus tops, cockscombs and the yolks of 4 eggs boiled hard; spread more forcemeat on the top, bake it, and turn it out in a dish, with rich gravy poured round. *Pigeons en Compote.*—Parboil 2 large pigeons; take them out of the water, and squeeze the juice of half a lemon over the breast of each. Have prepared in a stew-pan ¼ lb. of butter, a table-spoonful of flour, and 2 tea-cupsful of weak broth, a faggot of herbs, pepper, salt, a piece of ham and 8 mushrooms in quarters: place the pigeons in this, and stew them slowly till tender. Blanch 12 button onions, and a ¼ of an hour before they are done, put them in the stew-pan. When done, take out the herbs and ham, skim the gravy, pour it over the pigeons, in a dish, and the onions round.

Ducks with Peas.

Season them with salt, pepper, cayenne and mixed spices. Lay some very thin slices of bacon in a stew-pan, the ducks on them, more slices over them, moisten with broth, or water, and stew them from half to a whole hour, according to their age, and size. While they are stewing, parboil, and fry in butter, or with bits of bacon, 2 or 3 pints of young green peas, pour off the fat, put them in a stew-pan with a very little water or broth, salt, pepper, sugar, a bunch of parsley, and some young onions. Take the onions and parsley out from the peas, skim off the fat, and pour the gravy over the ducks.—*Or*: half roast the ducks, and stew them in a pint of good gravy, a little mint, and 3 sage leaves chopped small, cover close and let it stew half an hour. Boil a pint of green peas as for eating, and put them in, after you have thickened the gravy: put the ducks into a dish, and pour the gravy and peas over.

Ducks to Ragout.

Prepare them the same as pigeons to stew, brown them all round, in the frying-pan, then stew them in good broth, till tender. Season well with pepper, salt, onions, sage, and what other herbs you like. Thicken the sauce with browned flour and butter. Add a glass of Port, if you like, and pour it over them.

Ducks to Hash.

Cut them up, as at table, and if you have not any gravy suitable, prepare some of the trimmings, 3 onions, a bunch of herbs, pepper, salt, sugar, and spices. Strain, thicken it, and put in the pieces of duck; do not let the gravy even simmer, but keep hot by the side of the fire until the meat is heated through. Port wine or catsup, and cayenne may be added.—*Goose* may be hashed in this way, the legs scored, seasoned and broiled, laid on the hash, or served by themselves.

Wild Fowl to Ragout.

Half roast the bird, score the breast in 3 at each side, lightly strew mixed spices and cayenne into each cut, squeeze lemon juice over the spices. Stew it till tender, in good brown gravy, take it out and keep hot; add 1 or 2 finely shred eschalots to the gravy, also a glass of Port wine, and pour it over the wild fowl; any game may be re-warmed cut up, in good gravy, boiling hot, thickened with bread-crumbs, and seasoned with salt, spices to taste, wine, and lemon juice, or pickle.

Snipes, Landrails or Woodcocks to Ragout.

Pick 2 or 3 very carefully, take out the trail, and lard them with slices of fat and lean ham, dredge well with flour, and fry in butter of a light brown: then stew in good gravy, flavoured with sherry or Madeira, Port or claret, anchovy, oyster, and lemon pickle, and walnut catsup, 2 table-spoonsful of soy, cayenne and Gloucester sauce. Thicken with flour and butter. Just before serving add the juice of a lemon, and 1 table-spoonful of eschalot vinegar. Pound the trail with salt, lay it on slices of buttered toast, before the fire, put it in a deep dish, serve the ragout over.

Partridge or Wild Duck Salmi.

Par-roast two partridges, which have been kept long *enough*, when cold, skin and carve them, put them into a small saucepan with one eschalot, a bit of lemon peel, a very little dressed ham in small bits, all the trimmings of the birds, a large glass of Madeira, half a wine-glassful of the best olive oil, pepper, salt, cayenne and the juice of a lemon. When just heated through, dish the birds on a very hot dish, pour the strained sauce over, and serve very hot, with grilled toasts. A little good sauce of veal gravy, the trimmings, cayenne, and the juice of a bitter orange; then put in the pieces of duck, and simmer till hot.

Tripe to Fricassee.

Stew a piece of the thick part in well-seasoned veal stock. Cut it in strips, shake it over the fire in white sauce, five minutes; squeeze the juice of a lemon in the dish, pour the fricassee in, and garnish with slices of lemon. If maigre, cream and yolk of egg will enrich it.

Mock Brawn.

Having cleaned a hog's head, split it, take out the brains, cut off the ears, and rub the head well with salt. Let it drain for twelve hours, spread 2 oz. common salt and 1½ oz. bay salt over it, and the next day put it into a pan, cover with cold water, and let it stand a day and night. Then wash well, and boil it until the bone comes out; skin the head and tongue, and cut both into bits. Put half of the skin into a pan, spread the meat in layers, season with salt and pepper, press it down hard, and cover with the other half of the skin. If too fat, add bits of lean pork. Make a pickle of 2 oz. salt, a pint of vinegar, and a quart of the liquor; boil it three times, and when cold pour it over.

Tripe in the Scotch Fashion.

First boiled and cold; then simmer it gently in milk and water, with salt, and a piece of butter. When quite tender, take it out, and let it cool, whilst you prepare a thick batter of three eggs, three spoonsful of flour and some milk; add green onions or chives, parsley chopped fine, and ginger. Cut the tripe in square cutlets or strips, dip them in the batter, thick enough to form a thick crust, and fry in beef dripping.

A Scotch Haggis.

Having cleaned a sheep's pluck, cut some places in the heart and liver, to let out the blood, and parboil it all (during which the windpipe should hang over the side of the pot in a bowl, that it may empty itself). Scum the water, as the pluck boils: indeed, it ought to be changed. From half to three quarters of an hour will be sufficient. Take it all out, cut off about half of the liver, and put it back to boil longer. Trim away all pieces of skin and black-looking parts from the other half of the liver, the heart, and part of the lights, and mince all together, with 1 lb. of beef suet and three or four onions. The other half of the liver having boiled half an hour longer, put it in the air to get cold; then grate it to the mince, and put more onions if you like, but slightly parboiled. Toast a large tea-cupful of oatmeal flour; turn it often with a spoon, that it may be dried equally of a light brown. Spread the mince on a board, and strew the meal lightly over, with salt, pepper and cayenne. Have ready the haggis bag (it is better to have two, for one may burst), put in the meat, with broth to make a thick stew; the richer the broth the better; add a little vinegar, but take care that the bag be not too full, for the meat must have room to swell. When it begins to boil, prick the bag with a needle; boil it slowly, three hours. The *head* may be parboiled, minced and added.

Curry of Chicken, Rabbit, or Veal.

Read in the Chapter on Seasonings, the part relating to Curry Powder. —Curry may be made of cold meat, and makes a variety with the common mode of re-warming meat, but not so good a *Curry* as when made of undressed meat. Cut the meat into pieces, as are served at table, and brown them, in butter, with 1 or 2 sliced onions, over a quick fire. When of a fine amber colour, put it and the onions in a saucepan, with some veal, mutton broth, or stock of poultry and veal, or mutton trimmings; when this has simmered long enough to cook the meat, put in the curry powder, from 2 to 3 dessert-spoonsful, according to the quantity of meat, rubbed and mixed very smooth with a spoonful of flour; stir this carefully in the sauce, and simmer it five minutes; when done, put in the juice of a lemon, and stir in by degrees a coffee-cupful of thick cream. A small part of the meat and the livers of poultry may be pounded to thicken the sauce. —*Or:* rub the powder into a thin paste, with cream, and rub each piece of meat with it, when half cooked, then return it to the saucepan to finish stewing. —*Another*—Fry 4 large sliced onions in 2 oz. of butter, and put all into a stew-pan, with either a loin of lamb in steaks, a breast of veal cut up, chicken, duck or rabbit jointed, or any thing undressed and *lean*, with a pint of good stock, or more, according to the quantity of meat; stew till tender: then take out the meat, and mix with the gravy about 2 dessert-spoonsful of turmeric powder, 6 pounded coriander seeds, cayenne to taste, and 2 table-spoonsful of chili, or eschalot vinegar. Boil these till thoroughly mixed and thick, and till the turmeric has lost the raw flavour; then put in the meat, and give it one boil. Squeeze in the juice of a lemon or a lime, and serve it *very hot*, in a deep dish, with plenty of gravy; the rice in another.—Stewed onions, stewed cucumbers, or stewed celery, *brown*, are good with curry. Serve pickles (melon mangoes most suitable), and chili vinegar.—*Veal cutlets* fried with onions in butter, and stewed in gravy as above. *Lamb, Duck, Cow-heel*, and *Lobster* make good curries. Indeed tender *steaks* and *mutton chops* are also very good dressed in curry.

Curry Kebobbed.

Cut into bits, either chicken and tongue, or veal and ham; season with eschalot, and fasten them in alternate slices on small skewers. Mix with flour and butter 2 dessert-spoonsful of curry powder, or 1 of curry paste, 1 of turmeric, and add by degrees ½ pint of good gravy. Fry the meat with 3 onions, chopped in butter, and put all into a stew-pan with the gravy, a tea-spoonful of mushroom powder, a wine-glassful of sherry or Madeira, 2 table-spoonsful of lemon pickle, 2 of garlic or tarragon vinegar, 1 of soy, 1 of walnut pickle, 1 of claret or Port, and a tea-spoonful of cayenne vinegar.—Garnish with pickles.

Curry of Fish.

Slices of *cod, turbot, brill*, and *halibut*, also *whitings, haddocks*, and *codlings*, may all be curried. To be maigre, make the gravy of well-seasoned fish stock; if not, of beef or veal broth, in which an onion and carrot have been boiled; thicken with butter rubbed in browned flour. Bone the fish, and cut them into neat pieces, rub with flour, and fry them in butter, of a light brown. Drain them on a sieve. Mix very smoothly a table-spoonful of curry powder (more or less according to the quantity of fish), with a dessert-spoonful of flour, and mix it to a paste with a little of the broth; add 2 onions, beaten in a mortar, and ¼ pint of thick cream, mix this in the gravy, or roll the piece of fish in it, then put them in the gravy, and stew them gently till tender; place them in a dish, skim the fat off the sauce, and pour over the fish.—*Lobsters, prawns, shrimps, oysters*, and *muscles* are curried in the same way, to form a dish by themselves, or with other fish.—Slices of *cold* cod, turbot, or brill are re-warmed in curry sauce.

Beef or Ham Chutney.

To 1 oz. of grated meat, put 1 small onion chopped very fine, 1 tea-spoonful of grated ginger, and cayenne to taste; mix well together, adding vinegar or lemon juice.

Fish Chutney.

Parboil an onion, chop it very fine, and add to the fish, which should be rather salted, and chopped fine, or grated; add cayenne and vinegar to taste.

Rice to Boil for Curry.

Pick, and soak it in water; then boil very quickly, with a little salt in the water, till tender, but not soft; drain, and lay it on a sieve reversed, before the fire, to dry. Turn it with a fork, as lightly as possible, but do not use a spoon. Serve it in a dish by itself; or round the dish in light heaps, the curry in the middle. After it is boiled, some cooks pour cold water over, and then set it before the fire to dry. Every particle ought to be distinct, yet perfectly tender.—*Another* way is, to wash it in warm water, pick it carefully, pour boiling water over it in a stew-pan, cover that close, and keep it by the side of the fire to be quite hot. In an hour's time, pour off the water, set the stew-pan on the fire, and stir briskly with a fork till the rice is dry, but not hard.—The *Hindostanee* mode is this: when well picked, soak it in cold water a quarter of an hour; strain and put it into boiling water rather more than enough to cover it; boil it ten minutes, skimming, if necessary; then add a gill of milk for each lb. of rice, and boil it two or three minutes; take it off the fire, strain, and put it back into the saucepan over a slow fire; pour on it ½ oz. of butter melted, and a table-spoonful of the water in which it was boiled; boil it slowly, another eight minutes, and it will be ready.—In *Carolina* they soak the rice two hours in salt and water, wash it, put it in a bag of cheese cloth, then steam it twenty minutes, and each grain will be separated.

A Pillau.

Stew some rice in broth, or melted butter, till tender, season with salt, pepper, and mace. Prepare a boiled fowl, or mutton chops, or veal cutlets, dressed as you like; place them in a hot dish, and if fowl or veal, slices of boiled bacon over; cover the meat with the rice, glaze it with beaten egg, and place it before the fire, to brown. Garnish with hard-boiled egg and slices of lemon.—*Or*: half roast a breast of veal, cut it in pieces, season with pepper and salt (curry powder, if you like), and stew them in gravy, or broth. Place a high border of rice round a dish, the veal in the centre, thin slices of bacon on it, and cover with rice, glaze with yoke of egg, and brown it. A turkey capon, or old fowl, larded, may be dressed in this way; or cold poultry, or rabbit.

Sausages.

To the following receipts saltpetre may be added, to give a red hue. Mushrooms and oysters give a nice flavour, but the sausages do not keep well. Sausage meat may be cooked without skins: mould it into flat cakes, moistening with yolk of egg, to bind, and then fry them. These cakes form a pretty supper dish, garnished with curled parsley; also a garnish for roast turkey or fowl. The ingredients must be *well mixed*. Herbs ought to be used sparingly. *Pork Sausages.*—Cut 3 lbs. of fat, and 3 lbs. of lean pork, into thin slices, scrape each one, and throw away the skin; cut the meat altogether, as small as possible, with 2 oz. salt, ½ oz. pepper, 6 tea-spoonsful of sage, chopped fine, 2 nutmegs, and 2 eggs. Boil a pint of water, let it get cold, put in the crumb of a penny roll, to soak all night; the next morning mix it with the other ingredients, and fill the skins. *Oxford Sausages.*—To 1 lb. pork, add 1 lb. veal, 12 oz. beef suet, 3 oz. grated bread, 3 eggs, well beaten, with mace, black pepper, salt, and sweet herbs, these last chopped, then pounded in a mortar, before they are put to the other ingredients. Anchovy is an improvement.—*Or*: leave out the bread, herbs and suet, have plenty of fat to mix with the lean, mix it with yolk of egg, into long thin cakes, and fry them. *Epping Sausages.*—Equal portions of young tender pork, and beef suet. Mince them very finely, season with salt, pepper, grated nutmeg, and a little chopped sage. *Veal Sausages.*—Equal quantities of lean veal and fat bacon, ½ a handful of sage leaves, salt, pepper, and a few anchovies; beat all well in a mortar. Roll this into cakes and fry them. *Bologna Sausages.*—An equal portion of beef, veal, lean pork and fat of bacon, minced and mixed well together. Season with pepper, salt, and spices; fill a large skin, and boil it an hour.

Rissoles.

Any sort of cold meat, but veal, chicken, turkey and sweetbreads are best. Mince the meat, season with salt and pepper, and stew it two minutes in well-seasoned gravy; use no more than sufficient to moisten the mince. Let it get cold, then roll into balls; dip these into egg beaten; then into bread-crumbs, and fry them of a light brown. When done, place them in a dish, and pour good gravy into it.—*Or*: roll out thin puff paste, spread some mince on it, and roll up, in what shape you please; fry of a light brown. Rissoles may be made of cold turbot, shrimps, lobster and cod; season with cayenne and thin melted butter; add the yolk of an egg to bind it, then roll up in thin puff paste and fry them.

A Bread Border.

Cut slices of firm stale bread, the thickness of the blade of a knife, into any shape you like. Heat some top fat, or oil, in a saucepan, and put in the sippets. Take some out before they are much browned, and let the rest brown more. Drain well, fasten each one up with white paper, until you are ready to use them; then pierce the end of an egg, let out a little of the white, beat it up with a knife, and mix in a little flour. Heat a dish, dip one side or point of each sippet in the egg, and stick them, one by one, on the dish, in what form you please, and put the ragout or fricassee in the centre.

A Rice Border.

Soak the rice well, then stew it with salt and a blade of mace; to be richer, use butter and yolk of egg. When just tender, and no more, place it round the dish, as an edging; glaze with beaten yolk of egg, and set it in the oven, or before the fire, a few minutes; then put in the curry, or hash, &c. &c.

Potatoe Border.

Mash them nicely; and form a neat border round the edge of the dish; mark it and glaze with yolk of egg; brown it in the oven, and put the hash in the centre.

Omelets.

These with practice, are easily made, and are convenient to make out a dinner or supper, especially in the country, where fresh eggs may almost always be obtained. Omelets are so common in France, that the poorest inn by the road side will always furnish one. *Fresh* eggs are essential; the frying-pan should be round and small. The basis of most omelets is the following: beat well the yolks of 6 and the whites of 3 eggs, put to them a little salt and 2 table-spoonsful of water; put

1½ oz. fresh butter into the frying-pan, and hold it over the fire; when the butter is hot, pour in the eggs, shake the pan constantly, or keep stirring the eggs till they become firm, then with a knife lift the edge all round, that the butter may get under. If over done, it will be hard and dry. Gather the border up, roll the omelet, and serve in a hot dish. This may be flavoured in various ways: with grated lemon peel, nutmeg and mace; *or* with the juice of a Seville orange; *or* with grated ham, tongue, *or* veal kidney, pepper and salt; *or* finely chopped parsley, green onions, chives and herbs: *also*, for maigre dinners, lobster meat, shrimps or the soft parts of oysters may be pounded, seasoned and put into the eggs. A pounded anchovy, and, also, mushroom powder, may be used to give flavour. Potatoe or wheaten flour, about a table-spoonful, is sometimes added to the eggs.

Eggs to Poach.

Boil some spring water, skim it, and put in a table-spoonful of vinegar. Break off the top of the egg with a knife, and let it slip gently into the boiling water, turning the shell over the egg, to gather in the white; this is said to be a better way than to break the egg into a cup, then turn it into the water. Let the saucepan stand by the side of the fire till the white is set, then put it over the fire for two minutes. Take them up, with a slice; trim them, and serve on toasts, spinach, brocoli, sorrel, slices of broiled ham, or in the centre of a dish, with pork sausages round.

Eggs to Fry.

Melt a piece of butter in a frying-pan, and slip the eggs in.—*Or*: lay some thin slices of bacon in a dish before the fire, to toast; break the eggs into tea-cups, and slip them gently into boiling lard, in a frying-pan. When done, little more than two minutes, trim the white, and lay each one on a slice of bacon. Make a sauce of weak broth, cayenne, made mustard and vinegar.

Eggs to Butter.

Beat 12 eggs with 2 table-spoonsful of gravy; melt ¼ lb. butter, stir the eggs and this together, in a bason with pepper, salt, and finely minced onion, if liked. Pour this backwards and forwards from one bason to another, then into a stew-pan on the fire, and stir constantly with a wooden spoon, to prevent burning. When of a proper thickness, serve on toast.

Eggs to Fricassee.

Boil them hard, then cut the eggs in slices, pour a good white sauce over, and serve with sippets round the dish.

Eggs to Ragout.

Boil 8 eggs hard, take off the shell, cut them in quarters. Have ready a pint of gravy, well seasoned and thickened, and pour it hot over the eggs.—*Or*: melt some butter, thicken with flour, season with nutmeg and mace, add a tea-cupful of cream, and pour hot over the eggs.

Swiss Eggs.

Put a piece of butter the size of a small egg into a saucepan with ¼ lb. grated cheese, a little nutmeg, parsley and chives finely chopped, and ½ a glass of white wine. Stir it over a slow fire, till the cheese is melted; then mix in 6 eggs well beaten, set it on the fire, and keep stirring till done. Serve in the centre of a small dish, with toasted sippets round.

Scotch Eggs.

Boil 4 eggs hard, as for salad, peel and dip them, first in beaten egg, then in a forcemeat of grated ham, crumbs and spices. Fry in clarified dripping, and serve in gravy. *Or*: in white sauce.

Eggs à la Tripe.

Fry 4 sliced Spanish onions in butter, then dust in some flour, let it catch to a light brown, put in a breakfast cupful of hot milk, salt and pepper, and let it reduce. Then add 12 hard-boiled eggs, some in halves or quarters, others in slices, mix these gently in the sauce (a tea-spoonful of made mustard if you like), and serve it.

Eggs à la Maitre d'Hotel.

Fry onions as in the last receipt, add melted butter, with plenty of parsley chopped in it, put in the eggs and serve quite hot.

Fondu.

Mix an equal quantity of grated parmesan and Gloucester cheese, add double the weight in beaten yolk of egg and cream, or melted butter; beat all well together, add pepper and salt, then the whites of the eggs, which have been beaten separately: stir them lightly in, and bake in deep tin dish, or in paper cases, but fill only half full, as it will rise very much. Serve quite hot.

Ramakins.

Beat an equal portion of Gloucester and Cheshire cheese in a mortar, with the crumb of a French roll, soaked in milk, and the yolks of 3 eggs; season with salt and pepper, and when beaten to a paste, add the whites of 2 eggs, and bake them in saucers, in the Dutch oven.—*Or*: roll paste out thin, lay a thin slice of cheese on it, cover with paste, and bake like puffs.—*Or*: beat ¼ lb. Cheshire cheese with 2 eggs and 2 oz. butter, and form it into cakes to cover thin pieces of bread cut round with a wine-glass. Lay these on a dish, not touching one another, put it on a chaffing dish of coals, hold a salamander over till quite brown, and serve hot.

Asparagus and Eggs.

Beat 4 eggs well, with pepper and salt. Cut some dressed asparagus into pieces the size of peas, and stir into the eggs. Melt 2 oz. of butter, in a small stew-pan, pour in the mixture, stir till it thickens, and serve hot on a toast.

Mushrooms and Eggs.

Slice and fry some large onions and a few button mushrooms; drain them well; boil some eggs hard, and slice them; simmer in good gravy, or melted butter, with pepper, salt, mustard, and eschalot vinegar.

Devils.

These are made of legs, rumps, backs and gizzards of cold turkey, goose, capon, and all kinds of game, venison, mutton kidney, the back bone of mackerel well buttered, biscuits and rusks. The meat must be well scored for the seasonings to find their way into it: salt, pepper, cayenne, curry, mushroom, truffle, and anchovy powder, must be used according to taste. Broil, over a quick strong fire, and serve them dry, if to eat with wine; but they may be served with anchovy, or any *piquant* sauce. Served in a hot water dish. — *Biscuits* are spread with butter, heated before the fire and sprinkled with the seasonings.

Anchovy Toasts.

Fry thin slices of bread, without the crust, in butter. Spread them with pounded anchovies mixed with butter.

Mock Caviare.

Bone 6 anchovies, pound them in a mortar with dried parsley, a clove of garlic, cayenne, salt and salad oil, also lemon juice if you like. Serve on toast or biscuit.

Sandwiches.

The bread should be cut in thin slices with a sharp knife. Various things are used. Slices of beef, ham, or tongue, or either of the last two grated or scraped; also German or pork sausage, anchovies and shrimps; forcemeat, and all kinds of potted meat. Some persons cut the meat in very little pieces, and spread them over the bread; a mixture of ham and chicken in this way makes delicate sandwiches: or ham and hard-boiled yolk of egg, seasoned with salt, mustard, or curry powder, according to the meat. Cheese sandwiches are made thus: 2 parts of grated parmesan or Cheshire cheese, one of butter, and a small portion of made mustard; pound them in a mortar; cover slices of bread with a little, then thin slices of ham, or any cured meat, cover with another slice of bread, and press it lightly down; cut these sandwiches small.

Maccaroni. (See to make the paste.)

Boil 2 oz. in good broth or gravy, till tender; add a small piece of butter, and a little salt, give it a turn in the stew-pan, and put it in the dish. Scrape parmesan, stilton, or any other dry rich cheese over, and brown it before the fire. — *Or:* mix a pint of milk and a pint of water, put in 2 oz. maccaroni, and simmer it slowly three hours, till the liquor is wasted, and the maccaroni tender. Add grated cheese, salt, and cayenne, mix well, and brown it before the fire. Maccaroni plain boiled, with a little salt, till tender, and the gravy of roast or boiled meat poured over it, is light and nourishing for an invalid. *Maccaroni in the Italian way.* — Mince about six livers of fowl or game with a very little celery, young onion, and parsley (blanched), and stew them in good butter. Then have six more livers cut small, not minced, and cooked in a little butter. Boil 2 oz. of maccaroni in white gravy, season it, if necessary, add powdered mace and cayenne; when done, put a layer of it in a deep hot dish, then a layer of the mince, a layer of grated parmesan, then maccaroni, and at top the chopped livers and more cheese, and enough of the gravy to moisten it sufficiently; put it before the fire a quarter of an hour, or on a slow stove: then brown it or not as you choose. *Another (Italian).* — Boil it in water, pass it through a cullender, and having ready prepared some tomata sauce (*which see*), lift a layer of the maccaroni lightly with two forks out of the cullender into a deep vegetable or hash dish, put a light sprinkling of grated cheese, then tomata sauce, then maccaroni, and again tomata sauce, till the dish be full; if the maccaroni be dry, add butter in little bits, and cayenne, if you think proper. This is not browned. You may omit the cheese. *Maccaroni Maigre.* — Simmer 2 oz. maccaroni in a pint of milk and a pint of water (mixed) three hours, and the liquor wasted: stir into it grated cheese, salt, and cayenne, and brown it before the fire.

Toast and Cheese.

Toast a slice of stale bread half an inch thick, without the crust, butter one side, and lay on slices of toasting cheese; put it into a cheese-toaster before the fire; when done, lightly pepper and salt it, and serve it hot.

Welsh or Scotch Rabbit.

There are many receipts for this, and the following is a good one. Mix some butter with grated cheese (unless that be so fat that the butter is not required), add salt, pepper, made mustard, and a tea-cupful of brown stout or Port wine; put this into a cheese-toaster, stir till the cheese be dissolved, then brown, and serve it quite hot: toasts in a separate dish.

CHAPTER XV.

Stuffing and Forcemeat

With regard to the flavouring ingredients to be used in making these, no precise instructions can be given, because what is disagreeable to one palate is indispensable to another one, therefore, practice alone will teach a cook how to succeed in the art of forcemeat making; and so many flavouring condiments may be used that she may vary her forcemeats to almost any variety of dishes, taking care that no one flavour predominates, but the whole be so blended that the proper zest be given without too much poignancy. Some choose the flavour of onions, thyme, and other herbs, to be strong, while others dislike even a very little of either. Onion is milder for being parboiled in two waters, and some think the flavour of eschalot preferable.—Suet is indispensable; but if it cannot be obtained, beef marrow, or good fresh butter, are the best substitutes.—Bread-crumbs are better soaked in milk, than grated dry; in the former case their quantity must be judged by bulk, not by weight: the bread should be stale. The French use *Panada*, and prepare it thus: Soak slices of bread in hot milk, when moist press out the milk from the bread, and beat the latter up, with a little rich broth or white sauce, and a lump of butter. Stir till somewhat dry, add the yolks of 2 eggs, and pound the whole well together. Sweetbreads make delicate forcemeat flavoured with tongue.

Stuffing and forcemeat require to be well pounded in a mortar, and thoroughly mixed: it ought to be firm enough to cut with a knife, but not heavy.

The following flavouring ingredients may all be used.

Ham.	Cayenne.
Tongue.	Cloves.
Eggs, boiled hard.	Curry powder.
Anchovy.	Onion.
Oysters.	Parsley.
Pickled ditto.	Tarragon.
Lobsters.	Savory.
Mushrooms.	Knotted marjoram.
Truffles.	Thyme and lemon
Morells.	thyme.
Salt.	Basil.
White pepper.	Sage.
Jamaica pepper.	Lemon peel.
Nutmeg.	Chervil.

| Mace. | Garlic. |
| Mushroom powder. | Eschalot. |

The French preparation, called Godiveau.

Scrape 1 lb. of fillet of veal, mince 1½ lb. beef suet, chop scalded parsley, young onions and mushrooms, enough to season the meat, add pepper, salt, allspice, and mace; pound the whole well, mixing in 3 raw eggs at different times, with a little water.

Another, called Gratin.

½ lb. fillet of veal (if for fowl the livers parboiled), veal udder skinned and parboiled, and panada, equal parts of each; pepper, salt, cayenne, and fine herbs; with 3 eggs.

Forcemeat for Veal, Turkey, Fowls, or Rabbits.

Scrape fine 2 oz. of lean undressed veal, the same of ham, beef or veal suet, and bread-crumbs; add parsley, salt, pepper, and nutmeg or mace; pound well, and add the yolk of an egg to bind it. Add, if you like, a little onion, parboiled and chopped; sweet herbs, according to taste. For *boiled* turkey, the soft parts of 12 oysters, or an anchovy may be added.—*Room should be given for stuffing to swell.*

Plain stuffing for Veal, Poultry, or Fish.

Chop ½ lb. of beef or veal suet, mix it with 4 oz. bread-crumbs, chopped parsley, thyme, marjoram, a bay leaf, salt and pepper, and 3 eggs.

Stuffing for Goose or Duck.

Mix together 4 oz. bread-crumbs, 2 oz. onion, parboiled, ½ oz. sage leaves, pepper and salt.—*Or*: the liver, some bread-crumbs, butter the size of a walnut, a sage leaf or two, a sprig of lemon thyme, pepper and salt.

For Hare.

About 2 oz. beef suet, 1 drachm of parsley leaves, the same of marjoram, lemon thyme, lemon peel, ½ a drachm of eschalot, and nutmeg, pepper, and salt; (an anchovy, and cayenne if you choose), mix with an egg; it must be a stiff stuffing; add the liver, parboiled and minced.

Forcemeat Balls for Made Dishes.

Pound a piece of veal with an equal quantity of udder, or a third part the quantity of butter; moisten bread-crumbs with milk; (or soak a piece of bread in warm milk), then mix in a little chopped parsley and eschalot, pound it together to a smooth paste; rub through a sieve, and when cold mix it with the veal and udder, and the yolks of three hard-boiled eggs; season with salt, pepper, curry powder or cayenne, add the raw yolks of two eggs, and mix well together in a mortar. This does for small balls to fry, or to boil in soup.

Egg Balls.

Boil four eggs ten minutes and put them into cold water; when quite cold, pound the yolks in a mortar with a raw yolk, a tea-spoonful of flour, chopped parsley, salt, black pepper and cayenne; roll into small balls, and boil them two minutes.

Curry Balls.

Panada, hard-boiled yolk of egg, and fresh butter, pounded well, and seasoned with curry powder. Boil two minutes.

Stuffing for a Pike.

Grated bread-crumbs, herbs to taste, 2 oz. beef suet, salt, pepper, mace, ½ pint of cream and the yolks of 4 eggs; mix well, and stir over the fire till it thickens.

Fish Forcemeats, for Fish Soup, Stews, or Pies.

Put about 2 oz. of either turbot, sole, lobster, shrimps or oysters, free from skin, into a mortar with 2 oz. fresh butter, 1 oz. bread-crumbs, the yolks of 2 eggs boiled hard, a little eschalot, grated lemon peel, and parsley, minced fine; season with salt and cayenne. Break in the yolk and white of one egg, mix well, and add an anchovy pounded.—*Another*: beat the meat and the soft parts of a middling sized lobster, ½ an anchovy, a large piece of boiled celery, the yolk of a hard egg, a little cayenne, mace, salt, white pepper, 2 table-spoonsful of crumbs or panada, 1 of oyster liquor, 1 of mushroom catsup, 2 oz. warmed butter, and 2 eggs well beaten: make into balls, and fry of a fine brown.

CHAPTER XVI.

READ the directions for making stock for soup.—A cook ought never to be without stock for gravy, as she may preserve all bones and trimmings of meat, poultry and game; also liquor in which meat (unsalted), and poultry have been boiled, and thus seldom buy meat expressly for the purpose.

Sauces in which cream and eggs or acids are mixed, must be constantly stirred to prevent their curdling. Cream heated first, then stirred in by degrees.—The greatest nicety should be observed in thickening gravy, both for look and taste. The common method is to rub flour in butter; but the French *roux* is better.

The following is a list of store sauces, to keep in the house, to flavour hashes and stews. A bottle of each lasts some time, and the cost not very great.—The basis of all sauces for made dishes of *fish* is soy and chili vinegar.—A little practice and *great attention* will enable a cook to use these judiciously, to suit the dish, and the taste of her employers. Some like a combination of flavours, others prefer one, or two at most.

Worcester Sauce.	Walnut Catsup.
Camp Sauce.	Mushroom Catsup.
Gloucester Sauce.	Chili Vinegar.
Harvey's Sauce.	Universal Sauce.
Oude Sauce.	Essence of Anchovy.
Reading Sauce.	Essence of Lobster.
Tomata Sauce.	Eschalot Vinegar.
Lopresti's Sauce.	Tarragon Vinegar.
Essence of Shrimps.	Lemon Pickle.
Oyster Catsup.	

Gravy ought to be perfectly clear and free from fat; flavoured, to suit the dish it is intended for; and always served hot; if in a tureen, that ought to be covered.

Some very good cooks use *brandy* in making sauces, particularly for ragouts; *sugar* also.

White Roux.

Melt slowly 1 lb. of good butter in a little water, then stir in 1 lb. of fine, well dried flour; stir till as thick as paste, then simmer it a quarter of an hour, stirring all the time, or it will burn. It will keep two or three days. The common mode of browning soup and gravy with burnt sugar is not so good as brown flour, but the browning is prepared thus: put ¼ lb. of fresh butter with ½ lb. of lump sugar into a saucepan, shake it often, and when of a clear brown bottle it for use.

To Brown Flour.

Spread flour on a plate, set it in the oven, or before the fire, and turn often, that it may brown equally, and any shade you like. Put it by in a jar for use.

Brown Roux.

Melt butter very slowly, and stir in browned flour; it will not require so long as to cook white *roux*, because the flour has been browned. Will keep two or three days. When you use either of these *Roux*, mix the quantity you wish (a table-spoonful for a tureen of soup), with a little of the soup or gravy quite smooth, then use it.

The basis of most English sauces is melted butter, yet English cooks do not excel in making it, and the general fault is deficiency of butter.

To Melt Butter, the French Sauce Blanche.

Break ¼ lb. of good butter in small pieces, into a saucepan, with 3 table-spoonsful of sweet cream, or milk, milk and water, or water alone; dredge fine dried flour over, hold the saucepan over the fire, toss it quickly round (always one way) while the butter melts, and becomes as thick as very thick cream; let it just boil, turn the saucepan quickly, and it is done.

Butter for oysters, shrimps, lobsters, eggs, or any thickening ingredient, should be made rather thin, and if to be rich, a great proportion of cream. If for catsup or any flavouring ingredient, melt the butter with water only, and stir the ingredients in, by degrees, just before you serve it.

To Brown Butter.

Toss a lump of butter in a frying-pan, over the fire, till it becomes brown. Skim, then dredge browned flour over, stir round with a spoon till it boils; it ought to be quite smooth. This, adding cayenne, and some flavouring vinegar, is a good fish sauce.

Parsley and Butter, or Maitre d'Hotel Sauce.

Tie the parsley in a bunch, and boil it in salt and water, 5 or 10 minutes, according to its age, drain it, cut off the stalks, mince very fine, and stir it into melted butter.

Fennel, basil, burnet, cress, chervil, and *tarragon* the same. When you have not the fresh vegetable, boil celery or parsley seeds in the water to be used with the butter.

Ham Extract.

Cut away all skin and the fat of an undressed ham; cut out the bone, and put it into a large saucepan, with 3 quarts of water, 2 large carrots, 3 onions (2 in slices), a bunch of sweet basil and parsley, 3 cloves, and a table-spoonful of mushroom powder: let this simmer by the fire two hours; stirring up the vegetables from time to time; then take out the bone, put in the meat, and stew it 3 hours, or till the liquor, when strained and cold, is a jelly. A table-spoonful will flavour a tureenful of soup, and half the quantity in melted butter, is good sauce for poultry and game. Also good in veal and chicken pie.

To Draw Plain Gravy.

Notch and flour 1 lb. of gravy beef, or an ox melt, and put it in 1½ pint cold water; scum carefully, and stew gently, till all the juice is extracted from the meat, and about half an hour before it is done, put in a piece of crust of bread. When done, strain and clear it from the fat, and pour it again into a saucepan to thicken, with butter rolled in flour; season with salt, black or cayenne pepper.

Beef Gravy.

This, the basis of many rich sauces, is made of lean juicy meat. Cut 4 lbs. into thin slices, and score them; place a slice of streaked bacon, or the knuckle of a ham, at the bottom of a stew-pan, the beef upon it, and bits of butter; add half a large carrot, 3 onions, half an eschalot, and 3 heads of celery, all cut up; also a bunch of sweet herbs. Brown it over the fire, shaking the saucepan occasionally; in half an hour the juices will be drawn; then put in 2 quarts of boiling water, scum well, and when that is no longer necessary, wipe the edges of the saucepan and lid, and cover close. Simmer 3 hours, by the side of the fire; let it stand to settle, then strain it into an earthen vessel, and put it by in a cool place. For hare, add an anchovy.

Savoury Gravy.

Line a stew-pan with thin slices of ham or bacon, and add 3 lbs. of fillet of veal, or 2 of beef, in slices, a carrot and onion; moisten this with a tea-cupful of broth. The juices will form a glaze. Take the meat out on a dish, pick it all over, put a little more broth, or boiling water, add young onions, parsley, and sweet herbs to taste, also celery, cayenne, a bay leaf, mushrooms, and garlic, if you like; and after it has been scummed, simmer very gently. Strain, and then stand it in a cool place. This gravy may be enriched and flavoured at the cook's discretion. Wine, flavoured vinegar, truffles, morells, curry powder, tarragon, anchovy, pickled mushrooms and oysters, may be used to suit the dish it is required for.—Some cooks use more carrots and onions than I have directed.

White Gravy Sauce.

Part of a knuckle of veal, and some gravy beef. (The quantity will depend upon the degree of richness required.) Cut it in pieces, and put it in a stew-pan, with any trimmings of meat or poultry. Moisten with broth or water, and add a carrot, 3 onions, parsley, thyme, 2 bay leaves, and chopped mushrooms, if convenient. Let the meat heat through, without burning, and prick it, to let the juices flow. When the knuckle is sufficiently cooked for the table, take it out, let the stew-pan stand by the fire a few minutes, skim the fat off the sauce, strain, and boil it again till reduced to the quantity you require; thicken it with white *roux* (it can be thinned afterwards), boil it again, and skim if needful; keep stirring, lifting it often in a spoon and letting it fall, to make it smooth and fine. Sweet thick cream is a nice substitute for white *roux*, in this sauce.—*Or*: put 2 lbs. of lean gristly veal, and ¼ lb. lean bacon or ham, in little bits, into a stew-pan, in which some butter has been melted, let the gravy flow, but do not brown the meat. Mix 2 table-spoonsful of potatoe or rice flour smooth, with a little water, put it into a stew-pan, with a quart or 3 pints of veal broth, water, or milk; also an onion, a bunch of parsley and lemon thyme, a bay leaf, a piece of lemon peel and a tea-spoonful of white peppercorns; stew it very slowly an hour and three quarters, then stand a few minutes to settle, strain it, add a tea-cupful of cream, boil it up, and strain again.—A nice sauce for boiled fowls is made of thin veal broth and milk, seasoned as above, and thickened with the yolk of an egg stirred in, just before you serve it.—Mushrooms may be put in this sauce.—*Another* very good sauce for boiled fowls, veal, rabbits, and fricassees, is as follows: to ½ pint of the liquor in which either of these have been boiled, an onion sliced, a small bunch of parsley, lemon thyme and basil, a little pounded mace, nutmeg, and a few white peppercorns. Strain, boil it again, with a piece of butter rolled in flour, and at the last a little cream. If for boiled fowls, put the peel of a lemon in this, and add the juice just at the last.

Gravy without Meat.

Slice a large onion, flour, and fry it in butter; put it into a saucepan with a breakfast-cupful of good fresh beer, the same of water, a few peppercorns, salt, grated lemon peel, 2 cloves, and a table-spoonful of catsup. Simmer nearly half an hour, then strain it. An anchovy may be added.

Gravy that will keep a Week.

Put some lean beef, in thin slices, into a stew-pan with butter, and what herbs and roots you like, strewed over: cover close, and set it over a slow fire. When the gravy is drawn, keep shaking the stew-pan backwards and forwards several minutes, that it may dry up again, then put in as much water as you require, let it simmer an hour and a half. Keep it in a cool place. A thin slice of lean ham may be added.

Jelly for Cold Meat

May be made of the knuckle of a leg or shoulder of veal, or a piece of the scrag, and shanks of mutton, or a cow heel. Put the meat, a slice of lean ham or bacon, some herbs, 2 blades of mace, 2 onions, a tea-spoonful of Jamaica peppers bruised, the same of black pepper, and a piece of lemon peel, into a stew-pan; cover with about 3 pints of water, and let it boil; scum well, and let it simmer till the liquor is strong: strain it, and when nearly cold take off all the fat. Put it rough round cold poultry or veal. Eaten with cold meat pies.

Savoury Gravy for Venison.

Make a pint of good gravy, of the trimmings of venison, and mutton shanks; the meat should be browned first in the frying-pan, then stewed slowly, in water, to make the quantity required; scum carefully and strain it when done: add salt, pepper, walnut pickle, and a wine-glass of Port or claret.

Mutton Gravy, for Venison or Hare.

Broil a scrag of mutton, in pieces, rather brown; put them into a stew-pan, with a quart of boiling water; cover close, and simmer gently an hour: uncover the stew-pan, and let it reduce to ¾ pint; pour it through a hair sieve, take the fat off, add a little salt, and serve it quite hot.

Orange Gravy Sauce, for Game and Wild Fowl.

Put into a pint of clear good veal broth, an onion, twelve leaves of basil, a large piece of orange or lemon peel, and boil it slowly ten minutes; then strain, and put it back into the saucepan, with the juice of a Seville orange or a lemon, ½ a tea-spoonful of salt, the same of pepper, and a wine-glass of Port. Serve quite hot. Add cayenne, unless it be the practice to introduce it into cuts in the breast of the birds, at table.

Relishing Sauce for Goose, Duck, or Pork.

Steep 2 oz. of fresh sage leaves, 1 oz. lemon peel, 1 oz. minced eschalot, the same of salt, ½ a drachm of cayenne and of citric acid, in a pint of claret, a fort-night; shake it well every day. Let it stand 24 hours, to settle, then strain into a clean bottle, and cork it close. A table-spoonful to ¼ pint gravy or melted butter, heat it up, and serve quite hot.—*Another*, to make at once: stir a tea-spoonful of mustard, ½ tea-spoonful of salt, a little cayenne, and a wine-glass of Port or claret, into a ¼ pint of good melted butter or gravy.—*Or*: the mixture may be heated by it-self and poured into the goose, by a slit made in the apron, just before you serve it.

Sauce Robert, for Broils of every kind.

Put 1 oz. butter into a saucepan, with half a large onion, minced very fine; shake the saucepan frequently, or stir the butter with a wooden spoon, till the onion be of a light brown. Rub a table-spoonful of browned flour smooth, into a little broth or water, add salt and pepper, a table-spoonful of Port wine, and of mushroom catsup, and put this with ½ pint more of broth or water into the sauce-pan with the onions; boil it, add a tea-spoonful of made mustard, the juice of ½ a lemon, and two tea-spoonsful of any flavouring vinegar you like. *Another Grill Sauce* is: To ½ pint of clear drawn gravy, add 1 oz. butter, rubbed smooth in flour, a table-spoonful of mushroom catsup, 2 tea-spoonsful of lemon juice, 1½ tea-spoon-ful of made mustard, the same of capers, 1 tea-spoonful of essence of cayenne, ½ a one of black peppers, and 1 of chili vinegar; simmer it a few minutes, pour some over the grill, and serve the rest in a tureen.

Sauce for Turkey or Fowl.

Season veal gravy with pepper and salt, the juice of a Seville orange and a lemon, 2 wine-glassfuls of Port wine, and serve it in a sauce tureen.

Liver Sauce for Fowl.

Parboil the liver, and mince it fine; pare a lemon thin, take off the white part, and cut the lemon in small bits, picking out the seeds; mince a quarter part of the peel very fine, and put it with the lemon, the minced liver, and a little salt, to ½ pint of melted butter. Heat it over a gentle fire, but if it boil it will become oily. Parsley may be chopped with the liver.—*Or*: chop the parboiled liver, and stir into thin melted butter, boil it up, and then thicken it with the yolk of an egg; add a tea-spoonful of made mustard, and the same of walnut catsup.

Egg Sauce for Poultry and Salt Fish.

Boil 4 eggs hard, dip in cold water, and roll them under your hand, that the shell may come off easily; chop the whites and yolks separately, stir first the whites, then the yolks, into boiling hot melted butter. Serve directly.

Mushroom Sauce.

Wash and pick, a bason full of small button mushrooms, take off the thick skin, and stew them in veal broth, with pepper, cayenne, salt, mace, and nutmeg, 3 lumps of sugar, also enough butter rolled in flour, or arrow root, to thicken the sauce. Stew gently, till tender, stirring occasionally. When done, keep the sauce hot, and pour it over fowls, veal, or rabbit.—*Or*: stew the mushrooms in thin cream, instead of broth, and thicken as above. Pickled mushrooms, may be fried to make this sauce, instead of fresh ones.

Celery Sauce, for Boiled Turkey and Fowls.

Cut a young head of celery into slices of 1½ inch long, season with salt, a very little white pepper, nutmeg and mace, and then simmer till the celery be quite tender, in weak broth, or water. Thicken with butter rolled in white flour. The juice of a lemon may be added, when the sauce is ready. Pour it over the fowls, or serve in a tureen. This may be made brown, by thickening with browned flour, and adding a glass of red wine.

Rimolade, for Cold Turkey or Fowl.

Chop an eschalot very fine with 5 sprigs of parsley; beat 2 yolks of egg, and mix 3 table-spoonsful of olive oil with them, beat the mixture till quite thick, then stir in the eschalot and parsley with a tea-spoonful of good vinegar, a salt-spoonful of salt and the same of cayenne.

Tomata Sauce.

Put the tomatas into a jar, and place it in a cool oven. When soft, take off the skins, pick out the seeds, beat up the pulp, with a capsicum, a clove of garlic, a very little ginger, cayenne, white pepper, salt and vinegar; rub it through a sieve, and simmer it, a very few minutes. A little beet root juice will improve the colour.—*Or*:

stew them in weak broth or water with salt and pepper, when done, pass them through a rather wide sieve, add butter, stir well and serve it hot.—Italians, who use tomatas a great deal, cut them open, squeeze them gently to get rid of their liquor, and just rinse them in cold water, before they dress them.

Apple Sauce.

Pare, core, and slice 5 large apples, and boil them gently, in a saucepan, with a very little water, to keep them from burning; add lemon peel to taste. When they are soft, pour off the water, and beat them up, with a small bit of butter and some sugar. Some add a table-spoonful of brandy.

Gooseberry Sauce.

Cut off the tops and tails of a breakfast-cupful of gooseberries; scald them, till tender, then stir them into melted butter.—*Or*: mash the gooseberries after they are scalded, sweeten to taste, and serve, without butter.

Cucumber Sauce.

Pare the cucumbers, slice, and cut them in small pieces, stew them in thin broth or melted butter, till tender, then press them through a sieve into melted butter, stir and beat it up; season with mace, nutmeg, lemon peel, and finely grated ham. A dish of *stewed* cucumbers answers the purpose.

Onion Sauce.

Peel 12 onions, and lay them in salt and water a few minutes, to prevent their becoming black. Boil them in plenty of water, changing it once. When done, chop fine, and rub them with a wooden spoon, through a sieve; stir this pulp into thin melted butter, or cream, and heat it up. The onions may be roasted, then pulped, in place of being boiled. A very little mace, or nutmeg, may be added to onion sauce having cream in it. *Brown onion sauce* is made by frying, in butter, some sliced Spanish onions; simmer them in brown gravy, or broth, over a slow fire, add salt, pepper, cayenne, and a piece of butter, rolled in browned flour. Skim the sauce, add ½ a glass of Port or claret, the same of mushroom catsup, or a dessert-spoonful of walnut pickle, or eschalot vinegar. To make the sauce milder, boil a turnip with the onions.

Eschalot Sauce.

Chop enough eschalot to fill a dessert-spoon, and scald it in hot water, over the fire; drain, and put it into ½ pint of good gravy or melted butter, add salt and pepper, and when done, a large spoonful of vinegar.—*Or*: stew the eschalots in a little of the liquor of boiled mutton, thicken with butter rolled in flour, add a spoonful of vinegar, and this is good sauce for the mutton.

Sauce Partout.

Take 1 pint of walnut pickle liquor, the same of catsup, ½ pint of white wine,

½ lb. anchovies unwashed, 2 cloves of garlic, one stick of horse-radish, a faggot of sweet herbs, the rind of a lemon, and cayenne to cover a sixpence. Boil together till the anchovies are dissolved. Strain and bottle it for use.

Chetna Sauce.

Pour heated vinegar over 12 eschalots, let it stand twelve hours, then strain and add ½ pint of walnut, and ½ pint of mushroom catsup, 2 wine-glassfuls of soy, a tea-spoonful of cayenne, ½ a tea-spoonful of chili vinegar: boil five minutes, then bottle and rosin it.

Carrier Sauce, for Mutton.

Boil some chopped eschalots in gravy, seasoned with salt and pepper, and flavoured with vinegar.

Horse-radish Sauce.

Scrape fine, or grate, a tea-cupful of horse-radish, add salt, and a little cupful of bread-crumbs, stew this in white gravy, and add a little vinegar.—This may be made brown by using browned gravy; a tea-spoonful of made mustard is an improvement. Vinegar may be used alone, instead of gravy.—*Or*: to 3 table-spoonsful of cream, put 2 table-spoonsful vinegar, 1 tea-spoonful made mustard, a little salt, and grated horse-radish.

Mint Sauce.

Wash and pick some young mint, and mince the leaves very fine; mix them with powdered sugar, put these into the sauce tureen, and pour good white vinegar over.

Sauce for Cold Meat.

Chop some eschalots, parsley, and mint, and put to them an equal portion of olive oil, vinegar, and a little salt.—*Another*: chopped parsley, vinegar, oil, and a tea-spoonful of made mustard.—You may add to either of these an equal portion of tarragon and chervil.

Coratch Sauce.

Half a clove, or less, according to taste, of garlic pounded, a large tea-spoonful of soy, the same of walnut pickle, a little cayenne, and good vinegar.

Miser's Sauce.

Chop 2 onions, and mix them with pepper, salt, vinegar, and melted butter.

Poor Man's Sauce.

Mince parsley and a few eschalots, and stew them in broth or water, with a few peppercorns; add a little vinegar when done. Good with broils of poultry and game.

Sauce for Roast Beef.

Mix 1½ table-spoonful of grated horse-radish with a dessert-spoonful of made mustard, the same of brown sugar; add vinegar to make it as thin as mustard.

Lemon Sauce.

Pare a lemon, and take off all the white part; cut the lemon in thick slices, take out the seeds, and cut the slices into small pieces; mix them by degrees into melted butter, and stir it, that the butter may not oil.

Caper Sauce.

Mince 1 table-spoonful of capers very fine, and another one not so fine, put a spoonful of good vinegar to them, and mix all into ½ pint of melted butter, or gravy. Stir it well or it may oil.—This is a good sauce for fish, with a little of the essence of anchovies.—A very good substitute for capers, is made by chopping pickled gherkins or nasturtiums or radish pods: a little lemon juice will improve these.—Walnut sauce made in the same way, is good with boiled mutton.—Some persons deem it better not to mince capers, but have them whole.

Bread Sauce.

Put a small tea-cupful of grated bread-crumbs into a small saucepan, and sufficient to moisten them of the liquor in which fresh meat, or poultry, has been boiled; let it soak, then add a small onion (parboiled), salt, mace, and six or eight peppercorns. Beat it up from time to time, and when the bread is smooth and stiff, take out the onions and peppercorns, and put to the sauce two table-spoonsful of cream. Some persons add cayenne, a *little*.

Rice Sauce.

By some preferred to bread sauce. Wash and pick 2 oz. rice, and stew it in milk, with a parboiled onion, salt, and 6 peppercorns. When tender, take out the onion and peppercorns, rub the rice through a cullender, and heat in milk, cream, or melted butter.

Sweet Sauce.

Melt some white, or red currant jelly, with a glass or two of red, or white wine. *Or*: send the jelly to table in glasses, or glass dishes.

Sharp Sauce.

Melt ¼ lb. of loaf sugar-candy in ½ pint of champagne vinegar; take off the skim as the sugar dissolves.

Store Sauces for Ragouts, &c., &c.

To ¼ pint good mushroom catsup, add the same of walnut catsup, of eschalot and basil wine, and soy, 1 oz. of slices of lemon peel, 1 drachm of concrete of lemon, a wine-glassful of essence of anchovies, 1 drachm of the best cayenne, and

2 wine-glassfuls of tarragon or eschalot vinegar. Let these infuse ten days, then strain and bottle for use: 2 table-spoonsful will flavour a pint of gravy. *Another, for Roast Meat, Steaks, or Chops.*—Take ½ pint of mushroom or oyster catsup, the same of walnut pickle, add ½ oz. Jamaica pepper in powder, the same of scraped horse-radish and of minced eschalot, and 4 grains cayenne. Infuse these ten days, strain and bottle for use. A table-spoonful or two, according to the quantity of gravy. Melted butter flavoured with this, to pour over steaks or chops.

Sauce for Tench.

To ½ a tea-cupful of gravy an equal quantity of white wine, 2 anchovies, 2 eschalots and a small piece of horse-radish: simmer till the anchovies are dissolved, then strain and thicken it: add a tea-cupful of cream, also a little lemon juice.

A Good Store Sauce for Fish, Stews, &c.

To 1 pint of sherry add ½ pint of walnut pickle, ¼ pint of soy, ¼ pint of lemon pickle, 1 pint of white wine vinegar, a wine-glassful of eschalot and the same of chili vinegar, ¾ pint of essence of anchovy, the peel of 2 and the juice of 1 lemon, 10 eschalots, 10 blades of mace, 2 nutmegs, 12 black and 12 white peppers, some cayenne, and mushroom powder: boil ten minutes, and when cold strain and bottle it. Good with all fried fish, and with salmon.

An excellent Fish Sauce.

Chop 6 cloves of eschalot, 4 of garlic, a handful of horse-radish and 24 anchovies; put them into 1 pint of white, and 1 pint of Port wine, also 2 wine-glassfuls of soy, the same of walnut catsup, and 1 wine-glassful of chili vinegar. Boil well, strain, and when cold, bottle and rosin it.

A Plain Fish Sauce.

Boil in ¼ pint water 3 anchovies, 2 onions, and a faggot of herbs, all chopped, a little horse-radish (scraped), and a large spoonful of vinegar. Boil till the anchovies are dissolved, then strain it, and mix what proportion you like with melted butter, or send it to table in a cruet.

Lobster Sauce.

A hen lobster is best. Pound the coral and spawn with a bit of butter, and rub it through a coarse sieve into melted butter, mix smooth, and season with cayenne; then add the meat of the tail, cut in very small dice, and let the sauce heat up, but not boil. A little essence of anchovy, or catsup, and spices may be added; also cream, heated first. *Crab sauce* the same way.

Oyster Sauce.

Do not open them till ready to make the sauce, then save all the liquor; put it and the oysters into a small saucepan, and scald them; lift them out on a sieve with a spoon with holes in it; let the liquor settle, and pour all but the sediment into good melted butter; beard the oysters, put them into a saucepan, and pour the butter over them; let it nearly boil, then stand by the side of the fire till they are tender, for boiling makes them hard. When ready, stir in a little cream.—A very little mace, lemon peel, and a tea-spoonful of oyster catsup, or essence of anchovy, may be added.

Anchovy Sauce.

Bone and pound 3 anchovies, with a piece of butter, and stir into thick melted butter. Add cayenne, soy, essence of anchovy, mustard, horse-radish or vinegar.

Shrimp and Cockle Sauce.

Shell and wash carefully, put them into thick melted butter, let it boil, and then stand covered two minutes.

Roe Sauce.

Boil 2 or 3 soft roes, take off all the filaments which hang about them, bruise in a mortar with the yolk of an egg, and stir them in thin parsley, or fennel, and butter; add pepper, salt, and a small spoonful of walnut pickle.

Dutch Fish Sauce.

Boil equal quantities of water and vinegar, season with pepper and salt, and thicken with beaten yolk of egg; stir the egg in, but do not boil, or it will curdle.

Sauce for Devils.

Thicken some good gravy (of either fish or meat stock,) with browned flour, till it is a batter, add a dessert-spoonful of walnut catsup, a tea-spoonful of essence of anchovies, the same of made mustard, 12 capers and a bit of eschalot, all finely minced, a tea-spoonful of grated lemon peel, and a little cayenne. Simmer for a minute, pour a little of it over the broil, and serve the rest in a tureen.

CHAPTER XVII.

EXCEPT in the matter of plain roasting, boiling, or baking, the test of good cooking is the taste and skill displayed in giving *flavour* to the composition. Care is not all that is required here; there needs study, and practice. No rules can be given, except to avoid over flavouring, and to suit the ingredients, as much as possible, to the compound which is to be flavoured. In order to be able always to do this, some forethought is requisite on the part of the housekeeper, who will save herself much vexation and trouble by keeping a small assortment of seasonings always ready for use in her *Store Room*; and by taking some little pains, to have a sufficient *variety*.

Many prefer cayenne made from English chilies to any other: they are in season in September and October; cut off the stalks, and lay them before the fire to dry for twelve hours. When dry, pound them in a mortar with one fourth their weight in salt, till they are as fine as possible, and put the mixture into a close stopped bottle.

Before spices are rubbed into meat, they should be pounded, and well mixed. For the convenience of the cook they may be kept prepared in the following manner.

Kitchen Pepper.

Fill little square bottles with an equal quantity of finely ground or pounded ginger, nutmeg, black pepper, allspice, cinnamon and cloves. Keep these corked tight, and when "kitchen pepper" is required, take the proper proportion of each, and mix them, with common salt. For *white sauces*, use white pepper, nutmeg, mace, lemon peel (dried), ginger and cayenne; pounded or grated, and kept in bottles.

Savoury Powder.

1 oz. of salt, ½ oz. mustard, ¼ oz. allspice, ¼ oz. ginger, ¼ oz. nutmeg, ½ oz. black pepper, ½ oz. lemon peel, and 2 drachms cayenne; grate and pound well together, pass the mixture through a fine sieve and bottle it.—Some leave out allspice and ginger, substituting mace and cloves.

Curry Powder.

Take 12 oz. of coriander seeds, 2 oz. cummin seeds, 1 oz. fenugreek seeds, 1 oz.

ginger, 1 oz. black pepper, 4 oz. cayenne, and 2 oz. pale turmeric. Pound the whole and mix well together. Put these ingredients before the fire, stir and rub them frequently, till quite dry. Then set them by to get cold, rub through a hair sieve, and put them into a dry bottle, cork close, and keep in a dry place. A table-spoonful will make curry sufficient for one fowl.—*Another*: Take ¼ lb. coriander seed, 2½ oz. turmeric, 1 oz. cummin seed, ½ oz. black pepper, and cayenne to taste; then proceed in the same way.—*Another*: 2 oz. coriander seeds, ¼ lb. turmeric; of black pepper, flour of mustard, cayenne and ginger, each 1 oz.; of lesser cardamoms ½ oz., cummin seed ¼ oz., and fenugreek seeds ¼ oz.—*Another*: 4 oz. turmeric in powder, 4 oz. of coriander, 2 oz. carraway seeds in powder, 2 oz. fenugreek, and cayenne to taste.—*Curry paste* is very good, but it may be better to prepare curry powder at home; for different curries require different flavouring; as fish and veal require more acid than fowls, rabbit, &c., &c. The ingredients may be kept in bottles, and mixed when used.

Herbs.

As these cannot always be procured green, it is convenient to have them in the house, dried and prepared, each in the proper season. The common method is to dry them in the sun, but their flavour is better preserved, by being put into a cool oven, or the meat screen, before a moderate fire, taking care not to scorch them. They should be gathered when just ripe, on a dry day. Cleanse them from dirt and dust, cut off the roots, put them before the fire, and dry them quickly, rather than by degrees. Pick off the leaves, pound and sift them; put the powder into bottles, and keep these closely stopped.

Basil, from the middle of August, to the same time in September.

Winter and Summer Savory, July and August.

Knotted Marjoram, July.

Thyme, Orange Thyme, and Lemon Thyme, June and July.

Mint, end of June and through July.

Sage, August and September.

Tarragon, June, July, and August.

Chervil, May, June, July.

Burnet, June, July, August.

Parsley, May, June, July.

Fennel, May, June, July.

Elder Flowers, May, June, July.

Orange Flowers, May, June, and July.

The following mixture of herb powder is good for soups or ragouts: 2 oz. each of parsley, winter savory, sweet marjoram, and lemon thyme, 1 oz. each of sweet basil and lemon peel, cut very thin. For made dishes, the cook may keep this mixture, with one fourth part of savory powder mixed in it. Dried herbs may be infused in spirits of wine or brandy ten days or a fortnight; then strained, the spirit closely corked, and put by for use.—Some recommend the following mixture: infuse in 1 pint of wine, brandy, vinegar, or spirits of wine, ½ oz. each of lemon thyme, winter savory, sweet marjoram, and sweet basil, 2 drachms grated lemon peel, 2 drachms minced eschalots, and 1 drachm celery seed: shake it every day for a fortnight, then strain and bottle it.

Horse-Radish Powder.

In November and December, slice horse-radish the thickness of a shilling, and dry it, *very gradually*, in a Dutch oven; pound and bottle it.

Pea Powder.

This gives a relish to pea soup. Pound 1 drachm celery seed, ¼ drachm cayenne pepper, ½ oz. dried mint, ½ oz. of sage; when well mixed, rub through a fine sieve, and bottle it.

Mushroom Powder.

Wash ½ a peck of large mushrooms, quite fresh, and wipe them with a piece of flannel; scrape out the black clean, and put them into a saucepan without water, with 2 large onions, 4 cloves, ¼ oz. mace, and 2 tea-spoonsful of white pepper, all in powder; simmer and shake them till all the liquor be dried up, but do not let them burn; lay them on tins or sieves, in a slow oven, till dry enough to beat to a powder, then put it in small bottles, and keep them in a dry place. Cayenne, if you choose; a tea-spoonful sufficient for a tureen of soup. To flavour gravy for game, and for many made dishes. *Mushrooms to Dry.*—Wipe them clean, and take off the brown and skin; dry them on paper, in a cool oven, and keep them in paper bags. They will swell, when simmered in gravy, to their own size.

Anchovy Powder.

Pound the anchovies, rub them through a hair sieve, then work them into thin cakes with flour, and a little flour of mustard. Toast the cakes very dry, rub them to a powder, and bottle it. For sauces, or to sprinkle over toasts, or sandwiches.

CHAPTER XVIII.

General and particular Instructions for Cooking Vegetables, and also for Mixing Salads

Persons who live in the country, may generally have fresh vegetables; but in towns, and especially in London, the case is different; and vegetables not quite fresh are very inferior to those which have been only a short time out of the ground.—Take the outside leaves off all of the cabbage kind, and plunge the part you mean to cook into cold water, the heads downwards; let there be plenty of water, and a large piece of salt, which helps to draw out the insects. Examine the leaves well, and take off all the decayed parts. They should be boiled in soft water, to preserve their flavour, and alone, to preserve their colour. Allow as much water as the vessel will hold, the more the better; and a handful of salt. The shorter time they are in the water the better, therefore see that it boil fast, before you put the vegetables in, and keep it boiling at the same rate afterwards; let the vessel be uncovered, and take off all scum. When done, take them out of the water instantly, and drain them; they ought then to go to table, for vegetables, particularly green ones, suffer in look and in taste, every moment they wait.

In dressing vegetables, as well as in making soup, the French greatly excel us, for they always cook them enough. Besides they make more of them than we do, by various ways of dressing them, with gravy and cream. Several receipts are here given, by which a side or supper dish, may be prepared at very little cost, particularly in the country, where fresh vegetables are always at hand.

Salads, if mixed with oil, are not injurious, except in peculiar cases, for they are cooling and refreshing in hot weather, and beneficial in many respects, in the winter. Most persons, particularly the Londoners, eat cucumbers, but strange to say, they do not, generally, value a well made salad so highly.

Potatoes to Boil.

The best way, upon the whole, is to *boil*, not steam them. Much depends upon the sort of potato, and it is unfair to condemn a cook's ability in the cooking of this article, until it be ascertained that the fault is really hers, for I have seen potatoes that no care or attention could boil enough, without their being watery, and others that it would be difficult for any species of cookery to spoil. They should be of equal size, or the small ones will be too much done before the large ones are done enough; do not pare or cut them; have a saucepan so large that they will only half fill it, and put in cold water sufficient to cover them about an inch, so that if it waste, they may still be covered; but too much water would injure them. Put the saucepan on the fire, and as soon as the water boils, set it on one side, to simmer slowly till the potatoes will admit a fork; the cracking of the skin being too uncertain a test; having tried them, if tender, pour the water off, and place the saucepan by the side of the fire, take off the cover, and lay a folded cloth, or coarse flannel, over the potatoes. Middling sized ones will be boiled enough in fifteen minutes. Some (and I believe it is the practice in Ireland), when they have poured off the water, lay the potatoes in a coarse cloth, sprinkle salt over, and cover them a few minutes, then squeeze them lightly, one by one, in the folds of a dry cloth, peel and serve them. Some peel potatoes for the next day's dinner and put them into cold water enough to cover them, over night; the water is poured off just before the potatoes are boiled. After the beginning of March potatoes should be peeled before they are boiled, and after April they should always be mashed. Potatoes may be dressed in various ways to make supper or side dishes, and there are sauces suitable to enrich them. *Young Potatoes.*—Rub the skin off with a cloth, then pour boiling water over them in a saucepan, let it simmer, and they will soon be done.

Potatoes to Fry, Broil, or Stew.

Cold potatoes may be cut in slices and fried in dripping, or broiled on a grid-iron, then laid on a sieve to drain; serve on a hot dish, and sprinkle a little pepper and salt over them. Garnish with sprigs of curled parsley, or the parsley may be fried and strewed over.—*Or*: when the potatoes are nearly boiled enough, pour off the water, peel and flour them, brush with yolk of egg, and roll them in fine bread-crumbs or biscuit-powder, and fry in butter or nice dripping.—*Or*: stewed gently with butter; turn them, while stewing; pour a white sauce in the dish.

Potatoes to Mash.

Peel them, cut out the specks, and boil them: when done, and the water poured off, put them over the fire for two or three minutes, to dry, then put in some salt and butter, with milk enough to moisten sufficiently to beat them to a mash. The rolling-pin is better than anything else. Cream is better than butter, and then no milk need be used. Potatoes thus mashed may be put into a shape, or scallop-shells, with bits of butter on the top, then browned before the fire; either way makes a pretty dish.—*Or*: they may be rolled up, with a very little flour and yolk of egg into balls, and browned in the dripping-pan under roast meat. These balls are pretty as a garnish.—*Or*: make them up into a *Collar*, score it, and brown it before the fire, then serve it with a brown gravy in the dish.

Colcannan.

Boil 4 lbs. potatoes, also as many of the inside leaves of curled kale as will fill a saucer. Mash the two together in the saucepan the potatoes were boiled in, to keep them hot; put a piece of butter in the centre, when you serve it. Some prefer parsley to kale, but use less.

Potatoes to Roast.

Some cooks half boil them first. They should be washed and dried. If large, they will take two hours to roast, and should be all of a size, or they will not all be done alike.—*Or:* pour off the water, peel and lay them in a tin pan, before the fire, by the side of roasting meat. Baste, from the dripping-pan, and turn them to brown equally.

Potatoe Pie.

Having washed and peeled the potatoes, slice them, and put a layer into the pie dish, strew, over a little chopped onion, small bits of butter, salt, and pepper (and, if you like, hard-boiled egg in slices), then put more potatoes, and so on, till the dish is full; add a little water, then stick over the top nearly ¼ lb. of fresh butter, in bits; cover with a light puff paste, and bake an hour and a half.

Potatoe Balls.

Mash quite smooth 7 or 8 mealy potatoes, with 3 oz. of butter, 2 table-spoonsful cream, 1 of essence of anchovy, and 1 or 2 eschalots *very finely* chopped; make up into balls, dip them into egg beaten, and brown them. Garnish with curled parsley, for a side or supper dish.

Potatoe Ragout.

Mash 1 lb. of potatoes with butter (no milk or cream), and grate in some ham, nutmeg, salt, pepper, 2 eggs beaten, and a very little flour. Mix well together, and form it into loaves, or long thin rolls, fry or stew of a light brown, for a garnish to veal cutlets, or a dish by themselves.

Potatoes à la Maître d'Hotel.

Boil, peel, and cut the potatoes in slices ½ an inch thick, put them into a stewpan with some young onions skinned, chopped parsley, butter (a large piece), pepper, salt, and a little broth to moisten the potatoes. Toss them till the parsley is cooked; serve with parsley and butter poured over.

Cabbages to Boil.

Wash well, and quarter them, if large. A young cabbage is done in from twenty minutes to half an hour, a full grown one will take nearly an hour. Have plenty of water, that they may be covered, all the time they are boiling; scum well. Serve melted butter. *Savoys, Sprouts, and Young Greens.*—Boil the same as cabbages, but twenty minutes will be sufficient.

Cabbage à la Bourgeoise.

Wash and pick quite clean a large cabbage; take the leaves off one by one, and spread upon each some forcemeat, made of veal, suet, parsley, salt, and pepper, mixed with a little cream and an egg; then put the leaves together, in the form of a whole cabbage, tie this up securely at each end, and stew it in a braise. When it is tender, take it out, and press in a linen cloth to clear it from the fat. Cut in two, in a dish, and pour good gravy over it.

Red Cabbage to Stew.

Melt sufficient butter, to stew the quantity of cabbage; cut it into shreds and put it into a saucepan, with a chopped onion, 2 cloves, a bay leaf, cayenne pepper and salt. Keep the saucepan covered close, and when done, add a good spoonful of vinegar. This may be spread in a dish, and sausages served on it.

Cabbage, Greens, or Spinach to Curry.

After they are boiled, drain, chop and stew them in butter with curry powder to taste; the powder previously mixed with salt, pepper, and vinegar. It is an improvement to spinach, to add sorrel; and some like a small quantity of chopped onion. To these curries you may add minced veal, chicken or rabbit, and serve with a gravy of veal; *or*, if to be maigre, minced cold fish, prawns or oysters, and fish gravy.

Spinach.

As spinach harbours insects, and is often gritty, wash it in two or three waters; then drain it on a sieve. Some boil it in very little water, but this is not a good way. Put a small handful of salt into the water, and when it boils, scum well; put in the spinach, and boil it quickly till quite tender, ten minutes will be enough. Pour it into a sieve, then squeeze between two plates or trenchers, chop fine, and put it into a small saucepan, with a piece of butter and a little salt. Stir with a spoon, five minutes over the fire, spread in a dish, score nicely, and serve it hot.—*Spinach, Sorrel, and Chicory*, may be stewed, the two former in equal portions together, or all separately, for fricandeaus. Wash, pick, and stew very slowly, in an earthen vessel, with butter, oil, or broth, just enough to moisten them.—*Or*: do not put any liquid at all, but when tender, beat up the sorrel, &c. &c. with a bit of butter.

Spinach au Gras.

When boiled, pour through a sieve and press it, to squeeze the water out; put a large piece of butter or dripping into a saucepan, and, when it has melted, put in some sippets of toasted bread for a few minutes, take them out and put in the spinach chopped fine, and a little good gravy of the day before, or out of the dripping-pan, if you be roasting meat, or some good broth, pepper, salt, nutmeg, and flour; simmer a few minutes, and serve with the toasts round it. *Au Sucre*.— Having boiled and squeezed all the water from spinach, chop, and put it into a saucepan with a good sized piece of butter, pepper, salt, nutmeg, and a little flour. Shake the saucepan over the fire a few minutes, then put in some cream or very good milk, to moisten the spinach, and 2 or 3 lumps of sugar, according to taste. Simmer very gently, and serve it garnished with toasts.

Asparagus and Sea Kale.

Scrape the stalks quite clean, and throw them into a large pan of cold water. Tie them in bundles of equal size with tape, not string, as that is likely to break off the heads; cut the ends of the asparagus even, and having a pot of boiling water ready (it ought to be scummed when the water boils), put in the bundles. When the stalks are tender, the asparagus is done; but loses flavour by being a minute too long in the water; indeed, it is the only one which will bear being a *little firm*. Before it is done, toast the round of a loaf, dip it into the boiling water, lay it in a dish, and the asparagus on it. Serve melted butter with asparagus and kale. The French, when the butter is melted, beat up the yolk of an egg, and stir in it, by degrees, a small quantity of vinegar, enough to flavour it; stir well for two minutes over the fire, and it is an excellent sauce for asparagus, or any green vegetable.

Cauliflower and Brocoli.

Choose middling sized ones, close and white, trim off the outside leaves, and cut off the stalks at the bottom. Strip off all the side shoots, peel off the skin of the stalk, and cut it close at the bottom. Boil and scum the water, then put the vegetables in; cauliflower will be done in fifteen or twenty minutes, and spoiled if it boil longer. Brocoli in from ten to fifteen minutes. Lift out of the water with a slice. Serve melted butter. Both may be served on toasts, and the sauce for asparagus served with them, either for the second course or for supper.

Cauliflower with Parmesan.

Boil nicely and place it in a dish (not a close one), grate cheese over, and then pour white sauce over. Brown it, grate more cheese, then pour more white sauce over. Brown it again before the fire, or with a salamander. Serve it with white sauce, or melted butter in a dish.

Cauliflower to Stew.

Boil a large cauliflower till nearly done, then lift it out very gently, separate it into small pieces, put these into a stew-pan, with enough rich brown gravy to moisten, and let it stew till tender. Garnish with slices of lemon.—*Or*: if you have no gravy, put into a stew-pan a piece of fat bacon, 2 or 3 green onions, chopped small, a blade of mace, and a very little lemon thyme, shake the stew-pan over the fire, ten minutes, then put in the cauliflower, let it brown, add a very little water, and let it stew.—*Or*: if to be a maigre, put a lump of butter into a saucepan, an onion minced, some nutmeg, salt, and pepper, shake the saucepan over the fire a few minutes, then put in the pieces of cauliflower, and pour in enough boiling water to moisten; simmer it a few minutes, add the yolks of 3 eggs well beaten, turn the saucepan over the fire till the eggs are cooked, then serve the cauliflower.

Cauliflower or Brocoli to Fry.

Boil till nearly tender enough to eat, then pick it in nice pieces, dip them in a batter made of ¼ lb. flour, the yolks of 3 eggs and a coffee-cupful of beer, pepper, and salt. Then fry the pieces in boiling lard, of a light brown, and put them on a sieve to drain and dry before the fire.—*Or*: dip them first in egg, then in fine crumbs of bread, and then egg again, before you fry them.—Celery and onions the same.—Serve white sauce.

Peas.

They should be shelled but a short time before they are cooked. The younger, of course, the better. When the water boils, scum it, put the peas in, with a little salt, and a piece of sugar, and let them boil quickly from fifteen to twenty minutes. When done, drain, and put them in a dish with some bits of fresh butter; stir the peas with a silver spoon, and cover the dish. Some like mint boiled with peas; others boiled alone, chopped, and laid in little lumps round them.—*Or*: after they are partly boiled, drain and stew the peas in a little broth, with a lettuce, a little green onion, and mint, or a sliced cucumber in the place of the lettuce; stew them till nearly done before you put in the peas; add a little salt, pepper, and brown or white sugar. Essence of ham, or mushroom catsup, may be added.—*Or*: when the peas are partly cooked, drain, and rub in some butter kneaded in flour, then stew them in weak broth, till quite done; add salt, a bunch of parsley, and green onions. Before you serve the peas, drain them, dip a lump of sugar into boiling water, stir it amongst them, and grate parmesan over. For maigre dinners, use more butter, instead of broth. *In White Sauce.*—Put quite young peas into a stew-pan, with a piece of butter, a cabbage lettuce, and a little each of parsley and chives. Do not add any liquor, but stew them very gently over a slow fire. When done, stir, by degrees, ½ pint cream, and the beat yolks of 3 eggs, into the peas; let it thicken over the fire, but not boil, then serve it. The peas which are eaten in their shells may be dressed in this way.

Windsor Beans.

Boil in plenty of water, with salt, and a bunch of parsley. Serve parsley and butter; garnish with chopped parsley. The French parboil them, take off the skins, stew them, and when done pour a rich veal gravy over.

French Beans.

Cut off the stalks, and if the beans are not young, string them, cut them in two, slantways; if old, split first, then cut them slantways; if very young, do not cut them at all. Lay them in water, with a little salt, for about half an hour. Then put them into water, boiling fast, and boil till tender. Serve melted butter. These beans may be stewed in all the ways directed for peas. *Beans à la Maitre d'Hotel.*—Warm them up in parsley and butter.

Turnips.

Some think turnips are most tender when not pared before they are boiled, but the general practice is to cut off a thick peel. Most persons slice them also, but it is not the best way. An hour and a half of gentle boiling is enough. When done, lift them out with a slice, and lay them on a sieve to drain; when dry, serve them. To very young turnips leave about an inch of the green top. *To Mash Turnips.*—Squeeze them as dry as possible between two trenchers, put them into a saucepan with a little new milk or cream, beat well with a wooden spoon, to mash them, add a piece of butter and a little salt; stir over the fire till the butter is melted, then serve them. It is an improvement to put in with the cream a table-spoonful of powdered sugar. *To Ragout.*—Turnips may be made a ragout to serve under or round meat.

Cut in slices an inch thick, and parboil them; then stew them in broth, which, if not already seasoned, may be seasoned at the time the turnips are put to it. When done, skim off the fat, and serve in the dish with any stew or braise, or by themselves. *Turnips and Parsnips to Stew White.*—Parboil, cut in four, and stew them in weak broth, or milk and water (enough liquid to keep the turnips from burning); add salt and mace. As the liquid diminishes, put in a little good cream, and grated nutmeg. When done, mix with them a piece of butter rolled in flour.

Turnip Tops.

When they have been carefully picked, let them lie in cold water an hour. Boil in plenty of water, or they will taste bitter. If quite fresh and young, twenty minutes will be enough. Drain them on the back of a sieve.

Parsnips.

Boil them the same as turnips; or longer, according to their size and quality.

Carrots.

Boil the same as turnips; but if old, longer.—*Turnips, carrots,* and *parsnips* may be dressed together, or separately, in the following way:—Cut up 2 or 3 onions (or less, according to the quantity of roots), and put them into a stew-pan, with a large piece of butter kneaded in brown flour. Shake the saucepan a few minutes over the fire, then put in a little broth, let it stew slowly while you prepare the roots. Scald, or parboil, turnips, carrots, parsnips, and celery, cut them in thin slips, and put them to the onions; season with salt and pepper. When done, add a little made mustard and vinegar.—*Or:* wash and parboil them, cut in thin slices, and put them in a saucepan with a large piece of butter, a bunch of parsley, sweet basil, chives, a clove of garlic, and an eschalot. Shake them over the fire, add a little salt, whole pepper, a blade of mace, and some flour, then put in a very little broth or milk and water. Stew it gently till they are tender, and the liquid reduced. Lift out the herbs, and put in some cream (according to the quantity required), with 2 or 3 eggs beaten up in it. Turn the saucepan, over the fire, till the sauce thickens. When done, add a little vinegar.

Beet Root and Mangel Wurzel.

Wash but do not scrape it, for if the skin be broken, the colour is lost. A middling-sized beet root will take from three to four hours to boil, and the same sized mangel wurzel another hour. When quite tender it is done. Serve it, cut into thin slices; thick melted butter poured over.

Onions to Boil.

Peel and boil them till tender in milk and water. The time required must depend upon their size.—They may be served in white sauce. *Onions to Stew.*—Spanish onions are best. Peel and parboil very gently; then stew them in good broth, or milk and water, and season with white pepper and salt. When done, thicken the sauce with butter rolled in flour, lift out the onions, place them in a dish, and pour the sauce over. —*Or*: stew them in rich, brown gravy. *Onions to Roast.*—Roast them before the fire, in their skins.

Cucumbers to Stew.

Pare the cucumbers, and cut them in four, longways; to each one put a *small* onion, sliced; then stew them in broth, with cayenne, pepper, salt, and nutmeg. When done, lay them in a dish, thicken the sauce with butter rubbed in flour, and pour over them. For maigre dinners, stew them in enough water to moisten them, with a large piece of butter: when done, pour some cream, mixed with beaten yolk of egg, into the saucepan, enough to make a sufficiency of sauce, let it thicken over the fire, lay the cucumbers in a dish, and pour the sauce over. —*Or*: cut onions and cucumbers in halves, fry in butter, and pour good broth or gravy over them; then stew till done, and skim off the fat.

Celery to Stew.

Cut the head in pieces of 3 inches long, and stew as directed for cucumbers. Some cooks stew it whole, or, if very large, divided in two, and in strong brown gravy. —*Or*: if to be white, in rich veal broth, and add some cream. It must be cooked till quite tender to eat well.

Mushrooms and Morels.

Both are used in sauces and ragouts. For stewing, button mushrooms, or the smallest flaps, are best. Trim them carefully, for a little bit of mould will spoil the whole. Stew them, in their own gravy, in an earthen vessel, with a very little water to prevent their burning. When nearly done, add as much rich brown gravy as is required for sauce, a little nutmeg, and, if you like, finely sliced ham, cayenne, pepper, and salt, if required; thicken, by mixing the yolk of an egg, by little and little, into the gravy. If to be white, squeeze lemon juice over the mushrooms, after they have stewed in their own gravy: add a tea-spoonful of cream, a piece of butter rolled in flour, cayenne, white pepper, salt, and nutmeg; thicken with the yolk of an egg. *Mushrooms to Broil.*—The largest flaps are best, but should be fresh gathered. Skin them, and score the under side. Lay them, one by one, into an earthen vessel, brushing each one with oil, or oiled butter, and strewing a little pepper and salt over each. When they have steeped in this, an hour and a half, broil, on both sides, over a clear fire, and serve with a sauce of melted butter, minced parsley, green onions, and the juice of a lemon.

Salsify.

Boil the young shoots, about a year old, as asparagus.

Scorzonera and Skirrets.

The same as carrots; and are good in soup.

Artichokes.

Take off the outer leaves and cut off the stalks. Wash well in cold water, and let them lie in it some time. Put them head downwards, into the pot, take care to keep the water boiling, and add more as it diminishes, for they ought to boil two hours, or more. Float a plate or dish on the top to keep the artichokes under. Draw out a leaf, and if tender, they are done, but not else. Drain them dry, and serve melted butter, in a tureen. *To Fry.*—Cut off an inch or more, of the leaves, and cut the artichoke down in slices of ¾ of an inch thick, taking out the choke. Parboil the slices in salt and water, then fry them in a pan nearly full of boiling lard, to be quite crisp, and of a fine colour. Drain them before the fire a few minutes.

Jerusalem Artichokes.

Boil, but do not let them remain in the water after they are done, or they will spoil; pour melted butter over.—*Or*: they may be cooked in a rich brown gravy, or white sauce, and served with sippets of toasted bread.

Artichoke Bottoms.

If dried, soak them, then stew in gravy.—*Or*: boil in milk, and serve them in white sauce.

Endive to Stew.

Trim off all the green part, wash, cut in pieces, and parboil it till about half done; drain well, and chop it, not very fine; put it into a stew-pan with a little strong gravy, and stew gently till quite tender; season with pepper and salt, and serve as sauce to roast meat or fricandeaus.

Lettuce to Stew.

Wash, parboil, and stew, in rich brown or white gravy; if to be white, thicken with cream and yolk of egg. Lay them in a dish and pour gravy over.

Cabbage Lettuce with Forcemeat.

Parboil gently, for half an hour, then dip into cold water, and press them in your hand. Strip off the leaves, spread a forcemeat, rich or maigre as you please, on each leaf:—*Or*: put the forcemeat into the middle of each lettuce; tie them up, neatly, in their original shape, and stew them in gravy. When done, serve with the gravy poured over.

Vegetable Marrow.

This may be boiled and served on toast, like asparagus; serve melted butter.—*Or*: when nearly cooked enough by boiling, divide in quarters, and stew gently in gravy like cucumbers.—*Or*: serve it in white sauce.

Marrow to Stuff (Italian).

Cut very young ones, about six inches long, in two, lengthways; take out the seeds and pulp with a small spoon, put a little salt on each one, and lay them between 2 cloths, the hollow part down, to draw the water out. Soak some crumb of bread in warm broth or milk and water, beat it up like thick pap, add pepper, salt, the beaten yolks of 2 eggs, nutmeg and lemon peel; to this the Italians add grated parmesan; pour off the water, and fill the vegetable marrow with this stuffing; put the halves together, bind them slightly with thread, brush over beaten yolk of egg, cover with bread-crumbs, and lay them, singly, in a broad shallow stew-pan, well rubbed round the sides and the bottom with butter. Place the stew-pan over a slow fire, cover it, and when the butter is dried up, keep the marrow moistened with broth. When nearly cooked enough, put in some tomata sauce, and then put hot coals on the lid of the stew-pan to brown the vegetables. Minced fowl and grated ham may be added to the stuffing. *To Fry.* — Cut the long shaped ones (quite young), in four, longways, and each piece into long thin slices, lay these between cloths, sprinkle salt over to draw out the water, and let them lie half an hour: during which, prepare a smooth batter of flour, water, and 2 eggs, dip the marrow into it, and fry in lard, of a light brown. Shake the pan gently, but do not touch the fry, lest the paste should break and the fat get in, and make it greasy. Spread a sheet of paper on a sieve, lay the fry on it, before the fire a few minutes to dry, then serve it.

Cardoons.

Choose the whitest, and cut them into pieces of 2 inches long; half boil them in salt and water, with a very little vinegar; pour off the water, take out the cardoons, and peel off the threads; finish by stewing them, in stock of fish or meat, and butter, if required, to enrich it. Mix some flour with a little oil, the whites of 2 eggs, and a little white wine. Cut the pieces of cardoon in 2, dip them in the above mixture, and fry them in lard, of a light brown.

Lentils

Are chiefly used to make cullis for soups and made dishes, as follows: pick and wash ½ a pint or more, according to the quantity wanted. Stew them in broth; when done, pulp them through a sieve, and season as you like.

Samphire to Boil.

Boil in a good deal of water, with salt in it, till quite tender. Serve melted butter.

Laver.

This is generally prepared at the sea coast, and requires only to be heated. This is done best over a lamp, or, at a distance over the fire. When hot stir in a piece of butter, and a very little lemon juice or vinegar.

Haricots Blanc.

These should be soaked, at least, all night. Then be poured from the water, and stewed in broth, or with butter, salt, pepper, chopped parsley and young onions. They must be cooked till tender, or they are not eatable.

SALADS.

Lettuce, endive, and small salading, are the most commonly used, but there are many other greens which eat well, as salads. They should be fresh gathered, well washed, picked, and laid in water with a little salt in it. When you take them out, which should not be till just before they are wanted, shake them well, lay them in a cloth, shake that, to make them as dry as possible, but do not squeeze, for that will destroy their crispness.

In countries where salad is in more general request than in England, the greatest pains are bestowed to have it in perfection. It is essential to a good salad, that the leaves of lettuces should be crisp; and the French people shake them in a basket, made for the purpose, which answers better than anything. The French are justly famed for their salads, but the main cause of their superiority in them, is attributable to the abundance and goodness of both the oil and the vinegar used in the mixture.

To dress Salad.

Do not cut it up till you are going to mix it. Strew a little salt, and then pour over it, 3 table-spoonsful of oil to 1½ of vinegar, add a little pepper, and stir it up well with a spoon and fork. There ought not to be a drop of liquid at the bottom of the bowl. To this may be added hard-boiled yolk of egg, also beet root well boiled and sliced. Any kind of salad may be dressed in this way. Good oil is not dear, but exceedingly wholesome. The least degree of the flavour of garlic is liked by some in salad, and may be obtained by cutting open a clove and rubbing it a few times round the salad bowl. Some persons like a very little grated parmesan, in their salad.

Where oil is not liked, use oiled butter, or cream. Rub very smooth on a soup plate the yolks of hard-boiled eggs, with thick cream; when this is done, add more cream, or oiled butter, vinegar, pepper, and salt to your taste, and mix the salad in it: or pour the mixture into the bowl, the salad on the top, and do not stir it up at all, but leave this to be done at table.

The top of a dressed salad should be garnished with slices of beet root, contrasted with rings of the white of hard-boiled eggs; or a few young radishes and green onions, or cresses, tastefully arranged on the top. Plovers and sea birds' eggs may be laid on the top, arranging some herb to form each one's nest; or all in one nest, in the centre. A pretty salad is a great ornament to a table, and not an expensive one.

The following list may be imperfect, but though there may be other herbs which would be useful in salads, all these are good.

Lettuce.	Coriander.
Radishes.	Tarragon.
Water Cresses.	Nasturtiums.
Young Onions.	Sorrel.
Corn Salad.	Young Spinach.

Endive.	French Fennel.
Celery.	Burnet.
Mustard and Cress.	Basil.
Chervil.	Chicory.

The French make salads of cold boiled cauliflower, celery, French beans, and haricots. A mixture of either with some green herbs, dressed with oil, is very good; by way of variety.

Lobster Salad.

Prepare a mixture of white lettuce, and green salading, mix it with cream or oil; take out the coral of the lobster, and dispose it amongst the vegetables so as best to contrast the colours.—*Or*: lobster may be cut up, dressed as eaten at table, then mixed with lettuce and small salading also cut up and dressed; the dressing of each must be according to taste. Some persons dress their lobster with lemon juice and cayenne. Put the mixture into a salad bowl, light sprigs of cresses on the top, and heaps of the coral amidst them.

Italian Salad.

About three hours before the salad is wanted, bone and chop 2 anchovies, and mix them in a salad bowl, with an eschalot, and some small salading, or lettuce, or any herbs, fresh gathered; boil 2 eggs hard, bruise the yolks, then mix them with 2 spoonsful of oil, 1 of vinegar, a little pepper, and a little made mustard. To this sauce, put very thin slices of cold roast meat of any kind, fowl, game, or lobster (and any cold gravy), and leave them to soak. Garnish it prettily. Cold fish may be dressed in this way; then hard-boiled eggs may be added; and, with either meat or fish, cold boiled vegetables. Nicely garnished, these salads are pretty for supper tables. Capsicums, barberries, and pickled fruit are of use in ornamenting them.

Cucumbers

Should be fresh, mixed with onion, and never eaten without oil.

CHAPTER XIX.

*General Instructions for making Pastry, with particular Directions
relating to Meat, Fish, and Fruit Pies*

PRACTICE is more requisite than judgment to arrive at perfection in making
pastry, particularly raised crusts, and very little can be given in the way of general
instruction on the subject.—The flour should be of the best quality, dried before
the fire, and then allowed to get cool before it is wetted.—Good salt butter, washed
in several waters, to extract the salt, is cheaper in some seasons, and is as good as
fresh butter. Fresh butter should be worked, on a board, with a wooden spoon, or
the hand, to extract the butter-milk, before it is used for delicate pastry; after you
have well worked, dab it with a soft cloth.

Finely shred suet makes very good crust for fruit, as well as meat pies, and,
if good, is more delicate and wholesome than lard; veal suet is the most delicate.
Some cooks cut the suet in pieces, and melt it in water, then, when cold, press
out the water, pound the suet in a mortar, with a very little oil, till it becomes the
consistence of butter, and use it for pie crust; but I prefer fresh suet very finely
shred, not chopped. For this purpose it must be quite sweet.—Lard varies much
in quality; and if not good, the paste will not be light. Sweet marrow is very good.

A marble slab is very useful for making pastry, particularly in hot weather.
Pastry is never good made in a warm room, neither will it bear being exposed to
a draught of air. The sooner it is baked, the lighter it will be. There is ample room
for display of taste in ornamenting pastry, both for meat pies and sweets. Paste
cutters are not expensive, and if kept in good order, will last a long time; but, if not
delicately clean, the paste will be spoiled.

For very *common meat pies*, a crust may be made of mashed potatoes, spread
thickly over the top. For more delicate pies, rice may be boiled in milk and water
till it begins to swell, then drained, and mixed with 1 or 2 eggs well beaten, and
spread in a thick layer over the meat.

A glazing for meat pies is made of white sugar and water; yolk of egg and water; yolk of egg and melted butter.

To ice paste, beat the white of an egg, and brush it over the tart, when half
baked; then sift finely powdered sugar over that.—*Another way*: pound and sift 4
oz. refined sugar, beat up the white of an egg, and by degrees add it to the sugar,
till it looks white, and is thick; when the tarts are baked, spread the iceing over
the top with a brush, and return them to the oven to harden, but take care that the
iceing do not burn.

Be careful to keep the pasteboard and rolling-pin quite clean; and recollect that the best made paste will be spoiled, if not nicely *baked*.

Plain Crust for Meat Pies.

To 2 lbs. of fine, well dried flour, put 1 lb. finely sliced fresh suet, and a little salt, mix it up lightly, with enough cold water to mould it, then roll out thin, fold it up, roll again, and it is ready. Put more suet to make it richer. *Another.*—Common bread dough, or French roll dough, makes very good crust for plain pies. Roll it out, and stick bits of butter and lard into it, and roll up again. If the dough be good the crust will be light.

Richer Crust.

For 2 lbs. of flour, break in pieces 1½ lb. washed salt butter, rub it in the flour, wet it up with the yolks of 3 eggs well beaten, and mixed in from ½ to a whole pint of spring water. Roll the paste out thin, double it, and roll out again; repeat this three times, and it is ready.

An Elegant Crust.

Wash ¾ lb. of very good butter, and melt it carefully, so that it do not oil, let it cool, and stir into it an egg well beaten: mix this into ¾ lb. of very fine well dried flour. It should not be a stiff paste, and must be rolled out thin.

A Flaky Crust.

Wet 1 lb. of well dried flour, with as much water as will make it into a stiff dough. Roll it out, and stick bits of butter over. ¾ lb. of butter should be divided in 3, and rolled in at three different times.

Puff Paste.

Weigh an equal quantity of fine flour, and fresh, or well washed salt butter: crumble one third part of the butter into the flour, mix well together, and wet it with cold water to make it into dough. Dust some dry flour over the pasteboard, and work the dough well, with your hands, into a stiff paste; then roll out thin, and stick little bits of butter into it, sprinkle flour lightly over, fold the paste, roll out again; stick in more butter, fold up again, and repeat the same till all the butter is used. Lay a wet cloth in folds over, till you use it. *Another.*—Rub ½ lb. fresh butter into 1 lb. fine flour, with the yolks of 2 eggs beaten, and some finely sifted sugar: rub all together very smoothly, wet with cold water, and work it into a stiff paste.

Crisp Paste.

Rub ¼ lb. butter into 1 lb. flour, add 2 table-spoonsful of sifted loaf sugar, and the yolks of 3 eggs, work it well with a horn spoon, roll it out very thin, touching it as little as possible.

A Good Light Crust.

Rub a piece of butter the size of an egg, the same of lard, and soda to lie on a shilling, into 1 lb. flour; mix it into a stiff paste with 1 egg and a little water; roll it out 3 times, spread lightly, once with butter, and twice with lard.

Short Crust not Rich.

Rub into 1 lb. of flour, 6 oz. butter, 2 oz. sifted white sugar, and the yolks of 2 eggs mixed with a little cream or new milk. To make it richer, use more butter and perfume the paste with orange or rose water, or flavour with lemon juice. The butter must all be crumbled into the flour before it is wetted; the less it is rolled the better.

A Nice Crust for Preserved Fruits, Cheesecakes, &c.

Beat ½ lb. good fresh butter, in a bason, with a spoon, till it becomes cream, add 2 oz. finely sifted sugar, and mix in 1 lb. fine flour, then wet it with the whites of 3 eggs well beaten, and roll out the paste. If not stiff enough, use more flour and sugar.—*Or*: rub together equal quantities of flour and butter, with a little sifted sugar; work it into a paste with warm milk, roll it out thin and line your patty pans. *Another.*—Melt 4 oz. of butter in a saucepan, with a tea-spoonful of water, 2 oz. sifted sugar, and a bit of lemon peel; when the butter is melted, take out the lemon peel, and first dredge a little flour into the liquid, shake the saucepan, then put in as much more flour, with a spoon, as the butter will take, keep the saucepan over the fire, and stir briskly with a wooden spoon. Turn it out into another saucepan and let it cool; then put it over the fire, and break in, first 1 egg, stir it well, then 3 more eggs, and stir well again, till the paste is ropy.

Raised Crust for Meat Pies.

Put ¾ of a pint of water and ½ lb. lard into a saucepan, set it on the fire; have ready on the paste-board, 2½ lbs. of flour, make a hole in the middle, and when the water in the saucepan boils, pour it into it, gently mixing it by degrees with the flour, with a spoon; when well mixed, knead it into a stiff paste. Dredge flour on the board, to prevent the paste from sticking, continue to roll, and knead it, but do not use a rolling-pin. Let it stand to cool before you form the crust for the pie, as follows: cut out pieces for the bottom and top, roll them of the proper thickness, and roll out a piece for the sides; fix the sides round the bottom pieces, cement them together with white of egg, and pinch the bottom crust up round to keep it closed firmly; then put in the meat and lay on the top crust, pinching the edges together closely.—It must be thick in proportion to the size of the pie.

Rice Paste.

Mix ½ lb. rice flour into a stiff paste with the yolk of an egg and milk, beat it out with a rolling-pin, and spread bits of butter over, roll it up, and spread more butter till you have used ½ lb. This will boil as well as bake.

Maccaroni Paste.

Work 1 lb. flour into a paste with 4 eggs; it will be very stiff; must be well kneaded, and then beaten for a long time with a rolling-pin, to make it smooth; then roll out very thin, and cut it in strips. This is rather toilsome than troublesome, because it is difficult to roll thin enough, on account of its stiffness; yet is well worth the trouble, to those who like maccaroni. It cooks in much less time than that which is bought, and is much more delicate.

Meat Pies.

Some cooks say that meat should be a *little* stewed with seasoning, a piece of butter, and only a *very* little water, before it is put into a pie.—Common meat pies should have a thin under crust; but the covering must be thick, or it will be scorched up, before the meat is cooked. Meat pies require a hot, but not a fierce oven.

Venison Pasty.

Make a stiff paste of 2 lbs. of flour and 1 lb. of butter, or fresh suet shred finely, wet it with 4 or 5 eggs well beaten and mixed in warm water. Roll it out several times, line the sides of the dish, but not the bottom.—Some cooks *marinade* or *soak* the venison for a night, in Port wine and seasonings.—Take out all the bones, season the meat with salt, pepper, pounded allspice and mace, and a little cayenne, then put it into a stone jar, and pour over some gravy of the trimmings, or of mutton or beef; place the jar in a saucepan of water, and simmer it over the fire, or on a hearth two or three hours, but the meat should not be over done. Put it by till the next day; remove the cake of fat from the top, lay the meat in alternate pieces of fat and lean in a pie dish, add more seasoning if required, the gravy, and ¼ pint of Port or claret; also a little eschalot or any flavouring vinegar. If the venison want fat, slices of mutton fat may be substituted.—The breast is best for a pasty, but the neck is very good; also the shoulder if too lean to roast. If any gravy be left have it ready to pour hot into the pasty.

Beef Steak Pie.

Cut small steaks from the rump: season, and roll up as olives, or lay them flat, fat and lean mixed, seasoned with salt, pepper, and spices. Then put in ½ pint of gravy, or ½ pint of water, and a table-spoonful of vinegar. If you have no gravy, a piece of kidney will enrich the gravy of the beef, and is a valuable addition to a meat pie. Forcemeat in layers between the slices of beef, or in small balls, makes this much richer; if to be eaten cold, suet must not be used: some cooks put in a few large oysters also. Walnut or mushroom catsup. A good gravy may be poured into the pie, when baked.

Pork Pie.

This is generally made in a raised crust, but in a common pie dish, with a plain crust, it is very good. Season with pepper and salt. Cut all the meat from the bones, and do not put any water into the pie. Pork pie is best cold, and small ones are made by laying a paste in saucers or small plates, then the meat; cover with paste, turning the two edges up neatly.—The griskin is best for pies.

Sausage Rolls.

Use sausage meat; or, take equal portions of cold roast veal and ham, or cold fowl and tongue; chop these very small, season with a tea-spoonful of powdered sweet herbs and a tea-spoonful of mixed salt and cayenne: mix well together, put 3 table-spoonsful of the chopped and seasoned meat, well rolled together, into enough light paste to cover it, and bake half an hour in a brisk oven.—These may be tied in a cloth and boiled; the crust plainer.

Mutton Pie.

Cut cutlets from the leg, or chops from the neck or loin, season with pepper and salt, and place them in a dish, fill this with gravy or water, and, if you choose, strew over a very little minced onion or eschalot and parsley, and cover with a plain crust.—*Squab Pie*, is made of mutton, and between each layer of meat, slices of apples, potatoes, and shred onions.

Lamb Pie.

The same as mutton pie; only being more delicate, it does not require so much seasoning, and is best, made to turn out of patty pans.

Veal Pie.

Cut chops from the neck or breast, or cutlets from any other part, season with salt, pepper, mace, nutmeg, lemon peel, or what herbs you like, lay them in the dish; very thin slices of bacon over them; pour in a little gravy, made from the bones or trimmings, or a little water. Forcemeat balls, hard-boiled yolks of eggs, scalded sweetbreads, veal kidneys, truffles, morels, mushrooms, oysters and thick cream, may be used to enrich this pie.—*Or*: slices of veal, spread with forcemeat, and rolled up as olives; make a hole in the top part of the crust, and when it comes out of the oven, pour in some good gravy.—To be very rich: put the olives in a dish, and between and round them, small forcemeat balls, hard-boiled yolks of eggs, pickled cucumbers cut in round pieces, and pickled mushrooms; pour in good gravy, a glass of white wine, the juice of a lemon, or lemon and oyster pickle.

Maccaroni Pie.

Swell ½ lb. in broth or water; put a thick layer at the bottom of a deep dish, buttered all round, then a layer of beef steak cut thin, or thin slices spread with forcemeat, and rolled up like olives; season the beef, then another layer of macca-roni, then more beef, the top layer maccaroni; pour over gravy or water to fill the dish, and cover with a *thin* crust, and bake it. As the maccaroni absorbs the gravy, there ought to be more to pour in, when it comes from the oven. A light sprinkling of cheese over each layer of maccaroni is an improvement. This pie may be made of fowl, or veal and ham. It is excellent. To be eaten hot.—The *white chedder* is as good as parmesan cheese.

Calf's Head Pie.

Clean and soak, then parboil the head for half an hour, with part of a knuckle of veal, or 2 shanks of mutton, in a very little water, with 2 onions, a bunch of parsley, and winter savory, the rind of a lemon, a few peppercorns, and 2 blades of mace. Take it up, and let it cool, cut it into neat pieces, skin and cut the tongue into small bits. Boil in the liquor a few chips of isinglass, till of a strong jelly. Spread a layer of thin slices of ham, or tongue, at the bottom of a dish, a layer of the head, fat and lean assorted, with forcemeat balls, hard-boiled yolks of eggs, and pickled mushrooms: then strew over salt, pepper, nutmeg, and grated lemon peel; put another layer of slices of ham, and so on, till the dish is nearly full; pour in as much of the jelly as there is room for, cover with a crust, and bake it. Good cold only, and will keep several days.

Sweetbread Pie.

Boil ½ a neck of veal and 2 lbs. gravy beef in 4 quarts of water, with ½ a tea-spoonful of grated nutmeg, and equal quantities of mace and cayenne, and a tea-spoonful of salt; simmer this till it is reduced to ½ pint, and strain it off. Put a good puff paste round your dish; put in 6 sweetbreads, stuffed with green truffles, and 12 oysters with their liquor (omit either or both, as you choose); but take care that the fish and meat are distributed; then fill the dish with the gravy, put on the top crust, and bake, in a quick oven, an hour and a quarter. To be eaten hot.

Pigeon, Rook, or Moorfowl Pie.

Season them inside with salt and pepper, and put in each a bit of butter, rolled in flour. (Some parboil the livers, minced with parsley, and put them inside also.) Lay a beef steak (some stew it first) at the bottom of the dish, or veal cutlets, seasoned, and thin slices of bacon; put in the pigeons, the gizzards, yolks of hard-boiled eggs (forcemeat balls, if you like), and enough water to make gravy. Cover with a puff paste, and bake it. Some cooks cut up the pigeons, and use no beef steak, as they say that the pigeons, if cut up, will produce a sufficiency of gravy. Port and white wine may be added; also catsups, sauces, and mushroom powder.—*Rooks* must be skinned; the back-bone cut out.—*Moorfowl pie* must not be over-baked: when done, you may pour in a hot sauce of melted butter, lemon juice, and a glass of claret.

Hare Pie.

Cut up a leveret, and season it well; to be very rich, have relishing forcemeat balls, and hard-boiled yolks of eggs, to mix with the meat in the dish. Put plenty of butter, rolled in flour, and some water, and cover with a paste. This pie will require long soaking, as the meat is solid; but, unless it be a leveret, much the best way is, to stew the hare first, like venison for pasty.

Chicken, or Rabbit Pie.

Cut up the chickens, season each joint with salt, white pepper, mace, and nutmeg, lay them in the dish, with slices of ham or bacon, a few bits of butter, rolled in flour, and a little water, cover with a crust, and bake it. This pie may be made richer, by putting veal cutlets or veal udder, at the bottom of the dish, adding forcemeat balls and yolks of hard-boiled eggs; also a good jelly gravy, seasoned with peppercorns, onions, and parsley, and poured over the chickens before the pie is baked. Mushrooms are an improvement. Forcemeat for *rabbit* may be made of the livers, suet, anchovies, eschalot, onion, salt, and pepper.

Goose Pie.

Bone, then season well, a goose, and a large fowl; stuff the fowl with the following forcemeat: 2 oz. grated ham, the same of veal and suet, a little parsley, salt, pepper, and 2 eggs to bind it. Place the fowl within the goose, and put that into a raised crust; fill up round with slices of tongue, or pigeons, game, and forcemeat; put pieces of butter, rolled in flour, over all, and cover with a crust. Bake it three hours.

Giblet Pie.

Stew the giblets in broth, with peppercorns, onions, and parsley. When quite tender, take them up, to get cold, then divide, and lay them, on a well-seasoned beef steak, in a pie dish, and the liquor in which they were stewed, and cover with a plain crust. When done, pour in a tea-cupful of cream.

Partridge, also Perigord Pie.

Made the same as pigeon pie. — Or: instead of the steak (some use veal), at the bottom of the dish, spread a thick layer of forcemeat, put in the partridges, bits of butter rolled in flour, and a few scalded button mushrooms, or a table-spoonful of catsup. Cover with a good crust, and bake (if 4 partridges), an hour. — *Perigord Pie*: Singe and truss 6 partridges, lard, season highly, and stuff them with a forcemeat made of 2 lbs. of truffles (brushed, washed, and peeled), the livers of the partridges, and a piece of veal udder parboiled; season with salt, pepper, spices, minced onion and parsley, all pounded; put a little into each partridge, and fill up with whole truffles; line a raised crust with thin slices of bacon and forcemeat, put in the partridges, cover the pie, and bake it.

Pheasant Pie.

Cut off the heads of two pheasants, bone and stuff them, with the livers, bread-crumbs, lemon peel, ham, veal, suet, anchovies, mace, pepper, salt, mushroom powder, and a little eschalot; stew them in good gravy a few minutes, then put them into a baking dish, with some balls of the forcemeat and pickled mushrooms; fill up with good gravy, flavoured with lemon, oyster, and mushroom pickle, a table-spoonful of brandy, and the same of camp sauce. Cover with puff paste, and bake it. Good either hot or cold.

Sea Pie.

Cut up a fowl or two, and thin slices of salt beef, the latter soaked in lukewarm water. Make a good paste of half flour and half mashed potatoes, with butter, lard, or dripping; roll out thin, put a layer at the bottom of a deep tin baking dish, then a layer of fowl and beef, season with pepper, salt, and a little shred onion; then another layer of paste, and one of meat, till the dish is nearly full, fill up with cold water, and bake it; when done, turn it out and serve quite hot. —*Or*: slices of bacon, and no beef.

Parsley Pie.

This may be made of veal, fowl, or calf's feet, but the latter partly cooked first; scald a cullender full of fresh parsley in milk, drain it, season it with salt, pepper, and nutmeg, add a tea-spoonful of broth, and pour it into a pie dish, over the meat. When baked, pour in ¼ pint of scalded cream.

Herb Pie.

One handful of spinach, and of parsley, 2 small lettuces, a very little mustard and cress, and a few white beet leaves; wash, then parboil them, drain, press out the water, mix with a little salt, cut them small, and lay them in a dish: pour over a batter of flour, 2 eggs, a pint of cream, and ½ pint of milk: cover with a rich crust and bake it.

Fish Pie.

The fish should be boiled first; indeed, the remains of the previous day's dinner may answer the purpose. As any and every sort of fish is good in pies, one receipt will do for all, leaving it to the taste of the cook to enrich or flavour it. —If *Turbot*, cut the fish in slices, put a layer in the dish, strew over a mixture of pepper, salt, pounded mace, allspice, and little bits of butter, then a layer of fish, then of the seasoning and butter, till the dish is full. Having saved some of the liquor in which it was boiled, put it on to boil again, with all the skin and trimmings of the fish, strain and pour this into the dish for gravy. Lay a puff paste over, and bake in a slow oven half an hour. *Cod Sounds* must be washed well, then soak several hours, and lay them in a cloth to dry. Put into a stew-pan 2 oz. fresh butter, and half an onion sliced, brown these, and add a table-spoonful of flour rubbed into a small piece of butter, and ½ pint boiling water; let it boil up, put in about 8 cod sounds, season with pepper, the juice of a lemon, and essence of anchovies, stir it a few minutes over the fire, put it in a pie-dish, cover with a light paste, and bake it an hour. —*Another and richer*: Cut the fish into fillets; season them with pounded mace, pepper, cayenne, and salt; or, if whitings, eels, trout, or any fish that will admit of it, do not cut them up, but season the inside, and turn the fish round, fastening with a thread. Have some good fish stock, warm it, add seasoning, and any catsup you like. If you wish it to be *very* rich, line the dish with fish forcemeat, lay some bits of butter at the bottom, put a thick layer of the fish, then strew over chopped shrimps, prawns, or oysters, then the rest of the fish, strain the stock over it, enough for gravy, cover with a light puff paste, and bake it.

Lobster Pie.

This is a rich compound, at its very plainest, and may be made very rich indeed. Parboil 1, 2, or 3, according to the size of your dish. Take out all the meat, cut it in pieces, and lay them in the dish, in alternate layers, with oysters cut in two, and bread-crumbs, moisten with essence of anchovies. Whilst you are doing this, let all the shells and the spawn of the lobster be stewed in half water and half vinegar: add mace and cayenne; when done, strain it; add wine and catsup, boil it up, and pour over the lobster. Lay a light puff paste over, and bake it.

Herring, Eel, or Mackerel Pie.

Skin eels, and cut them in pieces 2 inches long. Season highly, and put a little vinegar into the sauce. This, and all fish pies, may be baked *open*, with a paste edging.

Shrimp and Prawn Pie.

Having picked, put them into little shallow dishes, strew bits of butter over, season as you like, but allspice and chili vinegar should form a part, white wine, also 2 anchovies, if you like. Cover with a puff paste.

Salt Fish Pie.

Soak the fish a night. Boil it till tender, take off the skin, and take out the bones. If the fish be good, it will be in layers, lay them on a fish drainer to cool. Boil 5 eggs hard, cut them with 2 onions, and 2 potatoes in slices; put a layer at the bottom of a pie dish, season with pepper and made mustard, then a layer of fish, season that, another layer of the mixture, and so on till the dish be full; lay some bits of butter on the top, pour in a tea-cupful of water, with a tea-spoonful of essence of anchovy, and of catsup and oyster pickle. Cover with a puff paste, and bake it an hour.—The *sauces* appropriate to fish, are suitable to fish pies. *Fresh Cod Pie.*—Salt a piece of the middle of a fish, one night; wash, dry, and season it with pepper, salt, and nutmeg; lay it in a deep pie dish, with some oysters, put bits of butter on it, pour in some good broth, and cover with a crust. When done, pour in a ¼ pint of hot cream, with a bit of butter rolled in flour, nutmeg, and grated lemon peel.

Patties.

These are convenient for a side dish at dinner, or a principal one at supper or luncheon. An expert cook may contrive to reserve meat or fish, when cooking a large dinner, to provide a dish of patties. The compound must be very nicely minced, suitably seasoned, and sent to table in baked paste; or fried in balls, for a garnish.

Crust for Savoury Patties.

If you can, get from the pastry-cook empty puff patties, it will save you trouble; if not, make a thin puff paste, and line the patty pans; cut out the tops, on white paper, with a thin stamp, and mark them neatly; put a piece of soft paper crumpled, in the middle of the lined patty pan, to support the top; put it on and bake them. Prepare the mince, and when the patties are baked enough, lift off the top, put the mince in (not so much as to run over the edges), and lay the top on.

Chicken, or Turkey and Ham, or Veal Patties.

Mince very finely, the breast, or other white parts of cold chicken, fowl, turkey, or roast veal, and about half the quantity of lean ham, or tongue. Have a little delicate gravy, or jelly of roast veal or lamb, thicken it with butter, rolled in flour, add pepper, salt, cayenne, and lemon juice; put the mince in, and stir it over the fire till quite hot, and fill the baked patties with this quite hot. A few oysters may be minced with the meat.

Rabbit and Hare Patties.

Mince the best parts with a little mutton suet. Thicken a little good gravy, and season with salt, pepper, cayenne, nutmeg, mace, lemon peel, and Port wine, also the stuffing that may be left of the hare or rabbit; heat the mince in it, and fill patties, as above.

Beef Patties.

Mince a piece of tender, underdone meat, with a little of the firm fat; season with salt, pepper, onion, a chopped anchovy, and a very little chili or eschalot vinegar; warm it in gravy, and finish, like other patties.

Oyster Patties.

Beard and wash in their own liquor, some fresh oysters; strain the liquor, and if of 12, put to it 1 oz. butter rolled in flour, with the oysters cut small, a little salt, white pepper, mace, nutmeg, and lemon peel, add to the whole 1 table-spoonful of thick cream; warm, and put it hot into the baked patties.—*Or*: 2 parts of oysters, prepared as above, and one part of fresh mushrooms, cut in dice, fried in butter, and stewed in enough gravy to moisten them; stir the oysters to the mushrooms, and fill the patties.

Lobster and Shrimp Patties.

Chop finely the meat of the tail and claws of a hen lobster; pound some of the spawn, with ½ oz. of butter, and a little meat gravy or jelly, or a table-spoonful of cream; season with cayenne, salt, lemon peel, and essence of anchovy.

Gooseberry, or Green Currant Pie.

Top and tail fruit enough to fill your dish; lay a strip of paste round the edge, put in half the fruit, then half the sugar, the rest of the fruit, more sugar, and cover with a good puff paste. Mark the edges neatly, and ornament the top. When it comes out of the oven, sift powdered sugar over.—First put a little cup in the centre of the dish, to preserve the juice.

Rhubarb Pie.

When old and stringy, peel the skin off, cut the stalks slantways, and make it into a pie, the same as gooseberry: if young, do not peel it.—Some like lemon peel in it.

Red currants, raspberries, ripe gooseberries, cherries, plums, all sorts of damsons, apricots, and peaches, make excellent pies; allow plenty of sugar, put in a little cup, and fill the dish high in the middle with fruit. Divide the apricots and peaches.

Green Apricot Tart.

The fruit should be stewed till tender in a very little water and some sugar; baked in a pie dish with a covering of puff paste, and is an excellent tart.

Apple Pie.

Russetings, ribstone pippins, and such apples as are a little acid, are best. Pare, core, and slice them; sprinkle sugar between, as you put them in the dish, also a little pounded cinnamon and cloves. Slices of quince are an improvement, or quince marmalade, or candied citron or orange peel. Put a strip of paste round the edge of the dish, and cover with a light paste. If they are dry, put in a little lemon juice, and a wine-glassful of white wine.

Green Codling Tart.

Make the pie as directed in the last receipt, and when it comes out of the oven, with a sharp knife cut round the crust, an inch from the edge, take it off, and pour over the apples, a plain or rich custard; have ready baked on a tin, some paste leaves, and stick round the tart; or else cut the top, you have taken off, into lozenges, or the best shape you can, and stick them round.

In the country, fresh cream ought to accompany fruit pies. Clouted cream is excellent with fruit pies.—*Apples, gooseberries,* and *rhubarb* stewed, with sugar enough to sweeten, are better for children, than cooked in paste.—*Or:* fruit thus prepared, may be spread on very thin paste, covered up in turn-overs, and baked on tins.

Cranberry Tart.

The cranberries should be stewed first, with brown sugar, and a very little water, then baked in open tarts, or in patty-pans lined, and covered with light puff paste.

Tarts of Preserved Fruits.

Cover patty-pans, or shallow tins or dishes with light puff paste, lay the preserve in them, cover with light bars of paste, or with paste stars, leaves, or flowers. For delicate preserves, the best way is to bake the paste, first, then put in the preserves, and ornament with leaves baked for the purpose, on tins.

Small Puffs.

Roll out light paste nearly ½ an inch thick, cut it in pieces of 5 inches wide, lay preserves on each, fold it over, wet the edges, and pinch them together, lay these on buttered paper, and bake them.—*Or:* cut the paste into squares, lozenges, and leaves, bake them on tins, and then lay different preserves on each one, and arrange them tastefully in a dish.

Spanish Puffs.

Boil ½ the rind of a lemon, a small stick of cinnamon, and a bit of butter the size of a nut, in ¼ pint of milk, strain it, and set it on the fire in a stew-pan; when it boils, stir in 2 spoonsful of flour, and a large table-spoonful of brandy, take it off, and rub it well together; when quite cold, add 4 eggs, one at a time, rubbing well all the while; divide the mixture into tea-spoonsfuls, or on a plate, let it stand to grow firm, then fry in plenty of boiling lard.

Apple Puffs.

Stew the apples, pulp them through a sieve, and sweeten with white pow-dered sugar; make them as directed for *small puffs*, and bake in a quick oven.

Orange and Lemon Puffs.

Grate the peel of 2 Seville oranges, or 3 lemons, and mix with it ¾ lb. grated lump sugar. Beat up the whites of 4 eggs to a solid froth, put that to the sugar, beat the whole, without stopping, for half an hour, pour it in little round cakes, on buttered paper laid on tins, and bake them in a moderate oven. When cold, tear off the paper.

Minced Pie Meat.

Par-roast, or slightly bake, about 2 lbs. of lean beef (some prefer neat's tongue); when cold, chop it finely; chop 2 lbs. beef suet, also 2 lbs. apples, peeled and cored, 1 lb. stoned raisins, and the same of currants; mix these together in a pan, with 1 lb. of good moist sugar, 2 nutmegs, grated, 1 oz. salt, 1 oz. ginger, ½ oz. coriander seeds, ½ oz. allspice, ½ oz. cloves, the juice of 6 lemons and their rinds, grated, ½ lb. candied citron, the same of candied lemon, ½ pint of brandy, and the same of sweet, ginger, or Madeira wine. Mix well, and it will keep some time, in a cool place. To use it, stir it, and add a little more brandy. Cover patty pans or shallow dishes with a puff paste, fill with the mince, and put a puff paste over: bake in a moderate oven.—*Or*: 1 lb. beef, 3 lbs. suet, 3 lbs. raisins, 4 lbs. currants, 3½ lbs. sugar, 3 lbs. apples, the rind of 3 lemons, and the juice of 2½ lbs. candied lemon; nutmeg, ginger, and pepper to taste. These receipts are both good.

A Bride's Pie.

Boil 2 calf's feet quite tender, and chop the meat. Chop separately 1 lb. suet and 1 lb. apples, quite fine; mix these with the meat, add ½ lb. currants, ½ lb. rai-sins (chopped fine), ¼ oz. cinnamon, 2 drachms nutmeg, and mace (all pounded), 1 oz. candied citron and lemon peel, sliced thin, a wine-glass of brandy, and of Madeira. Line a tin pan with puff paste, put in the mince, cover with a paste, and ornament it.

Maigre Mince Meat.

To 6 lbs. currants add 3 lbs. raisins, 2 oz. cloves, 1½ oz. mace and 1 nutmeg, 3 lbs. fine powdered sugar, the rinds of 2 lemons, and 24 sharp apples, all these ingredients chopped or pounded separately, and then mixed together; add a pint of brandy. Let it stand a day or two, and stir it from the bottom once or twice a day. It will keep in a dry place, for months. Add butter or suet, when you make it into pies, also citron, if you like.

Note.—Mince meat is improved by the currants being plumped in brandy. Raisins should be chopped *very* fine.

CHAPTER XX.

General and particular Directions for making Puddings

PRACTICE, which, generally speaking, is every thing in cooking, will not ensure success in making puddings, unless the ingredients be good.

For pudding crust, nothing is so good as veal suet finely shred, though beef suet and beef marrow make light crust. Fresh dripping is also very good. Lard is not so good, for either meat or fruit puddings. Meat puddings (or dumplings, as they are called, in some of the counties in England) are generally liked, and are, either in crust or in batter, an economical dish, when made of the trimmings of beef or mutton, or the coarser parts of meat, which, though very good, would not so well admit of any other species of cooking. The meat should be quite fresh, and a due mixture of fat and lean. A piece of kidney, cut in bits, will enrich the gravy of beef steak or hare pudding. The crust for these puddings should be less rich, and thicker than for fruit puddings. Puddings will not be light unless the flour be fresh, and dried before the fire.

The number of eggs must be regulated by their size, for a small egg is but half a large one. Break them separately into a tea-cup, and put them into the basin one by one; by this means you ascertain their freshness before you mix them together, for if one be the least stale, it will spoil any number with which it may be mixed. Beat them well, the two parts separately, and strain them to the other ingredients.

Butter, whether salt or fresh, should be perfectly sweet; and milk or cream, if only a little upon the turn, will render of no avail all the labour that has been bestowed upon either pudding or custard.

Let all seasoning spices be finely pounded; currants washed, rubbed dry, carefully picked, and laid on a sieve before the fire to plump; almonds must be *blanched*, namely, covered with hot water, and then peeled.

Puddings of both meat and fruit may be boiled in a mould or bason, but they are lighter in a cloth; but then the crust must be thicker, for if it break, the gravy or juice will be lost. Spread the cloth in a cullender, or bason, flour it, lay in the crust, then the fruit or meat, put on the top, and pinch the edges firmly together, but do not let them be so thick as to form a heavy lump at the bottom, when the pudding is turned out.

Pudding cloths should not be washed with soap, but boiled in wood ashes, rinsed in clear water, dried, and put by in a drawer. When about to use it, dip the cloth in boiling water, squeeze dry, and dredge it with flour. Do not put a pudding in the pot till the water boils fast, and let there be plenty of it; move the pudding from time to time for the first ten minutes; and, as the water diminishes, put in more, boiling hot. The water should boil *slowly*, and never for a minute cease to boil during the time the pudding is in. When you take it out of the pot, dip the pudding into cold water for an instant, and set it in a bowl or cullender, for two or three minutes; this will cause it to turn more easily out of the cloth.

A pudding in which there is much bread should be tied up loosely, to allow it to swell. A batter pudding tied tight. Batter requires long beating; mix the milk and eggs by degrees into the flour, to avoid making it lumpy; this will be the case sometimes, and then the batter may be strained; but such waste may be avoided, by care in mixing at first. Tie meat puddings up tight.

More care is necessary in baking than in boiling puddings. They should not be scorched in a too hot, nor made sodden, in a too cool oven.

It is an improvement to puddings, custards, and cakes, to flavour them with orange flower, or rose water, or any of the perfumed distilled waters.

Paste for Meat Puddings.

Shred ½ lb. suet and rub it into 1¼ lb. flour, sprinkle a little salt, and wet it into a stiff paste with cold water; then beat it a few minutes with a rolling pin. Clarified dripping is not so good, but more economical.

Beef Steak Pudding.

The more tender the steak, the better, of course, the pudding. Cut it into pieces half the size of your hand, season with salt, pepper, and grated nutmeg. Spread a thin crust in a buttered bason, or mould; or a thicker one in a cloth: put the meat in, and a little water, also a wine-glassful of walnut, the same of oyster catsup, or 6 oysters, and a table-spoonful of lemon pickle; cover it with the top crust, fasten the edges firmly, and tie it up tightly. Finely minced onion may be added. A piece of kidney will enrich the gravy. A beef pudding of 2 lbs. of meat ought to boil *gently* four hours.

Hare, rabbit, and chicken, make good puddings, the same as beef; slices of ham or bacon are an improvement to the two latter. Boil *hare pudding* as long as beef. *Dumplings.*—Chop beef small, season well, and put it into dumplings, the same as apple dumplings, and boil one hour.—*Sausage* meat, or whole sausages, skinned, may be boiled in paste, and are very good.

Suet Pudding and Dumplings.

Chop 6 oz. suet very fine, put it into a basin with 6 oz. flour, 2 oz. bread-crumbs, and a tea-spoonful of salt, stir well together, and pour in, by degrees, enough milk, or milk and water, to make it into a light pudding; put it into a floured cloth, and boil two hours. For dumplings, mix the above stiffer, make it into 6 dumplings, and tie them separately in a cloth; boil them one hour. 1 or 2 eggs are an improvement. 6 oz. of currants to the above quantity, make *currant dumplings*.

Meat in Batter.

Cut the meat into chops or steaks, put them in a deep dish, season with pepper and salt, and fill up the dish with a batter, made of three eggs, and 4 large table-spoonsful of flour, to a pint of milk; then bake it.—*Or*: bake the meat whole, and if a large piece, let it be in the oven half an hour before you pour in the batter, or else they will be cooked unequally.

Kidney Pudding.

Split and soak 1 or 2 ox kidneys, and season well; line a bason or cloth with a crust, put them in, and boil it two hours and a half; rather less, if in a cloth.

Fish Pudding.

Pound some slices of whiting in a mortar, with ¼ lb. butter; soak slices of 2 French rolls in cold milk, beat them up with pepper and salt, and mix with the fish. Boil this, in a buttered bason, about an hour and a half. Serve melted butter.—*Mackerel* is made into puddings; for this follow the directions for beef steak pudding.

Black Pudding.

They are made of hog's blood. Salt, strain, and boil it *very slowly*, or it will curdle, with a little milk or broth, pepper, salt, and minced onion; stir in, by degrees, some dried oatmeal and sliced suet; add what savoury herbs you like, fill the skins, and boil them. Some put in whole rice or grits (parboiled), in place of oatmeal.

Hog's Puddings, White.

Mix ½ lb. almonds blanched and cut in pieces, with 1 lb. grated bread, 2 lbs. beef or mutton suet, 1 lb. currants, some cinnamon and mace, a pint of cream, the yolks of 5 and whites of 2 eggs, some Lisbon sugar, lemon peel, and citron sliced, and a little orange-flower water. Fill the skins rather more than half, and boil in milk and water.

Apple Pudding to Boil.

Make a paste in the proportion of 4 oz. suet, or 2 oz. butter, lard, or dripping, to 8 oz. flour, and a little salt. Some use an egg or two, others cold water only, but it should be a *stiff* paste. Line a mould, bason, or cloth, with this paste, rolled smooth, put in the apples, pared, cored, and sliced; sweeten with brown sugar, and flavour with cloves, cinnamon, or lemon peel, as you like. Some persons put in 3 or 4 cloves, or a small piece of cinnamon, also lemon peel.

Green Apricot Pudding.

The same as the last, and is delicious. Let the crust be delicate, and use white powdered sugar.

Roll Pudding.

Roll out a paste as directed for apple pudding, spread jam or any other preserve you like on it, roll it over, tie it in a cloth, and boil it.—A very nice mixture to spread over paste in place of preserves, is composed of apples, currants, and a very little of mace, cinnamon, and sugar. *Another Jam Pudding*: line a bason with a thin paste, spread a layer of preserve at the bottom, then a thin paste to cover it, then a layer of preserve, and so on, till the bason is filled, cover with paste, pinch it round the edges, and boil it.

Apple Dumplings.

Peel large apples, divide them, take out the cores, then close them again, first putting 1 clove in each. Roll out thin paste, cut it into as many pieces as you have apples, and fold each one neatly up; close the paste safely. Tie up each dumpling separately, very tight, and boil them an hour. When you take them up, dip each one into cold water, stand it in a bason two or three minutes, and it will turn more easily out of the cloth.

Green currants, *ripe currants*, *and raspberries*, *gooseberries*, *cherries*, *damsons*, and all the various sorts of *plums*, are made into puddings, the same as *apple pudding*.

Plum Pudding.

For this national compound there are many receipts, and rich plum puddings are all very much alike, but the following receipts are very good:—To 6 oz. finely shred beef suet, add 2 oz. flour, 4 oz. stoned raisins, 4 oz. well picked and plumped currants, pounded allspice, cinnamon, nutmeg, and sugar to taste, and a tea-spoonsful of salt; mix these ingredients well, and wet them with 3 eggs well beaten, and as much milk as is required to mix it into a rather stiff pudding. You may add a wine-glassful of brandy, or 2 of sweet white wine; indeed, brandy is rarely omitted; some prefer the flavour of orange flower or rose-water. This pudding may be made richer by the addition of 1 oz. candied lemon peel, and ½ oz. citron. It should boil at least four hours.—Or: ½ lb. of slices of stale bread, pour ½ pint of boiling milk over, and cover close for fifteen or twenty minutes; beat this up with ½ lb. suet, ½ lb. raisins, and the same of currants, all chopped fine; add 2 table-spoonsful of flour, 3 eggs, a little salt, and as much milk as is required. This may be either boiled or baked.—Or: to ¾ lb. currants, ¾ lb. raisins, and ½ lb. suet, add ½ lb. bread-crumbs, 6 eggs, a wine-glassful of brandy, ½ a tea-cupful of fine sugar, ½ a nutmeg grated, and as much candied orange or lemon peel as you like: mix well, and boil three hours. No other liquid is required.

A Christmas Pudding.

To 1 lb. suet add 1 lb. flour, 1 lb. raisins, 1 lb. currants (chopped fine), 4 oz. bread-crumbs, 2 table-spoonsful sugar, 1 of grated lemon peel, a blade of mace, ½ a nutmeg, a tea-spoonful of ginger, and 6 eggs well beaten. Mix well and boil five hours.

Marrow Pudding.

Pour a quart of boiling milk over a large breakfast-cupful of stale crumbs, and cover a plate over. Shred ½ lb. fresh marrow, mix with it 2 oz. raisins, 2 oz.

currants, and beat them up with the soaked bread; sweeten to your taste, add a tea-spoonful of cinnamon powder, and a very little nutmeg. Lay a puff paste round the edge of a shallow pudding dish, and pour the pudding in. Bake from twenty-five minutes to half an hour. You may add lemon peel, a wine-glassful of brandy, some almonds blanched and slit; also candied citron and lemon peel.

Sauce for Plum Pudding.

Melt good fresh butter, thicken it, and stir in by degrees, a wine-glassful of white wine, the same of brandy or old rum; sweeten to your taste, and add grated lemon peel and cinnamon. *A Store Pudding Sauce.* — To ½ pint brandy, and 1 pint sherry, add 1 oz. thinly pared lemon peel, and ½ oz. mace; infuse these two or three weeks, then strain and bottle it. Add as much as you like to thick melted butter, and sweeten to taste.

French Plum Pudding.

Mix 6 oz. suet, 7 oz. grated bread, 2 oz. sugar, 3 eggs, a coffee-cupful of milk, a table-spoonful ratafia, or 2 of rum, and ½ lb. French plums; let it stand two hours, stir well again, and boil it in a mould, two hours.

Plum Pudding of Indian Corn Flour.

To 1 lb. corn flour add ½ lb. shred suet, and what currants, raisins, and spices you choose; mix the whole well together, with a pint of water, and boil the pudding in a cloth three hours.

Maigre Plum Pudding.

Simmer in ½ pint milk, 2 blades mace, and a bit of lemon peel, for ten minutes; strain into a basin, to cool. Beat 3 eggs, with 3 oz. lump sugar, ¼ of a nutmeg grated, and 3 oz. flour; beat well together, and add the milk by degrees; then put in 3 oz. fresh butter, 2 or 3 oz. bread-crumbs, 2 oz. currants, and 2 oz. raisins; stir all well together. Boil it in a mould two hours and a half. Serve melted butter sweetened, and flavoured with brandy.

Bread Pudding.

Pour a pint of boiling new milk over a breakfast-cupful of stale bread-crumbs, cover till cold, then beat them with a spoon; add 2 oz. currants, or a few cut raisins, a little sugar, cinnamon, nutmeg, and 3 or 4 eggs, well beaten; beat well together, and either boil in a buttered mould, or bake in a dish. It may be enriched by candied citron, or lemon peel, and flavoured with orange flower or rose water. This may be baked in little cups, turned out into a dish, and served with sweet sauce. *Brown Bread Pudding.* — Grate ½ lb. stale brown bread, and mix it with ½ lb. shred suet, and ½ lb. currants; sugar and nutmeg to taste, 4 eggs, 1 table-spoonful of brandy, and 2 of cream. Boil it three hours, and serve with sweet sauce.

Sweet Sauce.

Flavour thick melted butter with cinnamon and grated lemon peel, sweeten to taste, add 1 or 2 wine-glassfuls of white wine.—*Or*: sweeten some thin cream, put in a little piece of butter, heat it, then flavour with cinnamon or lemon peel, and white wine; pour it hot over the pudding, or serve in a tureen.—*Or*: break a stick of cinnamon into bits, boil it ten minutes, in water enough to cover it, add ¼ pint of white wine, 2 table-spoonsful of powdered sugar, and boil it up, strain, and pour over the pudding.

Bread and Butter Pudding.

Lay thin slices of stale bread and butter in a pudding dish, sprinkle currants over, then another layer of bread and butter, and so on till the dish is full to about an inch; pour over an unboiled custard (3 eggs to a pint of milk), sweeten to taste, soak it an hour, and bake half an hour.

Custard Pudding.

Boil a stick of cinnamon and a roll of lemon peel, in a pint of new milk, or cream, and set it by to cool. Beat 5 eggs, pour the milk to them, sweeten to taste, and bake in a dish lined with puff paste twenty minutes. You may add a wine-glassful of brandy. *To Boil.*—Prepare a mould as follows; put into it enough powdered sugar, to cover it, set it on the stove for the sugar to melt, and take care that the syrup cover the whole inside of the mould; grate lemon peel over the sugar, and pour the above mixture of milk or cream and eggs into it; tie a cloth over, and put instantly into boiling water, and boil it half an hour. Turn it out, and garnish with preserves. These puddings are good, hot or cold.

Little Puddings.

Grate a penny loaf, and mix well with a handful of currants, a very little fresh butter, nutmeg, and the yolk of an egg; make it into little balls, flour them, tie separately in a cloth, and boil them half an hour. Serve quite hot, with wine sauce.

An Excellent Pudding.

Boil a bit of cinnamon in a pint of milk, pour it over thin slices of French roll, or an equal quantity of rusks, cover with a plate to cool; beat it quite smooth with 6 oz. shred suet, ¼ lb. currants, 3 eggs beaten, and a little brandy, old rum, or orange-flower water. Bake an hour.

Oatmeal Pudding.

Steep the oatmeal all night in milk. Pour off the milk, and stir into the meal some cream, currants, spice, sugar, or salt, to your taste, and 3 or 4 eggs; or, if no cream, use more eggs. Stir well, and boil it in a basin an hour. Pour melted butter, sweetened, over it.

Batter Pudding.

Beat 4 eggs and mix them smoothly, with 4 table-spoonsful of flour, then stir in by degrees, 1 pint of new milk, beat it well, add a tea-spoonful of salt, and boil in a mould an hour, or bake it half an hour.—*Black Cap Pudding* is made in the same way, with the addition of 3 oz. currants; these will fall to the bottom of the basin, and form a black cap when the pudding is turned out.—*Batter Pudding with Fruit* is made as follows: pare, core, and divide, 8 large apples, put them in a deep pudding dish, pour a batter over, and bake it.—Cherries, plums, damsons, and most sorts of fruit, make nice puddings in this way.—Serve sweet sauce with batter puddings.—*Or*: raspberry vinegar, such as is made at home, clear, and possessing the flavour of the fruit.

Yorkshire Pudding.

This is batter, the same as the last receipt, baked, and eaten with roast meat; but in some houses it is not baked, but cooked under the meat thus: pour it into a shallow tin pan, put it under roasting meat, and stir till it begins to settle. After one or two trials a cook will know when to put the pudding under the meat, for that must depend upon the size of the joint, as it ought to go to table as soon as it is done, or it will be heavy. They are much lighter not turned. The fat will require to be poured off, once or twice.

Potato Puddings.

Boil in a quart of milk, a bit of lemon peel, and some nutmeg. Rub smooth, in a little cold milk, 4 table-spoonsful of potato flour, and stir it, by degrees, into the hot milk; when cool, add sugar, and 3 or 4 eggs, or more as you like, put it into a dish, and bake an hour. Add brandy or orange-flower water.

Carrot Pudding.

Mix ½ lb. grated raw carrot with ½ lb. grated bread, and stir these into a pint of thick cream and the yolks of 8 eggs well beaten, then stir in ½ lb. fresh butter, melted, 3 spoonsful of orange-flower water, ½ a wine-glassful of brandy, a nutmeg grated, and sugar to your taste; stir all well together, and if too thick, add a very little new milk, pour it into a dish lined with paste and bake it an hour.

Hasty Pudding.

Beat the yolk of an egg into ½ pint new milk with a little salt, stir this by degrees into 3 table-spoonsful of flour, and beat it to a smooth batter. Set 1½ pint of milk on the fire; when scalding hot pour in the batter, keep stirring that it may be smooth and not burn: let it thicken, but not boil. Serve it directly.

Buttermilk Pudding.

Use fresh buttermilk, and make the same as batter pudding, but without eggs. This is very good, with roast meat.—*Or*: warm 3 quarts of milk with a quart of buttermilk, then pour it through a sieve; when the curd is dry, pound it with ½ lb. sugar, the peel of a lemon boiled till tender, the crumb of a roll, 6 bitter almonds, 4 oz. butter, the yolks of 5 and whites of 3 eggs, a tea-cupful of good cream, a wine-glassful of sweet wine and of brandy; mix well, and bake in small cups, well buttered. Serve quite hot, with sweet sauce.

Save-all Pudding.

Put scraps of bread, or dry pieces of home-made cake, into a saucepan, with milk according to the quantity of bread; when it boils, beat the bread smooth, add 3 eggs, sugar, nutmeg, ginger, and lemon peel; put it into a buttered dish, and strew over the top 2 oz. shred suet, or butter. Bake or boil it three quarters of an hour. *Currants* or *raisins* are an improvement.

Camp Puddings.

Melt ¼ lb. butter in ½ pint of water, with a little salt, sugar to your taste, and grated lemon peel. When melted, stir in ¼ lb. flour, and when nearly cold, add 3 eggs well beaten. Bake in cups twenty minutes, or fry them in plenty of lard.

Pretty Puddings.

A pint of cream, or new milk, 4 eggs (leave out 2 whites), ½ a nutmeg grated, the pulp of 2 large apples (boiled), ¼ lb. butter melted, and a tea-cupful of grated bread. Beat it well together, sweeten to your taste, and bake it.

Nursery Pudding.

Cut the crumb of a twopenny loaf in slices, pour on it a quart of boiling milk, cover close for ten minutes; beat it and stir in ¼ lb. fresh butter, 4 eggs, a little nutmeg, and sugar. Bake in patty-pans, or in a dish, half an hour.

Arrow Root Pudding.

Rub 2 dessert-spoonsful of arrow root quite smooth in a little cold milk, pour upon it by degrees, stirring all the time, a pint of scalded new milk; put it on the fire a few minutes to thicken, but not boil; stir carefully, or it will be lumpy. When cold add sugar, and 3 yolks of eggs. Boil, or bake it half an hour.

Ground Rice Pudding.

Mix 2 oz. ground rice with ½ pint of cold milk; scald 1½ pint of new milk, and pour the rice and milk into it, stirring over the fire till it thickens: let it cool, then add 5 eggs well beaten, 6 oz. of powdered sugar, nutmeg, and a spoonful of orange-flower water, stir all well together, and bake in a dish, with a paste border, half an hour. Currants may be added. It may be boiled in a mould, an hour. Indian corn flour makes good puddings the same way; and there are preparations of Indian corn, such as *soujie, semolina,* and *golden polenta,* which may be dressed in the same way.

Semolina Pudding.

Mix 2 oz. of semolina quite smooth, with a little cold milk, then pour over it a pint of boiled milk, and sweeten to your taste, then put it into a saucepan, and keep stirring till it boils, take it off the fire, and stir till only lukewarm; add a slice of butter, the yolks of 4 eggs, the juice of a lemon, and a wine-glassful of brandy. Bake in a dish lined with paste, half an hour.

Indian Corn Mush.

The same thing as oatmeal porridge, but made of Indian corn meal. Boil 2 quarts of water with a little salt, and mix it, by degrees, into 1 lb. corn meal; boil very gently three quarters of an hour, stirring all the time, that the meal may not adhere to the bottom of the saucepan, and burn.

Hommony.

Boil one third of a pound of Indian meal in water to cover it, for twenty minutes, or until nearly all the water is wasted; it must be like thick paste. Put a piece of butter the size of a walnut into a vegetable dish, pour in the hommony, and serve it, like mashed turnips. Dip your spoon in the middle when you help it. In some parts of America, what they call *hommony* is made of the *cracked* corn: and if so, it must be something of the same kind as our peas-pudding, but not boiled in a cloth.

Polenta.

The best thing to prepare this in, is a three legged iron pot, hung over the fire. Let the fire be hot, and also blazing, if possible. To a quart of water, when it boils, put in a little salt, then add 12 oz. of meal, but be careful to do it in the following manner: while the water is boiling stir in half the meal first, but be sure to stir quickly all the time, or it may be lumpy, then you may put in the remainder at once, but keep stirring constantly. When it has been on the fire a quarter of an hour, cease to stir, take the pot off the fire and set it on the floor for two minutes, then put it on the fire again, and you will see the polenta first rise in a great puff, then break and fall; as soon as you perceive this, take it off the fire, and turn it out into a dish; it ought to come out quite clean, not leaving a particle adhering to the pot, else there has been some fault in the boiling. It is stirred with a long stick, thicker at one end than the other. Of this the Italians make an endless variety of dishes, some of which are the following: the most simple mode of dressing the polenta is thus: pour it from the boiling into a bowl, when cold turn it out; take a coarse thread in your two hands, put it on the side of the polenta away from you, draw the thread towards you, and you will find that it cuts a clean slice of polenta off, continue till you have cut it all into slices, and then you may dress them in different ways: the commonest is to cut the slices *thick* and brown them on a gridiron.

Whole Rice Pudding.

Rice should be soaked an hour in cold water. Wash well, and pick, a tea-cupful of good rice, boil it slowly ten minutes, in a little water, pour that off, and pour over the rice 1½ pint of new milk; let the milk boil up, pour it into a deep dish, stir in a bit of butter, sugar to your taste, a little pounded cinnamon, and grated lemon peel; bake it, and it will be a good plain pudding. This is made richer by adding to the rice and milk, when poured into the dish, some sliced suet, and raisins, or candied peel, also 3 or 4 eggs.—*Or:* apples pared, cored, and sliced, spread at the bottom of the dish, the rice and milk poured over them.—*Little rice puddings* are made by boiling the rice (after it has been parboiled in water) in a pint of cream, with a bit of butter; let it get quite cold, then mix with it the yolks of 6 eggs, sugar, lemon peel, and cinnamon; butter some little cups, lay slices of candied citron, or lemon, at the bottom, fill up with rice, bake, turn them out in a dish, and pour sweet sauce round. Ratafia is an improvement.

Rice Pudding to Boil.

Wash and pick ¼ lb. of rice, tie it in a cloth, leaving room to swell, boil it two hours. Turn it out in a dish, pour melted butter and sifted sugar over.—*Or:* apples sliced may be mixed with the rice when it is put into the pudding cloth.—*Or:* boil ½ lb. of rice in 1½ pint of milk till tender, then mix with it ½ lb. suet, and the same of currants and raisins chopped, 3 eggs, 1 table-spoonful of sugar, the same of brandy, a little nutmeg and lemon peel; beat well, put 2 table-spoonsful of flour to bind it, and boil in a mould or bason three hours.

Snow Balls.

Boil ½ lb. whole rice tender in water, with a large piece of lemon peel; drain off the water. Pare and core 4 large apples. Divide the rice into equal parts, roll out each one, put an apple in, cover with the rice, and tie each one tightly up in a cloth, and boil half an hour. Pour pudding sauce round.

Buxton Pudding.

Boil 1 pint new milk; rub smoothly with a little cold milk, 2 table-spoonsful of flour, and mix it by degrees to the boiled milk, and set it over the fire, let it boil five minutes, then cool; stir in 4 oz. melted butter, 5 eggs, 6 oz. lump sugar, and the rind of a lemon grated. Bake half an hour.

Vermicelli Pudding.

Boil 1½ pint of new milk, put to it 4 oz. fine vermicelli, boil them together till the latter is cooked; add ¼ lb. butter; the yolks of 4 eggs, ¼ lb. sugar, a little cinnamon, nutmeg, and lemon peel grated. Boil in a bason; or bake twenty minutes. Cream is an improvement.

Sago, or Tapioca Pudding.

Wash it in several waters, then soak it an hour. Boil 5 table-spoonsful in a quart of new milk, with sugar, cinnamon, lemon peel and nutmeg, to taste; when cold add 4 eggs, bake it in a dish with a paste border, in a slow oven. Some prefer the prepared sago powder.

Pearl Barley Pudding.

Wash 3 table-spoonsful of pearl barley in cold water, then boil it two hours or till quite soft, in a quart of milk, then beat in 2 eggs, some sugar, and 3 drops of essence of lemon: bake it in a pie dish.

Millet Pudding.

Wash 4 oz. of the seeds, pour on them 1½ pint of boiling milk, add 2 oz. butter, a little sugar, ginger, and nutmeg; cover with a plate, and let it remain till cold, then stir in 3 eggs: boil or bake it.

Maccaroni Pudding.

Simmer 3 oz. pipe maccaroni in 1½ pint of milk, and a little salt, till tender. (*Or*: simmer it in water, pour that off, then put the hot milk to the maccaroni.) Let it cool, add the yolks of 4 eggs, a little nutmeg, cinnamon, powdered sugar, and a table-spoonful of almond-flower water, and bake it.—*Or*: to make it richer, put a layer of any preserve in the centre of the maccaroni. Lay a paste round the edge of the dish.—*Or*: simmer 6 oz. maccaroni till tender, pour the water off, and let the maccaroni cool. Beat the yolks of 6 eggs, the whites of 3, and stir them into ½ pint of good cream, with a very little salt and pepper. Skin and mince the breast of a cold fowl, with half its quantity of lean ham; grate 1½ oz. parmesan over the mince, and mix it with all the rest; then pour it into a shape or bason; boil or steam it.—*Excellent.* Serve a good clear gravy with this.

A Pudding always liked.

Put ¼ lb. ratafia drops, 2 oz. jar raisins stoned and slit in two, 1 oz. sweet almonds slit and blanched, 1 oz. of citron and candied lemon (both sliced), in layers in a deep dish, and pour over a wine-glassful of sherry and the same of brandy; pour over a good, rich, unboiled custard, to fill up the dish, then bake it.

Cheese Pudding.

Grate ½ lb. of Cheshire cheese into a table-spoonful of finely grated breadcrumbs, mix them up with 2 eggs, a tea-cupful of cream, and the same of oiled butter; bake in a small dish lined with puff paste. Serve this quite hot.

Ratafia Pudding.

Blanch, and beat to a paste, in a mortar, ½ lb. of sweet, and ½ oz. of bitter, almonds, with a table-spoonful of orange-flower water; add 3 oz. of fresh butter, melted in a wine-glassful of hot cream, 4 eggs, sugar to taste, a very little nutmeg, and a table-spoonful of brandy. Bake in a small dish, or little cups buttered: serve white wine sauce.

Staffordshire Pudding.

Put into a scale 3 eggs in the shells, take the same weight of butter, of flour, and of sugar: beat the butter to a cream, then add the flour, beat it again, then the sugar and eggs. Butter cups, fill them half full, and bake twenty minutes in a slow oven. Serve in sweet sauce.

Baked Almond Pudding.

Beat 6 oz. of sweet and 12 bitter almonds to a paste; mix this with the yolks of 6 eggs, 4 oz. butter, the grated peel and juice of a lemon, 1½ pint of cream, a glass of white wine, and some sugar. Put a paste border round a dish, pour in the pudding, and bake it half an hour.

Wafer Pudding.

Melt 1 oz. butter and mix it with a gill of cream; when this is cold, work it into 1½ table-spoonful flour, and 4 eggs, mix well, and bake it in saucers, half an hour. Serve with wine sauce.

Orange Pudding.

Grate the rind of a large Seville orange into a mortar, put to it 4 oz. fresh butter and 6 oz. finely powdered sugar; beat well, and mix in, gradually, 8 eggs; have ready soaked in milk 3 sponge biscuits, and mix them to the rest; beat well, pour it into a shallow dish, lined with a rich puff paste, and bake till the paste is done.—*Or*: the yolks of 8, and whites of 4, eggs well beaten, 4 table-spoonsful of orange marmalade, 4 oz. pounded sugar, 4 oz. fresh butter, 2 oz. pounded Naples biscuits, 2 table-spoonsful of cream, 2 of sherry, and 1 of good brandy; mix all together, and bake in a dish with a very thin paste.

Lemon Pudding.

Put ½ lb. fresh butter with ½ lb. lump sugar into a saucepan, and stir it over the fire till the sugar is melted, turn it out to cool; beat 8 eggs, very well, add to them the juice of 2, and the grated peel of 3, lemons, and mix these well with the butter and sugar, also a wine-glassful of brandy; bake in a dish lined with puff paste, half an hour.—*Or*: boil in several waters the peel of 4 large lemons, and when cold pound it in a mortar with ½ lb. of lump sugar; add ½ lb. fresh butter beaten to a cream, 6 yolks of eggs, 3 whites, 2 table-spoonsful of brandy, and the juice of 3 lemons, mix well, and bake in a moderately quick oven; when done strew sifted sugar over.—Some persons put 2 sponge biscuits into the mixture.

Cabinet or Brandy Pudding.

Line a mould, first with raisins stoned, or with dried cherries, then with thin slices of French roll, then with ratafias or maccaroons, then put in preserved, or fresh, fruit as you like, mixed with sponge, and what other cakes you choose, until the mould be full, sprinkling in at times 2 glasses of brandy. Beat 4 eggs, yolks and whites, and put them into a pint of scalded and sweetened new milk or cream, add grated nutmeg and lemon peel; let the liquid sink gradually into the solid part, tie a floured cloth tight over, and boil the pudding one hour, keeping the bottom of the bason up.—*Another*: pour a pint of hot cream over ½ lb. of Savoy biscuit, and cover it; when cold, beat it up, with the yolks and whites of 8 eggs, beaten separately, sugar and grated lemon peel: butter a mould, stick some stoned raisins round, and pour in the pudding: boil or bake it.

Baked Apple or Gooseberry Pudding.

Having pared and cored them, stew 1 lb. of apples, or 1 quart of gooseberries, in a small stew-pan, with a very little water, a stick of cinnamon, 2 or 3 cloves, and grated lemon peel: when soft, pulp the apples through a sieve, sweeten them, or, if they want sharpness, add the juice of half, or a whole lemon, also ¼ lb. good fresh butter, and the yolks of 6 eggs well beaten; line a pudding dish, or patty-pans, with a good puff paste; pour the pudding in, and bake half an hour, or less, as required. A little brandy, or orange-flower water, may be used. — You may mix 2 oz. of Naples biscuit, with the pulp of gooseberries. *Another.* — Prepare the apples as in the last receipt: butter a dish and strew a very thick coating of crumbs of bread, put in the apples and cover with more crumbs; bake in a moderate oven half an hour, then turn it carefully out, and strew bits of lemon peel and finely sifted sugar over. — Rice may be used instead of crumbs of bread, first boiled till quite tender in milk, then sweetened, and flavoured with nutmeg and pounded cinnamon; stir a large piece of butter into it.

Quince Pudding.

Scald 1 lb. fruit till tender, pare them, and scrape off all the pulp. Strew over it pounded ginger and cinnamon, with sugar enough to sweeten it. To a pint of cream, put the yolks of 3 eggs, and stir enough pulp to make it as thick as you like. Pour it into a dish lined with puff paste, and bake it. Any stone fruit may be coddled, then baked in the same way.

Swiss Apple Pudding.

Break some rusks in bits, and soak them in boiling milk. Put a layer of sliced apples and sugar in a pudding dish, then a layer of rusks, and so on; finish with rusks, pour thin melted butter over, and bake it.

Peach, Apricot, and Nectarine Pudding.

Pour a pint of boiling, thin cream, over a breakfast-cupful of bread-crumbs, and cover with a plate. When cold, beat them up with the yolks of 5 eggs, sugar to taste, and a glass of white wine. Scald 12 large peaches, peel them, take out the kernels, pound these with the fruit, in a mortar, and mix with the other ingredients; put all into a dish with a paste border, and bake it. *Another Apricot Pudding.* — Coddle 6 large apricots till quite tender, cut them in quarters, sweeten to your taste, and when cold, add 6 yolks of eggs and 2 whites, well beaten, also a little cream. Put this in a dish lined with puff paste, and bake it half an hour in a slow oven: strew powdered sugar over, and send it to table.

For this and all delicate puddings requiring little baking, rather shallow dishes are best; and if the pudding is not to be *turned out*, a pretty paste border only is required; this formed of leaves neatly cut, and laid round the dish, their edges just laying over each other.

A Charlotte.

Cut slices of bread, an inch thick, butter them on both sides, and cut them into dice or long slips, and make them fit the bottom, and round the sides of a small buttered dish or baking tin, and fill up with apples which have been stewed, sweetened, and seasoned to taste; have some slices of bread soaked in warm milk and butter, cover these over the top, put a plate or dish on the top, and a weight on that, to keep it down, and bake in a quick oven: when done, turn it out of the dish.—This is very nice, made of layers of different sorts of marmalade or preserved fruit, and slices of stale sponge cake between each layer. *Another of Currants.*—Stew ripe currants with sugar enough to sweeten them: have ready a basin or mould buttered and lined with thin slices of bread and butter, pour in the stewed fruit hot, just off the fire, cover with more slices of bread and butter, turn a plate over, and a weight on that: let it stand till the next day, then turn it out, and pour cream or a thin custard round it, in the dish.

Bakewell Pudding.

Line a dish with puff paste, spread over a variety of preserves, and pour over them the following mixture:—½ lb. clarified butter, ½ lb. lump sugar, 8 yolks, and 2 whites of eggs, and any thing you choose to flavour with; bake it in a moderate oven. When cold you may put stripes of candied lemon over the top, and a few blanched almonds. To be eaten cold.—This without any preserves is called *Amber Pudding*.

Citron Pudding.

Mix ½ pint of good cream by degrees, with 1 table-spoonful of fine flour, 2 oz. of lump sugar, a little nutmeg and the yolks of 2 eggs; pour it into a dish or little cups, stick in 2 oz. of citron cut very fine, and bake in a moderate oven.

Maccaroon Pudding.

Pour a pint of boiling cream or new milk, flavoured with cinnamon and lemon peel, over ¼ lb. maccaroon and ¼ lb. almond cakes; when cold break them small, add the yolks of 6 and the whites of 4 eggs, 2 table-spoonsful of orange marmalade, 2 oz. fresh butter, 2 oz. sifted sugar, a glass of sherry, and one of brandy mixed: mix well, put it into cups, and bake fifteen minutes.

New College Pudding.

(The Original Receipt.)

Grate a stale penny loaf, shred fine ½ lb. suet, beat 4 eggs, and mix all well together, with 4 oz. of sifted sugar, a little nutmeg, a wine-glassful of brandy, a little candied orange and lemon peel, and a little rose or orange flower water. Fry these in good butter, and pour melted butter with a glass of white wine over them in the dish. The several ingredients may be prepared apart, but must not be mixed till you are ready to fry them.—*Another*: to 4 oz. of grated bread add 4 oz. suet shred fine, 4 oz. currants, 2 eggs, 3 table-spoonsful of brandy, with sugar, lemon peel, and nutmeg to your taste; mix well together, make into 4 little puddings, and boil them an hour.

Paradise Pudding.

Pare and chop 6 apples very fine, mix them with 6 oz. bread-crumbs, 6 oz. powdered sugar, 6 oz. currants, 6 eggs, 6 oz. of suet, a little salt, nutmeg, and lemon peel, also a glass of brandy. Boil in a bason one hour and a half.

Yeast or Light Dumplings.

Put 1½ table-spoonful of good yeast into as much lukewarm water as will mix a quartern of fine flour into dough; add a little salt, knead it lightly, cover with a cloth, and let it stand in rather a warm place, not exposed to a current of air, two hours. Make it into 12 dumplings, let them stand half an hour, put them into a large vessel of boiling water, keep the lid on, and they will be done in fifteen or twenty minutes. Serve melted butter.

Hard Dumplings.

Sprinkle a little salt into the flour and mix it up rather stiff with water, make it into dumplings, and boil them with beef or pork. They may be made in cakes as broad as a small plate, about an inch thick; place a skimmer in the pot, lay the cake on it, boil it half an hour; score it deeply, and slip slices of butter in, sprinkle a little salt over, and serve it quite hot. A very little *lard* may be rubbed into the flour.

Pancakes.

The batter requires long beating, but the great art consists in frying them. The lard, butter, or dripping must be fresh and hot, as for fish. Beat 2 eggs and stir them, with a little salt, into 3 table-spoonsful of flour, or allow an egg to each spoonful of flour, add pounded cinnamon, and, by degrees, a pint of new milk, and beat it to a smooth batter. Make a small round frying-pan quite hot, put a piece of butter or lard into it, and, when melted, pour it out and wipe the pan; put a piece more in, and when it has melted and begins to froth, pour in a ladle or tea-cupful of the batter, toss the pan round, run a knife round the edges, and turn the pancake when the top is of a light brown; brown the other side; roll it up, and serve very hot. Currant jelly, or marmalade, may be spread thinly on the pancake before it is rolled up. Cream and more eggs will make it richer; also brandy or lemon juice.

Whole Rice Pancakes.

Boil ½ lb. rice in water till quite tender, strain, and let it cool; then break it very fine, and add ½ lb. clarified butter, ½ pint of scalded cream, or new milk, a little salt, nutmeg, and 5 eggs, well beaten. Mix well, and fry them. Garnish with slices of lemon, or Seville orange.

Ground Rice Pancakes.

Stir, by degrees, into a quart of new milk, 4 table-spoonsful of ground rice, and a little salt; stir it over the fire till it is as thick as pap; stir in ½ lb. butter and grated nutmeg, and let it cool; add 4 table-spoonsful of flour, a little sugar, and 9 eggs; beat well, and fry them.

Fritters.

Make batter the same as pancakes, but stiffer; pour a large spoonful into boiling lard; fry as many at a time as the pan will hold. Sift powdered sugar over, and serve on a hot dish. Fritters are usually made with minced apple or currants, stirred into the batter, or any sweetmeat stiff enough to be cut into little bits, or candied lemon or orange peel.—*Or*: grate the crumb of a stale roll, beat it smooth in a pint of milk over the fire, then let it get cold, and mix it with the yolks of 5 eggs, 3 oz. sifted sugar, and ½ a nutmeg. Fry in boiling lard, and serve hot. Sweet sauce in a tureen. *Curd Fritters*—Rub a quart basin full of dried curd with the yolks of 8 and whites of 4 eggs; 3 oz. sugar, ½ a nutmeg grated, and a dessert-spoonful of flour; beat well, and drop the batter into boiling lard. *Apple Fritters*—Make a stiff common pancake batter. Boil ½ a stick of cinnamon in a breakfast-cupful of water, and let it cool. Peel and core some large apples, cut them in round slices, and steep them half an hour, or more, in the cinnamon water; then dip each piece in the batter, and fry them in lard, or clarified dripping. Drain, dust sugar over each one, and serve hot.—*Or*: to make a pretty dish, drop enough batter into the pan to form a fritter the size of the slices of apple, lay a slice of apple upon that, and drop batter on the top.—*Or*: the apples may be pared, cored, half baked (whole), then dipped in the batter, and fried.

A Rice White Pot.

Boil 1 lb. whole rice quite tender, in 2 quarts of new milk, strain, and beat it in a mortar with ¼ lb. blanched almonds, and a little rose water. Boil 2 quarts of cream with a blade or 2 of mace, let it cool, and stir into it 5 eggs well beaten, sweeten to taste, pour it into the rice, mix well, and bake half an hour. Lay some slices of candied orange and citron on the top before you put it into the oven.—*Or*: to a quart of new milk add the yolks of 4 and the whites of 2 eggs, a table-spoonful of rose water, and 2 oz. sugar; beat well, and pour it into a pie dish, over some thin slices of bread: bake it half an hour.

Pain Perdu.

Boil a pint of cream, or new milk; when cold, stir in 6 eggs and put in a French roll, cut in slices, to soak an hour. Fry the slices in butter, of a light brown, and serve with pudding sauce poured over.

CHAPTER XXI.

Directions for making Bread, Cakes, Biscuits, Rolls and Muffins

Almost every county has its peculiar fashion of making bread: and almost every hand differs in the practice. The receipt here given is the one followed by most persons in Hampshire; and I select it, being the one I am most familiar with, and not because that county is famed for excellence in bread; for much depends upon the goodness of the flour, and some other parts of England excel Hampshire in this respect.

Good bread is so essential, that no pains ought to be spared to procure it. For this purpose the flour ought to be well prepared, and kept in a dry place. Some persons like brown bread, but it is not, in general, so wholesome as that which is all white. Six pounds of rye flour, to a peck of wheaten flour, makes very good bread.

The advantages of making bread *at home*, in preference to buying it at the baker's, are stated in Cobbett's "Cottage Economy"; and I refer my readers to that little work, to convince them that they will benefit greatly by following the advice there given on this subject.

Small beer yeast is the best for making bread, as ale, or strong beer yeast, is generally too bitter.

To take the Bitter from Yeast. — Put the yeast to the water you use to mix the "batter," or as the country people call it, "set the sponge," and stir into it 2 or 3 good handfuls of bran; pour it through a sieve or jelly bag (kept for the purpose), and then mix it into the flour. The bran not only corrects the bitterness of the yeast, but communicates a sweetness to the bread. — *Or*: put into the yeast 2 or 3 pieces of wood coal, stir them about, pour the water in, and then strain it.

Household Bread.

(From Cobbett's Cottage Economy.)

"Supposing the quantity to be a bushel of flour, put it into the trough, and make a deep hole in the middle. Stir into a pint (or if very thick and good, ½ or ¾ pint), of yeast, a pint of soft warm water, and pour it into the hole in the flour. In very cold weather the water should be nearly hot, in very warm weather only lukewarm. Take a spoon and work it round the outside of this body of moisture, so as to bring into that body, by degrees, flour enough to form a *thin batter*, which you must stir about well for a minute or two. Then take a handful of flour and scatter it thinly over the head of this batter, so as to *hide* it. Cover a cloth over the trough to keep the air from the bread, and the thickness of this covering, as well as the situation of the trough as to distance from the fire, must depend on the nature of the place and state of the weather, as to heat and cold. When you perceive that the batter has risen enough to make *cracks* in the flour that you covered it over with, you begin to form the whole mass into *dough*, thus: you begin round the hole containing the batter, working the flour into the batter, and pouring in, as it is wanted, soft water, or half milk and half water, in winter a *little* warm, in summer quite cold; but before you begin this, you scatter the salt over the heap, at the rate of a lb. to a bushel of flour. When you have got the whole *sufficiently moist*, you *knead it well*. This is a grand part of the business; for unless the dough be *well worked*, there will be *little round lumps of flour in the loaves*; besides which, the original batter, which is to give fermentation to the whole, will not be duly mixed. The dough must, therefore, be well worked. The *fists* must go heartily into it. It must be rolled over; pressed out; folded up, and pressed out again, until it be completely mixed, and formed into a *stiff* and *tough dough*."

The loaves are made up according to fancy, both as to size and shape; but the time they require to bake will greatly depend upon the former, for the household loaf of a Hampshire farm-house takes three hours or three hours and a half, while that of a Norfolk farm-house does not, I should imagine, require half the time.

French Bread or Rolls.

Warm 1½ pint of milk, add ½ pint yeast; mix them with fine flour to a thick batter, put it near the fire to rise, keeping it covered. When it has risen as high as it will, add ¼ pint of warm water, ½ oz. salt, 2 oz. butter; rub the butter first with a little dry flour, mix the dough not quite so stiff as for common bread; let it stand three quarters of an hour to rise, then make it into rolls. Bake in a quick oven.

Rice Bread.

To ¼ lb. wheat flour, allow 1 lb. rice; the latter first boiled in four times its weight of water, till it becomes a perfect pulp, then mix by degrees, the flour with the rice, and sufficient yeast for the quantity of bread; knead and set it to rise.

It was the fashion in this country to present a variety of cakes, some hot and some cold, on the tea-table; but now, except in some of the northern counties, the good custom is obsolete.

In America, it is the general custom to dine early, to take tea rather late, and no supper; and there the tea table is a matter of as much consideration as the dinner table is in England or France. Every house in America, especially in the country, has one, two, or more cottage ovens of various sizes. I believe that these very useful things are known in some parts of England, but I never saw them except in America. They are particularly adapted to open fire-places, where wood or peat are burnt. They are much the same as the iron pots, which stand on legs, except that the bottom of the oven is flat, not round, and that the lid fits into the top, leaving a space sufficient to hold a layer of hot coals: the oven stands upon legs, at a little distance from the ground, to admit of hot coals being placed under it. A loaf the size of our quartern loaf may be baked in this way, as well as tarts, cakes, custards, apples, pears, &c., &c. By means of this little oven, much labour and fuel are saved. Another appendage to an American kitchen, is the *girdle* for baking many sorts of cakes, and crumpets; and on this girdle they cook their far-famed buckwheat cakes. It is a round iron plate with a handle over it, which is hung upon the crane upon which iron pots are hung, or it will stand upon a trivet, and then the crumpets are cooked in the same way as pancakes; and are much better thus, fresh made, than as they are generally eaten.

In the country, where eggs, cream, and flour (the chief ingredients), are always to be obtained in perfection, there is no excuse for an absence of cakes for the tea, or of rolls at the breakfast table. In most houses, there are young ladies who might attend to this department, with very little loss of time, and with much credit to themselves, and I should be glad if I saw reason to hope that those who are now growing up would not despise the practice. The more difficult and intricate articles of ornamental confectionary, may be too troublesome for any but professors of the art; but all *cakes* may be made at home. Nothing worth knowing, is to be learned without trouble; but in the art of making and baking cakes, few failures can arise after any number of trials.

Flour for cakes should be of the best quality, well dried, and sifted. The eggs fresh, beaten separately, and beaten well. Currants well washed, picked, and dried in a cloth, or before the fire. The ingredients thoroughly mixed, and the cake put into the oven *instantly*, unless there be yeast, and then time must be given for it to rise.

Sal Volatile is used, not to make cakes rise, but to prevent their flattening, after they have risen, but though the practice may not be injurious, it had better be avoided. Yeast ought to be sweet, white, and thick; and may be prepared in the manner directed for bread. Pearl-ash is sometimes used to lighten bread and cakes.

An iceing is made as follows: to ½ lb. finely sifted sugar put the whites of 2 eggs, beaten with a little water; beat all well with a whisk till quite smooth, and spread it thickly over the cake, with a spoon; for small cakes, put it on lightly, with a brush.

Ovens vary so much, that experience alone can teach what quantity of fuel, and what portion of time may be required to heat any particular one. When such knowledge is once obtained, it will be a matter of no great difficulty so to manage the oven that it be always of the right temperature; which it must be, or all labour is lost.

Cakes keep moist covered with a cloth, in a pan.

Common Currant Loaf.

Melt ¼ lb. butter in a pint of milk, and mix it with 4 oz. yeast and 2 eggs, then stir it into 2 lbs. flour, beat well with a wooden spoon, and set it before the fire to rise; then add 1 lb. currants, and 2 oz. sifted sugar, and bake it an hour in a moderate oven.

A Rich Plum Cake.

To 1 lb. each, of currants and flour, rubbed together, add 12 oz. fresh butter beaten to a cream. Beat the whites and yolks of 16 eggs, put to them nearly 1 lb. finely powdered sugar, set this mixture over the fire, and whisk it till the eggs are warm; then take it off, beat till cold, and stir in, first, the butter, then the flour and currants; beat well, add ½ oz. bitter almonds, beaten to a paste, 2 oz. sweet almonds, blanched, and cut the long way, ½ oz. pounded cinnamon and mace, and ½ lb. candied peel, either citron, lemon, or orange, or a portion of each; add a little brandy or any highly flavoured liquor. Paper a hoop and pour in the cake. An hour and a half, or two hours will bake it.—*Another*: beat 1 lb. butter to a cream, put to it ¾ lb. sifted sugar, and a little rose or orange flower water, beat it; then add 8 yolks of eggs, the whites of 4, ½ lb. almonds, blanched and beaten, 1½ lb. currants, a little each, of cinnamon, mace, cloves, nutmeg, and ginger, and 1 lb. flour. You may add 2 table-spoonsful of brandy, 1 oz. citron, 1 oz. candied lemon peel, and the same of orange peel. Bake two hours.

A very good Cake.

Beat 2 lbs. fresh butter, with a little rose water, till it is like cream; rub it into 2 lbs. well dried flour; add the peel of a lemon grated, 1 lb. loaf sugar pounded and sifted, 15 eggs (beat the whites by themselves, the yolks with the sugar), a ¼ pint of brandy, the same of Lisbon or Marsala, 2½ lbs. currants, ½ lb. almonds, blanched and cut in slices, beat well together, put it into a buttered tin or dish, bake two hours. Candied lemon or citron may be added.

Pound Cake.

To 1 lb. flour add 1 lb. butter beaten to a cream, and 8 eggs: beat well, add sifted sugar, and grated lemon peel. You may add currants or carraways, to your taste. Beat well, and bake in rather a quick oven, an hour.

Common Cake.

To 2 lbs. flour, add ½ lb. butter, ½ lb. sugar, 4 eggs, 1 lb. currants, 1 oz. candied citron or lemon, 1 oz. carraway seeds, a little nutmeg, and 3 table-spoonsful yeast. Beat well, for half an hour, then put it in the oven *directly*.

A Cake without Butter.

Take the weight of 5 eggs (in their shells), in sifted sugar, and the weight of 3 in flour: beat the eggs, add first, the sugar, then the flour, the rinds of 2 large lemons grated, and a wine-glassful of sherry or brandy. Bake in a tin mould in a quick oven.—*Another*: to a quartern of dough add ½ lb. butter, 4 eggs, ½ lb. currants, and ½ lb. sugar, beat all well together more than half an hour, and bake in a buttered tin.

A Rich Seed Cake.

Mix 1 lb. sifted sugar into 1 lb. flour, and stir in, by degrees, 8 eggs, beaten, whisk well together, and add 3 oz. sweet almonds blanched and cut, some candied citron, lemon, and orange peel, and 12 oz. butter, beaten to a cream; a little pounded cinnamon, mace, and carraway seeds. Pour it into a papered hoop, and strew carraways on the top. — *Or*: put 2 lbs. flour into a deep pan, and mix in ¼ lb. sifted white sugar. Make a hole in the centre, pour in ½ pint of lukewarm milk and 2 table-spoonsful good yeast; stir a little of the flour in, cover a cloth lightly over, and let it stand an hour and a half to rise. Then work it up, with ½ lb. melted butter, a little allspice, ginger, nutmeg, and 1 oz. carraway seeds; adding warm milk sufficient to work it to a proper stiffness. Butter a hoop or dish, and pour in the cake; let it stand in a warm place another half hour to rise, then bake it. You may add 2 table-spoonsful of brandy.

A Rice Cake.

Mix 6 oz. ground rice, 4 oz. sugar, the grated peel of ½ a lemon, the yolks of 5 and whites of 3 eggs, and 1 table-spoonful orange flower water; break the eggs into a deep pan, and put the rice flour to them at once, mix it with a wooden spoon, then add the sugar and the other ingredients; beat well for twenty minutes, and it will be a fine light sponge; then immediately half fill the moulds, put them into a moderate oven, and bake three quarters of an hour, of a light brown colour. *Little Rice Cakes* — 1 lb. ground rice, 1 lb. 2 oz. sugar, ¾ lb. butter, 8 eggs, and flour to make it into a stiff paste. — *Or*: 1 lb. sugar, ½ lb. flour, ½ lb. ground rice, 6 oz. butter, 8 yolks and 2 whites of eggs. Both these require long beating. Roll the paste out, cut it in shapes, and bake on buttered tins. Some persons add a few drops of the essence of lemon, and of almond flavour.

Harvest Cake.

Mix into 3 lbs. flour ¼ oz. of powdered allspice; in another bowl put ¾ lb. sugar, either moist or lump, 2 oz. butter, 2 eggs, 3 table-spoonsful of yeast; beat well, then mix in the flour, with ¾ lb. currants, and warm milk and water, to make up the cake; set it by the fire an hour to rise.

Temperance Cake.

Rub ¼ lb. butter into 1 lb. flour, add ½ lb. moist sugar, ½ lb. currants, and a tea-spoonful of carbonate of soda, dissolved in a ¼ pint of warm milk; mix well, and bake it in a tin.

Sponge Cake.

The weight of 12 eggs in sifted sugar, and the weight of 6 in fine flour; beat the eggs separately, stir the sugar into the yolks, and beat well, then put in the whites and beat again, add a little nutmeg and rose-water, and just before you put the cake into the oven, stir the flour lightly into the eggs and sugar. This cake must be beaten with a whisk. Bake, in rather a quick oven, three quarters, or nearly an hour. — *Or*: beat, separately, the yolks and whites of 5 eggs, put them together, add grated lemon peel, and 5 oz. fine sugar, beat again an hour and a half, then stir in as lightly as possible 4 oz. flour, previously dried before the fire. — *Or*: boil ¾ lb.

lump sugar in ½ pint of water to a syrup; beat 7 eggs well, and pour the syrup, boiling hot, into them, stirring all the time; then beat it three quarters of an hour, and just before it is put in the oven, stir in lightly 10 oz. of fine flour, pour it in a mould, and bake in a slow oven. Lemon peel may be added. Some persons put in a dessert-spoonful of essence of lemon.

Marlborough Cake.

Beat 8 eggs, strain, and put to them 1 lb. finely sifted sugar, and beat the mixture well half an hour; then put in ½ lb. well dried flour, and 2 oz. carraway seeds, beat well five minutes, pour it into shallow tin pins, and bake in a quick oven.

Gingerbread.

Put 1¼ lb. treacle on the fire, and as it gets hot, take off the scum; stir in ¼ lb. of fresh butter, and let it cool; then mix it into a paste with 1½ lb. flour, 4 oz. brown sugar, a little ginger, and allspice; cut it into shapes, and bake on tins. More butter, or a little cream may be added. Candied orange, lemon peel, or carraway seeds, may be added.—*Another*: mix 1 lb. flour, ½ lb. butter (rubbed in), ½ lb. brown sugar, lemon, ginger, and ½ lb. treacle; let it stand all night, and bake it the next day. *Soft Gingerbread*—Six tea-cupfuls of flour, 3 of treacle, 1 of cream, and 1 of butter, 2 eggs, a table-spoonful of pearl-ash, dissolved in cold water, a table-spoonful of ginger, 1 tea-spoonful of pounded cloves, and a few raisins, stoned; mix well, and bake in a rather slow oven. *Gingerbread Nuts*—They may be made the same way as the receipt before the last, adding more spice. Cut in small cakes, or drop them from a spoon, and bake on paper. *Parliament*—Melt ¾ lb. butter with 2 lbs. treacle, and 1 lb. sugar, add ½ oz. ginger, the juice and grated rind of a lemon, and sufficient flour to make it into a paste: roll out thin, cut it into cakes, and bake it.

Parkin.

Mix 4 lbs. of meal with 2 lbs. treacle, 1 lb. sugar, 1 lb. butter, and ½ oz. ginger, with a tumbler full of brandy and rum; add nutmeg and mace if you like, and bake in large cakes.

Volatile Cakes.

Melt ½ lb. butter, and stir in 4 eggs, 1 tea-spoonful of powdered volatile salts, dissolved in a tea-spoonful of milk, ½ lb. flour, ¼ lb. finely powdered loaf sugar, a few currants and carraway seeds. Mix well, and drop the cakes on tins. They will rise very much. Bake in a quick oven.

Ginger or Hunting Cakes.

To 2 lbs. sugar, add 1 lb. butter, 2 oz. ginger, and a nutmeg grated; rub these into 1 lb. flour, and wet it with a pint of warm cream, or as much as is sufficient; roll out in thin cakes, and bake in a slack oven.

Rough Cakes.

Rub 6 oz. butter into 1 lb. flour, ½ lb. sifted sugar, ½ lb. currants, and a little mace or lemon peel, break in 2 eggs, work it all into a rough paste, and drop on tins. You may add 1 oz. almonds.

Ginger Rock Cakes.

Pound 1 lb. of loaf sugar, leaving a part of it as large as hemp seed; beat the whites of 2 eggs to a froth, add a dessert-spoonful of refined ginger (sold by the druggists in bottles), mix well with a tea-spoon, drop it on tins, and bake in a moderate oven, a quarter of an hour.

Plain Biscuits.

To 1 lb. flour, put the yolk of 1 egg, and milk sufficient to mix it to a stiff paste, knead it smooth, then roll out thin, cut it in round shapes, prick with a fork, and bake them in a slow oven.—*Or*: to 1 lb. flour add ¼ lb. butter, beaten to a cream, 5 oz. loaf sugar, 5 eggs, and some carraway seeds: beat well for an hour, and pour the biscuits on tins, each one a large spoonful. If not sufficiently thin and smooth, add another egg, or a little milk.—*Or*: rub 4 oz. fresh butter very smooth into 8 oz. flour, add 3 oz. sifted sugar, and a table-spoonful of carraways: then add the yolks of 4 eggs, and a table-spoonful of cream. Bake in a quick oven.

Indian Corn Biscuits.

To ½ lb. butter, add 6 oz. pounded sugar, and 3 eggs; when well mixed, add ¾ lb. corn flour, a little nutmeg, and carraway seeds, beat well, and bake on little tins.—*Or*: into ¾ lb. flour, rub 4 oz. butter, add 4 oz. sifted sugar, and nearly 1 oz. carraway seeds; make into a paste with 3 eggs, roll out thin, and cut them in any shape you like.

Dr. Oliver's Biscuits.

Put 2 lbs. flour into a shallow pan, mix 1 table-spoonful of yeast with a little warm water, and pour it into a hole in the middle of the flour, work a little of the flour into the yeast, and set the pan before the fire a quarter of an hour. Melt ¼ lb. butter in milk to mix the flour into a stiff paste, and bake on tins.

Lemon Biscuits.

Beat the yolks of 12, and the whites of 6 eggs, with 1 lb. loaf sugar: when the oven is ready, add 2 table-spoonsful rose water, 12 oz. flour, the juice and rind of 2 lemons, grated, a few almonds if you choose. Bake in a quick oven.—*Or*: mix 1 lb. sifted sugar with ¼ lb. butter melted, the rind of a lemon grated, 2 eggs, and a very little flour: roll into little flat cakes, and bake on tins.

Rusks.

Boil a quart of milk, let it cool, then put to it ½ pint of yeast, 2 eggs, 2 oz. coriander seeds, 2 oz. carraway seeds, a little ginger, and ¼ lb. finely pounded sugar, beat these together and add flour to make a stiff paste: divide it into long thin bricks, put these on tins and set them before the fire a short time to rise, then bake them. When cold, cut in slices, and dry them in a slack oven. — *Or*: melt ½ lb. butter in a quart of milk, let it cool, add 1 egg, ½ pint yeast, and 4 oz. sifted sugar, beat this a few minutes, then work in flour to make a light dough, and set it by the fire to rise. Make this into little loaves, bake them on tins, in a quick oven; when half done take them out of the oven, split, and put them back to finish.

Maccaroons, and Ratafia Cakes.

Blanch, and pound, with the whites of 4 eggs, 1 lb. of sweet almonds, 2 lbs. fine sugar, and beat it to a paste; add 8 more whites of eggs and beat well again. Drop it from a knife, on buttered paper, and bake on tins. *Ratafia Cakes.* — The same as maccaroons, only use half bitter and half sweet almonds.

Jumbles.

Rub ½ lb. flour, ½ lb. sifted sugar, with ¼ lb. butter, add a table-spoonful brandy and 2 eggs; keep out part of the flour to roll them out with; twist them up, and bake on tins. If too soft, leave out 1 white of egg.

Small Plum Cakes.

Mix 2 lbs. flour with 1 lb. sugar, rub in 1 lb. butter, 1 lb. currants, add 6 eggs. When well mixed, roll out the paste equally thin and flat; cut it into small round cakes with a wine-glass, and bake them in a moderate oven. — *Or*: do not *cut*, but *pull* it into small cakes.

Small Carraway Cakes.

Mix 1 lb. flour, 14 oz. butter, 5 or 6 table-spoonsful of yeast, 3 yolks of eggs and 1 white, into a paste, with cream. Set it before the fire half an hour, to rise; add a small tea-cupful of sugar and ½ lb. carraway seeds. Roll out into cakes, wash them over with rose water and sugar, and prick the top, with a knife. The oven rather quick.

Shrewsbury Cakes.

Beat ½ lb. butter to a cream, mix it with 6 oz. sifted sugar, 8 oz. flour, pounded cinnamon, carraway seeds, 2 eggs, and a little rose water. Roll out the paste a ¼ inch thick, cut the cakes into shapes, and bake on tins in a slack oven.

Shortbread.

Melt 1 lb. butter and pour it on 2 lbs. flour, ½ a tea-cupful of yeast, and 1 oz. carraway seeds; sweeten to your taste, and knead well. Roll out thin, cut this into 4 pieces, pinch round the edges, prick well with a fork, and bake on tins. — *Or*: rub 1½ lb. butter, melted without water, into the 4th of a peck of flour, add 6 oz. sifted sugar, 2 oz. each of candied orange, citron and blanched almonds, all these cut in rather large pieces; work it together, but not too much, or the cake will not be crisp; roll the paste out, about 1½ inch thick, divide it into cakes, pinch the edges neatly, and mark them on the top with a fork; strew carraways, strips of citron, and little bits of almonds on the top, and bake on buttered papers.

Derby Short Cakes.

Rub 1 lb. butter into 2 lbs. flour, ½ lb. sifted sugar, 1 egg, and milk to make it into a paste. Roll out thin, cut the cakes in slices, and bake on tins, twenty minutes.

Cinnamon Cakes.

Beat 6 eggs, with a coffee-cupful of rose water, add 1 lb. sifted sugar, ¼ oz. pounded cinnamon, and sufficient flour to make it into a paste. Roll out thin, and stamp it into small cakes. Bake on paper.

Rout Cakes.

Beat 1 lb. butter to a cream, and stir in the yolks of 12 eggs, 12 oz. flour, some grated lemon peel, and a few pounded almonds, or some orange flower water. Mix well, and pour it into a mould not more than an inch high, and lined with paper; bake it, and when it has cooled, cut it into shapes, with a sharp knife; moisten the sides of these with sugar, and crisp them before the fire.

Queen Cakes.

1 lb. well dried flour, 1 lb. butter, worked to a cream, 1 lb. sifted sugar, and 8 eggs. Beat the yolks and whites separately, put half the sugar into the butter, and the other half into the eggs, beat them well, then beat all together, except the flour, which must be lightly dredged in as you continue beating the mixture, and shaking in ½ lb. currants.

Buns.

Mix ½ lb. moist sugar with 2 lbs. flour, make a hole in the centre, and stir in ½ pint of lukewarm milk and a *full* table-spoonful of yeast. Cover it for two hours, in a warm place. Melt to an oil, 1 lb. butter, stir it into the mixture in the middle of the pan, and, by degrees, work it into a soft dough, dust it over with flour, cover with a cloth, and let it stand another hour. Make it into buns the size of a large egg, then lay them on a floured paste-board, and put them before the fire to rise to the proper size; bake on tins, in a hot oven; when done, brush them over with milk. — *Cross Buns*: in the same way, adding to the plain buns, about 1 oz. of ground allspice, mace, and cinnamon; when half baked, take them out of the oven, and press the form of a cross on the top; brush them over with milk when done. — *Another for Plain Buns*: melt 6 oz. butter, mix it well with 4 eggs, ½ lb. sifted sugar, 1 lb. flour, and a tea-spoonful of volatile salts dissolved in a tea-spoonful of warm milk; add ¼ lb. currants, with seeds to taste, and bake ten minutes. A tea-spoonful of essence of lemon, and one drop of essence of almond may be added. — *Seed or Plum Buns*: mix into the same quantity of bun dough as the first receipt, 1 oz. carraway seeds, or currants, or Smyrna raisins. Butter small tart pans, mould the dough into buns, put one into each pan, and set them to rise; ice them, with white of egg, dust fine sugar over, and dissolve that by sprinkling water lightly over. Bake them ten minutes, in a quick oven. Mark the edges, and ice the top, or not, as you choose. — *Bath Buns*: rub ½ lb. butter into 1 lb. flour, wet it with 4 eggs, and a wine-glassful of yeast, set it before the fire to rise; add 4 oz. sifted sugar, and a few carraway seeds. Make into buns, brush them over with white of egg, and strew sugar carraways over the top.

Sally Lumm's Tea Cakes.

Warm a pint of new milk, or cream, with 2 oz. butter; then add ¼ lb. flour to make it a stiff dough. Roll to the size you choose, and bake it on a tin. When done, cut it in 3 or more slices, butter, and send it to table directly; if it wait before the fire it will quickly be spoiled. — Some add eggs, a little yeast, and sugar, to make it eat shorter.

Breakfast Cakes.

Rub 3 oz. butter into 1 lb. flour, and a little salt. Mix 1 egg with a table-spoonful of yeast, and a little warm milk, and wet the flour, using as much milk as is required to make a light batter, as for fritters; beat well with the hand, then cover, and let it stand three or four hours, in a warm place, to rise. Add flour to make it into a paste to roll out. Make the cakes the size you choose, let them stand half an hour before the fire, prick them in the middle, with a skewer, and bake in a quick oven. — *Or*: mix 1 pint of cream, 2 eggs, a table-spoonful of yeast, and a little salt, into ½ lb. flour. Cover and let it rise. Bake on tins. — *Or*: melt ¼ lb. butter in new milk enough to wet up 2 lbs. flour, add 4 eggs, 4 table-spoonsful yeast, and wet up the flour; let it stand ten minutes, make it into 6 cakes, prick them with a fork, and let them stand covered near the fire, half an hour; bake in a moderate oven, a quarter of an hour.

Yorkshire Cakes.

Mix 1½ pint of warm milk, with a tea-spoonful of good yeast, into flour to make a thick batter; let it stand, covered, in a warm place, to rise. Rub 6 oz. butter into a little flour, add 3 eggs, mix well, then mix it with the batter, add flour enough to work it into a stiff dough, and let it stand again a quarter of an hour; then knead again, and break it into small cakes, roll round and smooth, then put them on tins, cover lightly, and set them by the fire fifteen minutes, to rise, before you put them into the oven.

Roehampton Rolls.

To 1 lb. of flour, add the whites of 3 eggs, 3 oz. butter, and 1 spoonful of yeast, wet it with milk into a stiff dough; let this rise, before the fire, an hour, make it into rolls, and bake ten minutes. — *Or*: to ½ pint of yeast add 2 eggs, 2 lumps of sugar, a piece of butter the size of an egg, and 2 quarts of milk, beat well, and strain in as much fine flour as it will take up, mix well, and divide it into rolls; set them before the fire, an hour, then bake half an hour.

Muffins.

Mix a pint of scalded milk, with ¼ pint fresh yeast, and flour to make a thick batter. Set it in a warm place to rise. Rub 2 oz. butter in a little flour and add it to the batter, with flour to make it into dough; cover and let it stand again; knead well, and make it into muffins: put them on tins, let them stand a quarter of an hour, then bake them.

Crumpets.

Mix a quart of good milk into flour to make a thick batter, add a little salt, 1 egg, and a table-spoonful of small beer yeast; beat well, cover, and let it stand near the fire half an hour, to rise. Hang the girdle, or put the frying-pan over the fire, and when hot wipe it clean with a wet cloth. Tie a piece of butter in muslin, and rub it over the girdle: then pour on it a tea-cupful of batter, and as it begins to cook, raise the edge all round, with a sharp knife; when one side is done, turn it and bake the other side. When done, put it in a plate before the fire, rub the girdle with the buttered rag, and pour in another cupful of batter, then spread butter over the one in the plate, and so on, till they are all baked. Send a few at a time, quite hot, to table. Crumpets made thus are lighter than in the common way. Rye flour makes excellent cakes this way, and likewise Indian Corn meal. N.B.—Receipts for various ways of cooking *Indian Corn* flour or meal will be found in "Cobbett's Cottage Economy."

Scotch Slim Cakes.

Rub 3 oz. butter into ½ lb. flour, mix it into a light dough with 2 eggs and warm milk. Roll lightly out, and cut them round, the size of a saucer, bake them, as directed, for crumpets. Butter, and serve them quite hot.

CHAPTER XXII.

General Observations on Confectionary, and particular Instructions for making Jellies, Creams

As I should always have recourse to the confectioner for all ornamental dishes, I shall give under this head, only such things as may be prepared at home with comparatively little risk of failure, and consequent waste of materials; observing, at the same time, that the plainest custard requires as much attention as the richest cream, and that all sweet dishes require to be flavoured with judgment. It is impossible to produce delicate creams, jellies, &c., &c., unless the ingredients, particularly cream, milk, and eggs, be perfectly fresh, and unless there be *enough* of them. If served in glasses or dishes, use only eggs; but, if the cream is to be turned out of a shape, isinglass must be used to stiffen it. The quantity greatly depends upon the size of the shape; 1 oz. to a pint is the general allowance, but more is often necessary.—The sugar used in jellies ought to be clarified, for one point of excellence is clearness.—To prevent oiling, put a little rose water into the mortar in which you pound almonds.—Where there is much practice in making sweet dishes, all the vessels should be kept wholly for that purpose. Jelly bags and sieves delicately clean, always dipped into, and wrung out of, hot water, before they are used.

Common Custards.

To ½ pint new milk, put a little piece of lemon peel cut very thin, a little cinnamon, and 8 bitter almonds blanched and pounded. Simmer the milk ten minutes. Then strain, and when cool, put to it a pint of cream, the yolks of 5 eggs, 2 table-spoonsful sifted sugar, and set it in a saucepan over the fire. Stir one way, all the time; take care that it do not burn, and not boil. When thick enough it will be done, and a minute or two too much will cause it to turn. When taken from the fire, add half a glass of brandy, and stir a quarter of an hour before you pour it into cups. In case of no cream, use 3 more eggs.—*Or:* mix a table-spoonful of rice flour in a little cold milk, and add the beaten yolks of 6 eggs. Have ready boiled, a quart of new milk, with a bit of lemon peel, and cinnamon; let it cool, then stir the eggs and some sugar into it: let it thicken over the fire, but not boil, stirring all the time. Take it off the fire, pour it into a jug, and stir till cool. Serve in cups, or a glass dish, and grate nutmeg over. Some persons boil custards in a jug, set into a deep saucepan of water, which is kept boiling.

Rich Custards to Bake, or Boil.

Boil a quart of cream with mace and cinnamon. Take it off the fire, add sugar to taste, and let it stand till no warmer than milk from the cow; then add 10 eggs, well beaten. Strain it, and fill the cups very full. The oven must be as hot as for tarts, and the cups often turned; or finish by boiling them in a jug stood in boiling water, but keep stirring all the while. Brandy is an improvement, in the proportion of a wine-glassful to a quart. Some flavour with ratafia, peach water, or orange flower water. A dessert-spoonful of isinglass will add to the firmness of custards made entirely of milk.

Lemon Custards.

Beat the yolks of 8 eggs till they are as white as milk, add the grated rinds and juice of 2 lemons, sweeten to taste; pour in a pint of boiling water and stir over the fire till it thickens, add a wine-glassful of white wine, and the same of brandy, stir over the fire again for a few minutes, then pour it into cups.

Orange Custards.

Beat the rind of a Seville orange (previously boiled), to a paste, and mix it with a dessert-spoonful of brandy, the juice of a lemon, 5 oz. sugar, and the yolks of 5 eggs; beat it well, a quarter of an hour, and pour in, by degrees, a pint of boiling cream; keep on beating till cold, then pour it into cups, and set them in a deep dish in boiling water, till very thick.

Spanish Custards.

Set 1½ pint of thin cream over the fire, leaving out a tea-cupful; put in 6 or 8 bitter almonds, and ¼ oz. isinglass dissolved in a basin with boiling water enough to cover it; simmer for three-quarters of an hour, or till the isinglass is dissolved; mix smoothly into the cold cream a table-spoonful of ground rice, pour it into the hot cream, stirring all the time, and simmer it gently till it thickens sufficiently. Flavour with 2 table-spoonsful of orange flower, or rose water, or what you like; strain through a coarse hair sieve, and stir till nearly cold, when pour it into cups dipped in cold water. Let these stand in a cool place; when firm, turn them out on a dish, stick them with blanched almonds sliced, and garnish with preserved cucumber, citron, or other preserve; when about to serve, pour a little cold cream into the dish.—*Or*: boil a pint of cream with a stick of cinnamon, let it cool, strain it, add 3 table-spoonsful of rice flour, the whites of 3 eggs well beaten, sugar, and a little rose water; set it over the fire, and simmer till as thick as hasty pudding; wet a mould with rose water, pour the custard in; when cold, turn it out.

Custards with Apples.

Pare, core, and either stew or bake some apples, in an earthen pan, with as little water as possible, and sugar to sweeten. When they are fallen, put them into a pie dish, and let them stand to get cold; pour over an unboiled custard, and set the dish into the oven, or before the fire, until the custard is fixed.

Custard with Rice.

Boil some rice in milk till quite tender, with cinnamon and a very few bitter almonds; when cold, sweeten it, and form a thick high wall round a glass dish, and pour a boiled custard in the centre. Just before it goes to table, strew coloured comfits, in stripes, up the wall.

A Trifle.

Whisk a quart of good cream with 6 oz. powdered sugar, a glass of white wine, the juice and grated peel of 1 lemon, and a little cinnamon. Take off the froth as it rises, and lay it on a sieve, reversed, over a bowl. This should be done early in the morning, or the day before, that the froth may be firm. Place in a deep trifle dish 3 or 4 sponge cakes, some maccaroons, and ratafia cakes, also a few sweet almonds blanched and split, then pour over enough white wine, with a little brandy, to moisten them; when the wine is soaked up, spread over the cakes a layer of raspberry jam, or any good preserve, and pour over that a *rich* and boiled custard. Heap the whip lightly on as high as the dish will allow. The preserve used or left out, according to taste.

Gooseberry or Apple Trifle.

Scald the fruit, and pulp it through a sieve, sweeten it, and put a thick layer in a glass dish. Mix ½ pint of milk, ½ pint of cream, and the yolk of 1 egg, scald it over the fire, stirring all the time, add sugar, and let it become cold, then lay it on the fruit, and on it a whip, as directed in the last receipt.—*Or*: scald, pulp, and sweeten the fruit, then stir it over the fire, into a thin custard: when cooked enough, pour it into a glass dish, to get cold. If apple, grate nutmeg and cinnamon, or lemon peel, over the top, add also lemon juice, and lay a whip on the top.

A Tipsy Cake.

Put a stale sponge cake into a deep china or glass dish, pour round it some raisin wine or Marsala, and brandy to your taste, but enough to saturate the cake: when it is soaked up, strew sifted sugar over, and pour in the dish a rich custard. Ornament the top of the cake by sticking a light flower in the centre, or bits of clear currant jelly; *or*, sweet almonds blanched and split.

Crème Patisserie.

Boil a quart of new milk with cinnamon and lemon peel. Rub a heaped table-spoonful of flour quite smooth with a little cold milk; stir the boiled milk, by degrees, into it; add 5 eggs, and sugar to taste. Stir it over a slow fire till it thickens; pour it into a dish, and stir it slowly a few minutes. Flavour with vanilla, orange-flower water, ratafia, or brandy. This is flavoured with *tea* or *coffee*, in the following manner: put a heaped table-spoonful of green tea into the milk, boil it up, cover the saucepan, simmer it a few minutes, then strain it. This will give a strong flavour of tea. For coffee: make a breakfast-cupful of very strong coffee, and put it into the milk just before it boils: use no other flavouring ingredient, and sweeten the cream sufficiently.—*Or*: boil in a pint of thin cream, the peel of a large lemon grated or pared very thin, sugar to taste, and a very small piece of cinnamon. Work up a table-spoonful of flour with the juice of the lemon; pour the boiling cream to it, by degrees, and stir it over the fire till the flour is cooked; pour it into a dish, and stir slowly till nearly cold; garnish with candied sweetmeats.

Chocolate Cream.

Boil a quart of cream, having first scraped into it 1 oz. scented chocolate; add nearly ¼ lb. lump sugar, and 8 whites of eggs; whisk well, and, as the froth rises, take it off, and put into glasses.

A Plain Cream.

Boil together, or separately, a pint of cream and a pint of new milk, with lemon peel, cinnamon, and sugar to taste; then add 12 sweet and 3 bitter almonds, pounded to a paste, with a little rose water, also a table-spoonful of rice flour rubbed smooth in cold milk; scald it, pour into a jug to cool. Serve in glasses, or a glass dish.

Italian Cream.

Boil 1½ pint of sweet cream with ½ pint of new milk, the rind of a lemon cut thin, and sugar to taste; then let it cool. Beat the yolks of 8 eggs, add them to the cream, set it over the fire, stir till it thickens, and put in about 1 oz. of melted isinglass, to stiffen it. Whisk well, and strain it through a fine sieve into a mould, to turn out. First try a little in a saucer to ascertain if more isinglass be wanted. It may be flavoured with *curaçoa* or *noyeau*.

Ginger Cream.

The same as chocolate cream; using only cream, no milk. Flavour it by boiling in the cream either preserved, or essence of ginger. Serve it in cups.—*Or*: after the cream has thickened over the fire, add isinglass, as directed for Italian cream, and strain it into a mould.

Lemon Cream.

Beat the whites of 9 eggs with one yolk, till as thin as water, but not frothed, add 9 table-spoonsful cold water, and the juice of 2 lemons, with sugar to taste: strain it through a fine sieve, put in a piece of lemon peel, and stir it over the fire, till as thick as cream. Do not let it stay long on the fire, to get too thick.—*Or*: steep the peel of 2 lemons, cut very thin, in a pint of water, all night, then sweeten and boil it; stir in the whites of 6 eggs beaten to a froth, and keep stirring over the fire till thick, then add the yolks. You may add ¼ oz. of isinglass, which makes it more like ice.—*Or*: boil up a pint of thick cream with the beaten yolks of 2 eggs, 4 oz. sugar, and the thin rind of a lemon; stir till nearly cold, and pour it upon the juice of a lemon, in a bowl; stir it till cold.—*White lemon cream* is made by using whites of eggs only.

Orange Cream.

Pare a large orange very thin, put the peel into a bason, and squeeze 4 oranges over it; pour in 1 pint of cream, and set it over the fire; before it quite boils take out the peel, or the cream may be too bitter. Let the cream become cold, then stir in the yolks and whites of 4 eggs, and sugar to taste. Set it over the fire again, and just scald it. Pour into cups.—*Or*: squeeze and strain the juice of 11 oranges, sweeten well with pounded loaf sugar, and stir over a slow fire till the sugar be melted, taking off the scum as it rises; when cold mix it with the beaten yolks of 12 eggs, mixed with a pint of cream, stir it over the fire again to thicken, and serve in a glass dish or cups.—*Or*: boil ¾ oz. of isinglass in ½ pint of water, till half reduced, and when nearly cold stir in the juice of 4 oranges and 1 lemon well sweetened, and a pint of cream previously beaten to a froth, stir it over a slow fire till it begins to thicken, and then pour it into a mould.—N.B. the juice of any fruit may he used in the same way, always adding the juice of a lemon.

Lemon or Orange Cream frothed.

Squeeze the juice of a large lemon, or orange, into a glass or china dish. Sweeten a pint of cream, and let it just boil; pour it out to get cold, put it into a tea-pot, hold it up as high as possible, and pour it upon the juice.

Alamode Cream.

Grate 2 lemons into a bason, squeeze in the juice, add ¼ lb. sifted sugar; melt ½ oz. isinglass in a tea-cupful of hot water, strain it on the lemon, stirring all the time, then pour in a pint of cold cream, but stir all the while, or it may be lumpy. Pour it in a glass dish, and keep it in a cool place. Garnish with almonds and apple paste.

Velvet Cream.

Put into a deep glass or china dish, 3 table-spoonsful of lemon juice, a little grated peel, and preserved apricot cut small, 3 table-spoonsful of white wine or brandy, and powdered sugar. Scald a pint of cream, put in ¼ oz. of melted isinglass, stir it over the fire a few minutes, and continue to stir till no warmer than new milk; then strain, and pour it into the dish. Made the day before it is wanted.

Vanilla Cream.

Boil ½ a stick of vanilla in a tea-cupful of milk till the flavour is as strong as you like, and mix it with a jelly made of calf's feet, or made with 1 oz. of isinglass in a pint of water and a pint of cream, sweeten to taste, stir it till nearly cold, then pour it into a mould which has stood in cold water. The day before it is wanted.

Burnt Cream.

Boil a stick of cinnamon with a large piece of lemon peel, in a pint of cream; when nearly cold, stir in gently the yolks of 6 eggs; sweeten it, take out the spice and peel, strew pounded sugar over, and brown it with a salamander.

Snow Cream.

Pare, core, and stew, 10 or 12 apples and pulp them; beat the pulp nearly cold, stir in enough finely powdered sugar to sweeten, a little lemon peel, and the whites of 12 eggs, already beaten, whisk, till it becomes stiff, and lay it in heaps in a glass dish.

Currant and Raspberry Cream.

Mash the fruit and strain ¼ pint of juice through a fine sieve, add rather more than ½ pint of cream, sugar to taste, and a little brandy; whisk it the same as a trifle.—*Or*: put a very little sifted sugar into 1½ pint of cream, a tea-cupful of raspberry jelly, the grated rind of 1 and the juice of ½ a lemon, whisk well, for half an hour, till it be thick and solid, then pour it into a glass dish or cups.

Strawberry Cream.

The same as the last.—*Or*: sweeten some cream, and make a strong whip. Beat up what remains of the cream with yolk of egg (3 to ½ a pint), and scald it; let it cool, mix the fruit with it, pour it into glasses or a dish, and lay the fruit on the top. The pulp of apples, apricots, and plums may be mixed with cream, in this way.—*Or*: it may be formed in a mould by adding melted isinglass to the cream, just scalding, then straining it: when nearly cold, add the fruit and put it into a shape.

Clouted Cream.

Put 2 blades of mace and a wine-glassful of rose water, into a ¼ pint of new milk, scald and strain it; let it cool, stir in the yolks of 2 eggs, and a quart of cream. Stir it over the fire till scalding hot, and it is done. Excellent with fruit stewed, or with fruit pies.

Creams and jellies are *iced*, by putting the shape (the mixture being *perfectly cold*), in a bucket of ice broken in small bits. Let it stand till you are ready to send it to table, then take it out, wrap a towel, dipped into hot water, round the mould, and turn it out.

Strawberry Ice Cream.

Mash the fruit, strain off the juice, and sweeten it. Mix it, in the proportion of 1 lb. of fruit to a pint of sweet cream, whip it, pour it into glasses, and freeze as directed; or, add melted isinglass, and freeze it in a shape.—*Raspberry Ice Cream*, the same.

Pine Apple Ice Cream.

To 1½ gill of pine apple syrup, add the juice of 1½ lemon, and a pint of cream, sweeten, then stand it in the ice, and let it freeze as thick as butter. If you would have it the shape of a pine, take the shape and fill it; then lay half a sheet of brown paper over the mould before you put it into the ice, and let it remain some time; be careful that no water gets into it.

Coffee Ice.

A refreshing preparation, and suitable to entertainments. Make some strong coffee, sweeten with sugar candy, add what cream you like, pour it into a bowl, place that in an ice pail till the coffee is frozen: serve in glasses.

Paris Curd.

Put a pint of thin cream on the fire, with the whites of 6 eggs and the juice of a lemon; stir till it becomes a curd; hang it all night in a cloth, to drain; add 2 oz. sweet almonds, beaten to a paste, sugar to taste, and a little brandy. Mix well, and put it in shapes.

Blancmange.

Blanch 1 oz. sweet and ½ an oz. of bitter almonds and pound them with a little brandy, put them with ½ an ounce of isinglass into a bowl with ½ a pint of milk and ½ a pint of cream, and 2 oz. of pounded sugar, and let it stand 3 hours; then stir it over the fire till it begins to boil, when take it off and strain it, but keep stirring it till nearly cold, and then pour it into a mould. If you choose, have 12 bitter, no sweet almonds, a wine-glassful of brandy and a table-spoonful ratafia.—When about to turn it out, wrap a towel dipped in hot water round the mould, and draw a silver knife round the edge of the blancmange.

Rice Blancmange.

Boil 4 oz. of whole rice in water till it begins to swell, pour off the water, and put the rice into nearly a quart of new milk, with sugar, a little cinnamon and lemon peel. Boil slowly till the rice is mashed, and smooth. Do not let it burn. Put it into a mould to turn out. This may be in the centre of a dish with custard round it.

Blancmange with Preserves.

Boil 1 pint of cream with cinnamon and lemon peel; sweeten it, add 1 oz. isinglass dissolved in a little water, stir it over the fire till it is on the point of boiling, then pour it into a jug, stirring it occasionally; when milkwarm add a wine-glassful of brandy and a table-spoonful of ratafia. Have ready in a china or glass dish, some East or West India preserves, pour the blancmange on it, and set it by till the next day.

Jaunemange.

Dissolve 2 oz. isinglass in nearly a pint of boiling water; put to it ¾ pint of white wine, the juice of 2 oranges, and 1 lemon, the peel of a lemon shred fine, sugar to taste, a little cinnamon and brandy, and the yolks of 8 eggs. Simmer gently a few minutes, then strain it into moulds.

Rice Flummery.

Boil 5 oz. sifted ground rice in a quart of new milk, with ½ oz. bitter almonds, 2 table-spoonsful rose water, and sugar to sweeten; keep stirring till very thick, then put it into a mould. When cold turn it out, stick blanched almonds in, and pour round it some thick cream sweetened and flavoured with white wine; or no cream, but preserves in lumps.

Dutch Flummery.

Boil the rinds of 2 and juice of 3 lemons in ½ pint of white wine, ½ pint water, ¼ lb. sugar and 1 oz. of isinglass, ten minutes, then strain and mix it gradually with the yolks of 5 eggs, stir it over the fire five minutes, then stir till nearly cold, and pour it into a mould.

Rice Cups.

Sweeten a pint of new milk, with sifted sugar, and boil in it a stick of cinnamon, when it boils stir in 2½ oz. of sifted ground rice; then take it off the fire, and add the beaten whites of 3 eggs, stir again over the fire, for three minutes, and pour into cups, previously dipped in cold water. When cold, turn them out, pour a custard round, and ornament with preserves or stewed pears.

Syllabub.

Pour a bottle of sherry or Port into a china bowl, sweeten, and add plenty of nutmeg and cinnamon. Milk into it nearly double the quantity, and let it froth up high. Serve with sponge cakes. Some add a little brandy.

Solid Syllabub.

Scald a pint of cream, and sweeten it; when cold, add ½ a pint of white wine, the juice of a lemon, the peel grated: more sugar if required. Dissolve 1 oz. isinglass in water, strain, and when cold, stir it into the mixture, and put it into a mould the day before it is wanted.

Whipt Syllabub.

Rub ½ lb. sugar on lemon rind, and put into a deep narrow pan, with ½ pint white wine, the juice of ½ a lemon, the rind of a whole one, and a pint of thick cream; whisk well, always one way and without stopping, till it is all in a good froth; put it in glasses. It will be more firm the next day.—*Or*: to ½ pint of cream, add a pint of milk, ½ pint sack or white wine, sweeten with loaf sugar, and whisk it to a froth; pour a little white wine in the glasses, and the froth on the top.

Calf's Feet Jelly.

The day before you want jelly, boil a cow heel and one foot in 2½ quarts of water, till they are broken, and the water half wasted, strain and put it by till the next day. Then remove all the fat as well as the sediment, put the jelly into a saucepan with sugar, wine, lemon juice, and peel to your taste. Let it simmer, and when the flavour is rich, add the whites of 5 eggs well beaten, also their shells; let it boil gently twenty minutes, but do not stir it; then pour in a tea-cupful of warm water, let it boil gently five minutes longer, take the saucepan off the fire, cover close, and let it stand by the side, half an hour. It ought to be so clear as to require only once running through the jelly bag. Some mutton shanks (10 to 2 calf's feet), make the jelly richer. Raisin wine is generally used, but Marsala is better: it gives a more delicate colour to the jelly.—This is made *Noyeau Jelly* by using noyeau in sufficient quantity to give a strong flavour. Also *Madeira Wine Jelly*. But as the firmness of the jelly may be diminished by the wine, add a little isinglass. Some think that jelly eats best in the rough, not out of a mould.—*Another*: boil 4 feet in 2½ quarts of water, boil twelve hours, or till all their goodness is extracted. The next day remove all fat as well as sediment, put the jelly into a saucepan with 1½ pint of sherry or Marsala, the peel and juice of 7 lemons, and sugar to your taste. Finish in the same way as directed above, and when strained, add a wine-glassful of Champagne brandy. You may add 1 oz. isinglass to make the jelly very stiff, but some object to this, as it makes it tough as well as stiff. Some use a coarse brown bag, in preference to flannel.

Punch Jelly.

Boil 2 oz. isinglass in a pint of water, add the juice of 4 lemons, and the grated rind of one, put to this 6 oz. loaf sugar, previously boiled in a very little water till it is a rich clear syrup, then add 6 table-spoonsful of rum.—*Or*: make a good bowl of punch (*which see*), stronger if you like. To every pint of punch add 1½ oz. isinglass, dissolved in ¼ pint of water; pour this into the punch whilst hot, then fill the moulds, taking care that they are not disturbed until the jelly is completely set.

Savoury Jelly.

Boil 2 lbs. knuckle of veal, 1 lb. lean beef, and 4 mutton shanks, in 2 quarts of water, with salt, pepper, mace, and 1 onion; boil till the liquor is reduced one half, then strain it; when cold, put it into a saucepan with the whites of 3 eggs, stir well, then set it over the fire till it boils, and strain through a jelly bag. A table-spoonful of soy will improve the colour.

Orange and Lemon Jelly.

Grate the rinds of 2 Seville, 2 sweet oranges, and 2 lemons; squeeze the juice of 2 sweet, 6 Seville oranges, and 3 lemons; mix the rinds and juice together; boil slowly 1 lb. lump sugar in a pint of water to thick syrup, turn it into a bowl; when *nearly* cold, add the juice and stir well; boil ¼ lb. of isinglass in a pint of water till dissolved, let it cool, add it to juice, stir till cold, and fill the mould.—*Another, and much better*: rub the rinds of 8 oranges with lump sugar, and boil a quarter of an hour in the stock of calf's feet and ½ oz. isinglass, with sugar to your taste; have the juice of the oranges, the juice of 3 lemons, and the whites of 6 eggs in a bason, pour the stock in, stir well, and boil altogether ten minutes; then pour in a wine-glassful of cold water, let it stand ten minutes, then pour through a jelly bag.—*Lemon Jelly* is made the same way; the rind of 2 and juice of 3 large lemons, the rind and juice of 1 orange.

Colouring for Jelly.

Boil slowly in ½ pint water, for half an hour, 15 grains cochineal in fine powder, ½ drachm of cream of tartar, and a bit of alum the size of a pea; let it stand till the next day, then pour it off.

Arrow-root Jelly.

Put ¼ pint of water into a saucepan, with a wine-glassful of sherry, or a spoonful of brandy, sugar, and grated nutmeg. Boil up once, then mix it, by degrees, with a dessert-spoonful of arrow-root, rubbed smooth, and mixed with 2 spoonsful of cold water. Return it into the saucepan, stir, and boil it three minutes.—*Or*: steep for three hours the rind of a lemon, and 4 bitter almonds, pounded, in 2 table-spoonsful water, strain, and mix the water with 3 table-spoonsful arrow-root, and of lemon juice, 1 of brandy; sweeten, stir over the fire till thick, and put it into glasses.

Hartshorn Jelly.

To 3 quarts of water put 1 lb. hartshorn shavings, and 1 oz. isinglass, boil gently till it becomes a jelly (about four hours); the next day melt it, add the juice of 2 lemons, half the peel, and a pint of sherry, also the whites of 5 eggs beaten to a froth, and sugar to taste; boil for a few minutes, and pass it through a jelly bag till clear.

Apple Jelly.

Pare 12 firm apples, and simmer them in a quart of water till quite cooked, but not broken; strain the liquor, and put to it 2 oz. isinglass, the juice of 2 lemons, the peel of one cut thin, sugar to taste, and a little cochineal, tied in muslin; boil till the isinglass is dissolved and the jelly of a nice colour, strain, and pour it into a mould.

Isinglass Jelly.

Dissolve 1 oz. isinglass in ½ pint of water, and put to it ½ lb. lump sugar, the juice of a large lemon, the peel cut thin, and a pint of sherry; boil five minutes, then strain it into a mould.

Gâteau de Pomme.

Dissolve 1½ oz. isinglass in ½ pint water, and boil it with ½ lb. sugar, the juice and rind of a lemon and 1 lb. of apples, pared and cored; boil it three quarters of an hour, pour it into a mould; when quite cold, turn it into a glass dish, and pour a good custard round.

A Bird's Nest.

Make some clear jelly, of an amber colour, and fill a small round basin half full. Have some bird's eggs blown, fill them with blancmange; when the latter is quite cold, peel off the shells, and it will represent small eggs. Put some moss round a glass dish, turn the jelly out, into the middle, lay some lemon peel, cut in thin strips to represent straws, on the jelly, and the eggs on the top.

Strawberry Jelly.

Boil 2 oz. isinglass in ¼ pint of water till dissolved, skimming it all the time; then strain and let it cool. Mash a quart of fresh fruit in an earthen vessel, with a wooden spoon; add powdered sugar and a very little water. Pass it through a jelly bag, stir the melted isinglass into it, and fill your mould.—*Raspberry* and *red currant* jelly in the same way.

Lemon and Orange Sponge.

Dissolve ½ oz. isinglass in a pint of water, strain it, and the next day put to it the juice of 2 lemons, and the grated peel of 1; then rub some raspberry jam through a hair sieve into the mixture, and whisk it well, till it is like sponge; then put it into an earthen mould in a cool place. Any preserve may be used, or lemon only, or orange; or it may be flavoured with raspberry vinegar.—*Or*: dissolve ¾ oz. isinglass in a little water, add ¾ pint of cream, the same of new milk, and ½ pint of raspberry jelly, and the juice of a lemon: whisk well, one way, till it is thick, and looks like sponge; then pour it into the mould.—*Or*: pour a pint of boiling water on 2 oz. isinglass, when dissolved add the strained juice of 4 Seville and 4 sweet oranges or lemons, sugar to taste; whisk well, half an hour, then pour it into a mould.—*Or*: dissolve 2 oz. isinglass in ½ pint of water, strain and add to it, the juice of 10 sweet oranges, and the grated rind of 2, the juice of 1 lemon, and sugar to taste; when nearly cold whisk it till it looks like sponge, and pour it in a mould. Make it in the evening, to turn out next day. Some use more isinglass.

Rice Soufflè.

Boil 2 table-spoonsful ground rice very slowly, in ½ pint good milk, with a piece of lemon peel, stirring all the time. Let it cool, then stir in the yolks of 4 eggs, and some sugar, stir it over the fire a few minutes, and let it cool again. Then add the whites of 6 eggs, well whipped; put it into a deep and round dish, and bake in a rather slack oven till the *soufflè* rises; send it to table *instantly*, or it will flatten. *Potato Soufflè,*—Half the quantity of potato flour, as directed for rice flour, and make it the same way.

A Good Soufflè.

Soak 4 or 5 slices of sponge cake in sherry and brandy mixed, and sweetened, cover with a layer of preserves, then pour over a rich boiled custard; beat the whites of 4 eggs to a froth, and lay it over the top to look rough; brown it in a Dutch oven, and serve *directly*, or it will be spoiled.

Orange Soufflè.

Mix a table-spoonful of flour with a pint of cream, put it into a saucepan, with 2 table-spoonsful rose water, some orange and lemon peel; stir till it boils, then strain and sweeten it: when cold add 2 table-spoonsful orange marmalade. Beat 6 eggs, stir in a wine-glassful of brandy, mix with the other ingredients, and put all into a buttered shape; place it in a saucepan of boiling water, over a stove: let the water boil an hour and a quarter without any cover to the shape.

Lemon Soufflè.

Pour ¾ pint of boiling water over 1 oz. isinglass, the juice of 3 lemons, and 5 oz. sifted sugar; when dissolved, boil all together five minutes, pour it into a large bason, when the steam is gone off whisk it till it becomes spongy, then put it in a glass dish. It should be made the day before it is wanted, and requires long whisking.

Omelet Soufflè.

Beat the yolks of 6 eggs, and whip the whites; strain and sweeten the yolks with powdered sugar; add a little grated lemon peel; stir in lightly the whites, and pour the whole into a frying-pan, in which you have just melted a large piece of fresh butter. Cook over a slow fire, but do not let it scorch, and, when done, turn it carefully out, and set it in the oven to rise.

Sweet Omelets.

Mix a table-spoonful of fine flour, or potato flour, in ½ pint of new milk; then whisk together the yolks and whites of 4 eggs, and add to the milk. Put fresh butter enough to fry the omelet into a pan, about ¼ lb., make it hot over a clear fire, and pour in half the mixture; when this is a little set, put 4 table-spoonsful of red currant jelly, or any other preserve, or apple pulp in the centre, and the remainder of the mixture on the top; as soon as the upper portion is fixed, send the dish to table.—*Or*: the omelet being fried, spread the preserve on it, in the pan, and roll it. Apples boiled to a pulp and sweetened, may be used instead of preserve.

Soufflè of Apples.

Pick, wash, and scald 4 oz. whole rice, drain off the water, and put the rice into a quart of new milk, or thin cream, which has been boiled with a bit of cinnamon or lemon peel. Simmer it very slowly till the rice is swelled, (not broken), drain it, and having brushed the edge of the dish with white of egg, place the rice in the form of a high wall round it. Mix with some apple jam, or pulped apples, 2 oz. butter, sugar to taste, and the yolks of 6 eggs; stir this over the fire, a few minutes, to cook the eggs; then stir in by degrees, the whites of 8 or 9 eggs, whipped, put it in the centre of the dish, and bake till it rises sufficiently.

Gooseberry and Apple Fool.

Pick or pare the fruit, put it in a jar, with a tea-cupful of cold water, and a little moist sugar; set the jar in a vessel of boiling water, or on a stove, till the fruit will pulp; press it through a cullender, and when nearly cold, mix in it some good cream, or thin custard.

Orange Fool.

To a pint of cream add the juice of 3 Seville oranges, 3 eggs, nutmeg, cinnamon, and sugar to taste. Set this over a slow fire, and stir till as thick as melted butter; it must not boil; pour it into a dish to be eaten cold.

Stewed Oranges.

Pare 4 sweet oranges, and be careful to remove the white part without breaking the skin; pare 2 lemons very thin, cut the peel in narrow lengths, and boil it in ½ pint water, with ¼ lb. lump sugar, until it becomes a thick syrup, then add the oranges, the juice of 1 lemon, and ¼ lb. lump sugar, and simmer it a quarter of an hour.

Red Apples in Jelly.

Pare and core some fine pippins, and throw them into a pan of cold water, then boil them in a very little water, with some cochineal, and when done, put them in a dish; boil the water with sugar, lemon peel, and a little isinglass, till it jellies; let it cool, scoop it into heaps with a tea-spoon, and lay it amongst the apples. Garnish with rings or straws of lemon peel, and some green sprigs.

Pears to Stew.

After peeling them, cut the pears in halves, take out the cores, and lay the pears, flat side upwards, in a tin saucepan, with sugar to taste, ¼ pint of port wine, water to cover them, and a few cloves; spread the peel over the pears, and stew them gently till tender; the saucepan covered.

Apples to Bake.

Pare and core, but do not divide them, unless very large. Bake them in an earthen dish, with sugar, a little port wine, pounded cloves, and grated lemon peel.—*Or*: pare 16 large apples, and put them with 1 lb. sifted sugar, juice of 1 lemon, and a tea-cupful water, in a large flat dish; cut the rind of the lemon in strips, and put them over the apples; bake in rather a quick oven, and baste from time to time with the syrup. *Excellent.*—*Or*: pare fine large apples, scoop out the core, without dividing the fruit, and fill the hole with butter and sugar, bake in a deep dish, and baste frequently. *Also very good.*

Cheesecakes.

Beat the curd of 3 pints of milk quite smooth, mix with it ½ lb. currants, a little pounded cinnamon, and the rind of a lemon, rubbed off with lumps of sugar (add more sugar, as you like), the yolks of 4 eggs, ½ pint scalded cream, and a wine-glassful of brandy. Mix well, and bake in patty-pans, lined with a light puff paste, twenty minutes, in a quick oven.—For *Almond Cheesecakes*, mixed pounded sweet and bitter almonds, instead of currants.

Lemon Cheesecakes.

Boil the peel of one lemon in water, till tender, then pound it in a mortar with ¼ lb. lump sugar, the juice of 2 lemons, and a table-spoonful of brandy; stir in ¼ lb. fresh butter, melted, and 3 eggs; mix well and pour into saucers or patty-pans, lined with a very light paste.—*Or*: to 1 lb. lump sugar (in lumps), add ¼ lb. butter, the yolks of 6 eggs, the whites of 4, the juice of 3 lemons, and the rinds of 2, grated.

Simmer over a slow fire till the sugar is dissolved, begins to thicken, and looks like honey. Stir gently one way, or it will curdle. This will keep a long while, closely tied down in a jar, in a cool place.—*Or*: ½ lb. butter, ½ lb. lump sugar, stir over the fire till melted, let it get cold, then add the yolks of 8 eggs, juice of a large lemon, mix it very well, and bake in a crust to turn out.—*Or*: beat 12 eggs, leaving out 4 whites; melt ½ lb. butter in a tea-cupful of cream, stir in ½ lb. sifted sugar, and when cold, stir in the eggs, then the grated rind of 2 lemons, then the juice: stir it over the fire till near boiling, then fill your patty-pans, and put them in the oven, to brown of a light colour. You may add ½ lb. of sweet almonds, blanched and pounded with rose water.

Another Curd Cheesecake.

Beat the curd of 2 quarts new milk, quite smooth, with 4 oz. butter; then mix it with ½ oz. of sweet, and 4 bitter almonds, blanched and pounded with 3 table-spoonsful rose water, add a ¼ lb. lump sugar, the peel of 3 lemons, the yolks of 6 eggs, candied citron cut small, ¼ lb. currants, ½ pint of cream, and a wine-glassful of brandy. Mix well, and bake in patty-pans, lined with thin paste.

Orange Cheesecakes.

Beat ½ lb. sweet almonds with orange flower water, add ½ lb. sugar, 1 lb. butter, melted, and nearly cold, the beaten yolks of 10 and the whites of 4 eggs, beat 2 candied oranges, the peel of a fresh one (the bitterness boiled out), till they are as tender as marmalade, then beat all well together, and bake in little patty-pans, lined.

Apple Cheesecakes.

½ lb. each, of grated apples, sugar and butter, the juice of 1 lemon, and the rind cut thin, 4 eggs, yolks and whites beaten separately: mix well and bake in lined patty-pans.

Rice Cheesecakes.

Beat the yolks of 6 with the whites of 3 eggs, add 4 oz. sifted ground rice, the same of sugar and melted butter, a wine-glassful brandy, and the grated peel of 1 lemon; mix well and bake in patty-pans, lined with paste.

Lent Potatoes.

Blanch, then pound with a little rose water, 3 oz. of sweet, and 4 or 5 bitter almonds; add 8 oz. butter, 4 eggs beaten and strained, 2 table-spoonsful white wine, and sugar to taste; beat well, grate in 3 savoy biscuits, and make into balls with a very little flour, the size of walnuts; boil in lard of a pale brown, drain and serve with sweet sauce.

Stewed French Plums.

Stew 1½ pound in a pint of Rhenish wine, till tender, then set them by to cool in a glass dish. Some use half Port and half water.

Note.—Those who like to use *Gelatine* will find directions with the packets, when they buy it. It is useful as a means of taking wine and brandy in the form of jelly, and is quickly prepared, but has little else to recommend it.

CHAPTER XXIII.

General and particular Instructions for making Preserves

Fʀᴜɪᴛ for every sort of preserve, ought to be the best of its kind; ripe enough, but not over ripe; gathered *on* a dry day, and *after* a dry day. The sugar of the best quality, and plenty of it, otherwise they are not good, neither will they keep; and much is wasted by boiling up a second time. Long boiling injures the colour of preserves, and they *must* be boiled too long, if there be not sugar enough. The bags and sieves should be kept delicately clean; wring them out of hot water the moment before you use them. Do not squeeze the bag, or press the fruit much, or the jelly will not be clear; this is not wasteful, for the fruit which is left, and a little fresh added to it, will make jam, or black butter; a very useful preserve. In boiling jams, try a little in a saucer; if the juice runs off as it cools, the jam requires longer boiling.

Some persons clarify all the sugar they use, but, for common preserves for private families, good loaf sugar, not clarified, answers the same purpose. After the preserve is poured into the jar, let it stand uncovered two days, then put brandy paper over, and cover with bladders, or paper, tied down close. Keep in a dry place, or they will be musty; but very hot, they will dry up, and be spoiled.

To Clarify Sugar.

Break lump sugar in pieces, and to every pound you put into the preserving-pan, add ¼ pint of water, and to every 2 lbs. sugar, the white of 1 egg, beaten; stir over the fire, till the sugar dissolves. When it boils it will throw up scum; take that off, with a slice, and lay it on a sieve, reversed, over a basin, that the syrup may run off. Pour into the pan the same quantity of cold water as you put in at first, and boil it up gently. Take off the scum, and return into the pan all the syrup which drains from it; keep it gently boiling until no scum rises.—*To Candy Sugar,* boil it till the surface is covered with little clusters, in the form of pearls.—*Moist Sugar* is clarified in the same way, but requires longer boiling and scumming; it answers for common jams, for immediate use, but they will not keep so long as when made of lump sugar.

Red Currant Jelly.

Strip the currants and put them into an earthen pan or jar, set that in a vessel of boiling water, and keep it boiling till the fruit is all burst; then pass through a jelly bag, but do not squeeze it. When the juice has all run off, put it into a preserving-pan, and to each pint allow 1¼ lb. of lump sugar; less may do, but the jelly will not be so sure to keep. Boil the jelly, rather quickly, from fifteen to twenty minutes, scumming carefully all the time; try a little in a saucer, to see if it be stiff enough, then fill your pots or glasses; leave them uncovered two days; cover brandy papers over, and tie skins over tight. *White Currant Jelly*—The same; but rather less boiling. The sugar must be very fine, to insure delicate clearness for the jelly. *Black Currant Jelly*—The same as red currant jelly. When the juice is put into the preserving-pan, with the sugar, add a very little water. Less sugar *may* do. But boil it well.

Currant Jam.

When jelly is made, if the bag be not squeezed, the fruit in it will have juice enough for jam; or, if not, put a fourth part of fresh fruit to it, then boil it up, with its weight of sugar, fifteen or twenty minutes.

Raspberry Jam.

Take 4 parts of raspberries and 1 part of red currant juice, boil it fifteen or twenty minutes, with an equal weight of sugar. Skim off the dross, as it rises.—*Or*: use raspberries alone, and no juice.—*Or*: some persons recommend the *Antwerp*, they are so juicy as to require boiling by themselves until nearly dry; then add 1 lb. fine lump sugar to 1 quart fruit, then boil again fifteen minutes, and no more, or the colour will be injured.

Strawberry Jam.

Gather fine scarlet strawberries, just ripe, bruise, and put them into a preserving-pan, with about a fifth part of red currant juice; strew over nearly their weight of sifted lump sugar, and boil quickly fifteen minutes.

Gooseberry Jam.

This may be made of gooseberries only, in the same manner as directed for currant jam, or of a mixture of red or black currants and gooseberries.

Green Gooseberry Jam.

First crack them in a mortar, put them into a preserving-pan with ¾ lb. lump sugar, to 1 lb. fruit, and boil till it begins to look clear. A nice preserve for tartlets.

Damson Jam.

Boil 1 lb. sugar to 1 lb. fruit, till the juice adheres to the fruit. For *open tarts*.

Rhubarb Jam.

Boil an equal quantity of rhubarb, cut in pieces, and gooseberries, before they are quite ripe, with ¾ lb. loaf sugar to 1 lb. of fruit. Well boiled, it forms a rich jam, similar to apricot. *Or*: boil 6 lbs. fruit cut in square pieces, 6 lbs. lump sugar, and let it stand a few hours, to draw out the juice, boil the juice three different times, and pour over the rhubarb.

Black Butter.

A very nice preserve to spread on bread, and is a mixture of currants, gooseberries, cherries, raspberries, or strawberries. To every 2 lbs. fruit, put 1 lb. sugar, and boil it till reduced one-fourth.

Fruit for Puddings.

Pare apples, pears, plums, and any fruit you have, and put them in a stone jar with brown sugar, to sweeten. Place the jar in a cool oven till the fruit is cooked.

To preserve Damsons, Bullaces, Morella Cherries, Gooseberries, and Currants, for Winter use.

All these fruits may be put into wide-mouthed bottles, with about 6 oz. Lisbon sugar to each; put corks lightly in, and set them in a vessel of cold water, and then let it boil very gently till the syrup rises over the fruit; when the fruit is cold, make the corks tight, dip them in rosin, and tie bladders over.

To Bottle Green Gooseberries and Currants.

The same as the last receipt, only without sugar. Let them remain in the water till the fruit begins to shrivel; take them out, and when the fruit is cold, cork the bottles tight, and dip them in melted rosin. The rough sort is best.

To Bottle Raspberries.

Mix an equal weight of crushed fruit and powdered loaf sugar, put them into wine-bottles, cork tight, and rosin the corks.

Damsons for Tarts.

Gather damsons quite dry, put them into large stone jars, having pricked them with a pin, tie bladders over, and put the jars into a vessel of cold water; set that over the fire, and let it simmer (not boil) for two hours, or till you see the damsons begin to sink (the water should reach nearly to the top of the jars), then wipe the jars, and put them away in a dry place. — *Or*: choose jars to hold 8 or 9 lbs., of equal size at top and bottom; put in each jar one fourth of the fruit, then a fourth of good moist sugar (allow 3 lbs. sugar to 9 lbs. fruit), then another layer of fruit, and so on, till the jar is full; put it in an oven just hot enough to bake it through. When household bread is drawn the oven is generally hot enough for this purpose, and the jars may remain in all night. When the fruit is cold, put a clean stick, a little forked at one end, into the middle of the jar, leaving the forked end a little above the top; put a piece of white paper over the fruit (which ought to reach the neck of the jar), then run melted mutton suet over it, of an inch thick, and keep the jar in a cool place. When you open it, lift up the covering of suet by the stick.

Apricots for Tarts.

Cut the apricots in two, but do not pare them, take out the stones, and to every pound of fruit put 1 lb. lump sugar, pounded. Let them stand all night, then stew them gently over a slow fire till tender; skim them, as they simmer, till they are quite clear. Put them in pots, and when quite cold, cover with silver papers dipped in brandy, and tie down close.

Apple Marmalade.

Pare and core the apples, leave them in a cool oven all night; the next day boil them up gently with an equal quantity of sugar, a little lemon peel and pounded cinnamon.

Apple Jelly.

Take the blossoms and stalks out of 6 lbs. ripe apples, but do not pare them; put them into a stew-pan with scarcely enough water to cover them, cover close, and stew them to a pulp, pour it into a cloth, and hang that up to drain, but do not squeeze it. To a quart of juice allow 1½ lb. lump sugar, boil gently to the consistency of other jelly, and before it is quite done add the juice of 2 lemons.—*Or*: pare and core your apples as if for pies, put them in the oven till quite soft, then squeeze them through thin muslin: to every pint add 1 lb. of lump sugar, half a wine-glassful of white wine, and a tea-spoonful of brandy, with the rind of a lemon; boil twenty minutes, or till it sets.

Peach, Apricot, or Plum Marmalade.

Skin the fruit, take out the stones, and mash it in a bowl; put an equal weight of fruit and sugar into a preserving-pan, boil it fifteen minutes, taking off all the scum. The kernels may be bruised and added.

Quince Marmalade.

Cut the fruit in quarters, and to 5 lbs. weight, and 3 lbs. sugar, add a pint of water; cover a piece of white paper over to keep in the steam, and simmer gently three hours; then beat them up to a jam, add ½ lb. more sugar, and simmer the jam another half hour.—*Or*: take the parings and cores of 2 lbs. quinces, cover them with water, and let it boil well; add 2 lbs. sugar, and when that is dissolved in the liquor, set it over a slow fire, and let it boil till it becomes a thick syrup; but the scum must be taken off as it rises. Let it get cold, then put in the quinces, with a little cochineal, and set it over a slow fire; stir and beat with a pewter spoon till it is done.

Quince Jelly.

Weigh them and measure 1 pint of water to 1 lb. fruit; pare the quinces as quickly as possible, as they are done, throw them into the water, then simmer gently until they are a little broken, but not long enough to redden the liquid, which should be very pale. Turn the whole into a jelly bag, and let it drain without pressure. Weigh the juice and boil it quickly 20 minutes, take it from the fire and stir in till dissolved, ¾ lb. lump sugar to each pound of juice, or rather more, if the fruit be very acid; then boil gently from ten to twenty minutes, or until it jellies strongly in falling from the skimmer, but stir it all the while, and take off all the scum as it rises. Pour it into glasses or moulds: it ought to be firm enough to turn out of the latter, and be rich and transparent.

Damson and Bullace Cheese.

Put the fruit into a stone jar, cover it, and set it on a hot hearth, or in an oven, and let it coddle for about six hours, stirring it now and then. Pulp the damsons through a sieve, add ½ lb. lump sugar to every 2 lbs. of fruit, and some of the kernels, blanched, and beaten in a mortar. Put it all in a stew-pan, and boil very gently for two or three hours (it can hardly boil too long, as boiling makes it firm), skimming carefully all the time. Some persons boil it only one hour; it is clearer, but less firm. Some add a very few bitter almonds, blanched and cut small.

Apricot Cheese.

Pare, then boil them with their weight of sugar, previously melted with a very little water; as the fruit breaks, take out the stones, blanch and pound the kernels, and put them to the fruit. Let the apricots boil, not more than half an hour. Pour the cheese into shapes.

Orange Cheese.

Scrape off the outward rind of Seville oranges, take out the pulp and skin, boil the peel tender, in water, beat it in a marble mortar to a pulp, add its weight of loaf sugar (already dissolved in the juice), and boil it quickly an hour; when done pour it into moulds, or on plates, to cut in shapes. Keep it in a dry place.

Pine Apple to Preserve.

Pare off the rind, and divide the pine apple into rather thick slices; boil the rind in ½ pint water, with 1 lb. loaf sugar in powder, and the juice of a lemon, twenty minutes. Strain this liquor, and boil the slices in it for half an hour; next day pour off the syrup, and boil it, taking care to scum as it rises, and pour it hot over the fruit; tie down the jar with a bladder, brandied paper being over the preserve.

Cucumbers to Preserve.

Choose the greenest and most free from seeds, some small, to preserve whole, others large, to cut in long slices. Put them in strong salt and water, cover with vine leaves, and set them in a warm place till yellow; then wash, and set them over the fire, in fresh water, with a little salt and fresh vine leaves; cover the pan close, but take care the fruit does not boil. If they are not of a fine green, change the water, and that will help to green them; cover as before, and make them hot. When of a good colour, take them off the fire and let them get cold; then cut the large ones into quarters, take out the seeds and soft parts, put them into cold water, for two days, but change the water twice every day to take out the salt. Boil 1 lb. loaf sugar, and ½ pint of water, scum well, add the rind of a lemon, and 4 oz. scraped ginger. When the syrup is very thick, take it off the fire, and when cold, wipe the cucumbers dry, and put them in. The syrup should be boiled once in two or three days, for a fortnight, and you may add more to it if necessary. When you pour the syrup upon the cucumbers, be sure that it is cold. Cover close and keep in a dry place.

Strawberries to Preserve whole.

Choose fine scarlets, not over ripe; have their weight in sifted sugar, and sprinkle *half* over the fruit, and let it stand all night. Next day simmer it gently with the rest of the sugar, and 1 pint of currant juice, to 1 lb. of fruit, till it jellies.

Raspberries whole.

Gather them on a dry day, after a dry night. To 1 lb. fruit, ¾ lb. sugar; put these in alternate layers in a preserving-pan, and keep shaking till it boils, then boil ten minutes, taking off all the scum. When cold, cover with brandy papers and bladders.

Strawberries in Wine.

Fill a wide mouthed bottle three parts full of strawberries gathered quite dry, strewing amongst them 4 table-spoonsful of finely pounded sugar; fill up with fine old sherry, and cork it close.

Red Gooseberries whole.

They must be just ripe, but no more. Clip off the top of each berry, make a little slit in the side, with a needle, that the sugar may penetrate, and take an equal weight of fruit and of sugar: boil them together, very gently, scum well, and when the skins begin to look transparent, take out the fruit, with a skimmer, and put it into jars or glasses; boil the syrup till it jellies, then strain, and pour it over the fruit.

Morella Cherries.

Cut off the stalks, and prick the fruit with a needle, boil a fourth more than its weight of sugar, about five minutes, with ¼ pint of red or white currant jelly; then put in the cherries, and simmer gently till they look bright. Some take out the stones.

Cherries en Chemise.

Cut off half the stalk of large ripe cherries; roll them, one by one, in beaten white of egg, and then lightly in sifted sugar. Spread a sheet of thin white paper on a sieve reversed, and place that on a stove, spread the fruit on the paper, and send them from the stove to table. Bunches of currants, or strawberries, in the same way.

Cherries in Syrup.

Take out the stones, put the fruit into a preserving-pan, with 2 lbs. lump sugar to 6 lbs. fruit, let it come slowly to a boil, set it by till next day, boil up again, repeat this the third day, when they will begin to look bright and plump; then pot them in the syrup.

To dry Apricots.

Pare thin, then cut in half, 4 lbs. of apricots, weighed after they are pared, and add 3 lbs. sifted sugar. When the sugar is nearly all melted, put it into a pan, and simmer it very gently over a slow fire; as each piece becomes tender lift it out into a china bowl, and when all are done, let the syrup cool a little, then pour it over the fruit. In two days pour out the syrup, leaving only a little in each half. Keep the apricots in a sunny place, and turn them every day, till quite dry. Keep in boxes, between layers of paper.

Dried Cherries.

To every 6 lbs. cherries, stoned, allow 1 lb. lump sugar. Scald the fruit in a pre-serving-pan, with very little water, then take it out, dry it: put it into the pan, with the sugar powdered, and put it over the fire to get scalding hot, then set it aside to get cold, put it on the fire again, and repeat this a third time, then drain them from the syrup, and lay them singly to dry on dishes, in the sun, or on a stove. Keep in boxes, between layers of white paper.

Orange Chips.

Cut oranges in halves, squeeze the juice through a sieve; cut the peel off very thin, and steep it a night in water, and the next day boil it till tender in the same water. Then cut the peel in strips and put them with the juice, in an earthen pan, with an equal weight of lump sugar, set it high over a moderate fire or stove, till the chips candy, stirring frequently; then spread them out in a cool room for a fortnight, to dry.

Orange Marmalade.

Get the clearest Seville oranges you can; cut them in 2, scoop out all the pulp and juice into a basin, and pick out the seeds and skins. Boil the rinds in spring water, changing that two or three times, to take off their bitterness: if for smooth marmalade, heat the rinds in a marble mortar, if for thick marmalade cut the rinds in thin pieces, add it to the juice and pulp, put it all into a preserving-pan, with double the weight of lump sugar, boil it over a fire, rather more than half an hour. Put it into pots, cover with brandy papers, and tie down close.—*Or*: put 6 Seville oranges into a scale, and weigh their weight, and half their weight again, of lump sugar: to every lb. of fruit measure a wine-pint of cold spring water. Cut the fruit in quarters, remove the pips, and throw them into the water; then cut the oranges in slices on plates, so as not to lose any part of the juice or pulp, then take the pips out of the water, put all the fruit, juice, and sugar in, and boil it gently an hour, or until it is sufficiently consistent. Put by in pots. Both these are good receipts.

Oranges to Preserve.

Cut a hole at the stalk end, and scoop out the pulp, tie each one in muslin, and lay them in cold spring water, to cover them, for two days, changing the water twice a day; then boil them in the last water, till tender. Take the oranges out of the liquor and allow 2 lbs. of the best lump sugar, and 1 pint of water, to every lb. of fruit, and put it into the liquor; boil and scum till it is a clear syrup, let it cool, then put in the oranges, and boil them gently half an hour. Boil the syrup every day, for a week, or till it looks clear.—*Or*: grate the oranges, put them in water, change it twice a day, then boil gently, till tender, and put them in cold water again, for two or three hours. Cut a small piece off the top, take out the seeds, and to every orange allow ½ lb. of lump sugar, strew it over them in a preserving-pan, without any water, and set that over a gentle fire, turning the oranges occasionally: when clear, lift them out, put them into little pots, boil up the syrup, and pour it hot over the oranges. If the oranges do not look clear, boil them half an hour, for two or three days: then boil the syrup by itself, or make a fresh one thus: pare and core some green apples, and boil them to make the water taste strong; do not stir the apples, only put them down, with the back of a spoon; strain the water till quite clear, and to every pint put 1 lb. double refined sugar, and the juice of a lemon strained, boil it to a strong jelly, drain the oranges out of the syrup, each one in a jar the size of an orange, the hole upwards, and pour the jelly over. Cover with brandy papers, and bladders. Do *lemons* the same way.—*Or*: pare the oranges, tie them separately in cloths, boil them in water till tender, that a straw may pass through them: cut a hole in the stalk end, take out the seeds, but not the pulp. Make a syrup of sweet oranges, lemons, and sugar, and when clear, put in the oranges.

Apricots, Peaches, Magnum Bonum Plums, and Greengages.

Pare and stone the finest fruit, not over ripe, and weigh rather more than their weight of lump sugar. Spread the fruit in a dish, the split part upwards, strew the sugar over, and let them stand all night. Break the stones, blanch the kernels, and simmer the whole gently, till the fruit looks transparent: scum well, lift the fruit out carefully into pots, pour the syrup over, and, when quite cold, cover close.

To Preserve Green Apricots.

Spread vine or apricot leaves at the bottom of the pan, then fruit, then leaves, till the pan be full, but the upper layer thick of leaves, fill up with water, and cover quite close, to keep the steam in. Keep the pan at such a distance from the fire, that in four or five hours, the fruit may be soft, not cracked. Make a thin syrup of sugar and some of the water, and drain the fruit; when both are cold, put the fruit and syrup back into the pan, no leaves, and keep it over the fire till the apricots are green, but they must not boil or crack; repeat this for two or three days: then pour off as much of the syrup as you think necessary, and boil it with more sugar and some sliced ginger to make a rich syrup; when this is cold, drain the apricots, and pour it over them. What there is left of the *thin* syrup will be useful to sweeten fruit tarts.

Orlean Plums.

An equal quantity of sugar and of plums. The fruit gathered before it is quite ripe. Put it into a pan with cold water, simmer it till the skins appear to crack, so that you may peel them off. Have ready, a thin clear syrup made of 1 lb. sugar, and a gill of water, put in the plums, give them a gentle boil, and put them by in a basin, till the next day; if they then appear done enough, drain them from the syrup, if not, boil again, and remain till the following day; then drain them, add the remainder of the sugar to the syrup, boil it till rich, and quite clear; put the plums into jars, pour the syrup over, leave them open till the next day, then put brandy papers over, and over them run mutton suet.

Jargonelle Pears.

Pare smoothly and thinly, some large, well shaped pears. Simmer in a thin syrup, and let them lie two days. Then pour off the syrup, add more sugar: simmer and scum it; then put the pears in, simmer till they look transparent, lift them out into pots, pour the syrup over, and tie closely. Rather more than the weight of fruit in sugar. A grain of pounded cochineal may be put in the syrup; lemon juice is an improvement.

Quinces.

Pare the quinces very thin, and put them into a stew-pan; cover with their parings, and fill the saucepan with hard water, set it over a slow fire, and keep the lid close that the steam may not escape; when the fruit is tender take it out, and put to it 1 quart of water, 2½ lbs. lump sugar, to make a clear syrup: put in the quinces, boil them ten or twelve minutes, and set them by, for four or five hours; then boil again five or six minutes, take them off the fire, and set them by two days: boil again, ten minutes, with the juice of 2 lemons. Let the quinces be quite cold, put them into broad pans, singly, and pour the syrup over. Cover with brandy papers, and skins over the whole.—*Or*: cut them in quarters, and to 5 lbs. fruit, put 3 lbs. sugar, and ½ pint water; lay a piece of white paper over, to keep in the steam, and let them simmer gently, three hours.

Fruit *pastes* are made by boiling the fruit with clarified sugar to a thick marmalade; moulded into thin cakes, and dried in a stove.

To Candy Fruit.

Put fruit, finished in syrup, in a layer, in a new sieve, and dip it quickly into hot water; spread it on a napkin before the fire to drain, and do more in the sieve; sift double refined sugar over the fruit, till white all over. Spread it on the shallow ends of sieves to dry in a *warm* oven, turning it two or three times. Do not let it get cold before it is dry. Watch it carefully.

Almacks.

1 lb. each of baking pears, apples, apricots, and plums; slice the two first, and open the others, put them, in alternate layers, in an earthen jar, in a slow oven. When the fruit is soft, squeeze it through a cullender, put to it 1 lb. lump sugar, and simmer gently, stirring all the while, till it leaves the pan clear, then put it in small moulds, or drop it in little cakes; when cold, put them by.

Peaches, Apricots, and Plums in Brandy.

Gather peaches before they are quite ripe, prick them with a needle, and rub off the down with a piece of flannel. Pass a quill carefully round the stone to loosen it. Put them into a large preserving-pan, with cold water, rather more than enough to cover them, and let it gradually become scalding hot. If the water does more than simmer very gently, or the fire be fierce, the fruit may crack. When tender, lift them carefully out, and fold them in flannel, or a soft table cloth, in several folds. Have ready a quart, or more, as the peaches require, of the best brandy, and dissolve in it 10 oz. of powdered sugar. When cool, put them into a glass jar, and pour the brandy and sugar over. Cover with leather, or a bladder.

Cherries in Brandy.

Gather morella cherries on a dry day, when quite ripe; cut off *half* the stalk, and put them into wide mouthed bottles, strewing layers of finely pounded sugar between. Allow to each bottle half the weight of the fruit in sugar. When the fruit reaches the neck of the bottle, fill up with brandy; cork and rosin it tight.

Grapes in Brandy.

Put some close bunches, of any sort, into a jar (having pricked each grape), strew a good quantity of pounded sugar candy over them, and fill up the jar with brandy. Tie a bladder over, and keep in a cool place.

Barberries for Tartlets.

Pick barberries without stones, from their stalks, and put them into a stone jar, in a kettle of water, or on a hot hearth, and simmer very slowly till the fruit is soft: then put it into a pan with ¾ lb. lump sugar to 1 lb. barberries, and boil slowly for fifteen minutes. Use no metal but silver.

Barberries in Bunches.

Tie the stalks of the fruit on little flat pieces of wood, 3 inches long, a ¼ inch wide. Simmer these in syrup two successive days, and when cold, cover them with the syrup. On the third day candy them. (See to candy fruit.)

CHAPTER XXIV.

Instructions for making Pickles

The great art of pickling consists in using good vinegar, and in selecting the various articles, at the proper seasons.—Pickles are indigestible, but their liquor is good to give relish to cold meat, therefore the strongest vinegar should be used, because a less quantity will suffice. They should be kept in a dry place, and glass jars are best, because then it is easy to perceive whether the vinegar diminishes, and if it does, more should be boiled with spice, and poured over the pickles. Fill the jars 3 parts full with the pickles, but always let there be 3 inches above their surface of vinegar. If earthenware jars are used, let them be unglazed; and vinegar should always be boiled in unglazed earthenware; indeed, it ought never to *boil* at all, but be just scalding hot, for boiling causes much of the strength to evaporate. Keep the bottles closely stopped, with bungs, and a bladder, wetted in the pickle. When you have opened a bottle, cork it again, put a fresh bladder over, if you wish the pickles to keep. When the pickles are all used, the vinegar should be boiled up with a little more spice, and bottled when cold. The colour of pickles is a matter of no small difficulty, though of the greatest consequence, when used by way of ornament. A fine colour is sometimes preserved by keeping pickles a long time in scalding hot vinegar, the vessel being covered. When a bottle of capers or pickles is opened, it should be kept filled, by fresh boiled vinegar.

Artichokes are in season in July and August.

Cauliflowers, in July and August.

Capsicum pods, end of July and beginning of August.

Cucumbers, the end of July to the end of August.

French beans, July.

Mushrooms, September.

Nasturtium pods, middle of July.

Onions from the middle to the end of July.

Radish pods, July.

Red cabbage, August.

Samphire, August.

Tomatas, the end of July to the end of August.

Walnuts.

Make a strong brine of salt and water, about ¼ lb. salt to a quart of water, and steep the walnuts in it a week, previously pricking them with a large needle; then put them, with the brine, into a stew-pan, gently simmer them, pour off the liquor, lay the walnuts on a sieve to drain in the air two days, to turn them black. Have ready made a pickle of strong vinegar; add to each quart 1 oz. ginger, 1 oz. strong pepper, 1 oz. eschalots, 1 oz. salt, ½ oz. allspice, and ½ a drachm of cayenne (some persons add garlic, brown mustard-seed, bay leaves, cloves, mace, chopped chilies, and horse-radish); put all into a stone jar, tie over a bladder wetted with vinegar, and over that a leather; keep it close by the side of the fire two days and nights; shake it frequently. Put the walnuts into jars, and pour the pickle hot over them; when cold, put in bungs, and tie wetted bladder over.

Walnuts, Green.

The best time is while the shells are still tender, and before they are quite ripe. Lay them in a strong brine of salt and water for ten days, changing the brine twice during that time; put in a thin board to float over, that the air may not get to them and turn them black; then pour the brine from the walnuts, and run a large needle several times through each one; lay some vine leaves at the bottom of an earthen pan, put in the walnuts, and cover with more leaves, fill up the vessel with water, and put it on the fire till scalding hot; then pour off the water, put fresh in, let that become hot, pour it off, and repeat this once again; scrape off the husks, rub the walnuts smooth with flannel, and throw them into a vessel of hot water. Boil, three minutes, a quart of vinegar for every 50 walnuts, with white pepper, salt, ginger, cloves, and cayenne (in the proportion of the last receipt), and after rubbing the walnuts, dry them out of the water, and pour the vinegar over them.

Gherkins.

The best are about 4 inches long, and 1 inch in diameter. Put them into un-glazed jars, or open pans, and pour salt and water over (¼ lb. salt to a quart of water), cover, and set them by the side, when not convenient for them to stand before the fire; in two or three days they will be yellow; pour off the water, and cover them with scalding hot vinegar: set them again before the fire, and keep them of an equal heat, if possible, for ten days, and they will become green; then pour off the vinegar, and have ready to pour over the gherkins (in jars), the same pickle as that for walnuts, leaving out the eschalots if you choose. The vinegar poured from the gherkins should be bottled, for it will be good cucumber vinegar.

Onions.

Take off the tops and coats of small round silver button onions, the size of a nutmeg, and put them into a stew-pan three parts full of boiling water; put no more at once than just enough to cover the top of the water. As soon as the onions look transparent, take them up in a sieve, lay them on a folded cloth, whilst you scald the remainder. Make them quite dry with these cloths, then fill the jars three parts full, and pour over them the following pickle, quite hot: to a quart of strong vinegar put 1 oz. allspice, 1 oz. ginger, 1 oz. mace, 1 oz. scraped horse-radish, 1 oz.

black pepper, and 1 oz. salt; infuse it by the fire three or four days; when the pickle and the onions are cold, bung the jars, and cover them, first with bladder wetted in vinegar, then with leather.—*Or*: put the onions into salt and water, change that every day for three days, then put them in a stew-pan with cold milk and water, let that stand over a fire till *near* to a boil, take out the onions, dry, and put them into jars, and pour a pickle over of good vinegar, salt, mace, and pepper, boiled and become cold.

Cucumbers and Onions.

Boil in 3 pints of vinegar ¼ lb. flour of mustard, mixed as for table use; let it get cold; slice 12 large cucumbers, and ½ gallon large onions; put them into jars with 2 oz. ginger, ½ oz. white pepper, and a small quantity of mace and cloves, and pour the vinegar, cold, over them.

Red Cabbage.

Cut out the stalk, and divide a firm, dark coloured middling sized cabbage, then cut in slices the breadth of straws; sprinkle salt over, and let it lie two days; then drain the slices very dry; fill the jar, 3 parts full, and pour a hot pickle over them, of strong vinegar, heated with black pepper, ginger, and allspice. Cover the jar to keep the steam in, and when the pickle is cold, put in bungs, and tie bladders over.

Melon Mangoes.

Cut a small square piece out of one side, and take out the seeds; fill them with brown mustard seeds, garlic, eschalot, scraped horse-radish, ripe capsicums, and a little finely pounded ginger: stuff the melons as full as the space will allow, replace the square piece, and bind them up tightly with thread. Boil a gallon of white wine vinegar, with ¼ oz. mace, ¼ oz. cloves, ½ oz. ginger, ½ oz. black and long pepper, and ½ oz. cayenne; as it is coming to a boil, pour in a wine-glassful of essence of horse-radish, and of garlic vinegar.

Beet Root.

Boil them very gently from an hour and a half to two hours, or till 3 parts done; take them out of the water to cool; peel and cut them in slices about half an inch thick. Prepare a pickle of good vinegar, and to each quart 1 oz. black pepper, ½ oz. salt, ½ oz. horse-radish, ½ oz. ginger, and a little cayenne; infuse these by the fire three days, and let the pickle be cold before you pour it over the beet-root.

Mushrooms.

Take the red inside out of the large ones, and rub both large and small, with a piece of flannel and salt; put them into a stew-pan, with a little mace and pepper, and strew salt over; keep them over a slow fire, till the liquor which will be drawn, dries up again; shake the stew-pan often; then pour over as much vinegar as will cover them, let it become hot, but not boil, and put all into a jar.—*Or*: boil buttons in milk and water till rather tender, put them into a cullender, and pump cold water on them till they are cold; put them into salt and water, for twenty-four hours, then dry them in a cloth. Make a pickle of distilled vinegar, mace, and ginger, if to be *white*, if not, white wine vinegar. It must be cold before you pour it over the pickle.

India Pickle.

Put into a jar a gallon of white wine vinegar, 1 lb. sliced ginger, ½ oz. turmeric bruised, ½ lb. flour of mustard, ½ lb. salt, 1 oz. long pepper, bruised; peel ½ lb. garlic, lay it on a sieve, sprinkle it with salt, let it stand in the sun, or before the fire, three days to dry, then put it into the vinegar. Place the jar by the side of the fire, cover close, and let it remain three days, shake it every day, and it will be ready to receive the vegetables.—*Or*: boil in a gallon of vinegar, ten minutes, 2 oz. black and white peppercorns, 2 oz. flour of mustard, 2 oz. turmeric, and 2 oz. ginger, 1 oz. of the best cayenne, and a good quantity of young horse-radish: (you may add ½ oz. more turmeric, and 2 oz. white mustard seed), add curry powder and eschalots.—*Or*: to a gallon of the strongest vinegar allow 3 oz. curry powder, the same of flour of mustard, rub these together with ½ pint of olive oil, 3 oz. ginger bruised, 1 oz. turmeric, and ½ lb. of eschalots, and 2 oz. garlic (both these sliced and slightly baked in the Dutch oven), ¼ lb. salt, and 2 drachms cayenne; put it all into a jar, cover with bladder wetted in the vinegar, and keep it by the side of the fire three days, shake it several times during each day, and it will be ready to receive the vegetables. Great care is required, to prepare the vegetables; they should be gathered, as they come in season, on a dry day. Parboil in salt and water strong enough to bear an egg, then drain and spread them in the sun, before the fire, or on a stove, to dry; this will occupy two days; then put them into the pickle. The vegetables are, large cucumbers sliced, gherkins, large onions sliced, small onions, cauliflowers, and brocoli in branches, celery, French beans, nasturtiums, capsicums, white turnip radishes, coddling apples, siberian crabs, green peaches, a large carrot in slices, nicked round the edges, and a white cabbage cut up; neither red cabbage nor walnuts. Small green melons are good; cut a slit to take out the seeds, parboil the melons in salt and water, drain and dry, then fill them with mustard seed, and 2 or 3 cloves, tie round, and put them into the pickle.—Some persons boil it up after the vegetables are in. These receipts are all good.

Lemons.

Cut them across, about half way through, and put 1½ tea-spoonful of salt into each one, let them lie in a deep dish five or six days; to each lemon add 1½ nutmeg, grated, 1 table-spoonful of black mustard seed, and a little mace; boil till tender, in vinegar to cover them, then put them by. Keep the jar filled with vinegar.—*Or*: cut the lemons in 4 parts, but not through, fill with fine salt, put them in layers in a jar, and sprinkle fine salt over each layer. Examine and turn them, every five or six days, and in six weeks they will be ready. If dry, add lemon juice to them.—*Or*: grate the rind of 8 lemons, rub well with salt, and turn them every day for a week: put them into a jar with 2 oz. race ginger, a large stick of horse-radish sliced, 2 tea-spoonsful flour of mustard, 3 of cayenne, 1 oz. turmeric, and vinegar enough to cover them. Put more vinegar if required.

Cauliflower and *brocoli* before they are quite ripe, may be picked in neat branches, and pickled, the same way as *gherkins*; also *French beans*, nasturtiums and radish pods, in the same way.

CHAPTER XXV.

Instructions for making Vinegars

Vinegar is seldom made at home, and as the best is made from wine only, it is scarcely worth the trouble, for, for every purpose, the best vinegar is the cheapest.

Gooseberry Vinegar.

To every quart of bruised ripe gooseberries, put 3 quarts of spring water, stir well, and steep them eight and forty hours; then strain into a barrel, and to every gallon of liquor, put 2 lbs. white pounded sugar, and a toast soaked in yeast. Put it in the sun in summer, and by the fire in winter, for six months, without stopping the bung hole, but keep it always covered with a plate. White currants, stripped, in the same way. — *Or*: boil 1 lb. coarse brown sugar in a gallon of water, a quarter of an hour, scumming well; put it in a pan; when nearly cold put in a thick slice of toasted bread spread with yeast: let it work twenty-four hours, put it in a cask or jar, and place that in the sun, or near the fire. You may add some ripe gooseberries, bruised.

Good Common Vinegar.

To every gallon of water, put 2 lbs. coarse sugar, boil and skim. Put it in a pan or tub, and when sufficiently cold add a slice of toast, spread on both sides with fresh yeast. Let it stand a week, then barrel, and set it in the sun or by the fire, for six months.

Cider Vinegar.

To every gallon of cider, put 1 lb. white sugar, shake well, and let it ferment, four months.

Vinegar of Wine Lees.

Boil the lees half an hour, during which, skim well. Pour it into a cask, with a bunch of chervil. Stop the cask close, and in a month it will be ready.

Cayenne Vinegar.

Put into a quart of the best vinegar, 10 oz. cayenne, 1 oz. salt, 1 oz. cloves, 1 oz. garlic broken, and 2 grains cochineal bruised; shake it every day, for a fortnight.

Chili Vinegar.

Put 100 fresh gathered red chilies into a quart of the best white wine vinegar; infuse them, ten days, shaking the bottle every other day. ½ an ounce of really good cayenne will answer the purpose of the chilies.—A spoonful or two in melted butter, for fish sauce. *Chili Wine.*—The same way as the last, using sherry, or brandy, instead of vinegar. A fine flavouring ingredient.

Eschalot Vinegar or Wine.

Infuse in a pint of vinegar, 1 oz. eschalots, peeled and sliced, a little scraped horse-radish, and 2 tea-spoonsful cayenne: shake the jar or bottle, once a day for three weeks, then strain and bottle the liquor. *Wine.*—Very good for flavouring made dishes: peel, mince and pound in a mortar, 3 oz. eschalots and steep them in a pint of sherry ten days, pour off the liquor and put in 3 oz. fresh eschalots, and let it stand again ten days, then pour off and bottle it.

Tarragon Vinegar.

Pick the leaves on a dry day, about Midsummer, make them perfectly dry before the fire, then put them into a wide-mouthed bottle or jar, and pour in vinegar to cover them; steep them fourteen days, then strain through a flannel jelly bag, into half pint bottles; cork carefully, and keep in a dry place.

Vinegar for Salads.

Take of chives, savory, tarragon, and eschalots, each 3 oz., of balm and mint tops, a handful each. Dry, pound, and put them into a wide mouthed bottle or jar, with a gallon of the best vinegar, and cork close. Set it in the sun, for a fortnight, strain it, squeeze the herbs; let it stand a day, then strain and bottle it.

Garlic Vinegar.

Peel and bruise 2 oz. garlic, infuse it in a quart of vinegar, three weeks. Strain and bottle it. A few drops to a pint of gravy; a very slight flavour is approved of by some, which by others, is considered highly offensive.

Green Mint Vinegar.

Fill a wide mouthed bottle with the green leaves, cover with vinegar and steep them a week; pour off the vinegar, put in fresh leaves, let it stand another week, then bottle it.

Horse-radish Vinegar.

Prepare this about November. Scrape 3 oz., also 2 oz. eschalots, and 1 drachm of cayenne, pour on them a quart of vinegar, and let it stand a week, then strain, and it is ready.

Camp Vinegar.

Put into a pint of the best vinegar, 1 drachm of cayenne, 3 table-spoonsful soy, 4 table-spoonsful walnut catsup, a small clove of garlic, minced fine, and 4 anchovies chopped. Steep a month, shake it every other day, strain it, pour it into pint or ½ pint bottles.

Cucumber Vinegar.

Pare 8 or 10 large cucumbers, cut in thin slices, and put them into a china bowl, with 2 onions sliced, a few eschalots, a little salt, white pepper, and cayenne. Boil a quart of vinegar, let it cool, then pour it into the bowl; cover close, let it stand three days, and bottle it.

Basil Wine.

About the end of August fill a wide mouthed bottle with fresh leaves of basil, cover with sherry and infuse them ten days; strain and put in fresh leaves, infuse another ten days, then pour off, and bottle it. A table-spoonful to a tureen of mock turtle, just before it is served.

Raspberry Vinegar.

This, besides being a nice sauce for batter and other light puddings, is good with water, as a summer drink, also for colds, sore throat or fever. It will not be good unless made with fresh fruit; and the finer the sugar, the clearer the syrup.— To 1 quart of fruit add 1 pint of vinegar (cold); cover close for twenty-four hours; pour off the liquor, and put to it a quart of fresh fruit, cover close and let it again stand for twenty-four hours; repeat this for the third time. Then boil up the vinegar, with a lb. of lump sugar to each pint, until it becomes a syrup.

CHAPTER XXVI.

Instructions for making Essences

Some of the following are useful in culinary, others in medicinal compounds, and some in both.

Essence of Ginger.

Put 3 oz. fresh grated ginger, and 1 oz. thinly cut lemon peel into a quart of brandy, let it stand ten days, and shake it every day.—*Essence of Allspice*—Oil of pimento, 1 drachm, strong spirits of wine, 2 oz., mix them by degrees; a few drops will flavour a pint of gravy or wine.—*Essence of Nutmeg, Clove, or Mace*—Put 1 drachm of either into 2 oz. of the strongest spirit of wine. A few drops will be sufficient.—*Essence of Cinnamon*—2 oz. spirits of wine, and 1 drachm of oil of cinnamon.

Essence of Savoury Spice.

1 oz. black pepper, ½ oz. allspice finely pounded, ¼ oz. grated nutmeg, infused in a pint of brandy ten days.

Essence of Cayenne.

Steep 1 oz. good cayenne in 1 pint of brandy, or spirits of wine, a fortnight, then strain and bottle it, for use.

Essence of Seville Orange and Lemon Peel.

Rub lump sugar on the lemon or orange, till quite saturated with the rind, then scrape the sugar so saturated into the jar you keep it in, rub the rind again, and so on, till you have enough, press the sugar down close, and keep it for use. This imparts a very nice flavour to custards and puddings. Tincture of lemon peel is made by paring the peel, and steeping it in brandy.

CHAPTER XXVII.

Instructions for making Catsups

THESE should be made at home, as well as pickles. A small quantity of catsup every year is sufficient, and very little time and trouble will provide it. It should be put into small bottles (filled to the neck), for when a cork is once drawn, catsups, essences, and pickles begin to decay. The bottles kept lying on their side, because this tends to preserve the cork. Keep them in a dry place.

Mushroom Catsup.

Made in September. The large flaps are best. Break off whatever parts are dirty or decayed, and lay the rest in pieces, in an earthen pan in layers, with salt between; put a folded cloth over, and let it stand a day and night, or longer, by the side of the fire; then strain off the liquor into the saucepan, and to every quart, put ½ oz. black peppercorns, a ¼ oz. allspice, ½ oz. sliced ginger, a few cloves, and 2 or 3 blades of mace. Boil the liquor, fifteen minutes, over a quick fire, though it will be stronger and keep longer, if boiled until the quantity be reduced one half, and then the spices need not be put in until it has been boiling about twenty minutes. When you take it off the fire, let it stand to settle, pour off clear, and bottle it; the sediment may be strained and bottled also, for it answers for fish sauce and brown soup. Anchovies, bay leaves, and cayenne, may be added to the spices. Dip the corks in melted rosin. Some put a table-spoonful of brandy into each pint bottle. A table-spoonful of mushroom catsup is sufficient to flavour ½ pint of sauce.—*Or*: break them in a pan, sprinkle salt between and let them stand till the next day, when, if their liquor be not drawn, add fresh mushrooms and more salt: the next day pour off the liquor, boil it three hours, let it settle, strain and add to every 2 quarts, ½ oz. of cloves, ½ oz, nutmegs, ½ oz. mace, 1 oz. race ginger, 1 oz. jamaica, and 1 oz. black pepper, some eschalots and horse-radish, and 1 pint of Port wine, then boil it again half an hour. This will keep well.

Walnut Catsup.

Gather them green, prick them with a large needle, and let them lie three days, in an earthen pan, sprinkled with a handful of salt, and a very little water. Mash them well each day, with a rolling pin. On the fourth day, pour some scalding hot salt and water over, mash again, and let them stand the whole day; then with a spoon or cup, lift out what liquor there is, pound the walnuts well, and pour a little good vinegar and water over them, which will extract all their juice; pour this off, and put to it what you already have, boil it slowly, and scum well. When there is no longer any scum, put to every quart 1 oz. bruised ginger, 1 oz. allspice, 1 oz. black pepper, a ¼ oz. each of cloves, mace, and nutmeg; simmer it three quarters of an hour, when cold, bottle it.—*Or*: when of a full size, but tender, pound the walnuts, strain out the juice, let it settle and boil it up, taking off the scum as it rises: to each 2 quarts allow 3 lbs. anchovies, and boil gently till they are dissolved, then strain, and boil again with a small quantity of garlic and eschalots, a stick of cinnamon, ½ an oz. each of black pepper, cloves and mace, the rind of 2 lemons, 3 pints of vinegar, 4 wine-glassfuls of port wine, and the same of strong beer; boil it gently three quarters of an hour; scum well. The longer this is kept the better.

Oyster Catsup.

Use fresh Melton oysters. Pound them in a marble mortar, and to a pint of oysters add a pint of sherry. Boil them up, then add 1 oz. salt, 2 drachms of pounded mace, and 1 drachm of cayenne; boil up again, skim, then strain it through a sieve, and when cold, bottle it, and seal down the corks. Brandy will assist to keep it: it is a nice catsup for white sauces.—Cockles and muscles, the same way, but a pounded anchovy or two may be added to give flavour.—*Or*: boil 100 oysters in 3 pints of sherry, with 1 lb. of anchovies, and 1 lemon sliced, for half an hour; then strain it, add a ¼ oz. cloves, ¼ oz. mace, 2 oz. eschalots, and 1 nutmeg sliced, boil it a quarter of an hour: when cold, bottle it, with the spice and eschalots. If the oysters are large they should be cut.

Tomata Catsup.

Take 6 doz. tomatas, 2 doz. eschalots, 1 doz. cloves of garlic, 2 sticks of horse-radish, and 6 bay leaves; slice and put them in 1½ pint of vinegar, with a handful of salt, 2 oz. pepper, 2 oz. allspice, and a little mace. Boil well together, ten minutes, pour it into a pan, let it stand till the next day, add a pint of sherry, give it one boil, take it off the fire, skim it, and after it has stood a few minutes, add a tea-cupful of anchovy sauce, and a tea-spoonful of cayenne. Strain, and when cold, bottle it. The pulp may be rubbed through a sieve for sauce.

Lobster Catsup.

Get a lobster of about 3 lbs. weight, and full of spawn, pick out all the meat, and pound the coral with 6 anchovies in a marble mortar: when completely bruised, add the meat, pound and moisten it with ½ a pint of sherry or Madeira, a tea-spoonful of cayenne, a wine-glassful of chili or eschalot vinegar, and 1½ pint of eschalot wine; mix well, put it into wide-mouthed bottles, on the top put a dessert-spoonful of whole black peppers, to each bottle: cork tightly, rosin them, and tie leather over. Keep in a cool place. 4 or 5 table-spoonsful to a tureen of thick melted butter.

CHAPTER XXVIII.

General Remarks upon the Cellar, followed by Directions for Brewing Beer, and the making of Wines and Cordials

A GOOD cellar, besides its general convenience, in regard to a variety of household purposes, is indispensable to every one who wishes to have good beer. However skilful and successful the brewer, no beer, nor, indeed, any fermented liquors (with few exceptions), can be kept good, any length of time, especially in the summer months, unless they be secured from being turned sour by heat, and by sudden variations of the atmosphere. No cellar can be considered perfect which is not below the surface of the ground. Houses in the country are frequently without the convenience of underground cellaring; but every house ought, where it is practicable, to be built over cellars, which, independently of other advantages, contribute very materially to the dryness and warmth of the building.

The directions for brewing, given by my father, in his *"Cottage Economy,"* are so circumstantial, and so simple, clear, and intelligible, that any person, however inexperienced, who reads them with attention, may, without further instruction, venture to brew without risk of a failure. It is certain that many families, who had previously never thought of brewing their own beer, have been encouraged by the plainness and simplicity of his directions to attempt it, and have never since been without good home-made beer. Brewing is not, perhaps, in strictness, a feminine occupation; there are, nevertheless, many women who are exceedingly skilful in the art. It is obviously not within the province of the mistress of a house, even to superintend the brewing department, but, when circumstances may render it necessary that she should undertake the task, she cannot, when about to give her directions, do better than consult the *"Cottage Economy."*

The utensils necessary are: a copper, a mash-tub and stand, an under-back, to stand under the edge of the mash-tub, when the malt is put in, two buckets, a strainer, a cooler, a tun-tub, and a cask to put the beer in.

Having these utensils, the next thing is, materials for making the beer. These are, soft water, malt, and hops. The water should be *soft*, because hard water does not so well extract the goodness of the malt; but if you have none but hard water, soften it by letting it stand two days in some open vessel in the air. The malt should be (or, at least, usually is) ground or bruised into a very coarse meal. The hops should be fresh, of a bright yellow, and highly scented. Farnham hops are the cleanest and best. I give receipts for finings, but do not recommend them, though they certainly will make beer clear which might not be so without them.

The process is this: if you mean to make about a hogshead of beer, take 120 gallons of water (soft, or softened by exposure to the air), and put it into the copper. When it has boiled, pour it into the malt. This is rather a nice matter; if you put in the malt too soon, it cakes and becomes dough. The old-fashioned rule is, to let the steam keep flying off till you can see your features in the water; but as the weather frequently renders this an uncertain criterion, take your thermometer, and plunge it into the water now and then, and when the quicksilver stands at 170, the heat is about right. Pour the malt in gently, taking care to stir it about as it goes in, so as to separate it, and make every particle come in contact with the water; when it is all in, stir it for twenty minutes or half an hour; then put your stirring-stick across the mash-tub, and cover cloths all over to keep in the heat. Let this, which is called *mashing*, go on for four or five hours. It cannot well be too long about. When the malt has remained soaking all this time, draw off the liquor by means of your buckets, and put it into the copper again. This liquor is called the "*sweet wort.*" Light the fire under the copper, and pour into it, for *every bushel* of malt that you have mashed, ¾ lb. of *hops*, or, if not very good, 1 lb. for every bushel. Stir these well into the wort, and keep it on a good hard boil for an hour, being very particular to make it boil all the while. This being done, you have now to cool the beer: rake the fire out from under the copper, and again take out your liquor in your buckets; put the cooler in some place away from the chances of dirt falling into it, and where it may stand level; then strain the liquor into it. The next operation is, the *working*; and the most difficult part of this is, to ascertain when, precisely, the liquor is cool enough to bear it. Experienced brewers generally ascertain this by the feel of the liquor, by merely putting the finger into it; but it is better to use the thermometer again; plunge it in, and when the quicksilver stands at 70 the heat is right. Then, with your buckets again, put the whole of the liquor out of the cooler into the tun-tub; and take a pint, or thereabouts, of fresh yeast (balm), and mix it in a bowl with some of the liquor; then pour it into the tun-tub with the liquor that is now cool enough to be set to work; mix it up a little by dipping the bowl in once or twice, and pouring it down from a height of two or three feet above the surface of the liquor in the tun-tub; then cover the tun-tub with cloths, as you did the mash-tub. In a few hours it will begin to work; that is, a little froth, like that of bottled porter, will begin to rise upon the surface; when this has risen to its height, and begins to flatten at the top and sink, it should be skimmed off, and is good yeast, and the beer is ready to put into the cask in your cellar. When you put it into the cask, let it stand a day, without being bunged down, because it may work a little there. When you find that it does not, then, if you use finings, put them in, and bung down tightly.

The following receipt is given to me by a gentleman who is celebrated for the excellence of his beer.

Suppose the brewer is about to make a hogshead of beer of good strength. Eight bushels of malt will be sufficient. Let the water, if not *soft*, stand two days in some vessel in the open air, which will soften it. One hundred and twenty gallons will be sufficient; and, if he uses ground malt, let him remember to attend to the heat of the water in the mash-tub before he puts it in, and also to the stirring and separating as it goes in. When it has stood long enough in the mash-tub, he must draw it off, and put it into the copper, and then throw in ¾ lb. of good hops *for every bushel of malt*; or, if the hops be not really good and strong, 1 lb. *to the bushel*. Boil the liquor at least an hour; but be very particular to make it boil the whole time; for much depends on this. Beer that has not boiled well is always crude, and soon spoils. It is the great fault of most brewers, that, to save the evaporation caused by a good boiling, they cool the liquor before it is sufficiently cooked. When it has boiled the proper time, pour it immediately, hot as it is, into a clean cask; put the bung and vent-peg in lightly; watch the cask, and when you find fermentation going on, which will show itself by a little oozing out of froth round the bung, take out both bung and vent-peg, and let them remain out till the working is over, and the froth begins to sink down into the cask; then put the bung and vent-peg in tightly, and the brewing is over. The cask should not be filled to running over, yet very little space should be left below the bung when driven in, as the body of air that would fill this vacancy would deaden the beer.

This mode deviates from that practised by my father, in two essential points: namely, the *cooling* and the *working* of the beer; for, in the last receipt it is not cooled at all, and no yeast is required to work it. If it answers, it is a less troublesome, and, calculating the cost of the coolers, less expensive mode of brewing than that detailed in the "*Cottage Economy*."

The "Cottage Economy" speaks of the necessity of keeping the casks in good order; and this is a matter, though of great importance, often neglected. New casks should be seasoned before they are used; one way recommended is, to boil 2 pecks of bran or malt dust in a copper of water, pour it hot into the cask, stop close, and let it stand two days, then wash it out well, and drain the cask. Servants are negligent about vent-pegs and bungs. They should be put in tight, the tap taken out, and a cork put in, as soon as the last beer is drawn. If the casks were kept in proper order, beer would not so often be spoiled. Of equal consequence, is the cleanness of the brewing utensils. They should be scoured well with a brush and scalding water, after they have been used. Do not use soap or any thing greasy. A strong ley of wood ashes may be used, if there be any apprehension of taint. When hops are dear, gentian may be substituted in part for them, in the proportion of 8¼ oz. gentian, and 2 lbs. hops, to 12 bushels of malt.

To Fine Beer.

Draw out a gallon of ale, put to it 2 oz. isinglass, cut small and beaten; stir the beer, and whip it with a whisk, to dissolve the isinglass, then strain, and pour it back into the cask, stir well, a few minutes, and put the bung in lightly, because a fresh fermentation will take place. When that is over stop it close; let the vent-peg be loose. Fermentation is over, make the vent-peg tight; and in a fortnight the beer will be fine. Drink 3 parts, and bottle the rest.—A good way to fine new beer, is to run the wort through a flannel into the tun, before it has worked.

For Stale Small Beer.

Put 1 lb. chalk, in small pieces, into a half hogshead, and stop it close. It will be fit to drink on the third day.—*Or*: put half chalk, and the other half hops.

To Bottle Beer.

Stone bottles are best. The best corks the cheapest, put them in cold water half an hour before you use them. The bottles perfectly clean and sweet, fill them with beer, put in each bottle a small tea-spoonful of powdered sugar, and let them stand uncorked, till the next day: then cork, and lay the bottles on their sides; or, better still, stand them with the necks downwards.—When a bottle is emptied, the cork should be returned into it directly, or it will become musty.

To Make Cider.

The apples quite ripe, but not rotten. If the weather be frosty, gather the apples, and spread them from 1 to 2 feet thick, on the ground, and cover with straw; if mild, let them hang on the trees, or remain under, if fallen, until you are ready to make the cider. It should not be made in warm weather, unless they are beginning to rot, in which case you must not delay. Unripe fruit should be made by itself, as the cider never keeps.—Large cider mills will make from 100 to 150 gallons in a day, according to the difference in the quality of fruit, some sorts of apples being more tough and less juicy than others, consequently requiring more grinding. Not more than 7 or 8 bushels should be put into the mill at once. They should be ground, till the kernels and rinds are all well mashed, to give the flavour to cider. Pour the cider from the mill into a press; press the juice well, then pour it into hogsheads. When it has done fermenting, and the time for this is very uncertain, rack it off into other hogsheads, let it settle, and then bung it down.

ENGLISH WINES AND CORDIALS.

Fruit of every kind should be gathered in dry sunny weather, quite ripe. All home made wines are the better for a little brandy; though some persons never use any.

To Clear Wine.

Dissolve ½ lb. hartshorn shavings in cider or rhenish wine; this is sufficient for a hogshead.—*Or*: to 2 table-spoonsful boiled rice, add ½ oz. burnt alum in powder: mix with a pint, or more, of the wine, stir it into the cask, with a stout stick, but do not agitate the lees.—*Or*: dissolve ½ oz. isinglass, in a pint or more of the wine, mix with it ½ oz. of chalk in powder, and put it into the cask: stir the wine, but not the lees.

British Sherry, or Malt Wine.

Take 12 quarts of the best sweet wort, from pale malt, let it cool and put it into a 10 gallon cask. Take as much water as will be required to fill up the cask, put it on the fire, with 22 lbs. of the best lump sugar, stir from time to time, and let it boil gently about a quarter of an hour, taking off the scum as it rises. Take it off the fire, let it cool, pour it into the cask, and put in a little good yeast. It may, perhaps, continue to ferment two or three weeks; when this has ceased, put in 3 lbs. raisins, chopped fine; these may cause fresh fermentation, which must be allowed to subside; then put in the rinds of 4 Seville oranges, and their juice, also a quart of good brandy; at the end of three or four days, if a fresh fermentation have not taken place, put the bung in tight. Keep it a year in the cask, then bottle it; the longer it is kept the better.—*Or*: stir 42 lbs. good moist sugar into 14 gallons of water, till it is dissolved, then boil it twenty minutes; let it cool in a tub, then put in 16 lbs. good Malaga raisins, picked and chopped; when it is quite cold pour in 2 gallons of strong beer ready to be tunned, and let it stand eight days; then taking out the raisins, put it into a 16 gallon cask, with 2 quarts of the best brandy, 1 lb. bitter almonds blanched, and 2 oz. isinglass. Bottle it in a year.

British Madeira.

Boil 30 lbs. moist sugar in 10 gallons of water, half an hour, and scum well. Let it cool, and to every gallon put 1 quart of ale, out of the vat; let this work, in a tub, a day or two; then put it in the cask, with 1 lb. sugar candy, 6 lbs. raisins, 1 quart of brandy, and 2 oz. isinglass. When it has ceased to ferment, bung it tight, for a year.

English Frontiniac.

Boil 11 lbs. lump sugar in 4 gallons of water, half an hour; when only milk warm, put it to nearly a peck of elder flowers, picked clear from the stalks, the juice and peel of 4 large lemons, cut very thin, 3 lbs. stoned raisins, and 2 or 3 spoonsful yeast: stir often, for four or five days. When quite done working, bung it tight, and bottle it in a week.

Red Currant Wine.

To 28 lbs. of moist sugar, allow 4 gallons of water, pour it over the sugar, and stir it well. Have a sieve of currants (which usually produces between 10 and 11 quarts of juice), squeeze the fruit with the hand, to break the currants, and as you do so, put the crushed fruit into a horse-hair sieve, press it, and when no more will run through the sieve, wring the fruit in a coarse cloth. Pour the juice on the sugar and water, mix it, and then pour it all into a 9 gallon cask, and fill it with water, if the barrel should not be full.—The cask should be filled up with water every day, while the wine ferments, and be bunged up tight, when it ceases. This is a cheap and simple method of making currant wine.—*Or*: put a bushel of red, and a peck of white currants, into a tub or pan, squeeze well; strain them through a sieve upon 28 lbs. of powdered sugar; when the sugar is dissolved put in some water in the proportion of 1½ gallon to 1 gallon of juice, pour it all into the barrel, add 3 or 4 pints of raspberries, and a little brandy.

Raisin Wine.

Put the raisins in at the bung-hole of a close cask (which will be the better for having recently had wine in it), then pour in spring water, in the proportion of a gallon to 8 lbs. raisins; the cask should stand in a good cellar, not affected by external air. When the fermentation begins to subside, pour in a bottle of brandy, and put the bung in loosely; when the fermentation has wholly subsided, add a second bottle of brandy, and stop the cask close. In a year it will be fit to bottle, immediately from the cask, without refining. Malaga raisins make the finest wine: Smyrna, rich and full, and more resembling foreign wine.

Gooseberry Wine.

To every pound of green gooseberries, picked and bruised, add 1 quart of water, steep them four days, stirring twice a day. Strain the liquor through a sieve, and to every gallon add 3 lbs. loaf sugar; also to every 20 gallons, a quart of brandy, and a little isinglass. When the sugar is dissolved, tun the wine, and let it work, which it will do in a week, or little more, keeping back some of the wine to fill up the cask, before you stop it close. Let it stand in the barrel six months, bottle it, in six more begin to drink it.

To make 4 gallons of Elder Wine.

Boil 1 peck of berries in 4 gallons of water, half an hour; strain and add 2½ lbs. moist sugar. To every gallon of water add ½ oz. cloves, and 2 oz. ginger, tied in a linen bag, boil it again five minutes, and pour it into a pan. When cold, toast a piece of bread on both sides, spread it with good yeast, and put it in the wine. When worked sufficiently, put it into a spirit cask, and cork it down; take the spice out of the cloth, and put it into the cask, with a tumbler of brandy. Leave the vent peg out a few days; in three weeks or a month bottle it. *Elder Wine to drink cold.* — Boil 1 gallon of berries in 2 gallons of water, two hours and a half. Add 3 lbs. moist sugar to every gallon of wine; boil it twenty minutes. Next day work it with a yeast toast. When worked enough, cask it, with ½ a bottle of brandy, and 7 lbs. raisins.

Ginger Wine.

Boil in 9 gallons of water 12 lbs. loaf sugar, 12 lbs. of moist, 12 oz. good ginger sliced, and the rind of 8 lemons, half an hour, scumming all the time; let it stand till lukewarm, put it into a clean cask with the juice of the lemons, 6 lbs. chopped raisins, and a tea-cupful of yeast, stir every day for ten days, add ¾ oz. of isinglass and 2 quarts of brandy. Stop close, and in four months bottle it. —*Or*: in 12 gallons of water boil 12 lbs. loaf sugar, 12 oz. ginger, and the rind of 24 lemons, half an hour, scumming all the time; then put it in the cask with the lemon juice, 12 lbs. raisins, and the yeast, stir every day for a fortnight, add 2 oz. isinglass and 1 quart of brandy.

Mountain Wine.

To 5 lbs. of large Malaga raisins, chopped very small, put a gallon of spring water; steep them a fortnight; squeeze out the liquor, and put it in a barrel: do not stop close until the hissing is over.

Primrose Wine.

Boil 18 lbs. lump sugar in 6 gallons of water, with the juice of 8 lemons, 6 Seville oranges, and the whites of 8 eggs; boil half an hour, taking off the scum as it rises; when cool put in a crust of toasted bread, soaked in yeast, let it ferment thirty-six hours: put into the cask the peel of 12 lemons, and of 10 Seville oranges, with 6 gallons of primrose pips, then pour in the liquor. Stir every day for a week, add 3 pints of brandy; stop the cask close, and in six weeks bottle the wine.

Cowslip Wine.

Boil 3½ lbs. lump sugar in 4 quarts of water an hour, skim and let it stand until lukewarm, pour it into a pan, upon 4 quarts of cowslip flowers; add a piece of toasted bread spread with yeast, and let it stand four days: put in as many lemons, sliced, as you have gallons of wine, mix and put it into a cask, and stop close.

Grape Wine.

To 1 gallon of bruised grapes (not over ripe), put 1 gallon of water. Let it stand six days, without stirring, strain it off fine, and to each gallon put 3 lbs. moist sugar; barrel, but do not stop it, till it has done hissing.—*Or*: the fruit barely half ripe, pick from the stalks, and bruise it, then put it in hair cloths, add an equal weight of water, and let it stand eighteen hours, stirring occasionally: dissolve in it from 3 lbs. to 3½ lbs. lump sugar, to each gallon, as you wish the wine to be more or less strong. Put it in a cask, fill it to the brim, and have 2 or 3 quarts in reserve to fill up with, as it diminishes by fermenting. Let it ferment ten days, when that is over, and there is no danger of the cask bursting, fasten it tight, leaving a small vent to open once a week, for a month. Fine and rack the wine in March, and bottle it in October; for a *brisk* wine, it must ferment eight days longer, and be bottled the following March, in cold weather.

Parsnip Wine.

Boil 1 bushel of sliced parsnips in 60 quarts of water, one hour, then strain it, add 45 lbs. lump sugar, boil one hour more, and when cold ferment with yeast; add a quart of brandy, then bottle it.—*Or*: to each gallon of water add 4 lbs. of parsnips, washed and peeled, which boil till tender; drain, but do not bruise them, for no remedy will make the wine clear: to each gallon of the liquor add 3 lbs. loaf sugar, and ½ oz. crude tartar, and when cooled to the temperature of 75, put in a little new yeast; let it stand four days, in a tub, in a warm room; tun it, and bung up when the fermentation has ceased. March and October are the best seasons. It should remain twelve months in cask before it is bottled.

Almond Wine.

Warm a gallon of water, add 3 lbs. loaf sugar, stir well from the bottom, and put in the white of an egg well beaten. When the water boils, stir, skim, and boil it an hour, put it in a pan to cool, and add ½ pint of yeast. Tun it next day, work it ten days, stirring once a day, then add to every gallon 1 lb. of sun raisins chopped, and rather less than ¼ lb. of almonds (pounded), more of bitter than sweet, and a little isinglass. Stop the cask close, for twelve months.

Cherry Bounce.

To 4 quarts of brandy, 4 lbs. of red cherries, 2 lbs. of black cherries, and 1 quart of raspberries, a few cloves, a stick of cinnamon, and a bit of orange peel: let it stand a month, close stopped, then bottle it; a lump of sugar in each bottle.

Orange Wine.

To 10 gallons of spring water put 30 lbs. of lump sugar: mix well, and put it on the fire with the whites of 7 eggs well beaten; do not stir before it boils: when it has boiled half an hour, skim well, put it into a tub, and let it stand till cold. Then put to it a pint of good ale yeast, and the peels of 10 Seville oranges very thin, let it stand two days, stirring night and morning. Then barrel it, adding the juice of 40 Seville oranges, and their peels. When it has done working, stop it close for six months before it is bottled. — *Or*: to 10 gallons of water, put 32 lbs. loaf sugar, and the whites of 4 eggs, beaten, boil as long as any scum rises, take that off, pour it through a sieve, and boil again, until quite clear; then pour it into a pan. Peel 100 Seville oranges, very thin; when the steam is a little gone off the water, put the peel into it, keeping back about a double handful. When the liquor is quite cold, squeeze in the juice; let it stand two days, stirring occasionally; then strain it, through a hair sieve, into the cask, with the peel in reserve. If the fermentation has ceased, it may be bunged down in a week or ten days.

Orange Brandy.

Steep the rinds of 8 Seville oranges and 3 lemons with 3 lbs. lump sugar, in 1 gallon of brandy, four days and nights. Stir often, and run it through blotting paper.

A Liqueur.

Fill one third of a quart bottle with black currants and a quarter part as much of black cherries, fill up with brandy, put in a cork, and let it stand a month; strain it through linen, put in sugar to taste, let it stand again a month, then strain and bottle it. — *Quince* may he used the same way, but in *Rum*.

Shrub.

To 1 quart of strained orange juice, put 2 lbs. loaf sugar, and 9 pints of rum or brandy; also the peels of half the oranges. Let it stand one night, then strain, pour into a cask, and shake it four times a day for four days. Let it stand till fine, then bottle it. — *Lemon Shrub*: to 1 gallon of rum or whiskey, put 1½ pint of strained lemon juice, 4 lbs. of lump sugar, the peel of 9 lemons, and 5 bitter almonds. Mix the lemon juice and sugar first, let it stand a week, take off all the scum, then pour it from one jug carefully to another, and bottle it.

Currant Rum.

To every pint of currant juice 1 lb. lump sugar, and to every 2 quarts of juice, 1 pint of water, set it over the fire, in a preserving pan, boil it, take off the scum, as it rises, and pour it into a pan to cool, stir till nearly cold, add to every 3 pints of liquor, 1 quart of rum, and bottle it.

Ratafia.

Infuse 1 oz. each of anise, dill, carraway, coriander, carrot, fennel, and angelica seeds, in 2 quarts of brandy, a fortnight in summer, and three weeks in winter: in the sun in summer, and in a chimney corner in winter. Shake it every day; strain through a jelly bag, and to every pint put 6 oz. of sugar, dissolved in water. Strain again, that it may be quite fine.—*Or: for Pudding Sauces*: blanch an equal quantity of peach, apricot, and nectarine kernels, slit and put them into a wide-mouthed bottle, with 1 oz. white sugar candy; fill it with brandy.

Noyeau.

Put ¼ lb. sweet and ¼ lb. bitter almonds with 2 lbs. sugar and the rinds of 3 lemons into a quart of brandy (white is best), with ½ pint new milk: shake and mix well together, every day for a fortnight; then strain and bottle it.

Real Drogheda Usquebaugh.

1 oz. anise seeds, ½ oz. fennel, 1 oz. green liquorice, 1 drachm coriander seeds, of cloves and mace, each 1 drachm, 1 lb. raisins of the sun, and ½ lb. figs. Slice the liquorice, bruise the other ingredients, and infuse all in a gallon of brandy eight days. Shake it 2 or 3 times a day; strain it, add 1 oz. of saffron in a bag: in two days bottle it.

Milk Punch.

Take 2 quarts of water, 1 quart of milk, ½ pint of lemon juice, 1 quart of brandy, and sugar to your taste: put the milk and water together a little warm, then the sugar, then the lemon juice, stir well, then add the brandy; stir again, run it through a flannel bag, till very fine; then bottle it. It will keep a fortnight or more.—*Or*: steep the rinds of 6 lemons in a bottle of rum three days; add 1 quart of lemon juice, 3 quarts of cold soft water, 3 quarts of rum, 3 lbs. lump sugar, and 2 nutmegs grated; mix well, add 2 quarts boiling milk, let it stand five hours; strain through a jelly bag, and bottle it.

Excellent Punch.

Put a piece of lemon peel into 3 pints of barley water, let it cool, add the juice of 6 lemons, and ½ pint of brandy; sweeten to taste, and put it in the cool, for four hours. Add a little fine old rum.

Norfolk Punch.

Steep the pulp of 12 lemons and 12 oranges, in 4 gallons of rum or brandy, twenty-four hours. Boil 12 lbs. of double refined sugar in 6 gallons of water, with the whites of 6 eggs, beaten to a froth; scum well; when cold, put it into the vessel with the rum, 6 quarts of orange juice, the juice of 12 lemons, also 2 quarts of new milk. Shake the vessel, to mix it; stop close, and let it stand in the cask two months, before you bottle it.

Roman Punch.

To the juice of 12 lemons and 2 oranges, add the peel of 1 orange cut thin, and 2 lbs. pounded loaf sugar, mix well, pass through a sieve, and mix it, gradually, with the whites of 10 eggs, beaten to a froth. Ice it a little, then add champagne or rum to your taste.

Regent's Punch.

A bottle of champagne, a ¼ pint of brandy, a wine glass of good old rum, and a pint of very strong green tea, with capillaire or any other syrup, to sweeten.

A cool Tankard.

Mix 2 wine-glassfuls of sherry, and 1 of brandy, in a tankard, with a hot toast, and sugar to taste; pour in a bottle of clear nice tasted ale, and stir it with a sprig of balm: then let it settle and serve it.

Porter Cup.

Put a bottle of porter, the same of table ale, a wine-glass of brandy, a des-sert-spoonful of syrup of ginger, 3 lumps of sugar, and half a nutmeg grated into a covered jug, and set it in a cold place half an hour; just before you serve it stir in a table-spoonful of carbonate of soda.

Cider Cup.

Begin with whatever quantity of brandy you choose, and go on, doubling the other ingredients, namely: sherry, cider, soda water, a little lemon peel and cinna-mon, sugar to your taste, and a bush of borage. Some persons put in a very little piece of the peel of cucumber, but this must be used sparingly, as the flavour is strong.

Ginger Beer.

Boil 14 lbs. lump sugar in 1½ gallon of water, with 2 oz. ginger, bruised, one hour; then add the whites of 8 eggs, well beaten; boil a little longer, and take off the scum as it rises; strain into a tub, and let it stand till cold; put it into a cask with the peel of 14 lemons cut thin, also the juice, a pint of brandy, and half a spoonful of ale-yeast at the top. Stop the cask close for a fortnight: then bottle, and in another fortnight it will be ready. Stone bottles are best.—*Or*: 1 oz. powdered ginger, ½ oz. cream of tartar, 1 large lemon sliced, 2 lbs. lump sugar, to 1 gallon of water, simmered half an hour: finish as above. *Ginger Imperial.*—Boil 2 oz. cream of tartar, the rind and juice of 2 lemons, 4 pieces of ginger bruised, and 1 lb. of sugar, in 6 quarts of water, half an hour. When cool, add 2 or 3 spoonsful yeast, and let it stand twenty-four hours, then bottle in ½ pint bottles, and tie down the corks. In three days it will be ready. An improvement to this is ¾ lb. sugar, ¼ lb. honey, and 1 tea-spoonful of essence of lemon.

Spruce Beer.

Mix a pint of spruce with 12 lbs. of treacle, stir in 3 gallons of water, let it stand half an hour, put in 3 more gallons of water, and a pint of yeast, stir well, and pour it into a 10 gallon cask, fill that with water, and let it work till fine; bottle it; let the bottles lie on their sides three days, then stand them up, in three more days it will be ready.

Crême d'Orange.

Slice 16 oranges, pour over them 1 gallon of rectified spirits, and 1¼ pint of orange flower water; in ten days, add 7 lbs. of clarified syrup, a quart of water, and ½ oz. of tincture of saffron: keep it closed, and in a fortnight strain the liquor through a jelly bag, let it settle, then pour from the sediment, and bottle it.

Raspberry or Mulberry Brandy or Wine.

Bruise fine ripe fruit with the back of a wooden spoon, and strain into a jar through a flannel bag, with 1 lb. of fine powdered loaf sugar to every quart of juice; stir well, let it stand three days, covered close; stir each day: pour it off clear, and put 1 quart of brandy, or 2 of sherry, to each quart of juice; bottle it, and it will be ready in a fortnight.

Spring Sherbet.

Scrape 10 sticks of rhubarb and boil them, ten minutes, in a quart of water; strain the liquor through a tammis cloth into a jug, add the peel of 1 lemon, very thin, and 2 table-spoonsful of clarified sugar; in six hours it is ready.

FLIP.

While a quart of ale is warming on the fire, beat 3 eggs with 4 oz. moist sugar, a tea-spoonful of grated ginger or nutmeg, and a quart of rum or brandy. When the ale is near boiling, pour it into one pitcher, the eggs and rum into another, and turn it from one to the other, until smooth as cream.

Egg Wine.

To 1 quart of Lisbon white wine, put 1 quart of water, sweeten to taste, and add a little nutmeg. Have ready the yolks of 3 eggs well beaten; boil the mixed wine and water, and pour it quickly on the beaten eggs, and pour from one bason to another, until it froths high. Serve in cups.

To Mull Wine.

Boil the quantity you choose, of cinnamon, nutmeg grated, cloves or mace, in a ¼ pint of water; add a pint of Port, and sugar to taste, boil it up, and serve it hot.

The Pope's Posset.

Blanch, pound, then boil in a little water, ½ lb. sweet, and a very few bitter almonds, strain, and put the liquid into a quart of heated white wine, with sugar to sweeten; beat well, and serve hot.

CHAPTER XXIX.

General Observations relating to the fitting up, and the care of the
Dairy, with Directions for making Cheese and Butter

THIS, of all the departments of country house-keeping, is the one which most quickly suffers from neglect; and of all the appendages to a country dwelling, there is nothing which so successfully rivals the flower garden, in exciting admiration, as a nice dairy. From the show-dairy, with its painted glass windows, marble fountains and china bowls, to that of the common farm house, with its red brick floor, deal shelves, and brown milk-pans, the dairy is always an object of interest, and is associated with every idea of real comfort, as well as of imaginary enjoyment, attendant upon a country life.

The management of this important department in a country establishment, from the milking of the cows, to the making of the butter and the cheese, must necessarily be almost wholly intrusted to a dairy maid, who ought to be *experienced* in the various duties of her office, or she cannot be skilful in the performance of them. Those persons who have excelled in dairy work, have generally learnt their business when quite young, as a knowledge of it is not to be hastily acquired. The great art of butter and cheese-making, consists in extreme care and scrupulous cleanliness; and an experienced dairy maid knows, that when her butter has a bad taste, some of the dairy utensils, the churn, the pail, or the pans, have been neglected in the scalding, *or*, the butter itself not well made: unless, indeed, as is sometimes the case, the fault lies in the food provided for the cows.

Note.—COBBETT's "Cottage Economy" contains directions for the keeping and feeding of cows.

The utmost care and diligence, on the part of the dairy maid, may, however, prove ineffectual, if the dairy itself be not convenient, and provided with the proper utensils. The principal requisites of a dairy are, coolness in summer, and a temperature warmer than the external air, in very cold weather. The building should, therefore, be so constructed, as to exclude the sun in summer, and the cold in winter. The windows should never front the South, South East, or South West. They should be latticed, or, which is preferable, wired, to admit a free circulation of air, with glazed frames, to be shut and opened, at pleasure. The room should be lofty, and the walls thick, as nothing more effectually preserves an even temperature, or excludes extremes of cold and heat. It should be paved with brick or stone, and laid with a proper descent, so that all water may be drained off. The floor should be washed every day in summer, and three or four times a week in the winter.

The utensils should not be scalded in the dairy, as the steam from hot water is injurious to milk. Neither rennet, cheese, or cheese-press, should be kept in it, as they diffuse an acidity. The dairy should not be used as a larder; it cannot be too scrupulously devoted to its own proper purposes.

The cows should be milked twice a day, and as nearly at the same hour as possible; and they should be milked *quite clean*: this is a matter of great consequence, not only as being conducive to the health of the animals, but if neglected, very much diminishes the value of their produce; for that which is milked last, is much richer than that which is first milked.

Some persons when they strain the milk into pans, for creaming, pour into each one, a little boiling hot water (in the proportion of 1 quart of water to 3 pails of milk); this was never done in our dairy in Hampshire, but I believe the effect is, to destroy the taste of turnip. It is very good, for this purpose, to keep a piece of salt-petre in the cream pot. This latter should have a stick in it, and be well stirred up twice a day, or, every time the dairy maid goes into the dairy. The cream should not be kept longer than four days, before it is made into butter. If twice a week be too often to churn, it ought not to be less frequent than three times in a fortnight. In private families the milk is generally skimmed only once, and this leaves the milk very good; but where butter is made for sale, and quantity rather than quality, is the object, a second skimming is generally resorted to. Some dairy maids object to the second skimming, on account of the bitter taste, which they say the cream so skimmed is sure to give the butter.

To Make Butter.

In summer the churn should be filled with cold spring water, and in winter scalded with hot water, preparatory to churning; then pour the cream in, through a straining cloth. In warm weather the churning should be performed in a cool place; and, in a general way, the butter will come in an hour; but it often does come in half the time, though it is not the better for coming so quickly. In very cold weather the churning must be done in a warm place; indeed, it is sometimes necessary to bring the churn near the fire, but this should never be allowed but in extreme cold weather, when the butter will sometimes be five or six hours in coming: when this is the case, it is almost always of a white colour and a poor taste. The butter being come, pour off the buttermilk, leaving the butter in the churn, pour in a pailful of cold water, wash the butter about, pour off the water, and pour in a fresh pailful; let the butter stand in this ten minutes. Scald a milk-pan, and stand it half an hour or more in cold water, lift the butter out of the churn into it, pour fresh water over, and wash the butter about well, drain the water off as dry as possible, and then proceed to work the buttermilk out of the butter. Some persons do this with the hands (which should first be dipped in hot water), others with a straining-cloth: if the latter, scald and wring it dry; then work the butter by squeezing it, by degrees, from one side of the pan to the other, pour cold water over to rinse, and pour that off; then work the butter back again, and rinse again; repeat this till the rinsing water is no longer coloured with milk, and then you may be sure that the buttermilk is all worked out; for, if there be any of it left, the butter will have streaks of white when cut, and will not be sweet. Having worked out the milk, the next thing is, to put in the salt. The quantity must depend, in some measure, on taste; some persons like their butter very much salted, while others think that the flavour of salt should not be distinguishable in fresh butter. Roll it quite fine, and you may allow ½ lb. to 5 lbs. butter: press the butter out thin, sprinkle over it some salt, fold up the butter, press it out again, strew over more salt, fold it up again, and so on, till all the salt is in, work the butter about well, to mix the salt with it, and pour off whatever liquid there may be in the pan. Take the butter out, a piece at a time (if the quantity be great), on a square wooden trencher (previously scalded and dipped into cold water), and, either with the hand, a fresh cloth, or a flat, thin piece of wood (made for the purpose), beat the butter out thin, fold it up, beat it out again, and repeat this several times, till the water is all beaten out. By the time it has arrived at this latter stage, it ought to be quite firm, except in extreme hot weather, when no pains are sufficient to make it so. When the water is all out, make up the butter, in what form and size you choose; place it on a board, or a marble slab, in a cool place, but not before a window, as too much air will not benefit it; spread over it a cheese-cloth, first scalded, then dipped in cold water, and it will harden in a few hours.

Different parts of England vary so much in the butter they produce, that what is considered very good in one county would be regarded as inferior in another. This is caused by difference in the pasturage, and not by variation in the mode of preparing the cream or making the butter; except, indeed, in some parts of the West of England. In Devonshire the cream is always, I believe, prepared according to the following directions, which were written for me by a Devonshire lady.

To make Butter without a Churn.

Spread a linen cloth in a large bason, pour in the cream, tie it up like a pudding, fold another cloth over it, and bury it in a hole two feet deep, in light earth, put all the earth lightly in, lay a turf on the top, and leave it twenty-four hours; take it up, and it will be found in the state that butter is when it is just come. The buttermilk is lost, but this method answers very well in hot weather. We tried it in America.

Clouted Cream.

Strain the milk, from the cow, into glazed earthenware vessels, and let it stand twelve hours in summer, and twenty-four, or thirty-six, in winter, before you scald it. Then place the vessels over a very small fire or hearth, for half or three-quarters of an hour, until the surface begins to swell, and the shape of the bottom of the pan appears on it (but if made hot enough to simmer, it will be spoiled); then set it to cool, and in twelve hours' time in summer, and eighteen or twenty-four in winter, the cream may be taken off with a skimmer which has holes.

Butter from Clouted Cream.

Scald well a large wooden bowl, then rinse it with cold water, but do not wipe it dry. Put in the cream, work it well with the hand (in one direction only), until the milk comes from it, which should be drained off, and will serve for making cakes and puddings; when the milk is all beaten out, wash the butter with cold water to cleanse it from the milk, then salt it, thus: spread it out on the bottom of the bowl, sprinkle salt over, roll it up, wash it again with cold water, beat out again, then shape and print it, as you please. The hands should be well washed in hot water, before you begin to work the butter. In winter and in weather of a moderate temperature the butter is speedily made, but in very hot weather it will take nearly or quite an hour of stirring round, and working with the hand, before it will come into butter.

To Pot Butter for Winter use.

In the summer, when there is plenty of butter, care should be taken to preserve enough for winter use. But observe, that none but good butter, well made, and quite free from buttermilk, will pot well. Have potting pans, to hold from 6 to 10 lbs. of butter. Put a thick layer of butter in the pan, press it down hard, then a layer of salt, press that down, then more butter, and so on: allowing 1 oz. of salt to every lb. of butter. If too salt, it can be freshened by being washed in cold water, before it is sent to table. Always keep the top well covered with salt, and as that turns to brine, more salt may be required. Tie paper over, and keep the pan in the dairy, or cellar. Some persons use one quarter part of lump sugar, and the same of saltpetre, to two parts of common salt.

To Make Cheese.

The milk should be just lukewarm, whether skimmed or not. To a pailful put 2 table-spoonsful of rennet, cover the milk, and let it stand, to turn: strike down the curd with the skimming dish, or break it with the hand, pour off the whey, put the curd into a cheese-cloth, and let two persons hold the four corners, and move it about, from side to side, to extract the whey: lay it into the vat, fold the cloth smoothly over the cheese, cover it with the lid of the vat, and put a weight of 10 or 12 lbs. on the top. Let it stand twelve hours; then take it carefully out, put it on a wooden trencher, or a clean hanging shelf, and sprinkle salt thickly over the top. The next day, wipe it dry all over, turn it the other side upwards, sprinkle salt on the top, and repeat this every day, for a week: after that, turn it every day, and occasionally wipe it.—*Another*: to 6 quarts new milk, add 2 quarts lukewarm water, and sufficient rennet to turn it: when the curd is settled put it into a small vat, about a foot square, and 1½ inch deep, with holes in the bottom; place a lid on it, and put on that a lb. weight, for a day.—*Another*: put 5 quarts of the last of the milking into a pan, with 2 table-spoonsful of rennet; when the curd is come, strike it down with the skimming dish two or three times, to break it: let it stand two hours. Spread a cheese-cloth on a sieve, put the curd on it, and let the whey drain; break the curd with the hand, put it into a vat, and a 2 lbs. weight on the top. When it has stood twelve hours, take it out and bind a cloth round it. Turn it every day, from one board to another. Cover the cheese with nettle leaves, and put it between 2 pewter plates, to ripen. It will be ready in three weeks.

CHAPTER XXX.

Observations upon Cooking for the Sick, and Receipts for Broths, Jellies, Gruels

OFTEN when the Doctor's skill has saved the life of his patient, and it remains for the diligent nurse to prepare the cooling drinks and restorative foods, the taste and the appetite of sick persons are so capricious that they will reject the very thing which they had just before chosen: and frequently, if consulted upon the subject, will object to something which, if it had appeared unexpectedly before them, they would, perhaps, have cheerfully partaken of. Everything which is prepared for a sick person should be delicately clean, served quickly, in the nicest order; and in a small quantity at a time.

See, in the Index, Mutton and Chicken broths.

Mutton Chops to Stew.

Chops for an invalid may be stewed till tender, in cold water to cover them, over a *slow fire*; scum carefully, add 1 onion, and if approved, 3 turnips. The broth will be very delicate.

A Nourishing Broth.

Put 1 lb. lean beef, 1 lb. scrag of veal, and 1 lb. scrag of mutton, into a saucepan with water enough to cover, and a little salt, let it boil to throw up the scum, take that off, pour off the water, and take off all the scum hanging about the meat: pour in 2½ quarts of warm (not hot) water, let it boil, and simmer gently till very much reduced, and the meat in rags. A faggot of herbs may be added, and a few peppercorns: also an onion, if desired. When the broth is cold remove the fat. If to serve at once, the fat may be taken off, by laying a piece of blotting paper over the top.—*Tapioca* is very nice in broths for invalids.—*Or*: put a knuckle of veal, with very little meat, and 2 shanks of mutton, into an earthen jar or pan, with 3 blades of mace, 2 peppercorns, an onion, a thick slice of bread, 3 quarts of water, and salt: tie a paper over, and bake it, four hours: then strain, and take off the fat.

Calf's-feet Broth.

Boil 3 feet in 4 quarts of water, with a little salt: it should boil up first, then simmer, till the liquor is wasted half: strain, and put it by. This may be warmed (the fat taken off), a tea-cupful at a time, with either white or Port wine, and is very nourishing.—*Or*: boil the feet with 2 oz. lean veal, the same of beef, half a penny roll, a blade of mace, salt, and nutmeg, in 4 quarts of water: when well boiled, strain it, and take off the fat.

Eel Broth.

This is very strengthening, ½ lb. small eels will make 1 pint of broth. Clean, and put them into a saucepan with 3 quarts of water, parsley, a slice of onion, a few peppercorns, and salt; simmer, till the broth tastes well, then strain it.

Beef Tea.

Notch 1½ lb. of beef (the veiny piece), put it into a saucepan with a quart of water, let it boil, take off the scum, and let it continue to simmer two hours. Beef tea should be free from fat and scum, and not burned.

Beef Jelly.

Let a shin of beef be in water an hour, take it out, and drain it; cut it in small pieces, break the bones, and put all in a stew-pan or jar, with 6 quarts of milk. Put it in the oven, and stew it till reduced to 3 quarts; skim off the fat, take out the bones, strain through a jelly bag, and add 1 oz. hartshorn shavings and a stick of cinnamon. Boil again gently over a slow fire, but be careful not to burn. Take every morning fasting, and at noon, a tea-cupful, warmed with a glass of wine.

Shank Jelly (very strengthening).

Soak 12 shanks of mutton, then brush and scour them very clean. Lay them in a saucepan with 3 blades of mace, an onion, 20 Jamaica and 40 black peppers, a bunch of sweet herbs, a crust of bread, browned by toasting, and 3 quarts of water; set the saucepan over a slow fire or hearth, keep it covered, let it simmer, as gently as possible, five hours. Strain, and keep it in a cold place. You may add 1 lb. of lean beef.

For a Weak Stomach.

Cut 2 lbs. of lean veal and some turnips into thin slices. Put a layer of veal and a layer of turnips into a stone jar, cover close and set it in a kettle of water. Boil two hours, then strain it. You may not have more than a tea-cupful of liquor, which is to be taken, a spoonful at a time, as often as agreeable. This has been known to stay on a weak stomach, when nothing else would. — *Or*: put a cow heel into a covered earthen jar or pan, with 3 pints of milk, 3 pints of water, 1 oz. hartshorn shavings, and a little fine sugar. Let it stand six hours in a moderate oven, then strain it. — *Or*: bake a neat's foot, in 2 quarts of water and 2 quarts of new milk, with ½ lb. sun raisins, stoned. When the foot is in pieces, set it by to get cold, and take off the fat. A tea-cupful, dissolved in warm milk or wine.

Bread Jelly, for a Sick Person.

Pare all the crust off a penny roll, cut the crumb in slices, toast these on both sides, of a light brown. Have ready a quart of water, boiled, and cold, put the slices of bread into it, and boil gently until the liquor is a jelly, which you will ascertain, by putting some in a spoon, to cool. Strain through a thin cloth, and put it by for use. Warm a tea-cupful, add sugar, grated lemon peel, and wine or milk as you choose; for children the latter. This jelly is said to be so strengthening that one spoonful contains more nourishment than a tea-cupful of any other jelly.—*Or*: grate some crumbs very fine; put a large tea-cupful of water into a saucepan, with a glass of white wine, sugar and nutmeg to taste, make this boil, stir in the crumbs, by degrees, boil very fast, stirring all the time, till it is as thick as you like.

Jelly for a Sick Person.

Boil 1 oz. of isinglass, in a quart of water, with 40 Jamaica peppers, and a crust of bread; let the water reduce one half. A large spoonful of this may be taken in wine and water, milk, or tea.—*Or*: boil ¼ oz. of isinglass shavings in a pint of new milk, till reduced half; sweeten to taste, and take it lukewarm.

Panada.

Boil a chicken, till 3 parts cooked, in a quart of water, let it get cold, take off the skin, cut the white meat into pieces, and pound it in a marble mortar, with a little of the water it was boiled in, salt and nutmeg. Boil it in more of the liquid, till of the proper consistency.

Strengthening Jelly.

Boil ¾ lb. hartshorn shavings, 1½ oz. of isinglass and candied eringo root, in 5 quarts of water, to a strong jelly, strain it, add ¼ lb. brown sugar candy, the juice of a Seville orange, and ½ pint of white wine. A wine-glassful three times a day.—*Or*: put 2 oz. of the best isinglass, 1 oz. gum arabic, 2 oz. white sugar candy, and a little nutmeg, in a white jar with a pint of Port or sherry, and simmer it twenty-four hours in a vessel of water; then strain it. Take the size of a walnut three times a day.

Gloucester Jelly.

Boil 2 oz. hartshorn shavings, 2 oz. pearl barley, 1 oz. sago, ½ oz. candied eringo root, and 3 pints of water, till reduced to a quart. A tea-cupful, warmed, morning and evening, in wine, milk, broth, or water.

Port Wine Jelly.

Boil 1 pint of Port wine, 1 oz. isinglass, 1 oz. sugar candy, ¼ oz. gum arabic, and ½ a nutmeg, grated, five minutes, and strain it through muslin. Some add lemon peel and juice, cloves, and nutmeg. For table, colour it with cochineal.

Arrow-root Jelly.

If genuine, this is very nourishing. Put ½ pint of water into a saucepan, with a wine-glass of sherry, or a table-spoonful of brandy, sugar, and grated nutmeg; let it come quickly to a boil; rub smooth a dessert-spoonful of arrow-root in two table-spoonsful of cold water; stir this by degrees into the wine and water, put it all into the same saucepan, and boil it three minutes.—*Or*: pour *boiling* (not merely *hot*) water over the arrow-root, and keep stirring; it will soon thicken. Add brandy, lump sugar, and, if approved, lemon juice.

Tapioca Jelly.

Wash well, and soak it five or six hours, changing the water two or three times; simmer it in the last water, with a piece of lemon peel, until clear; add lemon juice, wine, and sugar to taste.

Sago to Boil.

Put a large table-spoonful into ¾ of a pint of water. Stir and boil very gently, till it is as thick as you require. Add wine, sugar, and nutmeg to taste.—*Tapioca* in the same way. Soak both these two or three hours before they are boiled. They may be boiled in milk, like rice.

Gruel.

Put 2 table-spoonsful of the best grits into ½ pint cold water; let it boil gently, and stir often, till it is as thick as you require. When done, strain, and serve it directly; or if to be put by, stir till quite cold. Boil in it a piece of ginger, and, if for caudle, lemon peel also. *Barley Gruel*—Wash 5 oz. of pearl barley, boil it in two quarts of water, with a stick of cinnamon, till reduced half; strain, then warm it with 2 wine-glassfuls of wine.

Barley Cream.

Boil 1 lb. of veal, free from skin and fat, with 1 oz. pearl barley, in a quart of water, till reduced to a pint, then rub it through a sieve till it is of the consistency of cream, perfectly smooth; add salt and spice to taste.

Water Gruel.

Put a large spoonful of oatmeal into a pint of water, mix well, and let it boil up three or four times, stirring constantly; then strain, add salt to taste, and a piece of butter. Stir till the butter is melted, and the gruel will be fine and smooth.

Caudle.

Make some smooth gruel, well boiled, strain, and stir it. Some like half brandy and half white wine; others, wine, sugar, lemon peel, and nutmeg.—*Or*: add to ¼ pint gruel a large table-spoonful of brandy, the same of white wine, capillaire, a little nutmeg and lemon peel. Some use *ale*; no wine or brandy. *Rice Caudle*—Soak 2 table-spoonsful of rice in water, an hour, then simmer it gently in 1¼ pint of milk till it will pulp through a sieve; put the pulp and milk back into the saucepan, with a bruised clove and a bit of sugar. Simmer ten minutes; if too thick, add warm milk.—*Or*: rub smooth some ground rice with cold water, then mix with boiling water; simmer it a few minutes, add lemon peel, nutmeg pounded, cinnamon, and sugar, a little brandy, and boil it for a minute.

Rice Milk.

Wash, pick, then soak the rice in water, boil it in milk, with lemon peel and nutmeg: stir often, or it may burn.—*Ground Rice Milk*: rub a table-spoonful quite smooth, with a little cold water; stir in, by degrees, 1½ pint of milk, with cinnamon, lemon peel, and nutmeg; boil till thick enough, and sweeten to taste.

A Mutton Custard for a Cough.

Into a pint of good skim milk, shred 1 oz. of fresh mutton suet, and let it boil; then simmer gently an hour, stirring it from time to time. Strain, and take it at bedtime. Old fashioned, but good for tightness of the chest.—*Another remedy for the same*: heat the yolk of a fresh egg, and mix with a dessert-spoonful of honey, and the same of oatmeal; beat well, put it into a tumbler, and stir in by degrees, boiling water sufficient to fill it.—*Or*: mix a fresh laid egg, well beaten, with ¼ pint of new milk *warmed*, a table-spoonful of capillaire, the same of rose water, and a little grated nutmeg. Do not warm the milk after the egg is added to it.

Artificial Asses Milk.

To ½ oz. candied eringo root, add ½ oz. hartshorn shavings, and ½ oz. pearl barley; boil them in a pint of water over a slow fire till the water is reduced half. Mix a tea-cupful, with the same quantity of warmed milk, and take it half an hour before rising.

Onion Porridge.

Put 12 small, and 6 large onions, cut small, into a saucepan with a large piece of butter, shake over the fire, but do not let them burn: when half cooked, pour in a pint of boiling water, and simmer it till they are cooked. Some thicken with flour.

French Milk Porridge.

Stir some oatmeal and water together, and let it stand to settle; pour off the liquid, add fresh water to the oatmeal, and let it stand: the next day pass it through a sieve, boil the water, and while boiling, stir in some milk, in the proportion of 3 parts to 1 of water.

White Wine Whey.

Let ½ pint new milk come to a boil, pour in as much white wine as will turn it; let it boil up, and set the saucepan aside till the curd forms: then pour the whey off, or strain it, if required. Some add ½ pint of boiling water, and a bit of sugar; lemon juice may be added.

Rennet Whey.

Steep a piece of rennet, about an inch square, in a small tea-cupful of water, boiled and become a little cool. Then warm a quart of new milk, to the same temperature as from the cow, and when in this state, add a table-spoonful of the rennet. Let it stand before the fire until it thickens, then in a vessel of boiling water, on the fire, to separate the curds from the milk.

Vinegar or Lemon Whey.

Pour into boiling milk as much vinegar or lemon juice as will make a small quantity clear, dilute with warm water till it be of an agreeable acid; sweeten it to taste.

Mustard Whey.

Strew into a pint of milk, just coming to a boil, flour of mustard to turn it; let it stand a few minutes, then strain it.

Treacle Posset.

Into a pint of boiling milk pour 2 table-spoonsful of treacle, stir briskly till it curdles, then strain it.

Orgeat.

Beat 2 oz. of sweet, and 2 or 3 bitter almonds, with a tea-spoonful of orange-flower water, to a paste: mix them with a quart of milk and water, and sweeten with sugar or capillaire. Some add a little brandy.

Lemonade.

Pare 6 lemons very thin, and put the rinds into 3 pints of boiling water, and keep covered till cold. Boil 1 lb. of lump sugar in water to make a thin syrup, with the white of an egg to clear it. Squeeze 8 lemons in a separate bason, mix all together, add a quart of boiling milk, and pass it through a jelly bag till clear. Keep it till the next day.—*Or*: pour boiling water on a little of the peel, and cover close. Boil water and sugar together to a thin syrup, skim, and let it cool; then mix the juice, the syrup and water, in which the peel has infused, all together, and strain through a jelly bag. Some add capillaire.

Barley Water.

Wash 1 oz. of pearl barley, boil it in very little water, pour the latter off, then pour a quart of fresh water over, and boil it till reduced to half the quantity. Some boil lemon peel in it, others add lemon juice or cream of tartar, and sugar. A small quantity of gum arabic is good boiled in it.—*Another*, and by some doctors considered the best, is merely to pour boiling water on the barley, let it stand a quarter of an hour, and then pour it off clear.

Capillaire.

Put 14 lbs. of loaf sugar, 3 lbs. coarse sugar, and 6 eggs well beaten, into 3 quarts of water; boil it up twice, skim well, and add ¼ pint of orange-flower water. Strain through a jelly bag, and bottle it. A spoonful or two in a tumbler of either warm or cold water is a pleasant drink.

Linseed Tea.

Boil 1 quart of water, and as it boils put in a table-spoonful of linseed; add two onions, boil a few minutes, then strain it, put in the juice of a lemon, and sugar to your taste. If it gets thick by standing, add a little boiling water.—*Or*: put the linseed in a piece of muslin, then in a quart jug, pour boiling water over and cover it close, an hour.

Lemon and Orange Water.

Put 3 slices lemon peel into a tea-pot, with a dessert-spoonful of capillaire, and pour ½ pint of boiling water over.—*Or*: pour boiling water over preserved orange or lemon.—*Or*: boil lemon or orange juice in some thin syrup of sugar and water.

Apple Water.

Pour boiling water over slices of apple in a covered jug.

Toast and Water.

Toast a piece of bread quite brown, without burning, put it in a covered jug, and pour boiling water on it; before the water is quite cold strain it off.

A Drink for Sick Persons.

Boil 1 oz. of pearl barley in 2 pints of water, with 1 oz. sweet almonds beaten fine, and a bit of lemon peel; when boiled to a smooth liquor, add syrup of lemons and capillaire.—*Or*: *to take in a fever*: boil 1½ oz. tamarinds with ¾ oz. raisins and 2 oz. currants stoned, in 3 pints of water, till reduced half; add a little grated lemon peel.

Saline Draughts.

Pour ½ pint spring water on 2 drachms salt of wormwood, and 4 table-spoons-ful lemon juice; 2 table-spoonsful lump sugar may be added, if approved.—*Or*: pour 4 table-spoonsful lemon juice on 80 grains of salt of wormwood, add a small piece of sugar, finely pounded. When the salt is killed, add 4 table-spoonsful of plain mint water, and the same of spring water; strain, and divide it into 4 draughts, 1 to be taken every six hours. If the patient be bilious, add 10 grains of rhubarb, and 4 of jalap, to the morning and evening draught.—*Or*: pour into one glass a table-spoonful of lemon juice, and dissolve in it a lump of sugar; dissolve ½ a tea-spoonful of carbonate of soda in 2 table-spoonsful of water, in another glass: pour the two together, and drink in a state of effervescence. For delicate persons, a wine-glassful of sherry takes away the debilitating effect.

Coffee.

To be good must be made of a good kind, for poor, cheap coffee, though ever so strong, is not good. A breakfast-cup, quite full, before it is ground, makes a quart of good coffee. When the water boils in the coffee-pot, pour in the coffee, set it over the fire; the coffee will rise to the top, in boiling, and will then fall; boil it slowly three minutes longer, pour out a cupful, pour it back, then another, and let it stand five minutes by the side of the fire. A small piece of dried sole skin will fine it, or 2 lumps of sugar.—Coffee requires cream or boiled milk.

Chocolate.

Some prefer milk alone, others milk, and half its quantity in water; let it boil (be careful it do not burn), and put in the chocolate, scraped; in quantity according to the strength desired; mill it quickly, and let it boil up, then mill it again.—For sick persons, use thin gruel, not milk.

Tea.

For invalids who do not take tea for breakfast, its flavour may be given, by boiling a dessert-spoonful of green tea in a pint of milk, five minutes, then strain it. This renders it comparatively harmless.

Barley Sugar.

Put the beaten whites of 2 eggs in an earthen pipkin with a pint of water, and 2 lbs. clarified lump sugar, flavoured with essence or oil of lemons; boil quickly, skimming all the time, till stiff enough. Pour into a shallow brown dish, and form it as you please.

Everton Toffy.

To ¼ lb. treacle, put ½ lb. sugar, and 2 oz. butter, boil them together until they become hard when dropped in cold water. Then take the pan off the fire, and pour the toffy immediately into a tin dish.

CHAPTER XXXI.

Medical Recipes

In almost every family little illnesses are likely to occur, which may require medicine, though not, perhaps, the aid of a Doctor; it is, therefore, convenient to keep a small supply of common medicines in the house, especially in the country. The list I give was written by a medical gentleman; but while I am induced to insert it in this work, from a belief that it may, in some cases, be found of use, I cannot refrain from observing that it is far from my desire to lead any young housekeeper to adopt the fatal error that *Doctors* may be dispensed with, when anything approaching to serious illness betrays itself. Too many instances have occurred wherein life has been lost, for the want of timely medical skill, which might, perhaps, have arrested the progress of disease at its feeble commencement, and before it had acquired sufficient strength to baffle opposition.

The following receipts have all been tried by the persons who gave them to me; many of them may be old fashioned, but some I can assert to be good. That for the *croup* has been resorted to, several times in our own family, and always with success. The complaint is a violent one, its attacks are sudden and the progress of the disease is so rapid that there ought not to be an *instant* of delay in administering the remedies. The *croup* is of common occurrence in America, and the following receipt came from that country.

For the Croup.

The healthiest children are the most liable to this complaint, which is caused by sudden changings in the atmosphere, draughts of cold air, and checking of the perspiration, It betrays itself by a hoarse croaking cough, something like the hooping cough.—Put the child into a warm bath placed opposite the fire; cover it all over with flannel, or a blanket; in the meantime chop an onion or two, squeeze the juice through a piece of muslin, mix it in the proportion of 1 tea-spoonful with 2 table-spoonsful treacle; get the child to swallow as much of this, from time to time, as you can: when it has been in the bath ten or twelve minutes, take it out in a blanket, and as quickly as you can, rub the stomach and chest with a mixture of rum and oil, or goose grease, wrap the child in a flannel and put it to bed, or keep it in the lap by the fire; if the child go to sleep, it will be almost sure to awake free from the disorder. These remedies may not succeed if there be delay in applying them.

For Weakness of Stomach.

1 drachm of prepared Columba root, and ½ drachm of rhubarb root, infused

in ½ pint of boiling water, one day: add 1 oz. tincture of Columba, and a little sugar. 2 table-spoonsful, twice a day.—*Or*: put about 25 camomile flowers into ½ a pint boiling water, with 3 cloves, and 2 hops, cover close and let it stand all night: a tea-cupful first in the morning, and again an hour before dinner. If giddiness ensues, the camomile does not agree with the patient, and must not be continued. Where it does agree, this will be found to restore the appetite.

Camphor Julep.

Rub ¼ oz. of camphor in a mortar, with a few drops of spirits of wine, and a few lumps of sugar; add, by degrees, a quart of water, boiled, and cold. Let it stand twenty-four hours, then strain through muslin, and bottle it.

For Bilious Complaints and Indigestion.

Pour over twenty grains each of rhubarb and ginger, and a handful of camomile flowers, a pint of boiling water. A wine-glassful the first in the morning, and an hour before dinner.

A Mild Aperient. (To take in the spring.)

Put 1 oz. of senna into a jar, and pour 1 quart of boiling water over it; fill up the vessel, with prunes and figs; cover with paper, and set it in the oven, with household bread. Take every morning, one or two prunes, and a wine-glass of the liquor.—*Or*: dissolve 3 oz. of Spanish liquorice in one pint boiling water, add 1 oz. socotrine aloes in powder, and 1 pint brandy. Take 1 tea-spoonful in a wine-glassful of water, either in the morning, at night, or both.—*Or*: a large tea-spoonful of magnesia, a lump of sugar, a dessert-spoonful of lemon juice, in ½ pint of spring water.

Gout Cordial.

Rhubarb 1 oz., senna, coriander seeds, sweet fennel seeds, cochineal, saffron, and liquorice root, of each, a ¼ oz., and of jar raisins 4 oz. Let the raisins be stoned, and all the ingredients be bruised. Put them into a quart of French brandy. Shake well every day for a fortnight. Take 1 table-spoonful, with peppermint, or plain water.

Hallett's Gout and Bilious Cordial.

Infuse in a gallon of distilled aniseed water, 3 oz. Turkey rhubarb, 4 oz. senna leaves, 4 oz. guaiacum shavings, 3 oz. elecampagne root, 1 oz. fennel seed, 14 oz. saffron, 14 oz. cochineal, 1 lb. sun raisins, 1 oz. aniseed; shake it every day for a fortnight; strain and bottle it.—A table-spoonful (or two) an hour after dinner.

For Nervous Affections.

Take a small wine-glassful of the following mixture: a tea-spoonful of sal volatile, of tincture of hops, and an equal portion of infusion of orange peel and of gentian.

Mustard Whey, for Dropsy and for Rheumatism.

Boil 1½ oz. bruised mustard seed, in a quart of milk and water, till the curd which forms is separated. Strain it and take a tea-cupful three times a day. *Another for Rheumatism.* — A handful of scraped horse-radish, and a table-spoonful of whole mustard seed, infused in a bottle of Madeira; the longer the better. A wine-glassful in bed at night, and another before the patient rises.

An Embrocation for Rheumatism.

Dissolve 1 oz. of gum camphor in 6 oz. of rectified spirits of wine; add by degrees, shaking the phial frequently, 2 oz. spirits of sal ammoniac and 2 drachms oil of lavender. This has been used with success. — *Another*: (known to mitigate the tic douloureux), is the *caja peeta oil*, but it *must* be genuine. It is also good for strains, bruises, and chilblains. — *Or*: a mixture of 6 drachms French soap, 6 drachms ether, and 1 oz. spirits of wine.

For a Sore Throat.

At the beginning of a sore throat, get fresh ivy leaves, tack them together, warm them, and put the shady side to the throat. — *Or*: wet bread-crumbs with brandy, and tie them round the throat. Make a gargle of 2 carrots, sliced and boiled, and use it often. — *Or*: dissolve 4 oz. camphor in a pint of rectified spirits of wine. Dip a piece of new Welsh flannel into this, and apply it to the throat. Be careful to wet frequently.

A remedy for a Common Cold.

3 grains compound extract of colocynth, and 3 grains of soap, in 2 pills, taken at going to bed. The following night, take 16 or 18 grains of compound powder of contrayerva, and ½ a pint vinegar whey. — Breakfast in bed the next morning.

Syrup for a Cough.

Boil 1 oz. balsam of tolu, very gently, two hours, in a quart of water; add 1 lb. white sugar candy, finely beaten, and boil it half an hour longer. Strain through a flannel bag twice; when cold, bottle it. You may add 2 oz. syrup of red poppies, and the same of raspberry vinegar. A spoonful when the cough is troublesome. — *Or*: 2 oz. honey, 4 table-spoonsful vinegar, 2 oz. syrup white poppies, and 2 oz. gum arabic: boil gently to the consistency of treacle; a tea-spoonful when the cough is troublesome. — *Or*: 1 table-spoonful treacle, 1 of honey, 1 of vinegar, 15 drops laudanum, and 15 drops peppermint. Simmer together a quarter of an hour. A dessert-spoonful to be taken at going to bed. — *Or*: mix together in a phial, 2 drachms of compound tincture of benjamin, 6 drachms ethereal spirits of nitre, 3 drachms of compound tincture of camphor, and 5 drachms of oxymel; a tea-spoonful in a wine-glass of warm water, when the cough is troublesome. — *Or*: mix 1 oz. gum arabic, 1 oz. sugar candy, and the juice of a lemon; pour on it a pint of boiling water; a little when the cough is troublesome.

Extract of Malt, for a Cough.

Over ½ a bushel of pale ground malt, pour hot (not boiling) water to cover it, let it stand eight and forty hours; drain off the liquor, without squeezing the grains, into a stew-pan large enough to boil quickly, without boiling over. When it begins to thicken, stir, till it is as thick as treacle. A dessert-spoonful three times a day.

For a Cold and Cough.

To 3 quarts of water, put ¼ lb. linseed, two pennyworth stick liquorice, and ¼ lb. sun raisins. Boil it, until the water be reduced half; add a spoonful of rum and of lemon juice. A ¼ pint at bed time, and in smaller quantities, during the night, if the cough be troublesome.

For the Hooping Cough.

Dissolve 1 scruple of salt of tartar in 1¼ pint of cold water: add 10 grains of pounded cochineal, and sweeten with lump sugar.—The dose increased in proportion to the age of the patient; for a child five years old, a table-spoonful is sufficient; for adults 2 table-spoonsful 3 times a day.—Abstain from all acids.

Garlic Syrup, for Hooping, or any other Cough.

Put 3 roots of garlic, sliced thinly and transversely, with 4 oz. honey, and 4 oz. vinegar, into a ½ pint bason, and set that into a large wash-hand bason; let it infuse half an hour, then strain it. Take the first in the morning, and the last at night, a tea-spoonful of the syrup, in an equal quantity of brandy and water; put the water in the glass first.

Almond Emulsion for a Cough.

Beat well in a marble mortar, 6 drachms of sweet almonds blanched, and 2 drachms of white sugar, add 1 pint cold water, by degrees; strain, then add 2 table-spoonsful of sweet spirits of nitre. Cork, and keep it in a cool place, or in cold water. A tea-spoonful three times a day.

For a Hoarseness.

Sweeten a ¼ pint of hyssop water with sugar candy, and set it over the fire; when quite hot, stir in the yolk of an egg well beaten, and drink it off; this may be taken night and morning.—*Or*: put a new laid egg in as much lemon juice as will cover it: let it stand twenty-four hours, and the shell will be dissolved. Break the egg, then take away the skin. Beat it well together, add 2 oz. of brown sugar candy pounded, ¼ pint of rum, a wine-glassful of salad oil, and beat all well together. A table-spoonful the first in the morning, and the last at night.

Plaster for a Cough.

Beat together 1 oz. each, of bees-wax, white Burgundy pitch, and rosin, ¼ oz. coarse turpentine, ½ oz. oil of mace; spread it on white leather, the shape of a heart; when it flies off, renew it, two or three times.

Bark Gargle.

Boil 1 oz. powdered bark and 1 drachm myrrh, in 1½ pint of water, over a slow fire, till one third is wasted; strain, then add a table-spoonful of honey, and a tea-spoonful of spirits of lavender.

An excellent Gargle for a Sore Throat.

Half fill a teapot with *dark* red rose leaves, pour boiling water over; when cold strain it into a 6 oz. bottle, add a tea-spoonful of tincture of myrrh, and 25 drops of elixir of vitriol: if the throat be ulcerated, a tea-spoonful of tincture of cayenne.

Chilblains.

Make a liniment, of 1 oz. of palma oil, 1 oz. of expressed oil of mace, and 2 drachms of camphor.

For Burns or Scalds.

Keep in a bottle, tightly corked, ½ oz. of trefoil, and the same of sweet oil; apply with a feather, immediately that the accident has occurred. *Linseed* or olive oil, applied instantly, will draw out the fire; *treacle* will have the same effect, and is recommended by some persons, in preference to anything else. Others say that *fine flour*, applied *instantly*, is the best thing; as soon as it becomes warm, replace it with fresh. *Wadding* also laid on the part instantly is good to draw out the fire.

For Bruises, Cuts, or Wounds.

Keep in the house a bottle containing a mixture of ¾ oz. of scented trefoil, of rum, and of sweet oil. — *Or*: have a bottle three parts full of brandy, fill it quite full with the white leaves of the flowers of the garden lily, and cork it close. Lay some of the leaves on the wound, and keep it wet with the liquor. The root of the same lily is used to make *strong* poultices.

For a Sprain.

Stir the white of an egg with alum, until it curdles; rub the part affected often.

Vegetable Ointment.

A small handful of smallage, red pimple, feverfew, rue, and pittory of the wall; simmer them in 1 lb. of unsalted butter, over a slow fire, half an hour: stir and press well, then strain it.

Opodeldoc.

Put a pint of rectified spirits of wine in a bottle, with 1 oz. camphor, and 6 oz. soft soap; shake it three times a day for three days, and it is ready.

Elder Ointment.

Melt 3 lbs. of mutton suet in 1 pint of olive oil, and boil in it 4 lbs. weight of el-

der flowers, full blown, till nearly crisp; then strain, and press out the ointment.—
Another: take 4 oz. each, of the inner bark of the elder tree, and the leaves, boil them
in 2 pints of linseed oil, and 6 oz. of white wax. Press it through a strainer.

A Carrot Poultice.

Boil washed carrots, and pound them to a pulp with a wooden pestle; add an
equal quantity of wheaten meal, and 2 table-spoonsful yeast, and wet it with beer
or porter. Let it stand before the fire to ferment. The *soft* part to be made into a
poultice with lard.

An Excellent Bitter.

Cut ½ oz. of gentian in thin slices into a stone jar, with the same quantity of
fresh orange peel and sliced ginger. Pour over them 1 quart of boiling water, and
let it stand ten hours. Strain it, add a gill of sherry, and bottle it. For a weak stomach, a wine-glassful the first thing in the morning will create an appetite.

For Weak Eyes.

(Dr. Bailey's.)

Boil 2 quarts of water, and stir into it ¼ oz. camphor, pounded in a mortar with
a bitter almond, 1 oz. bolalmanack, and ½ oz. copperas; when cold, bottle it. Bathe
the eyes often.—*Or*: dissolve in spring water, 10 grains of white vitriol, and 10
grains of sugar of lead. Wash the eyes four or five times a day.—*Or*: boil in spring
water five minutes, ¼ oz. white copperas and ¼ oz. of common salt. Put a drop in
the eye with a feather the last thing at night. The bottle to be marked *poison*.—*Another*, and very good: put 10 drops of laudanum and 6 drops of goulard into a ¼
pint of elderflower water: bathe the eyes with it.

For the Tooth-ache.

Each of the following remedies *have* been known to alleviate suffering. Turn
up a wine-glass, put a little powdered alum on the round part, rub it to a paste
with sweet spirits of nitre, and apply it directly to the cavity of the tooth, if there be
one, if not, on the gum round it. Repeat this often.—*Or*: mix 2 drachms of alum, in
impalpable powder, and 2 drachms of nitrous spirits of ether.—*Or*: 2 drachms of
alum powdered very fine, with 7 drachms of nitrous spirits of ether.—*Or*: a drop
of ether and of laudanum on cotton: this will also relieve the *ear-ache*.—*Or*: 1 oz.
tincture of myrrh, 1 oz. tincture of gumlac, ½ oz. tincture of bark: mix the two last,
shake well, add the myrrh by degrees, and shake well together. 1 table-spoonful
to 2 of hot water; wash the mouth frequently, holding it in for some time.—*For an
intermitting pain in the Teeth*: boil ½ oz. bark, grossly powdered, in a pint of cold
water, till it wastes to a pint; then strain through muslin and bottle it. When the
teeth are free from pain, put 2 table-spoonsful of laudanum, then gargle and wash
the mouth well with it. Repeat it several times in the day.

Peppermint Water.

Pour 5 drops of oil of peppermint on a lump of sugar. Put the sugar into a ½ pint phial, with a tea-spoonful of brandy, and fill up with water.

Soda Water.

To 40 grains of carbonate of soda, add 30 grains of tartaric acid in small crystals. Fill a soda bottle with spring water, put the mixture in, and cork it instantly, with a well fitting cork.

Medicinal Imperial.

Useful in the Spring, or in slight Fevers, or Colds.

Pour 3 quarts of boiling water over 1½ oz. of cream of tartar, 1 oz. Epsom salts, ¾ lb. lump sugar, the peel of 3 lemons, and the juice of 1; cover close half an hour, then boil up, skim and strain it through thin muslin, into decanters. — A wine-glassful before breakfast.

Lime Water.

Mix 4 oz. quick lime in 6 pints of soft water, and let it stand covered an hour; then pour off the liquid.

Seidlitz Powders.

Put into one tumbler, 2 drachms of Rochelle salts, and 2 scruples of carbonate of soda; into another tumbler put 2 scruples of tartaric acid, fill each tumbler rather more than a quarter part, then pour the two together. — *Or*: mix carefully 2 drachms of sulphate of magnesia in fine powder, with 2 scruples of bicarbonate of soda, and mark the packet No. 1; in another packet, marked No. 2, put 40 grains of tartaric acid in fine powder. Mix in two different tumblers, each a quarter part filled with water, and drink in a state of effervescence.

Medicines to keep in the House.

Camomile Flowers.	Sal. Volatile.
Camphorated Spirits.	Salt of Wormwood.
Castor Oil.	Senna Leaves.
Epsom Salts.	Soda Carbonate.
Hartshorn.	Spirits of Lavender.
Jalap Powder.	Sweet Spirits of Nitre.
Magnesia Calcined.	Tincture Rhubarb.
Peppermint Water.	Tincture Myrrh.
Rhubarb.	

CHAPTER XXXII.

Various Receipts

Eau de Cologne.

INTO 2 quarts spirits of wine, at 36, put 2 drachms essence of bergamot, the same of essence of cedrat (a superior kind of bergamot), 2 drachms essence of citron, 1 oz. essence of rosemary, and a ¼ drachm of the essence of neroly (an oil produced from the flowers of the Seville orange tree); let it stand 24 hours, then strain through brown paper, and bottle it.

Lavender Water.

Into 1 pint of spirits of wine put 1 oz. oil of lavender, ½ a drachm essence of ambergris, ½ a drachm essence of bergamot. Keep it three months.—*Or*: 8 oz. spirits of wine, 1 drachm oil of lavender, 10 drops of ambergris, and 20 drops of essence of bergamot.

Milk of Roses.

Thirty grains of salt of tartar, pulverised, 2 oz. oil of almonds, 6 oz. of rose water; mix the two first, then the rose water by degrees.—*Or*: 2 oz. of sweet almonds in a paste, 40 drops oil of lavender, and 40 oz. rose water.—*Or*: 1 oz. oil of almonds, 1 pint rose water, and 10 drops of oil of tartar.

Henry's Aromatic Vinegar.

Camphor, 2 drachms; oil of cloves, ½ a drachm; oil of lavender, 1 drachm; oil of rosemary, 1 drachm; and a ½ oz. of the best white wine vinegar; macerate for ten days, then strain it through paper.

Wash for the Skin.

An infusion of horse-radish in milk, or the fresh juice of house leek, are both good.—*Honey water*, very thick, is good in frosty weather.—Also, a wash made of 4 oz. potash, 4 oz. rose water, and 2 oz. lemon juice, mixed with 2 quarts of water; pour 2 table-spoonsful in a bason of water.

Pomade Divine.

Put ½ lb. of beef marrow into an earthen vessel, fill it with spring water, and change that every day for ten days, drain it off, put a pint of rose water to it, let it stand 24 hours; take the marrow out, drain and wipe it thoroughly dry in a thin cloth, beat it to a fine powder, add 1 oz. of benjamin, the same of storax, cypress nuts, florence, cinnamon, nutmeg, and ½ oz. of cloves: mix all these together first, then mix up with the marrow, and put into a pewter vessel with a close-fitting lid; put this vessel into a copper of boiling water, and boil it three hours, having boiling water to replenish the copper, so that the pewter vessel may be covered with water all the time. In three hours pour the mixture through fine muslin into pots, and, when cold, cover close with paper.

Lip Salve, very good.

Two oz. white wax, 2 oz. of unsalted lard, ½ oz. spermaceti, 1 oz. oil sweet almonds, 2 drachms balsam of Peru, a lump of sugar, and 2 drachms of alkali root; simmer together, then strain through muslin.

Pomatum.

Mix ½ lb. fresh lard with 4 oz. marrow, and beat them with a shilling bottle of essence of lemon.

Cold Cream.

To ½ a pint of rose water add ½ a pint of oil of almonds, 1 oz. virgin wax, and 1 oz. spermaceti; melt over a slow fire, and beat them together till quite cold.—*Or*: melt ½ lb. hog's lard in a bason over steam; add ¾ pint rose water, and ½ a wine-glassful of oil of almonds; stir together with care till of a proper consistency.

For Chapped Hands.

Mix ⅓ pint double distilled rose water, ½ oz. oil of almonds and 7 grains salt of tartar.—*Or*: yolks of 3 eggs, 3 table-spoonsful honey, 4 table-spoonsful brandy, and 4 sweet almonds, pounded.—*Or*: dissolve a tea-spoonful of pulverised borax in a tea-cupful of boiling soft water, add a tea-spoonful of honey, and mix well together. After washing, wipe the hands very dry, and put the mixture on with a feather.—*Oil of Almonds* or spermaceti rubbed on at night are soft and healing.

Almond Paste for the Hands.

To 1 lb. stale bread grated, ½ lb. bitter almonds (blanched and pounded), ¼ lb. honey, and 3 table-spoonsful of oil of almonds. Beat well together and keep it in jars with bladders tied over. As you use it add more honey and oil, if it requires moisture.

Tooth Powder.

Bol ammoniac, gum mastic, red coral, and myrrh, of each an equal quantity finely powdered.—*Another*: 3 oz. camphor, 1 oz. powdered cinchona bark, 1 oz. prepared charcoal, and sufficient spirits of wine to dissolve the camphor. Mix thoroughly, and pass through a fine sieve.—The mixture of chalk and camphor is very good for preserving as well as cleansing teeth.

Curling Fluid.

Melt a bit of bees-wax, about the size of a filbert kernel, slowly, in 1 oz. of oil of almonds, and then add a drop or two of ottar of rose.

To clean Carpets.

Mix ox gall and water; rub the carpet with a flannel dipped into the mixture, then with a linen cloth. Sometimes carpets shrink after being wetted, therefore fasten them to the floor.

To clean Silk Dresses.

The dress must be taken to pieces. Take out all grease spots, with spirits of turpentine; rub the silk over, with a sponge dipped in an equal quantity of honey, and soft soap, with spirits of wine, sufficient to make it nearly liquid. When well cleaned, dip the silk in cold spring-water, hang it up to dry; when nearly cold, smooth it on the wrong side, with a cool iron.—*Or*: make some strong salt and water, in the proportion of a handful of salt to a bucket of cold water, lay in the breadths of silk, do not rub, but occasionally lift them up and down singly, for three days, rinse the silk in cold spring-water, hang it up to dry, and when nearly dry, smooth it out; iron it on the wrong side with a cool iron.

To take Grease out of Silk or Stuff.

Moisten ½ lb. fuller's earth with water, dry it before the fire, then pound, sift, and mix it with 2 oz. starch (beaten and sifted), ½ the white of an egg, ¼ pint camphorated spirits, and of turpentine; mix well, and bottle it. Spread it over the spot: if too dry moisten with soft water.

To remove Grease from Satin, Silk, Muslin, Drawing-paper, and other things.

Drop pure water upon the spot, and scrape on it caked magnesia, until it is saturated with the powder. When dry brush it off, and the grease, in most cases, will be removed. Some find *soda* to answer.

To clean Blond.

Soap it well, with curd soap, in lukewarm water, and let it lie all night; then wash it out, rinse in cold water, made blue, fold in a cloth, and iron it, with a cool iron.

To Wash Silk Stockings.

Put them into lukewarm water to cover them, soap the feet well, and rub that part which is soiled, with smelt blue; lay them smooth in the water, strew some blue between the folds, and let them lie all night; be careful in washing to rub them well, as the blue is hard to come out: the second lather must be of equal heat, but not quite so blue. Cut bear is used to tinge them pink.

To clean Floor Cloths.

Sweep, then rub the floor cloth with a damp flannel, then with milk or milk and water, and polish with a clean dry cloth. This is better than wax.

To clean Stone Stairs.

Boil in 2 quarts of water ½ pint of size, the same of stone blue, 2 table-spoonsful of whitening, and 2 cakes of pipe-maker's clay. Wet a flannel with this, wash the stones with it, and when dry, rub with a clean flannel and brush.

To take Oil from Stone or Boards.

To a strong ley of pearl-ashes, add some unslacked lime, let it settle, pour it off clear; lower it with water, and scour the grease spots; but it must be done quickly.

To get a Stopper out of a Decanter.

Drop a few drops of spirits of wine on it, and it will soon come out.

To take Rust from Steel.

Rub well with sweet oil, and two days after, rub with unslacked lime till the rust disappears.

To clean Steel Stoves and Fire Irons.

Rub with a piece of flannel dipped in oil, then in emery powder; polish with a leather and rotten stone.

To clean Paint.

Put a very little pearl-ash or soda into the water, to soften it, then wash the paint with a flannel and soft soap; wash the soap off, and wipe dry with clean linen cloths.

To clean Papered Walls.

The very best method is to rub with stale bread. Cut the crust off very thick, and wipe straight down from the top, then go to the top again, and so on.

To clean Tin Covers.

They should be wiped dry after being used, to prevent their becoming rusty. Mix a little fine whitening with sweet oil, and rub well, wipe this off clean, then polish with a leather and dry whitening.

To clean Copper Utensils.

If the kitchen be damp, or very hot, the coppers will turn black. Rub brick dust over, then a flannel dipped in oil; polish with leather and rotten stone.

Marking Ink.

Mix 5 scruples of silver caustic, 2 drachms of gum arabic, 1 scruple of sap gum, in 1 oz. distilled water, in a glass bottle. The *wash* to use previously; ½ oz. of soda subcarbonate in 2 oz. distilled water.

Ink.

Infuse in a gallon of rain or soft water, ¾ lb. of blue galls, bruised; stir every day, for three weeks. Add 4 oz. green copperas, 4 oz. logwood chips, 6 oz. gum arabic, and a wine-glassful of brandy.—*Or*: put 1½ oz. nut galls pounded, 1 oz. gum arabic, 1 oz. copperas into 1½ pint of rain water: shake every day for a fortnight, and it is ready.

Blacking for Shoes.

Boil 6 oz. ivory black, 1 oz. bees-wax, and 1 oz. mutton suet, in 3 pints of water till melted and mixed.—*Or*: 1 quart vinegar, 6 oz. treacle, 2 oz. ivory black, and the yolks of 2 eggs, well beaten. Boil together till well mixed, keep it covered close.—*Or*: mix into a pint of small beer, 4 oz. ivory black, 3 oz. coarse sugar and a table-spoonful sweet oil.

Pot Pourri.

Mix together one handful of orange flowers, of sweet marjoram, lemon thyme, lavender flowers, clove pinks, rosemary, of myrtle flowers, 2 of stock flowers, 2 of damask roses, ½ a handful of mint, and the rinds of 2 lemons, dried and pounded; lay some bay salt at the bottom of your jar, then a layer of the mixture, till the jar is full.

To Thicken the Hair.

Simmer ½ lb. of the best lard in a tea-cupful of olive oil half an hour, scumming all the time: add 9 drops of any scent. Rub it in three times a week.

To Destroy Bugs.

Corrosive sublimate, in spirits of wine, poured into crevices, or put on with a feather; it should be repeated as often as necessary. A deadly poison.

Paste.

Mix a very small portion of white lead in paste which is to be used about books, drawings, &c., &c. This will keep away the worm which is so destructive. *Poison.*

CHAPTER XXXIII.

Observations relating to, and Directions for Cooking for the Poor

I ʜᴀᴠᴇ selected such receipts as appear to be the most profitable to adopt; and the insertion of these will accomplish nearly all that I can hope to effect under the above head, for we all know that a supply of food alone can avert the misery of hunger, and that if there were a thousand different *systems* for feeding the poor by the means of voluntary aid, the success of each system must depend on the practical efforts made in its application.

Some persons object to making soups, &c., for the poor, on the ground that poor people are not so well satisfied with this mode of relief as they would be if the materials were given them to dispose of in their own way. This objection is just in some cases, but not so in all; because, as respects domestic management, there are two distinct classes among the poor, the one having learned arts of economy while faring well, and the other being ignorant of those arts from never having had enough means to encourage them to make such things their study.

It is true that the old-fashioned English cottagers, that class so fast falling into decay, are by no means wanting in the knowledge of housekeeping and of cooking in an economical manner. Not only does their labour in the fields produce fertility, bring the richest harvests, and cause those appearances on the face of the country which make it admired as one of the most beautiful in the world; but the habitations of the labourers themselves, their neat cottages, and their gardens so abounding at once with the useful and the elegant; these have always been regarded as one complete feature, and that not the least important, in the landscape of England. And, if we look at the interior of these dwellings, we there find every thing corresponding with what we have remarked without. Where the father, after having done a hard day's work for his master, will continue, in the evening, to toil upon his own small plot of ground for a couple of hours, and where the children are bred up to respect the edges of the borders, the twigs of the shrubs, and the stems of the flowers, and to be industrious and even delighted in such things, it is natural that the mother should take the same pains with all that belongs to the inside of the dwelling. And, accordingly, those who have occasionally visited the poor of the rural districts of England, must have observed, that if they are often deficient in the means of living well, they are, as often, patterns of cleanliness, and as anxious to make a respectable appearance with their scanty furniture, to polish their half dozen pewter platters, to scrub their plain table or dresser, to keep clean and to set in order their few cups and saucers of china-ware, as their betters are to make a display of the greatest luxuries of life. These excellent habits of the people are so fixed, that we see a portion of them still clinging to those labourers, perhaps the most of all to be commiserated, who are employed in the factories of the north of England.

But the condition of the other class is very different. Some of these have never, from their earliest infancy, been accustomed to any of those scenes in which, though there be difficulties, there are circumstances to excite perseverance, and to reward painstaking. These are born in absolute want; their experience under the roof of their parents has been but a course of destitution; and they go forth into the world rather as fugitives from misery than as seekers to be more prosperous. If they obtain employment, their labour is perhaps repaid by wages barely sufficient to keep them alive; destitute of the means of practising anything like household management, never having known what it is to have a home, worthy to be so called, for a single day, it is scarcely possible for them to obtain that knowledge, simple as it is, which is required to contrive the various modes of making much out of a little. Besides, if the poor people existing in this condition were ever so inclined to do well, there are the strongest inducements held out to them to mismanage their small stock of means; they are continually standing in need of some temporary sustenance; and, who can wonder if thus bereft of all power to *provide* or to *economise*, they yield to destruction, and suffer themselves to be allured by the glare of the gin-palace, or the revelry of the pot-house! It is one of the signs of misery with such persons, that they are little acquainted with the art of cookery. Here and there may be found a poor woman who has become skilful by serving in the kitchens of other persons: but this is only an exception, and too rare to be of account.

In almost every family there are, occasionally, things which may be spared from its consumption, to be converted, by an experienced cook, into palatable and nourishing food for poor people, but which, if given to them in the shape of fragments, they would be totally ignorant how to make use of. Such, for instance, as bones with very little meat on them, trimmings of meat, of poultry, &c., some cooked, some uncooked, crusts of bread, and pieces of dripping; yet these, with a little pepper, salt, and flour to thicken, may, by careful cooking and scumming, be made to produce an excellent meal for a family of children.—Few servants are unwilling to take the trouble of helping their poor fellow creatures, and, if the head of every family would give as much as she can spare to the poor who live immediately in her own neighbourhood, more general good would be done than ladies can reasonably hope to do by subscribing their money to "societies," which, though they may have been established by the best-intentioned persons, and for the kindest of purposes, can never be so beneficial in their effects as that charity which one individual bestows on another. The relief which is doled out by a "Society" is accompanied by very imperfect, if any, inquiries into the particular circumstances of the persons relieved; by no expressions of sympathy, by no encouraging promises for the future, to cheer the heart of the anxious mother as she bends her way homeward with her kettle of soup: the soup which has been obtained by presenting a ticket is apportioned to the little hungry creatures, without their being reminded who it is that has so kindly provided for them, and after it is eaten there is no more thought about the source whence it came than about the hunger which it has removed. The private mode of charity is superior to the public in every way. There are great advantages arising from the former which the latter can never procure. Not only must the attentions of a known individual be the most gratefully appreciated by a poor man and woman, but the child which has often gone to bed satisfied and happy, after a supper provided by some good neighbour, cannot be expected to grow up without some of those feelings of personal respect and attachment for its benefactor, which, while they prevent the contrast of riches with poverty from becoming odious, are the strongest assurances of union between him who claims a property in the soil and him whose labour makes that property of value. Self-interest and humanity are not the least at variance in this matter; the same course of policy is dictated to both. It may seem glorious to be advertised throughout Europe, and to be read of in newspapers, as a large subscriber to a public Institution; but the benefits which are confined to a single parish are the more lasting from being local, and the fame of the distributor, though bounded in distance, is all the more deserved, the longer kept alive and cherished, and, consequently, the better worth endeavouring to obtain.

The soup I would recommend for poor people, should be made of the shin, or any coarse parts of beef, shanks and scrags of mutton, also trimmings of any fresh meat or poultry. 1 pound of meat to every pint of soup (that is, every three ½ pints of water), and then all the meat should not be boiled to rags, but some be left to eat. There should be a sufficient quantity of turnips, carrots, onions and herbs; also pepper and salt; and dumplings, of either white or brown flour, would be a good addition. A quart of soup, made in this way, with about ½ lb. of meat, and a dumpling for each person, would be a good dinner for a poor man, his wife and children; and such a one as a lady who has a kitchen at her command, may often regale them with. Less meat will do where there is pot-liquor. The liquor of all boiled meat should be saved, in a clean pan, and made the next day into soup. That of a leg of mutton will require but little meat in addition, to make good soup. The liquor of any fresh meat, of boiled pork, if the latter be not very salt, will make good peas soup, without any meat.—Soak a quart of peas all night, in soft water, or pot-liquor, and, if the former, some bones or pieces of meat; a small piece of pork would be very good. Put in 2 onions, cut up, a head of celery, a bunch of sweet herbs, and what salt and pepper you think it requires. Let it boil, and then simmer gently *by the side* full three hours, or longer if the peas be not done; stir the peas up from the bottom now and then. When you have neither meat nor pot-liquor, mix 2 or 3 oz. of dripping with an equal quantity of oatmeal, and stir it, by degrees, into the soup, or boil in it some dumplings of flour and suet.

In houses where a brick oven is heated once a week or oftener, for bread, it would give little additional trouble to bake a dish of some sort or other for a poor family. Soup may be made in this way: first put the meat on the fire in just enough water to cover it; when it boils, take off the scum, pour off the water, put the meat into an earthen pan, with 3 carrots cut up, a turnip, 2 onions, pepper and salt, and stale dry crusts of bread; pour over boiling water, in the proportion of a gallon to 2 lbs. meat, and let it bake three hours. Shanks of mutton, cowheels, ox and sheep's head, may be cooked in this way, but the two latter must be parboiled, to cleanse them; and will require four or five hours' baking. The soup made of ox head is not so nourishing as that of shin of beef. If there be room in the oven, a plain pudding may be baked as follows. Pour boiling skim milk over stale pieces of bread, and cover with a plate or dish. When it has soaked up the milk, beat the bread, dust in a little flour, add sugar, an egg or two, or shred suet, or pieces of dripping, and more milk if required; butter a brown pan, pour in the pudding, and bake it three-quarters of an hour.—*Or*: a batter pudding, made with two eggs, a quart of milk; or if eggs be scarce, leave them out, and use dripping; rub it into the flour, with a little salt, mix this by degrees with some milk into a batter and bake it. A batter pudding of this kind, rather thick, is very good with pieces of meat baked in it; in the proportion of 1 lb. solid meat, to a batter made with 1 quart of milk. Pickled pork, not very salt, makes a very good pudding. A plain rice pudding, without egg or butter, made with skim milk, and suet or dripping, is excellent food for children. But rice costs something, and my object is to point out to young housekeepers how they can best assist the poor without injury to their own purses; and, therefore, I do not urge the use of barley, rice, sugar, currants, &c. &c. They do not, of themselves, produce much nourishment; sufficient, perhaps, for children, and for persons who do not labour, but for hard working people, the object is to provide as much animal food as possible; therefore, when money is laid out, it ought to be for meat.

Puddings with suet approach very nearly to meat. A thick crust, with a slice of bacon or pork in it, and boiled, makes a good pudding.

Hasty pudding, made with skim milk, in the proportion of 1 quart to 3 table-spoonsful of flour, would be a good supper for children, and the cost not worth consideration, to any lady who has a dairy.

Buttermilk puddings, too, are cheap and easily made.

Milk is of great value to the poor.

Where there is a garden well stocked with vegetables, a meal for poor people may often be prepared, at little expense, by cooking cabbages, lettuces, turnips or carrots, &c. &c. in the water which has been saved from boiling meat, or thin broth. The vegetables, stewed slowly till tender, with or without a small piece of meat, and the gravy seasoned and thickened, will be much more nourishing, as well as palatable, than plain boiled.

To dress Cabbages, Lettuces, Brocoli and Cauliflower.

Put ½ lb. bacon or pork, in slices, at the bottom of a stew-pan, upon them a large cabbage, or two small ones, in quarters; a small bunch of herbs, some pepper and salt, the same quantity of bacon or pork on the top, and a quart of water or pot liquor; let it simmer till the cabbage is quite tender.

Another: wash a large cabbage or lettuce, open the leaves, and put between them little pieces of bacon or pork, and any fragments of fresh meat cut up; tie up the cabbage securely, and stew it till tender in a very little broth or water, with a little butter rolled in flour, and some seasonings. A little meat will go a great way in making this a palatable dish. Turnips, carrots, and potatoes, either raw, or such as have been cooked the day before, may be just warmed up, or stewed till tender in a little weak broth, thickened with flour, and seasoned with salt and pepper, and then, poured with the gravy on slices of bread in a tureen, they will be good food for children.

In "COBBETT's *Cottage Economy*" there will be found a variety of receipts for cooking Indian corn meal.

THE END.

INDEX

C

F

M

Q

R

V

Lector House believes that a society develops through a two-fold approach of continuous learning and adaptation, which is derived from the study of classic literary works spread across the historic timeline of literature records. Therefore, we aim at reviving, repairing and redeveloping all those inaccessible or damaged but historically as well as culturally important literature across subjects so that the future generations may have an opportunity to study and learn from past works to embark upon a journey of creating a better future.

This book is a result of an effort made by Lector House towards making a contribution to the preservation and repair of original ancient works which might hold historical significance to the approach of continuous learning across subjects.

HAPPY READING & LEARNING!

LECTOR HOUSE LLP
E-MAIL: lectorpublishing@gmail.com